Manual of

Travel Medicine and Health

Manual of

Travel Medicine and Health

Robert Steffen, MD
Professor of Travel Medicine
Institute for Social and Preventive Medicine, University of Zurich
Chief, Division of Epidemiology and Prevention of Communicable Diseases
Director, WHO Collaborating Center of Travelers' Health
Zurich, Switzerland

Herbert L. DuPont, MD
Clinical Professor of Medicine
H. Irving Schweppe Chair, Baylor College of Medicine
Mary W. Kelsey Professor, University of Texas at Houston
Chief, Internal Medicine Service
St. Luke' Episcopal Hospital
Houston, Texas

1999
B.C. Decker Inc.
Hamilton • London • Saint Louis

B.C. Decker Inc.
4 Hughson Street South
P.O. Box 620, L.C.D. 1
Hamilton, Ontario L8N 3K7
Tel: 905-522-7017 / 1-800-568-7281
Fax: 905-522-7839
e-mail: info@bcdecker.com
Website: http//www.bcdecker.com

99 00 01 02 03 / PC / 6 5 4 3 2 1
ISBN 1-55009-078-X

Sales and Distribution

United States
B.C. Decker Inc.
P.O. Box 785
Lewiston, NY USA
Tel: 905-522-7017; 1-800-568-7281
Fax: 905-522-7839
e-mail: info@bcdecker.com

Canada
B.C. Decker Inc.
4 Hughson Street South
P.O. Box 620, L.C.D. 1
Hamilton, Ontario L8N 3K7
Tel: 905-522-7017; 1-800-568-7281
Fax: 905-522-7839
e-mail: info@bcdecker.com
Website: http//www.bcdecker.com

Japan
Igaku-Shoin Ltd.
Foreign Publications Department
3-24-17 Hongo, Bunkyo-ku
Tokyo 113-8719, Japan
Tel: 3 3817 5680; Fax: 3 3815 7805
e-mail: tmbook@ba2.so-net.or.jp

South Korea
Seoul Medical Scientific Books Co.
C.P.O. Box 9794
Seoul 100-697
South Korea
Tel: 82-2925-5800; Fax: 82-2927-7283

U.K., Europe, Scandinavia, Middle East
Blackwell Science Ltd.
Osney Mead
Oxford OX2 0EL
United Kingdom
Tel: 44-1865-206206; Fax: 44-1865-721205
e-mail: blackwell-science.com

Australia
Blackwell Science, Asia Pty, Ltd.
54 University Street
Carlton, Victoria 3053
Australia
Tel: 03 9347 0300
Fax: 03 9349 75001
e-mail: info@blacksci-asia.com.au

South America
Ernesto Reichman
Distribuidora de Livros Ltda.
Rua Coronel Marques
335-Tatuape, 03440-000
Sao Paulo-SP-Brazil
Tel/Fax: 011-218-2122

Foreign Rights
John Scott & Co
International Publishers' Agency
P.O. Box 878
Kimberton, PA 19442
Tel: 610-827-1640; Fax: 610-827-1671

Notice: The authors and publisher have made every effort to ensure that the patient care recommended herein, including choice of drugs and drug dosages, is in accord with the accepted standard and practice at the time of publication. However, since research and regulation constantly
change clinical standards, the reader is urged to check recent publications and the product information sheet included in the package of each drug, which includes recommended doses, warnings, and contraindications. This is particularly important with new or infrequently used drugs.

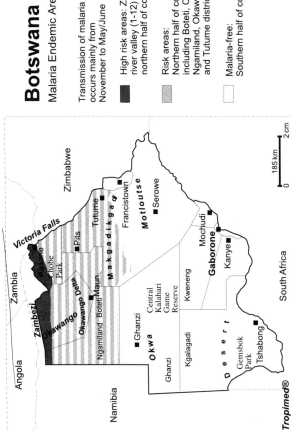

Botswana
Malaria Endemic Areas

Transmission of malaria occurs mainly from November to May/June

High risk areas: Zambezi river valley (1-12) and northern half of country (11-6)

Risk areas: Northern half of country (7-10) including Boteti, Chobe, Ngamiland, Okawango and Tutume districts/subdistricts

Malaria-free: Southern half of country

Tropimed®

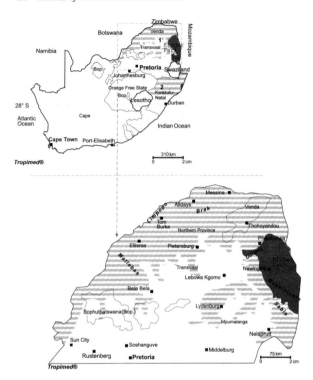

Tropimed®

South Africa

Malaria Endemic Areas

■ High risk all year in Krüger National Park and neighbouring parks, Kwazulu-Natal and Transvaal (north, east and west) from November to June

▨ The risk of malaria, mainly P.falciparum, exists all year in the low altitude areas of the north, east and west of Transvaal (1) and in coastal areas of Kwazulu-Natal (2) north of 28° S, from July to October

Erratum
These are corrected maps
for pages 471 and 480

CONTENTS

PART 3 **NONINFECTIOUS HEALTH RISKS AND THEIR PREVENTION**

PART 4 **DIAGNOSIS AND MANAGEMENT OF ILLNESS AFTER RETURN**

APPENDICES

To our colleagues and friends with whom we share
the challenges and pleasures of work and of travel—and
to the people abroad who receive us as guests.

PREFACE

Life is risky, and travel is even more so. The aim of this manual is to offer health professionals all they need to know to keep travelers in good health. The purpose is therefore to raise the standard of practice of preventive travel medicine.

Part 1 contains the basics necessary for every newcomer to the field. The subsequent parts contain epidemiologic data required for risk assessment, supported by numerous maps. They not only provide information about various diseases and risks encountered by travelers but also advice on avoidance of exposure to risk, immunization, drug prophylaxis, and recommendations for self-assessment and self-treatment while abroad. Also, the agents used in travel health, vaccines, drugs, and others, are described here in detail. There are innumerable information sources available on the diagnosis and therapy for some illnesses experienced by travelers or imported by migrants. For such, only the very basic information to be known by every general practitioner is included in this manual, with the focus on prevention and self-treatment.

Progress has been made toward a consensus on advice in travel medicine as this is of utmost importance to avoid confusion and resultant lack of compliance in travelers. However, there remains variation of opinion in some fields. Wherever this occurs, we describe the different positions; otherwise, we adhere to the advice published by the World Health Organization (WHO), the Centers for Disease Control and Prevention (CDC), other international expert groups, or universally accepted individual experts.

Travel medicine is a dynamic field. Any information provided in this manual will need continuous updating from other sources as new information becomes available. We plan to revise the book regularly and therefore invite all users to inform us about inadequacies or missing data to allow us to make subsequent editions even more valuable.

ACKNOWLEDGMENT

We wish to acknowledge the excellent advice and support we received in preparing this manuscript and its figures from the Zurich team: Drs. Marianne Debrunner, Maia Funk, Frank Peter Lücking, Patricia Schlagenhauf, Andrea Suhner, as well as Maja Rentsch, Janine Schiller, and particularly Hanspeter Jauss; from experts among various vaccine producing firms: Drs. Christian Herzog and Kent Larsson, and Sally Corinaldi; from Claudine Leuthold and her team at ASTRAL/TROPIMED in Geneva in preparing malaria endemicity maps; from copy editors Rohini Herbert and Craig Wilson, who greatly improved the quality of the text; and from the able production staff at B.C. Decker Inc., notably Rohini Herbert and Drew McCarthy.

Robert Steffen
Herbert L. DuPont

INTRODUCTION

Basic Concepts

Travel medicine is a new interdisciplinary field (Figure 1). The primary goal of travel medicine is to protect travelers from disease and death; the secondary one is to minimize the impact of illness and accidents through principles of self-treatment.

To achieve these goals, it is necessary initially to quantitate health risks through epidemiologic research. From such data, it is possible to rank preventive measures in the order of importance. The art of travel medicine lies in the careful selection of necessary preventive strategies, avoiding those measures which may cause unnecessary fear, adverse events, expense, or inconvenience. One basic precept is that potential travelers need not be given protective therapy against rare diseases while simultaneously being exposed to more frequently occurring diseases of comparable severity. Only in exceptional circumstances should travel health recommendations be as restrictive as advice to abandon travel plans.

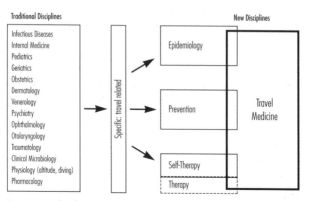

Figure 1   Travel medicine: an interdisciplinary field

Travel medicine is not merely a luxury service for individual travelers; it is also beneficial for public health. Collaboration between tourist-generating and tourist-receiving countries may result in improved hygienic conditions in resorts, and when health measures are copied and practiced, they will improve the situation for the local population as well. New drugs and vaccines developed for travelers, although initially costly, later become available on the market everywhere at lower prices. Surveillance of imported diseases and drug resistance patterns and data on sentinel cases in returning travelers are important to not only the developed world but also to the country where the disease originated, in the context of global concern over emerging or re-emerging infections.

The Travelers

Exposure of travelers to health risks depends on the destination, travel characteristics, and duration of stay. The importance of travel medicine is greatest for those venturing into the developing countries in tropic and subtropic regions where health standards and the health system are markedly substandard, and there is minimal regard for public safety. Therefore, travelers must carry the responsibility for their own health. Should they neglect to seek advice or be noncompliant, then they face a considerably higher risk of disease or even death.

Special attention must be given by the travel health community to ethnic groups visiting friends and relatives in their native countries and also to low-budget travelers who often do not go through a travel agent and use the cheapest means of travel.

Travel Industry

Travel industry professionals should inform potential travelers about health measures at the earliest opportunity. This may be done through brochures or guide books, which must be reviewed by competent travel health professionals. In some countries, it is now possible for travelers to receive travel advice when booking an airline ticket through a computerized reservation system.

Travel industry professionals (travel agents, tour operators, airlines) usually are the ones who have the earliest knowledge of an individual's travel plans. It should be travel industry policy to routinely refer for medical advice travelers who plan to visit areas with an elevated health risk. This should be done in a timely manner as some preventive measures need a few days or even weeks to become effective. This does not mean that all travel health consultation is useless and late for last-minute travelers. Travel industry collaborators need to be instructed accordingly. Detailed travel advice must be given only by travel health professionals and not by employees in travel agencies.

Ideally, tour operators' brochures and tour guides will use the opportunity to make a significant contribution by going even beyond health issues and encourage travelers to respect the people, the environment, and the culture at their destination.

Travel Health Professionals

Specialized travel clinics or vaccination centers in Europe are consulted by more than 50,000 potential travelers to the developing countries in one year. However, in North America, less than 500 travelers per year visit many travel clinics. There is divided opinion about the practice of travel medicine, whether it should be limited to specialized centers or whether any initiated general practitioner should be able to give travel health advice. To be able to give travel health advice, any health professional should have extensive travel experience and ideally should have visited the continent under discussion.

The family practitioner can certainly issue travel health advice to an individual with a low risk profile and who is visiting a developed nation. Basically, he only needs to give the potential traveler up-to-date information on immunity against tetanus and diphtheria, if necessary. Depending upon the frequency of travel to high-risk destinations from a travel-generating country, practicing physicians should be able to develop the expertise to give travel health advice to most travelers. Persons with a high-risk profile should be referred to experienced centers. Inclusion of the basic concepts of travel medicine in the curriculum of medical schools and continuing medical education is essential to ensure a high quality of service in travel medicine as part of general practice.

Even if most recommendations are amended less than once per year, travel health professionals must have access to a rapid up-to-date information system.

The Institutions

Various institutions play a significant role in travel medicine. Academic, international (World Health Organization), and national public health (Centers for Disease Control and Prevention) institutions carry the burden of research and dissemination of data. The International Society of Travel Medicine (ISTM), various national associations of travel medicine, the Wilderness Medical Society, the American Society of Tropical Medicine and Hygiene, the Federation of European Societies for Tropical Medicine and International Health, and other regional and national societies of tropical medicine are doing important work for the advancement of travel medicine, mainly by promoting the exchange of information among those working in this field. The private sector also plays a part by selling travel health software packages.

Conclusion

All of us in travel medicine are dependent on the regular receipt of up-to-date information and recommendations on important destination-specific risks and disease prevention strategies for our travelers. First steps have been taken on international, national, and local levels to urge travel health and travel industry professionals to collaborate. These efforts certainly need to be intensified.

PART 1

BASICS

TRAVELERS AND THEIR DESTINATIONS

Travelers

According to data provided by the World Tourism Organization (WTO) in Madrid, in 1995 there were 561 million recorded international tourist arrivals, the majority in the developed countries, e.g., 333 million in Europe. Each year, approximately 50 million travelers from a developed country visit a developing country (Figure 2). The health systems at their destinations, particularly the hygiene conditions, are of poor standard in most places, which poses considerable health risks for the traveler; this manual will concentrate on this particular section of the traveling population.

The projections show a substantial annual increase in travel from the developed to the developing countries (Table 1) although the recent economic crisis in Southeast Asia may cause some reduction in travel rates.

According to WTO definitions, "tourists" include a broad variety of travelers including business travelers, expatriates, crew members, etc. (Figure 3) while, according to Webster's Dictionary most "tourists" travel "especially for pleasure."

Financial Implications of International Travel

The international tourism receipts amount anually to 380 billion U.S. dollars. The worlds top tourism spenders were Germany (48 billion U.S. $), United States (46 billion), Japan (36 billion), United Kingdom, France, Italy, Austria, the Netherlands (all >10 billion). The top tourism earners were the United States (61 billion), France, Italy, Spain, United Kingdom, Austria, and Germany (all >10 billion).

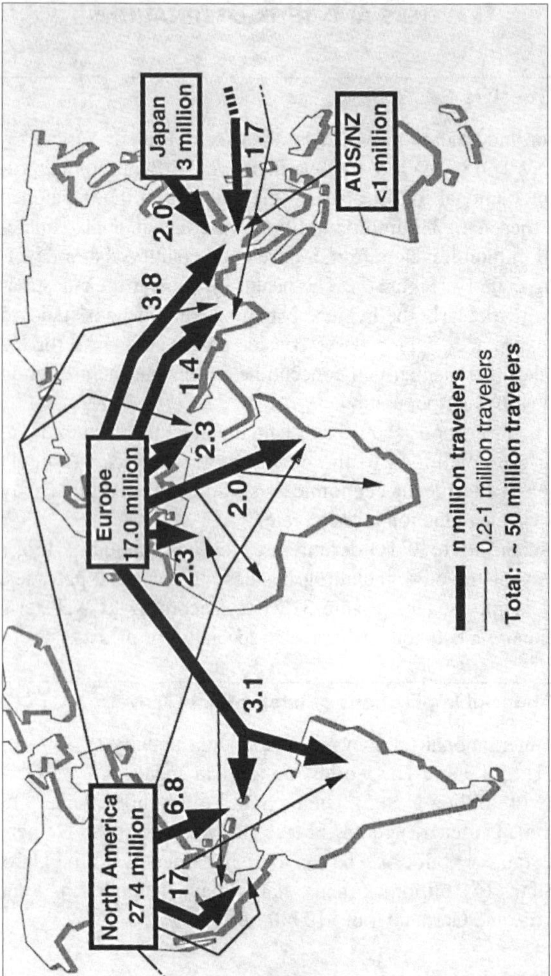

Figure 2   Travelers from the developed areas to the developing areas 1993 (WTO)

Table 1 Increase in Travelers from the Developed to the Developing Countries until 2010. Database 1995 Arrivals (Thousands) and Growth (% Per Annum)*

FROM: TO	USA/Canada Arrivals	Growth	Europe Arrivals	Growth	Japan Arrivals	Growth
Africa	500	4.5	6200	5.4	60	7.2
Middle East	600	10.0	3700	11.0	100	9.0
South Asia	400	7.7	1800	6.8	160	6.0
East Asia/Pacific	5000	5.5	9300	7.2	11,000	6.0
Americas	75,000	3.2	(16,000)	5.8	5300	6.9
Europe	(18,000)	2.0	(275,000)	2.4	5800	5.4
Long haul:	26.4%		11.8%		50.2%	

*Data from WTO.

Destinations

Geography

Those advising potential travelers must have comprehensive knowledge of world geography, the location of various countries, their capital cities (see Figures 5A to K) as well as the climates and altitudes of at least the most frequently visited destinations.

Environment

Environment plays an important role in most travels from the developed to the developing countries. A traveler may find the climate of the country he or she is visiting very different from that of the home country. Temperature, humidity, and rainfall have a direct impact on a traveler's health. Heat and humidity often lead to loss of energy and malaise initially and later to rapid exhaustion. Electrolyte and fluid depletion may lead to dangerous conditions, particularly in the elderly travelers and those with pre-existing illness. Excessive exposure to the sun rapidly results in sunburns, particularly at high altitudes. Some destinations in desert areas may be extremely dry, and very cold at night. When a traveler experiences extreme differences in temperature and humidity, it may produce undesired clinical symptoms.

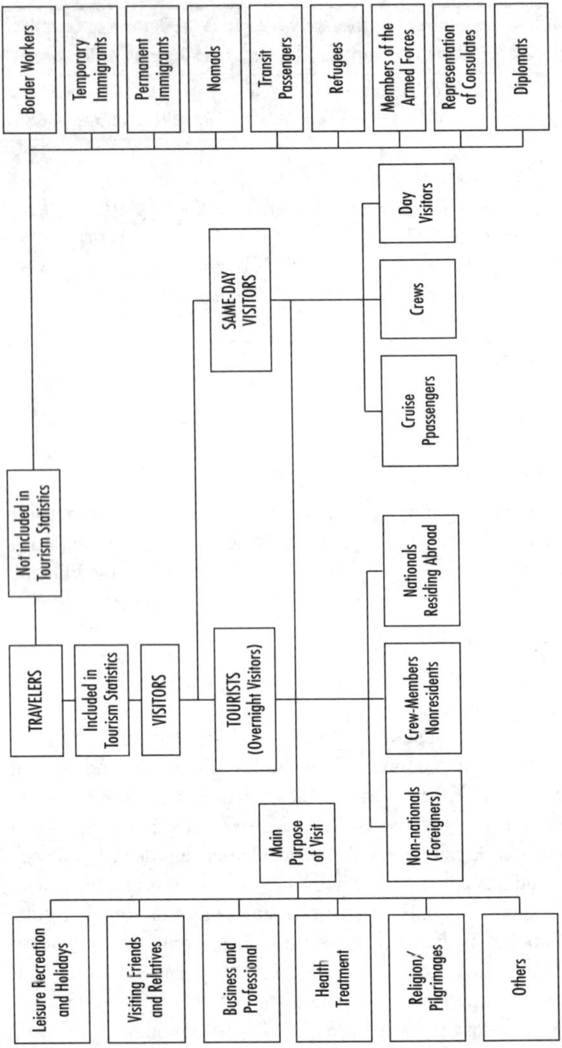

Figure 3 Classification of international visitors

TRAVELERS

Not included in Tourism Statistics
- Border Workers
- Temporary Immigrants
- Permanent Immigrants
- Nomads
- Transit Passengers
- Refugees
- Members of the Armed Forces
- Representation of Consulates
- Diplomats

Included in Tourism Statistics

VISITORS

SAME-DAY VISITORS
- Cruise Passengers
- Crews
- Day Visitors

TOURISTS (Overnight Visitors)
- Non-nationals (Foreigners)
- Crew-Members Nonresidents
- Nationals Residing Abroad

Main Purpose of Visit
- Leisure, Recreation and Holidays
- Visiting Friends and Relatives
- Business and Professional
- Health Treatment
- Religion/Pilgrimages
- Others

Heat, humidity, and overcrowding, especially in the poorer sections of cities promote the survival, multiplication, and spread of infectious agents and their vectors. Air pollution is a significant problem in many large cities in the world (e.g., Beijing, Mexico D.F., Athens). The air may become polluted after bush and forest fires. Dust from unpaved roads or in arid areas may cause increased susceptibility to infections of the upper respiratory tract.

Particular meteorologic conditions, such as El Niño currents in the Pacific, sometimes influence the weather worldwide causing prolonged heavy rains with subsequent floods and epidemics. However, highly efficient early warning systems with long-term predictions now enable public health officers to identify at-risk populations.

Many travel agencies publish information on climatic conditions at frequently visited tourist destinations. Many airlines also have such information available in print or as their computerized data.

At high altitudes, trekkers and climbers with pre-existing cardiac or pulmonary disease (Table 2) face a risk. Above 2400 meters, there is a risk of high altitude illness for any person staying for several hours. Details are discussed under "Altitude" in Part 3.

Time Zones

Travelers' health may be affected by time differences. Desynchronization of various physiologic and psychological rhythms occurs after rapid passage across several time zones. The Coordinated Universal Time (UTC) zones are shown in Figure 4. Jet lag is described in Part 3.

▎ Potential Health Hazards to Travelers by Region*

This section is intended to provide a general description of the health risks that travelers may face in various areas of the

---

*Reprinted from: International Travel and Health. Geneva: WHO; 1998. p. 43–52.

Table 2 Altitudes of Important Tourist Destinations
(Most Above 1220 m/4000 ft)

Cities and Countries	Meters	Feet
Addis Ababa, Ethiopia	926	3038
Albuquerque, USA	1620	5314
Andorra La Vella, Andorra	1080	3543
Antananarivo, Madagascar	1372	4500
Arieiro, Madeira Island, Portugal	1610	5282
Arusha, Tanzania	1387	4550
Asmara, Ethiopia	2325	7628
Aspen, USA	2369	7773
At Ta'if, Saudi Arabia	1471	4826
Banff, Canada	1397	4583
Bioemfontein, South Africa	1422	4665
Bishop, USA	1253	4112
Bogotá, Colombia	2645	8678
Boulder, USA	1611	5288
Bulawayo, Zimbabwe	1342	4405
Butte, USA	1693	5554
Byrd Station (Antarctica), USA	1553	5095
Cajamarca, Peru	2640	8662
Calgary, Canada	1079	3540
Caracas, Venezuela	1042	3418
Carson City, USA	1448	4751
Cherrapunji, India	1313	4309
Cheyenne, USA	1876	6156
Chihuahua, Mexico	1423	4669
Coban, Guatemala	1306	4285
Cochabamba, Bolivia	2550	8367
Colorado Springs, USA	1881	6172
Cuenca, Ecuador	2530	8301
Cuernavaca, Mexico	1560	5118
Cuzco, Peru	3225	10,581
Cyangugu, Rwanda	1529	5015
Darjeeling, India	2265	7431
Davos-Platz, Switzerland	1588	5210
Denver, USA	1625	5331
Durango, Mexico	1889	6198

Table 2 Continued

Cities and Countries	Meters	Feet
Erzurum, Turkey	1951	6402
Esfahan (Isfahan), Iran	1773	5817
Flagstaff, USA	2137	7012
Fort Portal, Uganda	1539	5049
Gangtok, India	1812	5945
Gilgit, Kashmir	1490	4890
Grand Canyon NP, USA	2015	6611
Grand Junction, USA	1481	4858
Guadalajara, Mexico	1589	5213
Guanajuato, Mexico	2500	8202
Guatemala, Guatemala	1480	4855
Gyumri (Leninakan), Armenia	1529	5016
Harare (Salisbury), Zimbabwe	1472	4831
Ifrane, Morocco	1635	5364
Iringa, Tanzania	1625	5330
Jasper, Canada	1061	3480
Jinja, Uganda	1172	3845
Johannesburg, South Africa	1665	5463
Jungfraujoch, Switzerland	3475	11,467
Kabale, Uganda	1871	6138
Kabul, Afghan	1815	5955
Kampala, Uganda	1312	4304
Kathmandu, Nepal	1337	4388
Kermanshah, Iran	1320	4331
Kerman, Iran	1859	6100
Ketama, Morocco	1520	4987
Kigali, Rwanda	1472	4828
Kisumu, Kenya	1149	3769
Kitale, Kenya	1920	6299
La Paz, Bolivia	3658–4018	12,001
Lake Louise, Canada	1534	5032
Laramie, USA	2217	7272
Leh, India	3506	11,503
Lhasa, Tibet, China	3685	12,090
Lichinga (Vila Cabral), Mozambique	1365	4478
Lubumbashi (Elisabethville), Zaire	1230	4035

Table 2 Continued

Cities and Countries	Meters	Feet
Lusaka, Zambia	1260	4134
Macchu Picchu, Peru	2380	7854
Marsabit, Kenya	1345	4413
Maseru, Lesotho	1528	5013
Mbabane, Swaziland	1163	3816
Mbala (Abercorn), Zambia	1658	5440
Medellín, Colombia	1498	4916
Merida, Venezuela	1635	5364
Mexico, Mexico	2308	7572
Morella, Mexico	1941	6368
Mt. Kilimanjaro, Tanzania	5890	19,340
Nairobi, Kenya	1820	5971
Nanyuki, Kenya	1947	6389
Ndola, Zambia	1269	4163
Nova Lisboa, Angola	1700	5577
Nuwara Eliya, Sri Lanka	1880	6188
Oaxaca, Mexico	1528	5012
Pachuca, Mexico	2426	7959
Petrified Forest NP, USA	1653	5425
Pretoria, South Africa	1369	4491
Puebla, Mexico	2162	7093
Queretaro, Mexico	1842	6043
Quetta, Pakistan	1673	5490
Quito, Ecuador	2879	9446
Reno, USA	1344	4411
Rock Springs, USA	2058	6752
Sa da Bandeira, Angola	1786	5860
Salt Lake City, USA	1288	4226
San Antonio de los Banos, Cuba	2509	8230
San Jose, Costa Rica	1146	3760
San Luis Potosi, Mexico	1859	6100
San Miguel de Allende, Mexico	1852	6076
San'a, Yemen Arab Republic	2377	7800
Santa Fe, USA	1934	6344
Seefeld, Austria	1204	3950
Shiraz, Iran	1505	4938

Table 2 Continued

Cities and Countries	Meters	Feet
Simla, India	2202	7224
South Pole Station (Antarctica), USA	2800	9186
Srinagar, India	1586	5205
St. Anton am Arlberg, Austria	1304	4278
St. Moritz, Switzerland	1833–3451	6013
Tabriz, Iran	1366	4483
Tamanrasset, Algeria	1400	4593
Tegucigalpa, Honduras	1004	3294
Tehran, Iran	1220	4002
Toluca, Mexico	2680	8793
Tsavo, Kenya	1462	4798
Tsumeb, Namibia	1311	4301
Ulaanbaatar (Ulan Bator), Mongolia	1325	4347
West Yellowstone, USA	2025	6644
Windhoek, Namibia	1728	5669
Yosemite NP, USA	1210	3970
Zacatecas, Mexico	2446	8025
Zermatt, Switzerland	1616–3900	5310–12700

world and not encounter in their home countries. It is impractical to try and identify problem areas accurately and to define the degree of likely risk in each of them. For example, even though viral hepatitis A is ubiquitous, the risk of infection varies not only according to area but also according to eating habits; hence, there may be more risk from communal eating in an area of low incidence than from eating in a private home in an area of high incidence. Generalizations would therefore be misleading. Current efforts to eradicate poliomyelitis worldwide are significantly reducing the risk of infection with wild poliovirus in almost all endemic areas.

Tourism is an important source of income for many countries, and to label any of them as high risk for a disease may cause serious economic repercussions. However, the national health administrations of these countries have a responsibility to provide travelers with an accurate picture of the risks from communicable diseases that may be encountered.

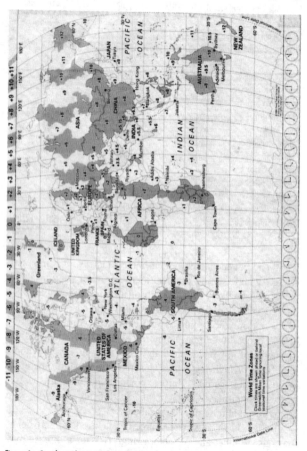

Figure 4   Coordinated Universal Time (UTC) zones

Africa (Figures 5A and 5B)

Northern Africa (Algeria, Egypt, Libyan Arab Jamahiriya, Morocco, and Tunisia) is characterized by a generally fertile coastal area and a desert hinterland, with oases that are often the foci of infections.

Arthropodborne diseases are unlikely to be a major problem to the traveler, although filariasis (focally in the Nile delta), leishmaniasis, malaria, relapsing fever, Rift Valley fever, sandfly fever, typhus, and West Nile fever do occur in some areas.

Foodborne and waterborne diseases are endemic, the most common being dysenteries and other diarrheal diseases. Hepatitis A occurs throughout the area, and hepatitis E is endemic in some regions. Typhoid fevers, alimentary helminthic infections, brucellosis, and giardiasis are common. Echinococcosis (hydatid disease) and sporadic cases of cholera are also encountered occasionally.

Other hazards. Poliomyelitis eradication efforts in northern Africa have been very successful, and virus transmission in most of the area has ceased. Egypt is the only country where confirmed cases of poliomyelitis were still reported in 1997. Trachoma, rabies, snakes, and scorpions are hazards in certain areas. Schistosomiasis (bilharziasis) is prevalent both in the Nile delta area and in the Nile valley; it occurs focally elsewhere in the area.

Sub-Saharan Africa (Angola, Benin, Burkina Faso, Burundi, Cameroon, Cape Verde, Central African Republic, Chad, Comoros, Congo, Côte d'Ivoire, Democratic Republic of the Congo, Djibouti, Equatorial Guinea, Eritrea, Ethiopia, Gabon, Gambia, Ghana, Guinea, Guinea-Bissau, Kenya, Liberia, Madagascar, Malawi, Mali, Mauritania, Mauritius, Mozambique, Niger, Nigeria, Réunion, Rwanda, São Tomé and Principe, Senegal, Seychelles, Sierra Leone, Somalia, Sudan, Togo, Uganda, United Republic of Tanzania, Zambia, and Zimbabwe). In this area, which lies entirely within the tropics,

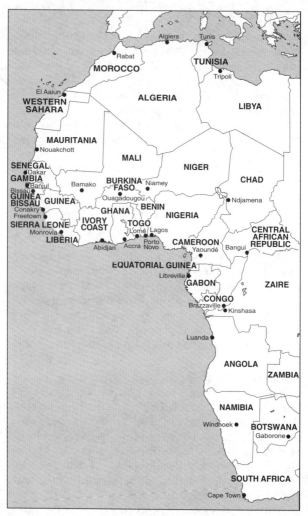

Figure 5A Western Africa

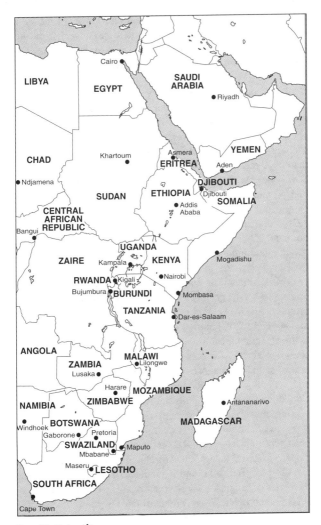

Figure 5B   Eastern Africa

the vegetation varies from the tropical rain forests of the west and center to the wooded steppes of the east, and from the desert of the north through the Sahel and Sudan savannas to the moist orchard savanna and woodlands north and south of the equator. Many of the diseases listed below occur in localized foci and are confined to rural areas. They are mentioned so that the international traveler and the medical practitioner concerned may be aware of the diseases that may occur.

Arthropodborne diseases are a major cause of morbidity. Malaria occurs throughout the area, except in places at more than 2600 meters altitude and in the islands of Réunion and the Seychelles. Various forms of filariasis are widespread in the region, and endemic foci of onchocerciasis (river blindness) exist in all the countries listed, except in the greater part of Kenya and in Djibouti, Gambia, Mauritania, Mozambique, Somalia, Zambia, Zimbabwe, and the island countries of the Atlantic and Indian Oceans. However, onchocerciasis exists in the island of Bioko in Equatorial Guinea. Both cutaneous and visceral leishmaniasis may be encountered, particularly in the drier areas. Visceral leishmaniasis is epidemic in eastern and southern Sudan. Human trypanosomiasis (sleeping sickness), in discrete foci, is reported from all countries except Djibouti, Eritrea, Gambia, Mauritania, Niger, Somalia, and the island countries of the Atlantic and Indian Oceans. The transmission rate of human trypanosomiasis is high in Sudan and Uganda and very high in Angola and the Democratic Republic of the Congo, and there is a significant risk of infection for travelers visiting or working in rural areas. Relapsing fever and louse-, flea-, and tickborne typhus occur. Natural foci of plague have been reported from Angola, the Democratic Republic of the Congo, Kenya, Madagascar, Mozambique, Uganda, the United Republic of Tanzania, and Zimbabwe. There is widespread incidence of tungiasis. Many viral diseases, some presenting as severe hemorrhagic fevers, are transmitted by mosquitoes, ticks, sandflies, and other insects which are found throughout this region. Large outbreaks of yellow fever occur periodically in the unvaccinated population. The natural focus of plague is a strictly delimited area, where ecologic conditions ensure the persistence of plague in wild rodents (and occasionally other animals) for long periods of time and where epizootics and periods of quiescence may alternate.

Foodborne and waterborne diseases are highly endemic in this region. Alimentary helminthic infections, dysenteries, diarrheal diseases such as giardiasis, typhoid fevers, and hepatitis A and E are widespread. Cholera is actively transmitted in many countries in this area. Dracunculiasis occurs in isolated foci. Paragonimiasis (oriental lung fluke) has been reported from Cameroon, Gabon, Liberia, and most recently from Equatorial Guinea. Echinococcosis (hydatid disease) is widespread in animal-breeding areas.

Other diseases. Hepatitis B is hyperendemic. Poliomyelitis (also a foodborne or waterborne disease) is probably endemic in most of these countries, except in Cape Verde, Comoros, Mauritius, Réunion, and the Seychelles. Schistosomiasis (bilharziasis) is present throughout the area, except in Cape Verde, Comoros, Djibouti, Réunion, and the Seychelles. Trachoma is widespread throughout the region. Among other diseases, certain arenavirus hemorrhagic fevers that are often fatal, have attained notoriety. Lassa fever has a virus reservoir in a commonly found multimammate rat. Studies have shown that an appreciable reservoir exists in some rural areas of West Africa, and people visiting these areas should take particular care to avoid rat-contaminated food or food containers but the extent of the disease should not be exaggerated. Ebola and Marburg hemorrhagic fevers are present but are reported only infrequently. Epidemics of meningococcal meningitis may occur throughout tropical Africa, particularly in the savanna areas during the dry season.

Other hazards include rabies and snake bites.

Southern Africa (Botswana, Lesotho, Namibia, Saint Helena, South Africa, and Swaziland) has varied physical characteristics ranging from the Namib and Kalahari deserts to the fertile plateaux and plains and to the more temperate climate of the southern coast.

Arthropodborne diseases such as Crimean-Congo hemorrhagic fevers, malaria, plague, relapsing fever, Rift Valley fever, tick-bite fever, and typhus (mainly tickborne) have been reported from most of this area, excepting Saint Helena; however, apart from malaria in certain areas, they are unlikely to be a major health threat for the traveler. Trypanosomiasis (sleeping sickness) may occur in Botswana and Namibia.

Foodborne and waterborne diseases, particularly amebiasis and typhoid, are common in some parts of this region. Hepatitis A is also prevalent in this area.

Other diseases. The southern African countries are on the verge of becoming poliomyelitis free; therefore, the risk of poliovirus infection is now low. Hepatitis B is hyperendemic. Schistosomiasis (bilharziasis) is endemic in Botswana, Namibia, South Africa, and Swaziland. Snakes may be a hazard in some areas.

The Americas

In 1994, an international commission certified the eradication of endemic wild poliovirus from the Americas. Ongoing surveillance in formerly endemic Central and South American countries confirms that poliovirus transmission remains interrupted.

North America (Bermuda, Canada, Greenland, Saint Pierre and Miquelon, and the United States of America [with Hawaii]) extends from the Arctic to the subtropical cays of southern USA (Figure 5C).

The incidence of communicable diseases is so low that it is unlikely to pose any hazard to the international traveler greater than that found in his or her own country. There are, of course, certain health risks but in general, only minimal precautions are required. Certain diseases such as plague, rabies in wildlife including bats, Rocky Mountain spotted fever, tularemia, and arthropodborne encephalitis occur on rare occasions. Recently, rodentborne hantavirus has been identified, predominantly in the western states of the USA and the southwestern provinces of Canada. Lyme disease is endemic in the northeastern, mid-Atlantic, and upper midwestern USA, with occasional cases being reported from the Pacific northwest. During recent years, the incidence of certain foodborne diseases, e.g., salmonellosis, has increased in some regions. Other hazards include poisonous snakes, poison ivy, and poison oak. In the northern most parts of the continent, exposure to very low temperatures in the winter can be a hazard.

Figure 5C   Map of North America

Mainland Middle America (Belize, Costa Rica, El Salvador, Guatemala, Honduras, Mexico, Nicaragua, and Panama) ranges from the deserts of the north to the tropical rain forests of the southeast (Figure 5D).

Of the *arthropodborne diseases*, malaria and cutaneous and mucocutaneous leishmaniasis occur in all eight countries of this region. Visceral leishmaniasis is encountered in El Salvador, Guatemala, Honduras, and Mexico. Onchocerciasis (river blindness) is found in two small foci in the south of Mexico and four dispersed foci in Guatemala. American trypanosomiasis (Chagas' disease) has been reported to occur in localized foci in rural areas in all eight countries. Bancroftian filariasis is present in Costa Rica. Dengue fever and Venezuelan equine encephalitis may occur in all these countries.

Foodborne and waterborne diseases, including amebic and bacillary dysenteries and other diarrheal diseases, and typhoid

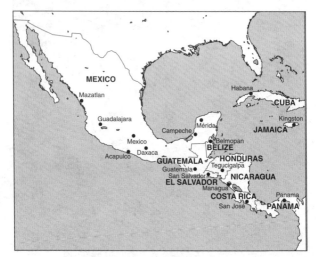

Figure 5D   Map of Central America

are very common throughout the area. All countries except Panama reported cases of cholera in 1996. Hepatitis A occurs throughout the area, and hepatitis E has been reported in Mexico. Helminthic infections are common. Paragonimiasis (oriental lung fluke) has been reported in Costa Rica, Honduras, and Panama. Brucellosis occurs in the northern part of the area. Many *Salmonella typhi* infections from Mexico and *Shigella dysenteriae* type 1 infections from mainland Middle America have generally been caused by drug-resistant enterobacteria.

Other diseases. Rabies in animals (usually dogs and bats) is widespread throughout the area. Snakes may be a hazard in some areas.

Caribbean Middle America (Antigua and Barbuda, Aruba, Bahamas, Barbados, British Virgin Islands, Cayman Islands, Cuba, Dominica, Dominican Republic, Grenada, Guadeloupe, Haiti, Jamaica, Martinique, Montserrat, Netherlands Antilles, Puerto Rico, Saint Kitts and Nevis, Saint Lucia, Saint Vincent and the Grenadines, Trinidad and Tobago, Turks and Caicos Islands, and the Virgin Islands [USA]). The islands, a number

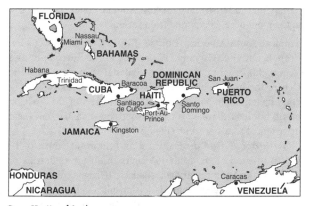

Figure 5E   Map of Carribean

of them mountainous with peaks 1000 to 2500 meters high, have an equable tropical climate, with heavy rain storms and high winds at certain times of the year (Figure 5E).

Of the *arthropodborne diseases*, malaria occurs in endemic form only in Haiti and in parts of the Dominican Republic. Diffuse cutaneous leishmaniasis was recently discovered in the Dominican Republic. Bancroftian filariasis is seen in Haiti and some other islands, and other filariases may occasionally be found. Human fascioliasis due to *Fasciola hepatica* is endemic in Cuba. Outbreaks of dengue fever occur in the area, and dengue hemorrhagic fever has also been encountered. Tularemia has been reported from Haiti.

Of the *foodborne and waterborne diseases*, bacillary and amebic dysenteries are common, and hepatitis A is reported particularly in the northern islands. No cases of cholera have been reported in the Caribbean.

Other diseases. Schistosomiasis (bilharziasis) is endemic in the Dominican Republic, Guadeloupe, Martinique, Puerto Rico, and Saint Lucia; control operations are in progress in these countries; it may also occur sporadically in other islands. Other hazards may occur from spiny seaurchins, coelenterates (corals and jellyfish), and snakes. Animal rabies, particularly in the mongoose, is reported from several islands.

Tropical South America (Bolivia, Brazil, Colombia, Ecuador, French Guiana, Guyana, Paraguay, Peru, Suriname, and Venezuela) consists of the narrow coastal strip on the Pacific Ocean, the high Andean range with numerous peaks 5000 to 7000 meters high, and the tropical rain forests of the Amazon basin, bordered on the north and south by savanna zones and dry tropical forest or scrub (Figure 5F).

Arthropodborne diseases are an important cause of ill health in rural areas. Malaria occurs in all ten countries or areas, as do American trypanosomiasis (Chagas' disease) and cutaneous and mucocutaneous leishmaniasis. There has been an increase of the latter in Brazil and Paraguay. Visceral leishmaniasis is endemic in northeast Brazil, with foci in other parts of Brazil; it is less frequent in Colombia and Venezuela, rare in Bolivia and Paraguay, and unknown in Peru. Endemic

Figure 5F Map of South America

onchocerciasis occurs in isolated foci in rural areas in Ecuador, Venezuela, and northern Brazil. The bite of blackflies may cause unpleasant reactions. Bancroftian filariasis is endemic in parts of Brazil, Guyana, and Suriname. Plague has been reported in natural foci in Bolivia, Brazil, Ecuador, and Peru. Among the arthropodborne viral diseases, jungle yellow fever may be found in forest areas in all countries of this region, except Paraguay and areas east of the Andes; in Brazil, it is confined to the northern and western states. Epidemics of viral encephalitis and dengue fever occur in some countries. Bartonellosis (Oroya fever), a sandflyborne disease, occurs in arid river valleys on the western slopes of the Andes in altitudes up to 3000 meters. Louseborne typhus is often found in the mountainous areas of Colombia and Peru.

Foodborne and waterborne diseases are common and include amebiasis, diarrheal diseases, helminthic infections, and hepatitis A. Paragonimiasis (oriental lung fluke) has been reported from Ecuador, Peru, and Venezuela. Brucellosis is common, and echinococcosis (hydatid disease) occurs particularly in Peru. Bolivia, Brazil, Colombia, Ecuador, Peru, and Venezuela all reported autochthonous cases of cholera in 1996.

Other diseases include rodentborne arenavirus hemorrhagic fever in Bolivia and Venezuela, and rodentborne pulmonary syndrome in Brazil and Paraguay. Hepatitis B and D (delta hepatitis) are highly endemic in the Amazon basin. The intestinal form of schistosomiasis (bilharziasis) is found in Brazil, Suriname, and north-central Venezuela.

Rabies has been reported from many of the countries in this area. Meningococcal meningitis occurs in the form of epidemic outbreaks in Brazil.

Snakes and leeches may be a hazard in some areas.

Temperate South America (Argentina, Chile, Falkland Islands [Malvinas], and Uruguay). The mainland ranges from the Mediterranean climatic area of the western coastal strip over the Andes divide on to the steppes and desert of Patagonia in the south and to the prairies of the northeast (see Figure 5F).

Arthropodborne diseases are relatively unimportant, except for the occurrence of American trypanosomiasis (Chagas' disease). Outbreaks of malaria occur in northwestern Argentina; cutaneous leishmaniasis is also reported from this part of the country.

Of the *foodborne and waterborne diseases* gastroenteritis (mainly salmonellosis) is relatively common in Argentina, especially in the suburban areas and among children below the age of 5 years. Some cases of cholera were reported from Argentina in 1996. Typhoid fever is not very common in Argentina but hepatitis A and intestinal parasitosis are widespread, the latter especially in the coastal region. Taeniasis (tapeworm), typhoid fever, viral hepatitis, and echinococcosis (hydatid disease) are reported from the other countries of this region.

Other diseases. Anthrax is an industrial or agricultural occupational hazard in the three mainland countries. Meningococcal meningitis is reported to occur in the form of epidemic outbreaks in Chile. Rodentborne hantavirus pulmonary syndrome has been identified in the north-central and southwestern regions of Argentina and in Chile.

Asia (Figures 5G and 5H)

East Asia (China [including Hong Kong Special Administrative Region], the Democratic People's Republic of Korea, Japan, Macao, Mongolia, and the Republic of Korea). This region includes the high mountain complexes, the desert and the steppes of the west, and the various forest zones of the east, down to the subtropical forests of the southeast.

Of the *arthropodborne diseases*, malaria occurs in China, and in recent years cases have also been reported from the Korean peninsula. Although reduced in distribution and prevalence, bancroftian and brugian filariasis are still reported in southern China. A resurgence of visceral leishmaniasis is occurring in China. Cutaneous leishmaniasis has been recently reported from Xin-

Figure 5G   Map of Western Asia

Figure 5H Map of Eastern Asia

jiang in the Uygur Autonomous Region. Plague may be encountered in China and Mongolia. Rodentborne hemorrhagic fever with renal syndrome and Korean hemorrhagic fever is endemic, except in Mongolia, and epidemics of dengue fever and Japanese encephalitis may occur in some countries. Miteborne or scrub typhus may be found in scrub areas in southern China, certain river valleys in Japan, and in the Republic of Korea.

Foodborne and waterborne diseases such as the diarrheal diseases and hepatitis A are common in most countries. Hepatitis E is prevalent in western China. Clonorchiasis (oriental liver fluke) and paragonimiasis (oriental lung fluke) are reported in China, Japan, Macao, and the Republic of Korea. Fasciolopsiasis (giant intestinal fluke) and brucellosis occur in China. Cholera may occur in some countries in this area.

Other diseases. Hepatitis B is highly endemic. The present endemic area of schistosomiasis (bilharziasis) is in the central Chang Jiang (Yangtze) river basin in China; active foci no longer exist in Japan. Poliomyelitis eradication activities have rapidly reduced poliovirus transmission in east Asia. Reliable surveillance data indicate that poliovirus transmission has been interrupted in China since 1994. Mongolia also no longer reports cases. Trachoma and leptospirosis occur in China. Rabies is endemic in some countries. There are reports of outbreaks of meningococcal meningitis in Mongolia.

Eastern South Asia (Brunei Darussalam, Cambodia, Indonesia, Lao People's Democratic Republic, Malaysia, Myanmar, the Philippines, Singapore, Thailand, and Vietnam). From the tropical rain and monsoon forests of the northwest, the area extends through the savanna and the dry tropical forests of the Indochina peninsula, and down to the tropical rain and monsoon forests of the islands bordering the South China Sea.

The *arthropodborne diseases* are an important cause of morbidity and mortality throughout the area. Malaria and filariasis are endemic in many parts of the rural areas of all the countries; however, in Brunei Darussalam and Singapore, normally only imported cases of malaria occur. Foci of plague exist in Myanmar; cases of plague also occur in Vietnam. Japanese encephalitis, dengue, and dengue hemorrhagic fever can occur in epidemics in both urban and rural areas of this region. Miteborne typhus has been reported in deforested areas in most countries.

Foodborne and waterborne diseases are common. Cholera and other watery diarrheas, amebic and bacillary dysentery, typhoid fever, and hepatitis A and E may occur in all countries in the area. Among helminthic infections, fasciolopsiasis (giant intestinal fluke) may be acquired in most countries in the area, clonorchiasis (oriental liver fluke) in the Indochina peninsula, opisthorchosis (cat liver fluke) in the Indochina peninsula, the Philippines, and Thailand, and paragonimiasis (oriental lung fluke) in most countries. Melioidosis can occur sporadically throughout the area.

Other diseases. Hepatitis B is highly endemic in the region. Schistosomiasis (bilharziasis) is endemic in the southern Philippines and in central Sulawesi (Indonesia) and occurs in small foci in the Mekong delta in Vietnam. The only known remaining focus of poliovirus transmission is in the Mekong delta area of Cambodia and southern Vietnam. Poliovirus transmission has probably been interrupted in the Lao People's Democratic Republic, Malaysia, and the Philippines and is very low in Indonesia, Myanmar, and Thailand. Trachoma exists in Indonesia, Myanmar, Thailand, and Vietnam.

Other hazards include rabies, snake bites, and leeches.

Middle South Asia (Afghanistan, Armenia, Azerbaijan, Bangladesh, Bhutan, Georgia, India, Islamic Republic of Iran, Kazakstan, Kyrgyzstan, Maldives, Nepal, Pakistan, Sri Lanka, Tajikistan, Turkmenistan, and Uzbekistan). Bordered for the most part by high mountain ranges in the north, the area extends from the steppes and desert in the west to monsoon and tropical rain forests in the east and south.

Arthropodborne diseases are endemic in all these countries; however, malaria is not endemic in Georgia, Kazakstan, Kyrgyzstan, the Maldives, Turkmenistan, and Uzbekistan. There are small foci of malaria in Armenia, Azerbaijan, and Tajikistan. In some of the other countries, malaria occurs in urban as well as rural areas. Filariasis is common in Bangladesh, India, and the southwestern coastal belt of Sri Lanka. Sandfly fever is on the increase in the region. A sharp rise in the incidence of visceral leishmaniasis has been observed in Bangladesh, India, and Nepal. In Pakistan, it is mainly reported from the north (Baltistan). Cutaneous leishmaniasis occurs in Afghanistan, India (Rajasthan), the Islamic Republic of Iran, and Pakistan. There are very small foci of cutaneous and visceral leishmaniasis in Azerbaijan and Tajikistan. There is evidence that natural foci of plague exist in India and Kazakstan. An outbreak of plague occurred in India in 1994. Tickborne relapsing fever is reported from Afghanistan, India, and the Islamic Republic of Iran, and typhus occurs in Afghanistan and India. Outbreaks of dengue fever may occur in Bangladesh, India, Pakistan, and Sri Lanka, and the hemorrhagic form has been reported from eastern India and Sri Lanka. Japanese encephalitis has been reported from the eastern part of the area and Crimean-Congo hemorrhagic fever from the western part. Another tickborne hemorrhagic fever has been reported in forest areas in Karnataka State in India and in a rural area of Rawalpindi District in Pakistan.

Foodborne and waterborne diseases are common throughout the area, in particular cholera and other watery diarrheas, dysenteries, typhoid fever, hepatitis A and E, and helminthic infections. Large epidemics of hepatitis E can occur. Giardiasis is common in the area. Brucellosis and echinococcosis (hydatid disease) are found in many countries in the area.

Other diseases. Hepatitis B is endemic. A very limited focus of urinary schistosomiasis (bilharziasis) persists in the southwest of the Islamic Republic of Iran. Outbreaks of meningococcal meningitis have been reported in India and Nepal. Poliomyelitis eradication activities have begun in all countries in the area, rapidly reducing the risk of infection with wild poliovirus. However, surveillance data are incomplete, and poliovirus transmission should still be assumed to be a risk to travelers in most countries, especially in the Indian subcontinent. Trachoma is common in Afghanistan and in parts of India, the Islamic Republic of Iran, Nepal, and Pakistan. Snakes and the presence of rabies in animals are hazards in most of the countries in the area.

Western South Asia (Bahrain, Cyprus, Iraq, Israel, Jordan, Kuwait, Lebanon, Oman, Qatar, Saudi Arabia, Syrian Arab Republic, Turkey, the United Arab Emirates, and Yemen). The area ranges from the mountains and steppes of the northwest to the large deserts and dry tropical scrub of the south.

Arthropodborne diseases, except for malaria in certain areas, are not a major hazard for the traveler. Malaria does not exist in Kuwait and no longer occurs in Bahrain, Cyprus, Israel, Jordan, Lebanon, or Qatar. Its incidence in the Syrian Arab Republic and United Arab Emirates is low but elsewhere it is endemic in certain rural areas. Cutaneous leishmaniasis is reported throughout the area; visceral leishmaniasis, although rare throughout most of the area, is common in central Iraq, in the southwest of Saudi Arabia, in the northwest of the Syrian Arab Republic, in Turkey (southeast Anatolia only), and in the west of Yemen. Murine and tickborne typhus can occur in certain countries, as may tickborne relapsing fever. Crimean-Congo hemorrhagic fever has been reported from Iraq and limited foci of onchocerciasis are reported from Yemen.

Foodborne and waterborne diseases are, however, a major hazard in most countries in the area. Typhoid fevers and hepatitis A exist in all countries. Dracunculiasis occurs in isolated foci in Yemen. Taeniasis (tapeworm) infestation is reported from many countries in the area. Brucellosis is reported from most countries, and there are foci of echinococcosis (hydatid disease).

Other diseases. Hepatitis B is endemic in the region. Schistosomiasis (bilharziasis) occurs in Iraq, Saudi Arabia, the Syrian Arab Republic, and Yemen. The risk of poliovirus infection is low in most countries in the area, with the exception of Yemen. Trachoma and animal rabies are found in many of the countries. The greatest hazards to pilgrims to Mecca and Medina are heat stroke and dehydration if the period of the Hajj coincides with the hot season.

Europe (Figures 5I and 5J)

Northern Europe (Belarus, Belgium, Czech Republic, Denmark [including Faroe Islands], Estonia, Finland, Germany, Iceland, Ireland, Latvia, Lithuania, Luxembourg, Netherlands, Norway, Poland, Republic of Moldova, Russian Federation, Slovakia, Sweden, Ukraine, and the United Kingdom [including Channel Islands and the Isle of Man]). The area consisting of these countries extends from the broadleaf forests and the plains of the west to the boreal and mixed forests to be found as far east as the Pacific Ocean. The incidence of communicable diseases in most parts of the area is such that they are unlikely to prove a hazard to the international traveler greater than that found in his or her own country. There are, of course, some health risks but in most of the area, very few precautions are required.

Of the *arthropodborne diseases*, there are very small foci of tickborne typhus in east and central Siberia. Tickborne encephalitis, for which a vaccine exists, and Lyme disease may occur throughout forested areas where vector ticks are found. Rodentborne hemorrhagic fever with renal syndrome is now recognized as occurring at low endemic levels in this area.

Foodborne and waterborne diseases reported, other than the ubiquitous diarrheal diseases, are taeniasis (tapeworm) and trichinellosis in parts of northern Europe, and diphyllobothriasis (fish tapeworm) from the freshwater fish around the Baltic Sea area. *Fasciola hepatica* infection can occur. Hepatitis A is encountered in the eastern European countries. The incidence of certain foodborne diseases, e.g., salmonellosis and campylobacteriosis, is increasing significantly in some countries.

Figure 5I   Map of Western Europe

Other diseases. All countries in the area where polio-myelitis was endemic are now making intense efforts to eradicate the disease. Within the Russian Federation, poliovirus transmission remains a possibility only in the area of Chechenia. Rabies is endemic in wild animals (particularly foxes) in rural areas of northern Europe. In recent years, Belarus, the Russian Federation, and Ukraine have experienced extensive epidemics of diphtheria. Diphtheria cases, mostly imported from these three countries, have also been reported from neighboring Estonia, Finland, Latvia, Lithuania, Poland, and the Republic of Moldova.

In parts of northern Europe, the extreme cold in the winter can be a climatic hazard.

Southern Europe (Albania, Andorra, Austria, Bosnia and Herzegovina, Bulgaria, Croatia, France, Gibraltar, Greece, Hungary, Italy, Liechtenstein, Malta, Monaco, Portugal [including Azores and Madeira], Romania, San Marino, Slovenia, Spain [including the Canary Islands], Switzerland, the Former Yugoslav Republic of Macedonia, and Yugoslavia). The area extends from the broadleaf forests in the northwest and the mountains of the Alps to the prairies and, in the south and southeast, the scrub vegetation of the Mediterranean.

Among the *arthropodborne diseases*, sporadic cases of murine and tickborne typhus and mosquitoborne West Nile fever occur in some countries bordering the Mediterranean littoral. Both cutaneous and visceral leishmaniasis and sandfly fever are also reported from this area. Leishmania and human immunodeficiency virus (HIV) co-infections have been notified from France, Italy, Portugal, and Spain. Tickborne encephalitis, for which a vaccine exists, Lyme disease, and rodentborne hemorrhagic fever with renal syndrome may occur in the eastern and southern parts of the area.

Foodborne and waterborne diseases—bacillary dysentery, diarrhea, and typhoid fever—are more common in the summer and autumn months, with a high incidence in the southeastern

Figure 5J   Map of Eastern Europe

and southwestern parts of the area. Brucellosis can occur in the extreme southwest and southeast and echinococcosis (hydatid disease) in the southeast. *Fasciola hepatica* infection has been reported from different countries in this area. Hepatitis A occurs in the eastern European countries. The incidence of certain foodborne diseases, e.g., salmonellosis and campylobacteriosis, is increasing significantly in some countries.

Other diseases. All countries in southern Europe where until recently poliomyelitis was endemic are conducting eradication activities, and the risk of infection in most countries is very low. However, a large poliomyelitis outbreak occurred in 1996 in Albania, also affecting Greece and Yugoslavia; the transmission was, however, interrupted by the end of 1996. Hepatitis B is endemic in the southern part of eastern Europe (Albania, Bulgaria, and Romania). Rabies in animals exists in most countries of southern Europe.

Oceania (Figure 5K)

Australia, New Zealand, and the Antarctic. In Australia, the mainland has tropical monsoon forests in the north and east; dry tropical forests, savanna, and deserts in the center; and Mediterranean-like scrub and subtropical forests in the south. New Zealand has a temperate climate, with the North Island characterized by subtropical forests and the South Island by steppe vegetation and hardwood forests.

International travelers to Australia and New Zealand will, in general, not be subjected to the hazards of communicable diseases to any extent greater than that found in their own country.

Arthropodborne disease (mosquitoborne epidemic polyarthritis and viral encephalitis) may occur in some rural areas of Australia. Occasional outbreaks of dengue have occurred in northern Australia in recent years.

Other hazards. Coelenterates (corals, jellyfish) may prove a hazard while bathing in the sea, and heat during summer is a hazard in the northern and central parts of Australia.

Melanesia and Micronesia-Polynesia (American Samoa, Cook Islands, Easter Island, Fiji, French Polynesia, Guam, Kiribati, Marshall Islands, [Federated States of] Micronesia , Nauru, New Caledonia, Niue, Palau, Papua New Guinea, Samoa, Solomon Islands, Tokelau, Tonga, Tuvalu, Vanuatu, and the Wallis and Futuna Islands). The area covers an enormous expanse of ocean, with the larger, mountainous, tropical, and monsoon-rain-forest-covered islands of the west giving way to the smaller, originally volcanic peaks and coral islands of the east.

Arthropodborne diseases occur in the majority of the islands. Malaria is endemic in Papua New Guinea, Solomon Islands, and Vanuatu. Filariasis is widespread but its prevalence varies. Miteborne typhus has been reported from Papua New Guinea. Dengue fever, including its hemorrhagic form, can occur in epidemics in most islands.

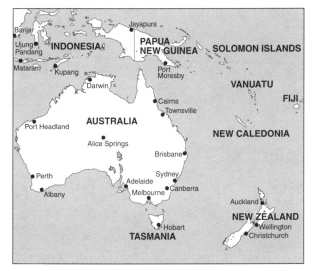

Figure 5K   Map of Australasia

Foodborne and waterborne diseases, such as the diarrheal diseases, typhoid fever, and helminthic infections, are commonly reported. Biointoxication may occur from raw or cooked fish and shellfish. Hepatitis A is reported in this area as well.

Other diseases. Hepatitis B is endemic in the region. Poliomyelitis cases have not been reported from any of these areas for more than 5 years. Trachoma occurs in parts of Melanesia. Hazards to sea bathers are the coelenterates, poisonous fish, and snakes.

OVERVIEW OF HEALTH RISKS IN TRAVELERS

Mortality

There are limited data on deaths of travelers occurring abroad, and no information is available on deaths that occur after return as a consequence of illness during the stay abroad. According to a Swiss study, the mortality rate of Swiss travelers in developing countries is 0.8 to 1.5 per 100,000 per month (excluding deaths due to acquired immunodeficiency syndrome [AIDS] occurring usually many years after HIV infection abroad). Trekking in Nepal is associated with a particularly high mortality rate of 15 per 100,000 whereas among the Swiss travelers staying in North America, it is only 0.3 per 100,000. Since those traveling to developing countries are supposed to be younger and healthier, mortality in such travelers is expected to be lower than the mortality in those remaining at home. However, many elderly Americans and Europeans also travel to escape from cold climates to go to a warmer region, such as the Caribbean or southern Europe. Here the average age is higher, and age-specific cardiovascular mortality rates are similar to those of the population remaining at home.

Accidents

High mortality has been observed in Americans traveling to Mexico and the Swiss going overseas, primarily due to accidents, particularly in young people. Deaths abroad due to injuries are higher by a factor of two to three in the 15 to 44-year-old travelers when compared with rates for nontravelers.

Fatalities are mostly due to traffic accidents. Use of motorcycles, lack of seatbelts in rental cars, chaotic traffic conditions in the developing countries, particularly at night are decisive factors (see Part 3). Drowning is another major cause of accidental death. Swimming after excessive drinking and lack of knowledge about sea currents often result in such tragedies.

Assaults and terrorism are statistically less important although there is significant concern regarding these mainly among travelers from the U.S. This may arise from the feeling of apprehension many Americans experience, as Americans are frequently political targets of terrorism. Among other countries, murder rates exceeding 10 are observed in Russia (20), Botswana (16), and Panama (14).

Infections

Infections claim a lower toll than many would expect; to a large extent, they may be effectively prevented. The most important is malaria, with a mortality rate exceeding 1 in 100,000 in travelers visiting tropical Africa. It is estimated that 6 in 100,000 travelers will ultimately die of AIDS, due to HIV transmission mostly through unprotected, casual sex during a stay in a developing country.

Morbidity

As many as 75% of short-term travelers to the tropics or subtropics report some health impairment and frequent use of self-medication. Short-term transatlantic travelers report a 50% rate of health impairment, often constipation. However, even in travelers to the developing countries, only a few of these self-reported health problems are severe; just 7% of all travelers need medical attention abroad, 16% upon return, 4% both abroad and upon return. Fourteen percent of travelers are incapacitated while abroad, and 2% of the time abroad is lost because of illness or accidents among all travelers. Less than 2% are unable to go back to work upon return; in all studies, about 1% of travelers have to stay in a hospital, usually for only a few days. One among 2000 travelers requires emergency aeromedical evacuation, be it by scheduled or ambulance flight (Figure 6).

A survey conducted among World Bank employees illustrates that travel is associated with increased morbidity and that this is not attributable only to infections. The risk per trip is greatest for first-time travelers; experienced travelers know how to diminish risks (Figure 7).

Infections

Since the initiation of epidemiologic surveys in the 1970s, there has been a definite reduction in the transmission of infectious diseases, mainly traveler's diarrhea, in southern Europe whereas the incidence rates of major infections affecting travelers in the developing countries have remained fairly constant. There are some exceptions, such as in Tunisia, where a joint action by the Ministries of Health and Tourism resulted in a reduction of the incidence of traveler's diarrhea from 50% to 30%; this finding has been validated by international teams.

It is important to be aware of frequent as well as rare infections in travelers (Figure 8). Traveler's diarrhea is the most fre-

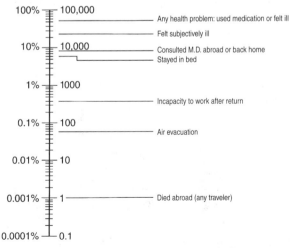

Figure 6   Incidence rate/month of health problems during a stay in developing countries

quent ailment encountered in those traveling from the developed nations to the developing countries, followed by upper respiratory tract infections without or, less frequently, with fever. In tropical Africa, Papua New Guinea, and on some islands in the Pacific, malaria is the most frequent among the life-threatening infections. Hepatitis A and hepatitis B are the most frequent among the vaccine-preventable diseases. Often there are concerns about exposure to rabies after animal bites. Regional and seasonal variations to these worldwide data are listed under the respective headings.

Sexually transmitted diseases, including HIV infection, continue to be of great concern since even in the presence of risk of possible HIV transmission, not all casual sexual contacts are protected by condoms (see below).

Risk Behavior and Compliance

Travel health professionals must recognize the fact that travelers often will not follow given recommendations. Travelers also may choose not to consult any travel health professionals prior to departure for fear of needles or side effects of medica-

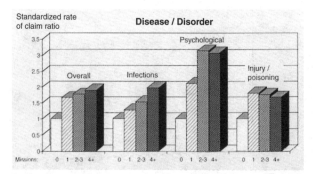

Figure 7   International business travel and insurance claims (5,672 male World Bank employees)

tion, high costs, or for psychological reasons. Many want to be "free" from rules and regimented behavior during their stay abroad. Some decide against travel health consultations as they have no confidence in the conflicting recommendations. Cost can be a major factor in a traveler's avoidance of health consultations. Some travelers prefer to use alternative medical methods such as herbal medicine or homeopathy in spite of their lack of safety or effectiveness. For example, homeopathic malaria prophylaxis has been demonstrated to pose a considerable health risk.

Behavior is hypothesized to originate from two factors: the value that an individual places on the behavior, and the individual's estimate of the likelihood that a given action will lead to the desired goal. The four following cognitive dimensions play a role: perceived susceptibility of an illness or accident, its severity, benefits from prevention, and disadvantages due to

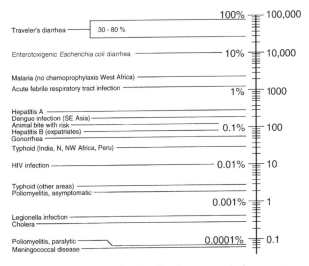

Figure 8   Incidence rate/month of health problems during a stay in developing countries

the preventive action, such as cost, adverse reactions, or discomfort.

More than 90% of travelers from Europe and North America succumb to gastronomic temptations and forget the old rule "boil it, cook it, peel it, or forget it." This leads to gastrointestinal disorders.

With respect to malaria, almost all travelers (> 99%) are informed about the risk in high transmission areas. The majority of travelers use medication as prescribed for the chemosuppression of malaria while abroad; however, only about 50% will do this regularly and continue this up to 4 weeks upon return. Most use some form of personal protection against mosquito bites but less than 5% systematically attempt to completely avoid such bites by using all possible methods that are available. Some travelers, although aware of the risk of malaria, decide not to consult a doctor within 24 hours of developing a febrile illness as instructed, and if unable to find a health professional within that time, they refuse to use the stand-by medication obtained prior to departure. This mistake has cost numerous lives.

Five percent of British, German, Swiss, or Canadian tourists, more often men than women, have casual sex abroad. When men travel alone, this rate may be 20%, according to one survey. These travelers are not all "sex tourists," who travel with the goal of having sex but many just stumble into a romantic affair more often with locals than with fellow travelers. The rate of unprotected contacts has recently decreased from half to one-third, with men above the age of 40 years being significantly more careless than young men perhaps because of fear of impotence when a condom is to be used. Also, women often fail to protect themselves or have their partners use condoms, even when their partners are natives of tropical Africa where HIV prevalence is particularly high.

Noncompliance has been associated with low quality of consultation prior to the journey, long duration of stay, multiple journeys, lower age, and adverse reactions. Businessmen, who are the least well informed, and those who visit relatives or friends in a developing country are less compliant than tourists, particularly when they travel in groups. Noncompliant travelers often forget preventive measures or consider them as unnecessary. Sometimes, they are encouraged by other travelers or friends to disregard travel health advice.

Pretravel Counseling

Standardized Pretravel Questioning

In pretravel consultations, the first thing to remember is that
the potential traveler is not a patient. He or she will usually
first register and indicate name, address, and birthdate. Nation-
ality may also be of interest in order to know which language
should be used for communication with the individual and to
obtain background on immune status. The potential traveler
should then indicate his travel plans, according to a minimum
checklist, such as the following:

- Destination(s): countries, city/resort/off-the-tourist-trail,
  itinerary
- Purpose: tourism/business or other professional (which?)/
  visit (to natives/expatriates), other (military, airline crew,
  adoption, etc.)
- Hygiene standard expected: high (e.g., multistar hotels)/low
  (e.g., low budget travel)
- Special activities: high altitude trekking, diving, hunting,
  camping, etc.
- Date of departure
- Duration of stay abroad

Potential travelers should also answer at least the following set
of questions on their health status and medical history:

- Do you currently use any medication?
  If yes, which ones:
- Do you currently have a fever?
  If yes, what temperature:
- Do you suffer from any chronic illnesses?
  If yes, which ones:
- Are you allergic to eggs or medication?
  If yes, describe:

- Are you pregnant or nursing?
  Details:
- Have you ever had seizures?
  Details:
- Have you ever had psychiatric or psychologic problems?
  Details:
- Have you ever had jaundice or hepatitis?
  Details:
- Are you or anybody in your household infected by HIV? Do you have any other immunodeficiencies?
  Details:

With future use of antimalarials, it may become essential to question travelers about glucose-6-phospate dehydrogenase (G-6-PD) deficiency; this is so far not routinely done.

Usually, travelers are unable to give accurate information about their immunization status; this is best discussed while reviewing the vaccination certificates, possibly also additional military documents as immunizations may have been performed during armed service duty. A useful standard procedure is to invite all visitors to a travel health consultation to bring those documents.

Whenever there is an indication that medical problems exist, these should be discussed and, if necessary, assessed. Otherwise, a medical check-up or examinations are usually not indicated, unless the traveler plans to become a long-term resident abroad or if extreme exertion is to be expected, such as in mountaineering at very high altitudes. Psychological evaluation may be particularly important in both these circumstances.

Pretravel Health Advice: Minimizing Exposure to Risks

Principles in the Practice of Travel Health Advice

To be able to minimize exposure to risks—among others, the German language has the useful term "exposure prophylaxis"—the traveler needs some knowledge and some discipline. Intelligent behavior reduces risks. Ideally, the travel health professional should provide potential travelers with counsel tailored to suit the specific trip planned and to the individual's health status.

Large travel clinics have often elected to use video programs to provide basic instructions to their customers. Such programs allow the travel staff to target the interview to specific items. Video programs should be based on "edutainment" rather than give rigid and strict do's and don'ts, and while the health professional must take good care to give all necessary advice, care should be taken not to overload the customer with unnecessary, or far too theoretical information. Studies have shown that only a limited amount of information can be absorbed in such consultations. The counseling medical professional should ensure that all the important messages have been understood. The goal is not to discourage customers from travel or to have them travel full of fears. Counseling families with children, long-term travelers, and persons with pre-existing medical conditions usually is very time consuming.

To be able to follow the basic rules of thoughtful behavior abroad, the traveler should be aware of the risks inherent in the 4 F and the 4 S (Table 3). There should be awareness about the risks as well as knowledge about the preventive measures to be taken.

Table 3 Main Instruction Targets for Travelers

Food	Boil it, cook it, peel it, or forget it
Fluids	Avoid tap water, drink plenty
Flies	Measures against mosquito bites
Flirts	No unprotected casual sex
Safe cars	Wear safety belt, no night driving
Swimming	Check currents, no alcohol
Sun	Don't get burned
Stress	Get rest, don't overload program

Avoiding Environmental Risks

Travel involves a considerable amount of physical effort. Various forms of environmental stress may impair a person's sense of well-being, reduce resistance to disease, or even cause disease. Such stress can, however, be avoided to a great extent (Table 4).

To begin with, stress can be avoided by not doing the packing in the last hour and having to rush to the airport. Those who suffer from claustrophobia or agoraphobia should try and book convenient seats ("a little cosy corner" or the first row of a section) in the aircraft.

At the destination, one should take necessary precautions to cope with the climate. Especially in hot, dry places, it is important to maintain sufficient fluid balance; particularly, senior travelers, whose thirst reflex is vastly reduced, must be reminded that they should consume a lot of fluids. An excellent indicator is the color of the urine, which should be light. Salt tablets are usually not indicated but after excessive sweating, travelers should take care to replenish their electrolytes by salt-containing food items or soups. Appropriate clothing, e.g., cotton which is highly absorbent, will contribute to well-being. Gradual acclimatization over the initial days by avoiding exertion is also of practical benefit.

It is unrealistic to just advise travelers to "avoid the sun." The practical thing to do is to avoid the sun at its highest intensity and to use ultraviolet (UV) blockers. This is discussed in detail in Part 3.

There are many risks associated with large bodies of water. Swimmers and divers should beware of currents (check warning signs, flags, ask the locals!). There may be contamination by sewage or industrial effluents. The visitor should find out if there is risk of schistosomiasis infection before swimming in lakes, ponds, and swamps; fast-flowing rivers pose lower risk of schistosomiasis. Pools are safe only if they are properly chlorinated. In all beach sports, accident prevention is paramount. Even a small bruise may become infected and result in a serious infection and

pain; the traveler may be incapacitated for any physical activity.
Life jackets should be used in potentially dangerous water sports.

Prevention of accidents related to the environment is
described in Part 3.

Table 4 How to Minimize Exposure to Risks

Risk Category	Type	Preventive Action
Psychological environment During travel	Stress	Allow sufficient time
	Claustro- and agoraphobia	Seat selection, cognitive therapy: avoid small boats and planes,
	Motion sickness	Seat selection, relaxed position of rest, preventive medication
	Jet lag	Melatonin or short-acting sleeping pill?
At destination	Climate	Clothing, fluids, minerals, frequent showers, avoid exertion
	Sun	Sun screen, minimal exposure
	Freshwater	Do not touch if risk of schistosomiasis, pools safe (?)
	Saltwater	Avoid currents, avoid bruises
	Soil	Do not walk barefoot or lie on soil
	Altitude	Slow ascent, warn high-risk subjects
	Traffic	Avoid night travel, motorbikes
Human to human	STD	Avoid unprotected sex
	Assault	Avoid risky areas, night strolls
Animal to human	Rabies	Do not pet unknown animals, do not touch cadavers
	Snakes (rare), scorpions	Wear shoes, check clothing
	Jellyfish, poisonous fish	Ask locals, wear goggles
Vectorborne	Malaria, dengue, etc.	Measures against mosquito bites
Foodborne	Traveler's diarrhea, etc.	"Boil it, cook it, peel it, or forget it" — as far as possible
Intoxicating drugs	Alcohol, marijuana, etc.	Abstain before casual sex, swimming, diving

Avoiding Human Risks

If travelers cannot abstain from casual sex, they should at least avoid unprotected sex. Travel health professionals, e.g., tour guides noting the plans of individuals in their group, must learn to raise the subject, particularly in persons likely to be lonely or under the influence of alcohol or drugs. Even though sexual encounters are not always deliberately planned, all travelers should be warned of risks associated with casual, unprotected sex. As previously mentioned, women often do not convince their partners to wear a condom, and often men over 40 years of age are afraid of being rendered impotent while using a condom.

To avoid assaults, it is wise to abstain from walks, particularly alone and at night, in areas which are considered unsafe. It may be beneficial to hire a taxi even for short distances in such situations and to lock the doors during the ride.

Avoiding Animal Risks

Most animals avoid human beings. The danger from animals often arises from unnecessary intrusion on the part of humans. To prevent the risk of rabies, one should not pet, terrify, or tease unknown animals. If bitten, one must assume that the animal may be rabid and take appropriate measures (see Part 2). Accompanying animals (dogs, and for many countries also cats) must be immunized against rabies before they are allowed to cross international frontiers.

While walking anywhere, including the beach, one should wear strong, thick shoes. This will protect against snake bites and scorpion stings as well as jigger fleas, *Tunga penetrans*, sandflies (phlebotomes), and thus *Leishmania* infection, fungal infections, and plantar warts.

Before putting on any clothing or shoes, one should first check for small animals or poisonous insects that may be hiding in them.

Avoiding Vectorborne Diseases

Female mosquitoes use visual, thermal, and olfactorial (the latter most important) stimuli to locate a human host required for their reproduction cycle. Male mosquitoes feed primarily on the nectar in flowers. During the day, dark clothing and movement of the host attract most mosquito species, and at night light colors attract them more. While dark colors attract the *Anopheles* mosquitoes, light ones attract the *Aedes* mosquitoes. The mosquitoes prefer to target male adults usually more than women and children. Fragrances from perfumes, soaps, or lotions may also attract mosquitoes.

Of the measures against arthropods transmitting a wide variety of communicable diseases, the most important is prevention of mosquito bites between dusk and dawn to avoid malaria infection. However, it must be remembered that *Aedes* mosquitoes transmitting dengue fever bite during the daytime. Therefore, personal protection measures (PPM) are paramount at all times, especially when increased mosquito activity is noted, such as after rainy periods.

Staying in air-conditioned rooms or those protected by wire meshes may be safe but few tourists will renounce outdoor activities just to avoid mosquito bites. Outdoors, one should use clothing to cover arms, legs, and particularly the ankles. Mosquito bites may penetrate thin clothes (<1 mm thick and openings >0.02 mm), which obviously are preferred in a tropical climate. Therefore, it is recommended to spray clothing with repellents or, even better, with insecticides. The uncovered skin should be protected with a repellent.

Repellents are chemicals that cause insects to turn away. Most contain DEET (N,N,diethyl-methyl-toluamide), a very effective substance that has been used for more than 40 years. Some others contain EBAAP (ethyl-buthylacetyl-aminopropionate), picaridin (1-piperidincarboxyl acid,2-(2-hydroxyethyl)-1-methyl-propylesther, Bayrepel), DMP (dimethylphtalate, reduced effect when temperature >23°C), ethylexanediol, indalone, or a mixture of these. Synthetic repellents are effective for several hours (most 3 to 4, never > 4) and thus need to be reapplied in prolonged exposure. While older generation DEET formulations are rapidly lost through sweating, newer ones containing polymers or other substances last longer but are frequently considered too sticky. The duration of protection depends on the following:

- Environment: temperature (each 10°C increase may result in up to 50% reduction in protection time), humidity, sunlight, wind
- Formulation: concentration, solvent (e.g., polymers)
- Host factors: sweating, percutaneous penetration of repellent in the skin
- Part of the skin exposed: body versus head
- Abrasion by clothing
- Behavior: swimming, washing off repellent
- Targeted insects: blood feeders versus stinging insects

There is risk of DEET toxicity, which usually occurs when the product is misused. This is due to absorption of 9 to 56% of the chemical, through the skin with higher rates in alcohol-based solutions. This is especially a concern in infants, in whom three cases of lethal encephalopathy with high concentrations (up to 100%) have been observed. The concentration is therefore limited to 35% in many countries. Any formulation with higher concentrations is not recommended (not >10% in children for DEET and EBAAP). Repellents should not be inhaled, ingested, applied on open wounds or irritated skin, or allowed to get into the eyes. Therefore, one must avoid applying repellents on children's hands as the chemical is likely to get into their eyes or mouth from the hands. Most repellents (with the exception of Bayrepel) are solvents of plastic materials; therefore, eye glasses or lenses, plastic watches, or varnish, must be protected or removed before the repellent is applied. The repellent should be washed off after returning indoors.

The repellent should always be applied sparingly on all exposed areas. Unprotected skin a few centimeters from a treated area may be attacked by hungry mosquitoes. Many consider repellents contraindicated in the following:

- Infants below the age of 1 year (mosquito nets are preferred)
- Long-term residents, for fear of accumulated toxicity
- Pregnant women, although no teratogenicity has been demonstrated

Natural repellents, such as citronella oil or other plant extracts, are rarely used anymore as their effectiveness is usually limited to less than an hour and are likely to cause an allergic reaction.

Insecticides are poisons that target the nerves of insects and other cold-blooded animals and thus kill them. Synthetic pyrethroid insecticides (permethrin, deltamethrin, and others) are more photostable and less volatile than the natural product pyrethrum (obtained from the flowers of *Chrysanthemum cinerariaefolium*). Pyrethrum acts as an insecticide as well as a repellent.

Pyrethroid-containing sprays should be used to eliminate mosquitoes from living and sleeping areas during evening and night-time hours. Such sprays are also used in aircraft for disinfection, i.e., to avoid the importation of mosquitoes to countries nonendemic for malaria. Most experts consider them nontoxic. Occasionally, mosquitoes may enter even air-conditioned rooms. Mosquito coils containing pyrethroids may be used although these coils last only a few hours. Many products are of questionable quality and may cause irritation of the mucous membranes.

Clothing sprayed with permethrin or deltamethrin provides residual protection for 2 to 4 weeks; the spraying causes no stains and minimal odor. For adults, this is considered nontoxic whereas in infants and children this is questionable. Permethrin, however, should not be applied directly on the skin.

If an accommodation allows entry of mosquitoes, sprays, dispensers, or pyrethroid mosquito coils should be used in addition to a mosquito net. Impregnation (soaking) of such nets with insecticide offers additional protection for 2 to 3 months, even when the net is slightly damaged. For impregnation of nets (or clothing, as used mainly by the military), use premixed Peripel; or measure 0.5 g/m^2 of permethrin or 0.05 g/m^2 of deltamethrin, soak and squeeze the clothing to absorb insecticide solution, wring gently, dry flat on a plastic sheet, avoiding direct sunlight, and after a while hang up the clothing to speed up the drying process.

Oral agents such as vitamin B, ultrasonic devices, and bug zappers which lure and electrocute insects are ineffective measures against mosquito bites.

Avoiding Contaminated Food and Beverage

Almost all travel counselors recommend avoidance of contaminated food; however, very few travelers consistently follow such advice. It is only rarely that travelers test the food with a thermometer and refuse it unless the core temperature is at least $60°C$. Such careful behavior will certainly reduce the size of inoculum of infectious organisms ingested. However, it is not practical and will not completely protect one from all gastrointestinal infections; sometimes, pathogens are found even in bottled water. Since it is not possible to convince all travelers to always avoid cold buffets or other potentially contaminated food or ensure satisfactorily hygienic kitchens in all parts of the world, a new strategy is necessary. Travelers should be educated about the risk scale (Figure 9), and emphasis should be made on abstaining from highly dangerous items and situations. Every traveler is free to decide what risks he or she wants to take but the decision should be made on an informed basis.

Basics on Immunization

The human immune system protects the body by eliminating or neutralizing materials recognized as foreign. The goal of

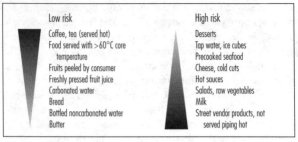

Low risk	High risk
Coffee, tea (served hot)	Desserts
Food served with >60°C core temperature	Tap water, ice cubes
Fruits peeled by consumer	Precooked seafood
Freshly pressed fruit juice	Cheese, cold cuts
Carbonated water	Hot sauces
Bread	Salads, raw vegetables
Bottled noncarbonated water	Milk
Butter	Street vendor products, not served piping hot

Figure 9   Food risk scale

immunization is to evoke an immune response, for instance, by production of antibodies. This is based on the fact that the immune system is capable of remembering previous encounters with immunogenic substances, which results in stronger responses upon rechallenge.

In active immunization (vaccination), an immunogenic substance (a vaccine), is administered. This is processed and modified by various cells of the human immune system until ultimately the B lymphocytes either differentiate into antibody-producing plasma cells specific for that vaccine or into long memory B lymphocytes. In passive immunization, antibodies produced by another (usually human) organism, often called immune globulins, are administered to provide immediate but short-lasting protection.

Live attenuated vaccines contain live, weakened microorganisms that induce active immunity; inactivated vaccines are composed of killed microorganisms or of components thereof that will induce active immunity.

The vaccines are described in detail in Part 2 of this manual. Because national standards for licensure differ, not all vaccines are available in all countries. Similarly, for vaccines against the same disease and for vaccine schedules, contraindications may differ by product and by country. Recommendations issued by national authorities and manufacturer's instructions should therefore be consulted for up-to-date information and details.

Strategy for Application of Immunizations

Appropriate immunizations prior to travel not only reduce the risk of vaccine-preventable diseases for the recipient, they also reduce the risk of international spread of the respective diseases. Several key factors should be considered when planning immunizations for individuals with travel plans as illustrated in this chapter. The essentials are as follows:

Host-related (part 1)
- Travel plans: destination, type of travel
- Personal immune status
- Personal state of health

Environment-related
- Required immunizations
- Risk assessment of other vaccine-preventable infections

On the basis of these issues, the travel health professional will determine the ideal immunizations for the traveler. This, however, may be altered by the following:

Host-related (part 2)
- Contraindications
- Time restraints
- Financial constraints

All travel-related vaccines are not necessarily indicated for all travelers; some may be medically contraindicated or there may be time or financial constraints. The travel health professional should be aware of priorities, with respect to incidence and severity of the various infections (Figure 10, Table 5). The health professional and the traveler should also take into account cost and risk of adverse reactions and decide on what and how much immunization is required. It is certainly not logical to immunize travelers against rare diseases that have a low case fatality rate with modern therapy and leave the travelers unprotected against more frequent and life-threatening infections for which no effective treatment is available. But lastly, it is an arbitrary decision on how far down the list in Table 5 one wants to recommend protection to a future traveler.

General Immunization Rules

Vaccine Administration. Vaccines should be stored as recommended by the manufacturer. In the case of vaccines in suspension form, the shelf life should be verified and the suspension shaken well before use. The vaccines should be administered as recommended by the manufacturer—intramuscularly (IM), subcutaneously (SQ), or intradermally (ID). Some vaccines

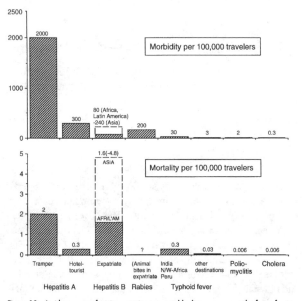

Figure 10 Incidence rate of various vaccine preventable diseases per month of stay for nonimmune travelers visiting a developing country

come with several options in the route of administration. While it is important to observe the required minimum intervals between vaccine doses, it is irrelevant if too many months, years, or decades have elapsed since the last dose, except that there may be inadequate immunity during the interval before the next dose. It is unnecessary to restart an interrupted series of vaccination or to add extra doses.

The skin at the injection site (deltoid region in adults and children > 1 year of age, anterolateral thigh in infants < 1 year of age, quadriceps muscle if intramuscular) should be cleansed with an antiseptic agent, such as 70% isopropyl alcohol, povidone-iodine or simply with soap and water. Ideally, one should wait 5 minutes for optimal germicidal effect before the vaccine is administered. A new needle and a new syringe are to be used for each injection.

Table 5 Rationale for Immunization of Travelers

Infection	Incidence	Impact	Total	Immunization	
				Yes	No
Hepatitis A	+++	++	+++++		
Hepatitis B	++	+++	+++++		
Rabies	++	++	++++		
Poliomyelitis	(+)	+++	+++(+)		
Yellow fever	(+)	+++	+++(+)		
Typhoid fever	++	+	+++		
Influenza	++(+)?	(+)	+++		
Diphtheria	(+)	++	++(+)		
Tetanus	(+)	++	++(+)		
Meningococcal disease	(+)	++	++(+)		
Japanese encephalitis	(+)	++	++(+)		
Cholera	+	+	++		
Measles	(+)	+	+(+)		

Text in immunization area: "The overcautious physician or traveler, those unconcerned about adverse events" / "Rational" / "Illogical" / "The hazardous, the cost conscious"

Rate per 100,000: +++ = >100; ++ = 1–99; + = 0.1–0.9; (+) = <0.1

Impact: +++ = high case fatality rate, serious residuals; ++ = >5% case fatality rate or incapacitation >4 weeks; + = low case fatality rate, brief incapacitation

Some health professionals find it useful to ask the traveler to take a deep breath just when the injection is administered as this may reduce the pain by distracting the patient.

Vaccination Rules and Requirements. The required vaccinations, based on the International Health Regulations (IHR) adopted by the 22nd World Health Assembly in 1969 are provided below.

As a condition for entry, various countries require proof of vaccination administered at an approved Vaccination Center; this must be documented on the International Certificate of Vaccination (Figure 11). While many countries require such proof only from travelers arriving from infected or potentially endemic areas, other require such evidence from all travelers, sometimes even those in transit. For international travel, the only certificate that is required now is the yellow fever vaccination certificate. As listed below, additional requirements exist, particularly for immunizations against cholera, diphtheria, and meningococcal disease. When immunizations are not required as a condition for entry, it is not necessary to transfer information on national or provincial vaccination documents to the International Certificate of Vaccination.

Travelers who have a contraindication to a required vaccination should obtain a validated waiver from the proper authorities. Additionally, waivers obtained from embassies or consulates of the countries to be visited may be useful, as on rare occasions the health authorities of some countries have refused to accept medical waivers.

Mainly in the U.S., proof of immunization against diphtheria, measles, poliomyelitis, and rubella is now universally required for entry into educational institutions. In addition, school entry requirements of most states include immunization against tetanus (49 states), pertussis (44 states), mumps (42 states), and hepatitis B (34 states).

Routine and Recommended Vaccination. All the developed countries have national plans and programs for routine childhood immunizations, with minor differences. They are, there-

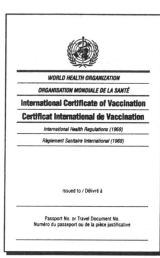

Figure 11   International Certificate of Vaccination

fore, not described in detail in this manual beyond the scope of international travel.

Travel brochures often refer only to vaccinations required by the IHR. It is of paramount importance to know and to convince travelers that generally recommended routine immunizations very often play a more significant role in maintaining a traveler's health than the legally required ones.

Schedule, Simultaneous Administration. In the past, travelers had to receive their immunizations on up to seven different dates. This certainly was not practical and may well have had a negative effect on compliance. As there are hardly any significant interactions between vaccines, all travel-related vaccines can be administered in one single session, except in cases where multiple doses are needed (Figure 12). This is, however, only needed in risk groups or in persons who failed to receive their routine childhood immunizations.

Most of the widely used antigens can be given on the same day without impairing antibody response or increasing the rate of adverse reactions. Different injection sites are to be used in

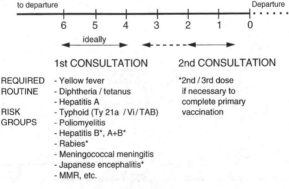

Figure 12   Routine schedule for travel-related vaccines

simultaneous vaccinations, with a distance of at least 2 cm between each site.

When simultaneous administration is not done, one should consider that the immune response to a live virus vaccine may theoretically be impaired if the vaccine is administered within 30 days of administration of another live virus vaccine. Whenever possible, live virus vaccines should therefore be given simultaneously or at least 1 month apart.

Contraindications. General contraindications for vaccines have been listed below. Details on each vaccine are listed in Part 2.

1. Acute illness. Usually persons with acute illness will not present themselves for immunization. Moderate or severe illnesses are a good reason to postpone immunization whereas mild ones (e.g., common cold with low-grade fever) are no reason for delay.

2. Lower age limit. Infants may be unable to produce antibodies to some vaccines; they may, however, be protected by maternal antibodies.

3. Hypersensitivity to vaccine components. Some people may have experienced hypersensitivity during previous vaccine administration. Some persons may be hypersensitive to thimerosal or trace amounts of antibiotics or proteins. No vaccine currently used in the developed nations contains penicillin or penicillin derivatives.

Allergy to egg proteins (found in yellow fever, influenza, measles-mumps-rubella [MMR], measles, and mumps vaccines) is no contraindication for immunization but vaccination should be performed in a setting where adverse reactions can be dealt with appropriately. Skin tests with a 1:20 to 1:100 saline diluted vaccine, whereby 0.1 ml is injected ID, or desensitization are obsolete.

4. Pregnancy. Although the risk in use of live vaccines during pregnancy is largely theoretical, it is wise to weigh the risk of infection against the risk of immunization (this also applies for the 3-month period before pregnancy); the concerns of the pregnant woman should be taken into consideration in the decision-making process. (See individual vaccines.)

5. *Lactation.* Although the risk in the use of live vaccines in lactating women is largely theoretical, it is wise to weigh the risk of infection against the risk of immunization, taking into account concerns of the lactating woman. (See individual vaccines.)

6. *Altered immunocompetence.* Congenital immunodeficiency, AIDS, leukemia, lymphoma, generalized malignancy, therapy with antimetabolites or alkylating agents, radiation, and large doses (2 mg/kg bodyweight/day or ≥ 20 mg/day) of prednisone or equivalents alter immunocompetence. After systemic treatment with high-dose corticosteroids for a period of ≥ 2 weeks, at least 3 months should elapse after stopping treatment before a live-virus vaccine is administered. In limited immune deficits such as asplenia or renal failure, higher doses of vaccines or additional vaccines may be indicated, but these subjects do not have contraindications for any particular vaccine.

Inactivated vaccines do not represent danger to immunocompromized recipients, but the immune response may be suboptimal. In contrast, live vaccines may lead to serious complications and are often contraindicated. Sometimes, e.g., with polio or typhoid vaccines, there are options to select an inactivated vaccine instead of a live one.

7. *Anticoagulation.* See Part 2.

Reactions to Travel-Related Vaccines. Although severe reactions are extremely rare in vaccines required for travel, anaphylaxis or serious hypersensitivity reactions are possible. Every clinic must have the necessary therapeutic agents (epinephrine, antihistamines, corticosteroids) immediately available and the personnel administering vaccines must be trained to handle such an emergency.

Local pain and swelling are common problems after a parenteral dose of vaccine; fever, rash, or other symptoms may rarely occur (see Part 2 for details). Illness resulting in long-term sequelae or death may occur after vaccination but the incidence rate for the routine or travel-related vaccines is below one per million.

Cost-Effectiveness of Travel Immunizations. No travel-related vaccination is considered beneficial costwise; the cost of vaccination is greater than the cost of avoided infection and death. Nevertheless, immunization before travel remains of vital importance for health reasons, and many travelers are willing to invest in safety just as they elect to invest in comfort while choosing a more expensive hotel.

Recommendations for Immunizations

As illustrated by Table 6, there is a considerable amount of consensus with respect to immunization recommendations issued by the WHO and other selected major national expert groups. On the basis of this consensus, the subsequent recommendations for specific vaccines for specific countries (see Appendix C) have been formulated. Details can be found in Part 2 of this manual where individual vaccines are discussed.

Basics on Malaria Prophylaxis

Malaria is a protozoan disease caused by four species of the genus *Plasmodium*. *Plasmodium falciparum* is the most important as it leads to malaria tropica whereas *P. vivax* and the less frequently occurring *P. ovale* and *P. malariae* only rarely cause life-threatening disease. *Plasmodia* are mainly transmitted through the bite of infected female *Anopheles* mosquitoes, feeding almost exclusively between dusk and dawn. As described in detail in Part 2, the risk of malaria varies according to the region, altitude, and season.

Malaria infection results in partial immunity ("semi-immunity") that provides protection at least from serious disease. This immunity seems to be directed primarily against the erythrocytic stages of the parasite and decreases rapidly (within 6 to 12 months) once the person leaves the endemic area, leaving him or her as susceptible to the disease as any nonimmune individual.

Prophylaxis for malaria and its complications is based on four principles:
- Information
- Personal protection measures against mosquito bites (discussed earlier and in Part 2)
- Chemoprophylaxis (usually, chemosuppression) where appropriate
- Prompt assessment and treatment of symptoms suggestive of malaria, including emergency self-therapy in special circumstances.

Table 6 Recommended Immunizations in Nonimmune Travelers to a Developing Country

Expert Group	WHO (World)	CATMAT (Canada)	CDC (USA)	PHLS (UK)	NHMRC (Australia)
REQUIRED					
• Yellow fever	**	**	**	**	**
ROUTINE					
• Diphtheria/tetanus	***	***	***	***	***
• Poliomyelitis	**	**	**	**	**
• Measles	***	***	***	***	***
RECOMMENDED					
• Hepatitis A	***	***	***	***/*	***/*
• Hepatitis B	*	*	*	*	*
• Rabies	*	*	*	*	*
• Typhoid fever	*	*	*	*	*
• Meningococcal disease	*	*	*	*	*
• Japanese encephalitis	*	*	*	*	*
• Tuberculosis	*	–/*	-	*	*
• Cholera	-	-	–/*	–	–
• Influenza	*	*	?	*	?

*** = all; ** = all when visiting endemic country; * = risk group only, – = none

Information

Travelers visiting countries where malaria is endemic should obtain essential information on the following:

- Location of endemic regions and also of areas free (or with negligable risk) of transmission (see Figure 13 and Appendix C)
- Mode and period of transmission: infected mosquitoes which bite almost exclusively at night, particularly around midnight
- Incubation period: minimum 6 days for *P. falciparum*, and may be up to several months and occasionally even exceeding 1 year, particularly in other *Plasmodium* species
- Early symptoms: usually flu-like, with fever, chills, headache, generalized aches and pains, and malaise. These symptoms may or may not occur with classic periodicity
- Options for prevention:
  1. Travelers should know that preventive measures against mosquito bites are the first line of defence.
  2. When indicated, chemoprophylaxis should be used but travelers should be cautioned that
     - this strategy is not 100% effective even when compliance is perfect, and
     - that the chemoprophylactic agent may cause adverse reactions.
  3. Travelers should be able to appreciate why the prophylactic regimen should be continued for 4 weeks after leaving the transmission area.
- Necessity for medical consultation within 24 hours when symptoms suggestive of malaria occur, as complications may develop very rapidly thereafter. The best advice is to "think malaria" when febrile symptoms occur.

Chemoprophylaxis

Chemoprophylaxis is essentially a misnomer as most currently marketed drugs actually do not prevent infection. These agents act

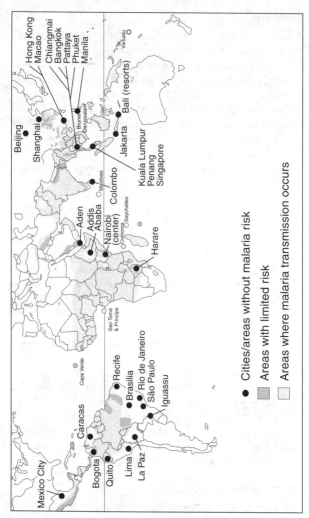

Figure 13 Worldwide malaria endemicity (adapted from WHO 1997)

rather by suppressing the proliferation and development of the malarial parasite and are better termed chemosuppressive agents.

Mode of Action. Prevention of malaria symptoms requires a disruption of the plasmodial life cycle. Several agents are available which act at one or more points in the parasite's cycle. Causal prophylactics (such as atovaquone) act on the hepatic (exoerythrocytic) cycle, interfering with early hepatic development of the plasmodium and thus preventing the next stage, the erythrocytic cycle. Other drugs (such as chloroquine and mefloquine) are blood schizontocides, which act by destroying the asexual intraerythrocytic parasites. The terminal prophylactic, primaquine, prevents relapses of *P. vivax* and *P. ovale* infection by eliminating the latent hepatic hypnozoites (Figure 14).

Risk-Benefit Analysis. All antimalarial agents have considerable potential for causing adverse events. Chemoprophylaxis

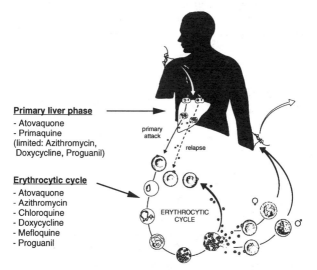

Figure 14   Site of action of antimalarials

should be recommended for travelers to endemic areas whenever the benefit of avoided symptomatic infections exceeds the risk of serious adverse events, i.e., events which require hospitalization. This is the case for most stays (except very short ones) in areas with high or intermediate transmission, such as tropical Africa, some Pacific areas, and certain provinces in Brazil (Figure 15 and Appendix C).

When the risk of acquiring an infection is low, such as in the most frequently visited destinations in Southeast Asia and Latin America, the frequency of adverse experience from prophylactic medication is greater than any expected benefit. According to the World Health Organization (WHO) and European expert groups, it is more appropriate to insist on personal protection measures against mosquito bites and to recommend consulting a doctor within 24 hours of onset of suggestive symptoms than it is to prescribe malaria chemoprophylaxis during short stays in low-endemic areas. If the traveler stays in an area where competent medical infrastructure is not present, stand-by or presumptive treatment may constitute an alternative strategy. This approach is discussed in detail in Part 2 of this manual; it is, however, not

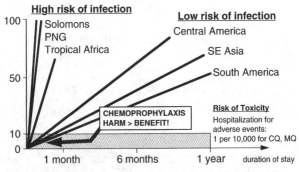

Figure 15 Risk of malaria infection without chemoprophylaxis versus risk of hospitalization for adverse events (per 100,000 travelers)

endorsed by the Centers for Disease Control and Prevention (CDC), USA and by various other national expert groups.

With regard to the occurrence of adverse events, there is near-total consensus that travelers should be cautioned in advance regarding possible side-effects and how to deal with them while some experts believe that over-emphasis of this promotes poor tolerability and is unnecessary because the manufacturer's product information is available for those who want such details.

Schedules for Chemoprophylaxis. Depending on the regimen, malaria chemoprophylaxis is administered as tablets taken daily or weekly. Most advisors recommend that prophylactic regimens

- begin 1 (to 2) weeks before travel;
- are continued for the duration of stay; and
- are maintained for 4 weeks after leaving the endemic area.

Treatment in the pretravel period allows analysis of tolerability prior to departure and ensures protective plasma drug concentrations. This is essential when mefloquine, 250 mg weekly, or chloroquine, 300 mg base/week, is prescribed; a sufficient plasma concentration would be achieved within 2 days with chloroquine, 100 mg base/day, or with doxycycline. In last minute travelers, a loading dose is recommended (see Part 2). The continued intake after return ensures that late infections will be dealt with by effective plasma concentrations when the merozoites emerge from the liver to invade the erythrocyctes. If an effective causal prophylactic drug is used, the duration of post-travel chemoprophylaxis could theoretically be shorter as the parasite's development will already have been interrupted in the hepatic cycle.

Choice of Agent. The selection of a prophylactic agent is often complex, and although there are generalized guidelines to minimize confusion, recommendations for travelers need to be tailored on an individual basis. Efficacy and tolerability are the most important factors to be considered.

Travel health professionals implementing WHO recommendations or national guidelines should be aware of

- destination factors, such as the degree of endemicity,
- predominant *Plasmodium* species, and
- extent of drug resistance (Figure 16), as this will define the efficacy of a particular agent.

Travelers' health and other characteristics (such as age and pregnancy) may also influence the choice of prophylaxis; certain regimens have clearly defined contraindications and precautions which need to be observed to ensure tolerability. The duration and mode of travel have also been shown to be important as have medication factors, such as compliance and acceptability.

Stand-By Emergency Treatment

When symptoms suggestive of malaria occur while abroad or after return, the traveler must obtain competent medical care within 24 hours of the onset of symptoms. Medical assessment must include blood sample screening, either by microscopic examination or with an appropriate rapid diagnostic test kit. Most travelers anywhere in the world have access to competent medical attention within the specified time frame. Only a small minority may find themselves with symptoms suggestive of malaria in a location remote from established medical facilities. In such a likelihood, those travelers may be advised to carry antimalarial medication for stand-by emergency treatment (SBET) and, if possible, a malaria test kit. These emergency supplies can be used for self-diagnosis and self-therapy or made available to the consulted physician.

The disadvantage of this strategy is both over- and under-use of SBET. For travelers using this approach, it is imperative to provide

- precise instructions on how to recognize malaria symptoms,
- the recommendation to seek local medical care, if at all possible,

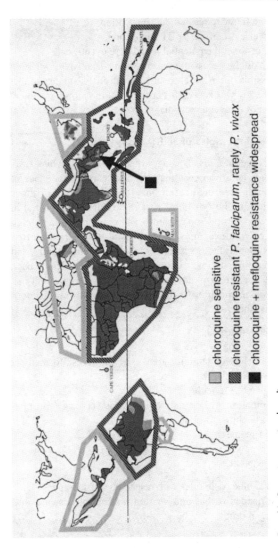

chloroquine sensitive

chloroquine resistant *P. falciparum*, rarely *P. vivax*

chloroquine + mefloquine resistance widespread

Figure 16   Drug resistance against plasmodia

- the time frame to reach medical attention,
- the precise use of the SBET medication,
- warning about the potential for adverse events, and
- advice on the necessity to also seek medical advice, as soon as possible, after initial treatment with SBET, to ensure that the therapy was successful or to obtain the proper treatment in case of erroneous self-diagnosis.

General Principles of Self-Therapy

Travelers feel at a disadvantage when they fall ill while away from home and from customary medical care. At the place of visit, the desired medication may be unavailable, or those available may be obsolete, past the expiry date, stored at wrong temperatures, or unknown and explained in a foreign language. Whatever may be the reason, travelers are often reluctant to consult a local doctor in a developing country, and it may not be possible to contact their own physicians back home. Therefore, it is advisable to arm travelers to high-risk areas with medications to treat common health problems or accidents, such as:

- traveler's diarrhea,
- common cold,
- malaria (low endemicity areas without access to medical care, see Part 2),
- insomnia due to jet lag,
- frequent ailments in certain types of travelers, e.g., constipation, bronchitis, low back pain,
- motion sickness,
- small wounds, and
- sprained ankles.

There are some basic rules with respect to self-therapy:
- Give proper verbal and written instructions on use and dosage of drugs.

- Set an upper time limit before a doctor is to be consulted.
- Inform about possible adverse effects of the medication.

Preference is to be given to medications the traveler has used previously.

Never recommend self-therapy to the traveler who obviously cannot understand procedures and limitations.

▌ The Travel Medical Kit

The content of the travel medical kit will be influenced by the destination (particularly if remote), the length of stay, the number of persons depending on the kit, potential health risks (e.g., diving), and the health of the traveler.

The minimum requirements for a travel medical kit are as follows:
- Medications regularly or occasionally used at home (including birth control)
- Malaria chemoprophylaxis, when indicated
- Medication for traveler's diarrhea, usually
  - antimotility agent, preferably loperamide
  - antibiotic, preferably quinolone
- Medication for common cold, bronchitis (possibly new fluoroquinolones, such as trovafloxacin/alatrofloxacin or levofloxacin, which may be used for both gastrointestinal and respiratory tract infections while older ones were rather limited to use in gastrointestinal infections)
- Analgesic/anti-inflammatory/antipyretic
- Sun block

Travelers should also consider taking with them
- condoms,
- thermometer,
- material to treat cuts and bruises: disinfectant, dressing, scissors, etc., and
- elastic bandage.

Some travelers may need or wish to take
- laxatives (if constipated during previous travels),
- rehydration powders,
- topical creams, such as steroids, anti-infective, anti-inflammatory,
- ear and eye drops,
- motion sickness medication,
- altitude medication,
- jet lag medication, sleeping pills,*
- narcotics for analgesia,* and
- syringes and needles.*

Travel Health Insurance

In countries where the usual health insurance does not cover treatment abroad and air evacuation, it may be recommendable to obtain special insurance coverage, particularly when a traveler has a pre-existing illness.

---

*It may be beneficial to have a letter of authorization explaining the reason for carrying these items to avoid problems with custom officers (Figure 17). Many countries have strict laws regarding importation of controlled substances; in some countries even benzodiazepines require special permits, although this is hardly ever enforced.

Traveler's Health Center

Complete Address

City and Country

Telephone or Fax

Date: _____, 199___

Mr/Mrs

I, _____, MD, certify

that Mr/Mrs _____ carries with

him/her a medical kit that includes prescribed medication,

syringes, and needles to be used by a doctor, during

his/her trip in case of emergency. These are recommended

for personal use only to avoid the risk of accidental

transmission of infectious diseases. They are not to be sold.

_____

Medical Director

Traveler's Clinic

Figure 17   Sample of letter to accompany the travel medical kit

Strategies in Host-Related Special Risks

Time Factor in Travel

In this manual, we have defined "short trips" as stays in the developing countries lasting 1 to 6 days, and "long term" stays as those that exceed 3 months. "Usual" stays abroad are for 7 days to 12 weeks (see previous section).

Short Trips Abroad

Usually, those visiting the developing countries for just 1 to 6 days are business people, politicians or other VIPs, airline crews, or, less often, transit passengers, who use the airline of a developing country to obtain a cheaper fare. Many among the short-term travelers are frequent travelers.

Epidemiology. Various studies illustrate that the attack rate (per stay) for illnesses such as traveler's diarrhea and the rate of accidents is lower in short-term travelers as compared to usual or long-term travelers but the incidence rate (per specified period of stay) is usually independent of the duration of stay. Exceptions with lower rates, such as for malaria, in short-trip travelers are usually due to the fact that these travelers stay in urban centers, which, to some extent, are a protected environment with limited exposure to pathogenic agents. The rate of traveler's diarrhea among international corporate business travelers staying abroad 1 week or less was < 6% but the proportion of travelers who visited high-risk destinations is not known. Several anecdotal cases of serious illness (including poliomyelitis and yellow fever) and accidents during and after short stays in the developing countries have been reported.

In long-haul airline crews, upper respiratory tract infections are the most common cause of lost work time, followed by gastrointestinal illness and trauma. Low back pain, fatigue, and insomnia, probably related to jet lag, are also frequently reported by airline crew members.

There is some evidence that seasoned travelers are less susceptible both to illness and to accidents abroad; on the other hand, business travelers are among the most negligent travelers, not taking any preventive measures or following outdated advice obtained during their first trip a long time ago. Often, business travelers rely on and use travel medical kits.

Pretravel Health Advice. The same basic rules for minimizing exposure and for immunizations apply for persons on short trips as for the usual travelers (see previous section). Often the total exposure time, over a year, may be similar as compared to a more typical vacationer. Recommendations for malaria chemoprophylaxis for short-term travelers may differ from those offered to the usual travelers. First, the risk of adverse reactions from prophylactic medication (1 per 10,000) may be in a similar order of magnitude or even exceed the benefit of avoiding infection. In rural areas of tropical Africa where malaria is transmitted, the risk is 1 per 3000 per day and probably no more than 1 per 10,000 per day in urban centers. In other parts of the world, the risk of malaria is usually much lower. The second factor to be taken into consideration is that for many frequent travelers the post-travel period of medication may overlap with the next trip. This means that the traveler would be taking chemoprophylaxis continuously, which often results in noncompliance.

Many short-trip travelers will have returned home within the incubation period of malaria and thus need to be reminded to consult a physician within a maximum of 24 hours if symptoms clinically compatible with those of malaria occur. Some airlines offer their crews stand-by emergency medication to be carried everywhere, in case a crew member, while being off duty, is staying in an area without access to medical facilities. This eventually needs to be considered in other short-term travelers as well.

Since many short-term travelers, among them the VIPs, usually are unable to refuse the food and beverages offered by their hosts, chemoprophylaxis of traveler's diarrhea may be more appropriate in them. This is not the case in airline crews, who often have organized, hygienically high-quality catering in the hotels even in high-risk destinations. Medication to treat traveler's diarrhea is a must in travel medical kits.

It may be worthwhile to explicitly warn short-term travelers to avoid unprotected casual sex.

Long-Term Travelers and Expatriates

This is a heterogeneous group, including students on a very low budget, missionaries and relief workers, employees of multinational firms, and diplomatic staff. Epidemiologic data have been presented earlier in Part 1 on the morbidity and mortality in this group of travelers.

Pretravel Health Advice and Assessment. Long-term travelers certainly need to devote more time to receive health advice than usual travelers; part of the information is probably best given as written documentation. After having read such documentation, these travelers should be given the opportunity at a second consultation to ask questions.

Persons who choose to live in another country must know that they will need to adjust to the new environment: climate, seasonal variations, and different kinds of food and beverages. The basic living conditions, the culture, the language, and people's attitudes may be all different, which can be stimulating for some and stressful and depressing for others. A new job in a developing country will require new skills, including diplomatic ones, and one must be prepared to take unusual responsibilities. Other members of the family may find life rather dull. Expatriates will often experience a sense of isolation. Cultural adaptation may be the most difficult, and the potential expatriate must know in advance that this is normal and to be expected.

Before departure, long-term travelers should ideally undergo a thorough medical assessment that should include:

- Medical history
- Physical examination and psychological evaluation

- Laboratory examination, particularly hematology, liver function tests, urinanalysis, HIV test (see Appendix C), and hepatitis serology
- Tuberculin test
- Chest radiography
- Dental assessment
- For women, pap smear and depending on age, mammography
- For older travelers, electrocardiography

The reports generated from the pretravel examination may be most useful when problems arise while abroad or upon return. On the basis of such examination, it can be determined whether the candidate is fit enough to live in the country where he or she plans to move, whether additional tests are to be recommended, or whether the person should be advised against a long stay in that region of the world. Reasons for advising against prolonged stays abroad are chronic or recurrent illness that requires frequent and continuous medical monitoring (see below under Pre-existing Health Conditions), an immunocompromized state, or a serious handicap.

It is essential to consider the physical and psychological aptitude of all members of the family that are making the move to a new country.

Last-Minute Travelers

People who decide to or need to travel within a few days (or who neglect to get travel health advice until shortly before departure) should be made aware that it is never too late to obtain pretravel health advice. They should be given the same recommendations for minimizing exposure to risks as those for the usual travelers.

For immunizations, some special aspects need to be observed. Booster doses usually grant protection almost immediately, and the same applies probably for hepatitis A vaccines. In contrast, oral typhoid immunization with Ty21a vaccine capsules or liquid needs 5 to 7 days for administration of the three (Europe) to four (North America) doses, and full protection is obtained 14 days after the last dose, that is, 19 to 21 days after the consultation for travel health advice. The last-minute traveler may already have returned home by then, which makes administration of this vaccine unnecessary whereas Vi vaccine given in a single dose more quickly offers protection in this situation.

For malaria chemoprophylaxis, particularly mefloquine, a loading dose should be considered for last-minute travelers (see Part 2).

Age and Gender

Infants and Children

Infants and small children may encounter health problems in tropical destinations; particularly, they are at considerable risk of gastrointestinal infections, which are frequent, and often serious, resulting in visits to a physician and occasionally hospitalization. Parents with very young children should be advised against vacationing in countries where such problems are likely to occur.

Even greater contraindications against travel to the developing countries exist for infants and children with immune deficiency, cystic fibrosis, diabetes, serious handicaps, and conditions which require repeated blood transfusions.

Infants and small children often cry during descent of an aircraft because of pain in the ears. To open their eustachian tubes and to reduce the negative pressure in the middle ear, they may be given a drink or chewing gum as soon as the aircraft descends. Parents must be reminded that motion sickness and bruises occur more frequently in children than in adults, and they should equip their travel medical kit accordingly. Acute mountain sickness is a greater risk for children and young adults than for healthy older travelers.

The parents of infants and small children will need detailed health advice on how to avoid illnesses during travel in the developing regions; this is even more important for expatriates. Skin hygiene is paramount, a daily bath in clean water (filtering and boiling are sometimes necessary) will reduce the risk of infections. This may, however, dry the skin, and therefore a moisturizing lotion should be used to avoid the risk of infection. Swimming pools in the developing countries with hot climates bear a higher risk of ear infections due to bacterial and fungal contamination. Excessive chlorination of water may cause conjunctivitis. Children who stay in the pool for prolonged periods of time should wear protective goggles and earplugs.

Children should wear light cotton clothes and closed shoes to avoid infection from cuts and scratches or parasitic infestation of the feet. Protection from ultraviolet radiation is of utmost importance as danger of damage to the skin and eyes is greater at that age than in adults. Photosensitizing agents must be avoided. It must be ensured that food and beverage preparation, especially in a hot climate, is done in a perfectly hygienic condition as described in the section on traveler's diarrhea.

Infants and small children will need routine vaccinations. If departure is imminent, the minimum age for the first dose and the minimum interval for doses one to two, and two to three are as follows:

- Diphtheria/tetanus/polio (OPV)
    first dose at 4 wk   intervals 4 wk
- Diphtheria-tetanus-polio-
    Haemophilus influenzae b
    (DTP-Hib) combined
    first dose at 6 wk   intervals 4 wk
- Polio (poliovirus vaccine live oral
    [OPV])
    first dose at 4 wk   intervals 6 wk
- Polio (poliovirus inactivated [IPV])
    first dose at 6 wk   intervals 4 wk/6 mo
- Measles/mumps/rubella
    first dose at 6 mo   repeat at 12 to 15 mo

- Hepatitis B

   first dose at birth   intervals 1 mo/2 mo

The same travel-related vaccinations are recommended for infants and children as for adults (check lower age limits!). This is described in detail in Part 2.

The first step against malaria is taking preventive measures against mosquito bites. This can be achieved, to some extent, by wearing long sleeves and full-length pants and with light treatment of the uncovered skin with DEET, EBAAP, or Bayrepel. It is better to avoid DEET concentrations of > 10% as they may be neurotoxic, and the agent should not be applied on children's hands to avoid contact with eyes and mouth. Many consider the agent contraindicated for children below the age of 1 year. Repellent cream on skin should be washed off after returning to a protected indoor area. Chemoprophylaxis for children follows the same basic rules as for adults, with doses determined according to body weight, as described in Part 2.

Children may sometimes need to travel by air unaccompanied; proper escort arrangements must be made for them with the airlines a few days prior to the journey.

Parents should also be briefed about crisis management in case of illness acquired abroad. This is particularly important when the child becomes febrile (see Part 4). Aspirin, often prescribed in the developing countries, may be a risk for Reye's syndrome; this may be avoided by using acetaminophen which should be included in the travel medical kit.

Female Travelers

For women who plan to travel alone on a long trip abroad, a gynecologic check-up before departure is recommended to avoid possible inconvenient or embarrassing experiences.

They should carry sufficient requirements of tampons, sanitary napkins, or pads, as in remote areas good quality products may not be available. Women who prefer not to menstruate while abroad may take oral contraceptives continuously, without interruption between packs. Such a solution may be beneficial for divers and swimmers to avoid attracting sharks, and also for visitors to game parks to avoid attracting animals. In some eastern countries entry into some temples are prohibited to menstruating women.

Women must know that the effect of hormonal contraceptives may be reduced by interaction with antibiotics, laxatives, or charcoal, and the same may occur in diarrhea. Pharmacokinetic properties of some contraceptives do not allow intervals exceeding 27 hours, thus women using low-dose products must be advised accordingly when they cross more time zones westbound.

If casual sex is a possibility, women should include condoms (or femidoms) in their travel medical kit.

Male Travelers

In pretravel health advice for male travelers three aspects need to be kept in mind: (1) a considerable proportion traveling alone will have casual sex, some unprotected; (2) men abuse alcohol more often; and (3) they are more accident prone because they take greater risks. Men above 40 years of age who have urinary system problems should consult with a urologist before long-term travel to assess the condition of the prostate.

Senior Travelers

With age there is a decrease in muscle tone and strength, joint flexibility, and cardiovascular performance. Elderly travelers are less tolerant of hot climates because of the reduced ability of peripheral blood vessels to dilate and the skin to perspire. Senior travelers are less sensitive to thirst. Because of decreased kidney function, they are more susceptible to fluid and electrolyte disturbances from diarrhea. Jet lag and the adverse side-effects of sedatives prescribed to counter jet lag are both seen more frequently in the older population.

With increasing age there is a decline in sharpness of vision and hearing, impairment of night vision and difficulty in turning the head sideways, and longer reaction times. Impaired hearing and sight may cause failure to detect approaching vehicles, and therefore elderly travelers driving cars are prone to greater accident risks. There is an increased risk of falling and fractures, especially fractures of the hip.

A medical check-up before the journey is wise, particularly if one suffers from a chronic disease. A way to overcome the limitations of age and infirmity is to take advantage of organized tours that cater to the elderly. A leisurely cruise is another alternative that allows the traveler to set his own pace. Luggage with wheels or a collapsible luggage cart is useful for all travelers. Encourage travelers with hearing loss to ensure that they have a hearing aid and to take along extra batteries.

Immunization requirements for the elderly traveler are no different from other adults, except that they require additionally pneumococcal vaccination and annual influenza vaccine administration.

Malaria prophylaxis is essential also for the older traveler at risk of exposure. Persons > 60 years of age tend to have less adverse events to chemoprophylaxis despite the frequent use of comedication.

Denture adhesive is often difficult to find in many countries, and travelers are advised to take along enough for the entire trip. Dentures should be soaked overnight in purified water; stains are not likely to occur from water treated with iodine. If a pure water source is not available, beer, soft drinks, or bottled mineral water can be used instead for a period of up to 4 weeks.

While abroad, elderly travelers are more likely to suffer fluid and electrolyte imbalances caused by diarrhea. Prompt therapy including oral rehydration solutions, is essential. Beware of potential drug interactions, e.g., trimethoprim/sulfamethoxazole combinations may potentiate oral hypoglycemics, and some quinolones prolong the half-life of theophyllines.

▍ Pregnant or Lactating Women

Medical establishments in many of the developing countries do not have all the facilities to treat complications of pregnancy should they occur. For travel during pregnancy, certain specific problems must be considered.

Malaria infection during pregnancy carries a bad prognosis, including maternal anemia, preterm delivery, low birth weight, intrauterine growth retardation, and fetal death. Therefore, there is universal consensus with the WHO statement, which "advises pregnant women not to travel on vacation to areas where transmission of chloroquine-resistant *P. falciparum* occurs." Other destinations far from competent medical facilities should also be avoided. If a pregnant woman decides to travel, the second trimester (weeks 18 to 24) is the safest period; at this time, there is lower risk of a spontaneous abortion or premature labor. Pregnant women should be strongly recommended to use malaria chemoprophylaxis if they need or elect to travel to high-risk areas. The use of chloroquine, proguanil, and at least during the second and third trimester also of mefloquine is not contraindicated in pregnancy and certainly no reason for interrupting a pregnancy.

The principal drugs used to treat traveler's diarrhea are not used in pregnant women for fear of adverse effects on the fetus.

Various relative contraindications exist for vaccines (see Part 2 for details). For other contraindications, see Table 7.

While abroad, fatigue, heartburn, gastrointestinal problems and discomfort, vaginal discharge, leg cramps, increased urination, varicose veins, and hemorrhoids may occur in pregnant women but with similar frequency as they would occur at home.

In road travel, seat belts should be fastened low over the pelvis; in case of most accidents, the fetus recovers quickly from the pressure caused by the seat belt when it is worn properly.

Air travel late in pregnancy might precipitate labor; therefore, most airlines have set (varying) limitations. In all prolonged travels, pregnant women should move around every 1 to 2 hours to reduce the risk of thrombosis.

Travel to destinations at altitudes of 2500 m and above (except for short excursions), diving, horse riding, safaris, and other expeditions to remote areas are not advisable during pregnancy.

In the event of traveler's diarrhea, doxycycline and quinolones are among the contraindicated antimicrobials; however, trimethoprim/ sulfamethoxazole or furazolidone may be used, if needed, together with loperamide.

Nursing mothers serve their infants well in nutritional and anti-infective aspects. To find a place for nursing may be a challenge, as in some societies nursing in public is not acceptable. Fluid intake and eating and sleeping patterns, and also stress invariably do affect lactation.

Breast milk will contain very small amounts of antimalarial drugs. However, there is no indication that this could be harmful to the infant. The quantity transferred is, however, too small to grant adequate protection against malaria; nursing infants should therefore receive the chemoprophylaxis dosage as recommended (see Part 2).

Lactating women should keep in mind that nursing does not grant complete protection against pregnancy, even if menstruation has not yet resumed.

Pre-existing Health Conditions

Pre-existing illness may be improved or aggravated during stay in tropical or subtropical climates. Each patient must be evaluated on the basis of the existing condition and of the travel characteristics, particularly the planned duration of stay. Such travelers should be reminded to check whether their insurance policy covers both hospitalization abroad and repatriation if their health condition deteriorates while abroad. If a patient has a particularly complicated medical problem, they should be provided with the name and phone number of a specialist at

Table 7 Relative Contraindications to International Travel During Pregnancy

Patients with obstetric risk factors

- History of miscarriage
- Incompetent cervix
- History of ectopic pregnancy (ectopic gestation in present pregnancy should be ruled out prior to travel)
- History of premature labor or premature rupture of membranes
- History of past or present placental abnormalities
- Threatened abortion or vaginal bleeding during present pregnancy
- Multiple gestation in present pregnancy
- History of toxemia, hypertension, or diabetes with any pregnancy
- History of infertility or difficulty becoming pregnant
- Primigravida age > 35 years or < 15 years

Patients with general medical risk factors

- Valvular heart disease or congestive heart failure
- History of thromboembolic disease
- Severe anemia
- Chronic organ system dysfunction that requires frequent medical interventions

Patients contemplating travel to destinations that may be hazardous

- High altitudes
- Areas endemic for or where there are epidemics of life-threatening food or insect-borne infections
- Areas where chloroquine-resistant *Plasmodium falciparum* is endemic
- Areas where live virus vaccines are required and recommended

Adapted from: Lee RV. The pregnant traveler. Travel Med Int 1989;7:51–58.

their destination, if at all possible. The International Association for Medical Assistance to Travellers (IAMAT) provides a directory of English-speaking physicians worldwide. (Their headquarters are located at 40 Regal Road, Guelph, Ontario N1K 1B5, Canada e-mail: iamat@sentex.net.)

Travelers on any medication should carry enough to last the entire trip, plus a few days' extra supply. Equivalent medications may not be available in other countries, and dosage and strength are frequently different, and conversion factors are not readily discernable. Most of the medication should be carried on the person or in the hand luggage to ensure a supply of medication in case of lost or stolen luggage. As hand luggage may also be stolen, in the case of serious medical disorders, it would be wise to have complete duplicate supplies of medication in both the hand luggage and the checked-in luggage.

Travelers with pre-existing medical conditions should carry their physician's office and emergency phone and fax numbers as well as a copy of all the pertinent medical records. When appropriate, the physician should also provide a copy of the most recent electrocardiogram and any significant test results. An official document detailing the necessary medical supply is advisable for patients carrying syringes or medications that are likely to be questioned by customs officials (see Figure 17).

The following is a general discussion of major conditions in the context of travel; the guidelines for each need to be tailored on an individual basis.

Cardiovascular Disease

Cardiovascular conditions do not necessarily preclude travel. Persons who are able to tolerate vigorous exercise at home will usually manage well during travel and at the destination, unless this is at an exceptionally high altitude (e.g., Altiplano in South America). However, unstable coronary artery disease and recent myocardial infarction are often a reason against travel, due to the stress of travel, exertion of carrying heavy luggage, and abrupt changes in climate that may aggravate the condition. Pretravel cardiology consultation, possibly with coronary angiography and 24-hour electrocardiography, may be considered in doubtful cases, particularly for prolonged stays abroad. See also the section on Fitness to Fly. Stable coronary heart disease is no contraindication for travel.

Patients with arrhythmias requiring medication, conditions requiring anticoagulation, or a risk of endocarditis should be advised against prolonged stays in the developing countries. In contrast, those with stable hypertension can tolerate a prolonged stay abroad or altitude exposure. If necessary, a patient can be instructed to self-check the blood pressure. Some antihypertensive medications such as beta-blockers may interfere with a compensatory increase in the heart rate at high elevations. This may result in shortness of breath and symptoms which mimic acute mountain sickness.

Low blood pressure may be aggravated in zones with a hot climate, and antihypertensive or diuretic medication may result in low blood pressure symptoms in any person.

Mild to moderate congestive heart failure usually causes no problems during air travel but may result in progressive problems upon arrival. Patients on diuretics are particularly prone to suffer electrolyte imbalance during bouts of traveler's diarrhea (or due to excessive perspiration), and in such cases, prophylactic antibiotics may be considered. Altitudes above 8000 ft can also compromise cardiopulmonary function in travelers with pre-existing heart or lung disease or severe anemia.

Long flights, or bus, car, and train rides may present a risk of venous (and rarely arterial) thrombosis for patients with varicose veins and similar risk factors, particularly if they have cramped, uncomfortable seats and are unable to move their legs for a long time. Such patients must be advised to request well in advance (possibly with a medical certificate) seats next to the aisle or in the first row, if there is ample space there. They must be reminded to maintain adequate fluid intake during the flight, to walk around periodically, and to avoid in-flight sleeping medication. In selected cases, pressure stockings, low-dose pre-flight heparin, or low-molecular-weight heparin may be considered; aspirin gives insufficient protection.

Travelers with cardiovascular conditions should have a cardiology consultation before travel, in case they have any concerns. They should always take care to minimize stress by allowing themselves ample time, get assistance in carrying heavy luggage, and, if necessary, ask for a wheelchair available at large airports. Patients with pacemakers or implanted defibrillators should get clearance from security staff and avoid passing through metal detectors. Although, theoretically, the metal detectors should not induce magnetic interference resulting in deprogramming of such instruments, this possibility cannot be be ruled out, particularly in the developing countries where the machines may be faulty.

Pulmonary Disease

Chronic respiratory insufficiency in patients with low arterial oxygen saturation and low forced expiratory volume who need oxygen supplementation for long periods on a daily basis are certainly unfit for pleasure travel but, if necessary, may be transported by air. Patients with chronic obstructive pulmonary disease with acceptable levels of arterial blood gases on the ground may well require oxygen during the flight since oxygen saturation will drop. Similarly, chronic obstructive pulmonary disease may be aggravated by high altitude, and these patients often suffer from increased dyspnea. In contrast, patients with asthma may experience easier breathing. During a flight, gases in the gastrointestinal tract will expand, and this may impair respiration to a critical point in some patients with more severe pulmonary disease (see also the next section).

According to statistics from British Airways, among all in-flight emergencies due to respiratory disorders, asthma (5.6%), dyspnea (3.3%), hyperventilation (1.6%), and hypoxia (1.3%) were the most frequent ones encountered. Rarely, a pneumothorax may occur or recur. Dry cabin air has been associated with a flare-up of bronchial irritation and asthma. The incidence of pulmonary embolism following venous thrombosis (as described above) during a flight is probably under-reported. Aggravation of sleep apnea syndrome after long flights have been described anecdotally.

Bronchopulmonic disease may be exacerbated, particularly in cities with smog whereas chronic bronchitis may improve in a humid, warm climate. Patients with chronic obstructive airway disease must be advised to take ample medication to cope with episodes of aggravation, as needed.

Metabolic and Endocrinologic Disease

The most frequent problem among this group of disorders is insulin-dependent diabetes. In such patients, travel is to be avoided unless they are stable, able to assess their blood sugar, and adapt the insulin dose. All long-term travelers should ensure that they are free of comorbid complications. There are potential problems of hypo- and hyperglycemia that may be caused by the disruption of daily routine and the stresses of travel. Diabetics should plan for increased monitoring of blood glucose during travel.

Before travel, patients with diabetes must make sure that they have in their hand luggage sufficient stock of

- insulin, as usually used (plus some extra)
- insulin (regular)
- injection material
- blood glucose meters (with extra batteries) and blood glucose testing strips
- urine ketone and glucose testing strips
- sugar and snacks for treating hypoglycemic episodes and in case of meal delays
- sugar substitutes
- glucagon emergency kit for use in case of hypoglycemia resulting in unconsciousness (Prior to travel, patients should instruct a travel companion both in the signs of hypoglycemia and in the use of the kit.)
- first aid kit
- diabetes log book
- medical certificate stating that the patient is diabetic
- insurance certificate guaranteeing coverage for hospitalization and/or evacuation

Diabetic travelers should request special diets for the flight at least 24 to 48 hours in advance. They should take appropriate preventive measures against motion sickness, which may result in hypoglycemia caused by decreased caloric intake. Selecting appropriate seats in the bus (front), plane (overwing), and on a boat (low, in the center, see Part 3) may be beneficial. Patients with insulin pumps should inform security staff that they should avoid passing through metal detectors. Although, theoretically, these should not induce magnetic interference resulting in deprogramming of an insulin pump, this cannot be be ruled out, particularly in the developing countries where the machines may be faulty.

Flights crossing no more than three time zones represent no problem to insulin-dependent diabetics but in further westbound flights with prolongation of the day, additional doses of regular insulin may be necessary. In contrast, for eastbound flights with shorter days, reduction of the insulin dose or regular insulin instead of prolonged action insulin may be indicated. When administering insulin during the flight, put half as much air in the bottle as normal due to the decreased air pressure at high altitude. Dehydration due to prolonged flights may make glucose control more difficult; therefore, plenty of nonalcoholic fluids should be consumed, and blood sugar should be monitored frequently. Each patient should consult their endocrinologist or another competent medical professional for detailed and personalized pretravel advice. Oral hypoglycemics for patients with non–insulin-dependent diabetes (type 2) can be taken as prescribed, without any adjustments for time zone changes.

In hot climates, during travel and at the destination, insulin should ideally be refrigerated. However, it will keep for at least 1 month unrefrigerated if protected from freezing or temperatures above 30°C (86°F). If insulin is likely to be exposed to heat above 50°C (approximately 120°F), it can be protected with a wide-mouthed thermos or insulated bottle. For trips lasting longer than 1 month, diabetics should check in advance the local availability and equivalent brand names of their usual form of insulin.

Diabetes increases susceptibility to heat-related problems. Symptoms of hypo- or hyperglycemia may mimic some of the symptoms of heat exposure, such as weakness, dizziness, headache, and confusion. Increased perspiration may result in an increased risk of cutaneous infection; therefore, measures of hygiene should be strictly followed. Diabetics with autonomic neuropathy, a condition which interferes with sweating, should avoid hot climates or make sure air-conditioned environments are available. Patients with diabetes must be reminded to drink lots of fluids. This is particularly important in senior travelers with type 2 diabetes to avoid dehydration and hyperosmolar coma. Before vigorous exercise, it may be necessary to slightly reduce the dose of insulin. Traveler's diarrhea may be prevented with chemoprophylaxis in a diabetic.

Diabetic foot care must be rigorously carried out and common sense rules obeyed. Diabetics must avoid going barefoot and frequently change their socks to keep the feet dry and comfortable. They must inspect their feet carefully each day and seek immediate medical attention if a foot infection or nonhealing cut or puncture wound is detected. If staying in humid climates, an antifungal powder is a useful addition to the first-aid kit.

If vomiting occurs and type 1 diabetics are unable to eat, insulin (preferably regular insulin) at a reduced dosage must still be used regularly. During any illness, blood sugar levels should be carefully monitored to accurately determine insulin requirements.

The names and addresses of local diabetes associations can be obtained by writing the International Diabetes Association (rue Washington 40, B-1050 Brussels, Belgium). Local diabetic associations can provide information about physicians specializing in diabetes in many parts of the world as well as restaurants offering special diets, pharmacies open 24 hours, and other useful information. The American Diabetes Association (1660 Duke Street, Alexandria, VA 22314) provides a wallet-size "Diabetic Alert Card" with emergency information in 13 languages.

Hyperuricemia may become a problem if recurrent bouts of gout occur. Hyperlipidemia is of comparatively little relevance with respect to travel.

Renal and Urinary Tract Disorders

Renal insufficiency may be complicated during long-term travel by dehydration due to excessive perspiration or diarrhea. Also, serious metabolic problems may occur following dietetic errors or diarrhea, resulting in hyperkalemia, hyponatremia, or metabolic acidosis. Finally, azotemia may increase the risk of infection through various mechanisms that decrease immunocompetence. This again may result in reduced efficacy of inactivated vaccines. For long-term travelers, renal insufficiency may be tolerated, if slight. However if severe, it is not advisable to plan extensive travel or a prolonged stay in a developing country.

Whenever a patient on hemodialysis wishes to travel, it is initially necessary to organize dialysis at the destination, indicating the characteristics of the patient and of the dialysis (see directories, e.g., Eurodial or International Dialysis Organisation [153 Rue du Port, F-69390 Fernaison, France, Phone +33-72-301230]; Creative Age Publications [7628 Densmore Ave, Van Nuys, CA 91406-2088, Phone +1-818 782-7328]). Various tour operators specialize in tours and cruises for patients on dialysis and kidney-transplant patients, with necessary access to medical resources. The patient may, however, need to be adequately equipped with all the required materials (e.g., erythropoetin), particularly for prolonged stays. Particular care must be taken to avoid infections, through immunization or chemoprophylaxis. Patients must be reminded to drink enough fluids to avoid thrombosis of the arteriovenous fistula. Insurance coverage for medical expenses must be obtained.

Patients with urolithiasis may have an increased risk of recurrence, especially during the first months of stay in a warm climate, and they need to be advised to drink lots of fluids. A predeparture ultrasonic evaluation may occasionally be indicated.

Gastrointestinal Disease

Chronic inflammatory bowel disease may predispose a traveler to enteric complications if he or she is staying in areas with high risk of gastrointestinal infection. Chronic hepatitis is a serious concern because of the risk of additional liver infections which may lead to deterioration of the condition. Patients with chronic hepatitis should therefore decide against traveling to those countries where other types of hepatitis are hyperendemic.

Patients on acetylsalicylic acid (e.g., aspirin) or those using nonsteroidal anti-inflammatory products must be aware of the risk of gastric mucosal injury and the risk of bleeding. Even though there are theoretic concerns that agents reducing gastric acidity may increase the risk of traveler's diarrhea, this has only been demonstrated in gastrectomy. There is some evidence that the proton pump inhibitors may be a risk factor for acquiring diarrhea whereas antacids and other H_2 blockers do not seem to cause an increased incidence of gastrointestinal infections. Patients with diverticulosis should carry antibiotics such as a quinolone and metronidazole to treat a bout of diverticulitis; such patients should abstain from antimotility agents in case of diarrhea as subsequent constipation may result in aggravation of diverticulosis or diverticulitis. Hemorrhoids may flare up after prolonged sitting, alcohol abuse (both risk factors of long flights!), and after consumption of spicy food. In patients with this ailment, the travel medical kit must contain the necessary medications.

In expedition participants going to remote areas, elective surgical care to prevent potential problems may be considered.

Dermatologic Disease

Sunlight, heat, moisture, cold dry climate, and positive or negative emotions may aggravate or alleviate some skin diseases. A few people have a genetically determined higher susceptibility to photosensitivity.

Psoriasis is usually improved by ultraviolet light but sunburn of the untanned skin may cause Koebner's phenomenon and lead to exacerbation. Ultraviolet light induces peeling of the skin and thus improves acne vulgaris; however, a minority of patients report an aggravation. Patients with atopic dermatitis usually observe a reduction of their skin lesions in summer but perspiration may aggravate the disease. Ultraviolet light improves T-cell lymphomas of the skin when used therapeutically. Vegetative disorders, like some forms of urticaria, may improve during a vacation with greater exposure to sunlight.

Sunlight may provoke symptomatic herpes simplex infection. This occurs often in people skiing in the sun (herpes solaris). Sunlight, or more specifically ultraviolet light, may also aggravate seborrheic dermatitis, rosacea, Mallorca acne (acne estivalis), and transient acantholytic dermatosis. Photosensitivity and sunlight can provoke discoid and systemic lupus erythematosus, respectively. Other serious dermatoses such as erythema multiforme, bullous pemphigoid, and pemphigus vulgaris are generally aggravated by sunlight. Porphyria cutanea tarda is a photosensitive disease with bullae formation on the light-exposed areas. Psoriasis is only rarely aggravated. The same applies for chronic venous insufficiency, tinea pedis, pityriasis versicolor, and actinic porokeratosis. Patients taking oral retinoids should be aware that they would easily get a sunburn in the mountains due to the higher amount of UV radiation at a higher altitude.

Heat plays a prominent role in intertrigo and hyperhidrosis. Persons with anhidrotic ectodermal dysplasia have no eccrine sweat glands and experience heat congestion when they are exposed to sun and heat. Travel to tropical countries may be life threatening in such cases.

A dry climate may unfavorably influence ichthyosis vulgaris and atopic dermatitis. Persons with dry skin should use a body lotion after a shower, take brief showers, and use soap only on the intertriginous areas.

Cold will aggravate Raynaud's disease and syndrome, peripheral vascular malperfusion, vasculitis due to cryoglobulins and cryofibrinogens, erythrocyanosis crurum, acrocyanosis, and cold panniculitis.

The recommended vaccinations generally given to potential travelers are usually well tolerated. In the past, the smallpox and BCG vaccines (hardly ever indicated now) had created problems.

In contrast, all agents used for malaria prophylaxis (chloroquine, amodiaquine, mefloquine, proguanil, doxycycline, and sulfadoxine/ pyrimethamine) may be associated with exacerbation of psoriasis or may result in phototoxicity.

Allergies

Travelers prone to allergies may be able to avoid during their travel the usual allergens they encounter at home but they face the risk of being exposed to new ones, and avoidance of allergens is more difficult in a foreign environment.

House dust mites thrive in tropical conditions and can be particularly sensitizing. The risk of seasonal reactions to pollens varies region by region. Food allergies are a constant threat due to unknown ingredients in exotic dishes. Various insect bites may result in anaphylaxis. Some medications recommended for use during travel in tropical areas may trigger hypersensitivity reactions.

Travelers with allergies should carry identification cards that include a list of substances they are allergic to and take with them a travel medical kit containing antihistamines and/or corticosteroids.

Rheumatologic Diseases

Degenerative rheumatologic disease is often improved during a stay in a warm climate. Depending on the type of aircraft seat, low back pain could often be aggravated during and after a long flight; it may be advisable to arrange for stop-overs during long journeys and spend a night in bed.

Neurologic Diseases

Among neurologic diseases, epilepsy is of particular relevance to travelers; mefloquine and, to a lesser extent, also chloroquine may lead to a recurrence of seizures and are therefore contraindicated. Headaches may improve while abroad; tension headaches, particularly, may disappear as during travel, the person is removed from the usual factors causing stress.

Psychiatric and Psychological Disease

Psychological and psychiatric diseases play an important role, particularly in the case of long-term residents in a foregin country. They are among the most frequent reasons for turning down an applicant who wishes to move to another country. Patients with substance abuse or of a history of it and persons who cannot easily adapt to new conditions are not good candidates for a prolonged stay abroad (see also Part 3).

HIV Infection and Other Immunodeficiences

Most immunodeficient travelers now encountered in travel medicine are infected by HIV. However, principles important to this group also pertain to travelers with immunodeficiency of different origin.

Overall, the increased risk of infection in the developing countries results in increased risks of diseases, particularly when the CD4 count is low. Persons with a CD4 count of $<200/mm^3$ should be recommended to cancel their travel plans to destinations with a high risk of infections. Additionally, medical facilities in many developing countries may not be sufficiently equipped to assess and treat such patients.

When a known HIV-infected individual is traveling to a developing country, pretravel evaluation should include the following:

1. Medical history
2. Travel plans (for recommended restrictions, see above)
3. Laboratory evaluation of hematologic parameters, including CD4 levels prior to departure. Consider tuberculin skin testing

In addition to the advice given to all travelers, the HIV-infected traveler should be instructed extensively on:

1. avoidance of unsafe sexual practices or the sharing of needles;
2. avoiding gastrointestinal infection by refusing potentially contaminated food and beverages, and carrying medication for rapid self-treatment. In AIDS patients, gastric secretory failure is common. This allows a larger number of viable pathogens to enter the small bowel. There may also be a depletion of CD4-positive T cells in the intestinal tissues, and there may be impaired mucosal immune function. Thus, HIV-infected travelers may well be more susceptible to diseases transmitted via the oral-fecal route;
3. the fact that there is an increased risk for developing respiratory infections during travel. In HIV-infected patients, there may be a risk of dissemination of disease or secondary complications; in those with tuberculosis, there is risk of the disease becoming active. Thus, self-treatment of sinusitis with decongestants, antihistamines, and antibiotics is important, especially before air travel.
4. avoiding sunlight since HIV-infected persons on a variety of medications are more prone to hypersensitivity reactions. In these patients, the sun may also reactivate herpes simplex infection.
5. personal protective measures against mosquito bites are of particular importance in this population to avoid vector-borne infections such as malaria or dengue fever.
6. seeking immediate evaluation and to receive prompt medical treatment, if illness occurs. If possible, a physician at the destination who is informed about HIV infection should be identified even before start of travel.

With respect to immunizations, the potential benefit and harm must be evaluated with particular care; the benefit of immunization may be reduced due to an impaired antibody response resulting in decreased protective efficacy. Those with CD4 counts >300/mm^3 usually develop antibodies but this does not necessarily mean that they will be clinically protected; those with CD4 counts <100/mm^3 will not form antibodies. The potential harm may be increased when using live vaccines as dissemination or increased reactions may occur. With the use of inactivated or toxoid vaccines (influenza, tetanus, hepatitis B) a small increase in the expression of HIV-1 has been observed but, nevertheless, they are considered safe. Multiple concomitant immunizations may accelerate the progression of HIV disease.

Generally, HIV-infected persons should be immunized or have protective antibodies against the following:

- Pneumococcal pneumonia (booster every 5 years until age 65)
- Influenza (annually, or at 6 month' intervals if the other hemisphere is visited, use appropriate vaccine for that hemisphere)
- *Haemophilus influenzae* B, single dose, no booster
- Hepatitis B (check serum antibodies to be certain that they are not already immune)
- Tetanus/diphtheria (booster every 10 years)
- Measles (check antibodies to see if immune)
- Hepatitis A (note impaired immune response, especially in patients with clinical signs of AIDS; in advanced disease, immune globulin may be considered)

Depending on the destination and travel characteristics, consider the following:

- Poliomyelitis (use inactivated vaccine)
- Yellow fever (protective and safe in those with CD4 count >500/mm^3; seroconversion limited to 85% and safe when CD4 count is 200 to 500/mm^3; contraindicated if CD4 count <200/mm^3)

- Typhoid (use inactivated vaccine)
- Meningococcal disease
- Rabies (in view of impaired immunogenicity, check antibody response)
- Japanese encephalitis.

For details on vaccines, see Part 2.

With respect to malaria chemoprophylaxis, there are no special recommendations but a minority of travel medicine experts prefer to use doxcycline chemoprophylaxis for the additional benefit in preventing traveler's diarrhea in HIV patients.

The travel medical kit should contain sufficient antimicrobial agents (e.g., a 7-day course against traveler's diarrhea is to be preferred in patients with HIV infection to short courses). There should be enough medication for the entire trip plus at least an extra week's supply. Labeling of medications to distinguish medicines such as co-trimoxazole for diarrhea from that for *Pneumocystis carinii* pneumonia helps avoid possible problems with the customs officials.

For long-term travelers with HIV infection, many countries issue restrictions beyond the WHO International Health Regulations (see Appendix C). Since entry requirements keep changing, it is best to get the latest information from the consulate of the host country at the time of making travel arrangements.

Asymptomatic patients returning from short trips who report having had no health problems during travel probably need no post-travel screening. Those who report diarrhea, respiratory problems, or other disease symptoms require appropriate evaluation.

For asymptomatic patients on extended trips, routine post-trip testing should include a complete blood count (CBC) with differential, stool examination for ova and parasites, and tuberculin testing with controls, if previously a skin test was negative for tuberculosis.

Handicapped Travelers

The benefits of modern travel are increasingly available to people with physical limitations, despite difficulties posed by physical and sometimes even cultural barriers. In many areas of the world, there is an increased awareness and support for their needs. Some agencies and tour operators have developed an expertise in dealing with handicapped travelers. Tours are available for people with a wide range of special physical or medical requirements. Information can be obtained from the following organizations:

- Society for the Advancement of Travel for the Handicapped (347 Fifth Avenue, Suite 610, New York NY, Phone +1-212 447-SATH, Fax +1-212 725-8253)
- Mobility International (25 rue de Manchester, B-1070 Brussels, Belgium)

Wheelchair users are usually advised that a lightweight folding chair or "junior" model is most convenient during travel. It is useful to carry the necessary tools for repairs as well. Most newer aircraft are designed for wheelchair access, and some older planes still in service have been retrofitted for wheelchair access. Many cities throughout the world publish accessibility handbooks; their tourist bureaus will be able to provide information on this.

Depending on the destination, transport of guide dogs for the blind across international borders can be a major problem. Lengthy quarantines for the animals may be imposed. It is advisable to check regulations with the embassy or consulate of the destination country prior to travel and obtain all the necessary medical and legal documents in advance. It is also important to inquire about requirements for re-entry into the country of origin.

Hearing-impaired travelers need to inform transportation and hotel staff of their handicap so that they do not miss travel announcements or emergency information and alarms. On airline flights, they should request preloading privileges and notify flight attendants of their hearing problem. Attendants will show the emergency equipment and exit locations and keep them informed of announcements.

There are no rules restricting travel of the mentally challenged or others with mental disabilities as long as they are self-sufficient. If the need for assistance is anticipated, requests for help en route, at airports, or elsewhere should be made well in advance. Tours and excursions exist in many countries for those with special needs. Some people may become disoriented in a strange town and lose their way. It is helpful for them to carry a card with the name, address, and phone number of their hotel or other residence as well as a card showing their destination so that they can obtain directions or assistance if they get lost.

Strategies in Environment-Related Special Risks

Air Travel

There is no doubt that for most travelers the destination itself is more hazardous than the process of getting there. However, there is some evidence that in international travel, the stress of going through all the procedures at airports is a greater health risk than the actual air travel itself. In Germany, for instance, the risk of a fatal aircraft accident is only 3.1 per billion kilometers, as compared to 10.6 in car travel.

Environmental Factors

Unlike the very small or antique aircraft, all modern aircraft now have pressurized cabins, with pressure equivalent to that at an altitude of less than 2500 m/8000 ft (usually 1800 to 2300 m). This is comparable to being a passenger in a bus on a mountain road, and healthy persons will experience a drop in hemoglobin saturation from 98% to 92 to 94%. The reduction of the oxygen partial pressure is almost 30%.

Motion sickness is only rarely a problem in modern aircraft (discussed in Part 3).

Air humidity within 2 hours of the aircraft reaching cruising altitude decreases to 5% in first class and to 25% in the economy class, where the passengers are more closely seated. This may cause problems primarily for contact lens wearers (irritation, corneal ulcer), who should therefore use glasses on long-range flights. Dry skin may be treated with moisturizing creams. There is a definite need on long flights for extra fluid consumption to avoid dehydration and raising plasma viscosity, which may be detrimental especially to patients with a history of arterial obstruction.

During and within 48 hours after long flights, there is a risk of venous stasis, thrombosis, and thromboembolism, sometimes labeled "economy class syndrome." At the Heathrow Airport in London, UK, pulmonary embolism has been the second leading cause of in-flight or post-flight death in the 1979 to 1983 period, and 81% of the cases were women. Patients with a history of deep vein thrombosis and recent hospital admission, smokers, obese passengers, and women on contraceptives are at greater risk; malignancy, pregnancy, congestive heart failure, presence of antiphospolipid antibodies, and familial thrombophilia are also risk factors.

Ozone may be an irritant but most ozone is converted to oxygen as the outside air is compressed before it enters the cabin; additionally, many aircrafts are equiped with catalytic converters.

Ionizing radiation from cosmic sources, with higher levels occurring over the poles, have been noted. However, even very frequent flyers, such as diplomatic couriers, hardly ever cross the 2000 hours per year (pregnant women 200 hours) limit set by the International Commission on Radiation Protection.

Disease transmission in aircrafts has been documented for influenza and tuberculosis. Most likely this was due to direct person-to-person transmission as the high-efficiency particle absorption (HEPA) filters in aircraft are reported to be effective in retaining bacteria, viruses, and aerosols; thus, recirculated air should be no risk to passengers. Microbiologic evaluation of airline cabin air shows levels of colony-forming units and molds that are much less than in public areas on the ground.

Fitness to Fly

Traditionally, experienced airline medical directors had a rule of thumb: those who were able to climb the stairs into a plane were fit to fly. This rule is still valid to assess travelers with respiratory disorders, anemias, or heart failure.

There are only very few contraindications for travel by air (see below). Cardiovascular, pulmonary, and other serious conditions do not necessarily preclude air travel; however, it must be kept in mind that more than 50% in-flight deaths are attributed to a cardiac cause. Hypoxia that is most likely due to chronic obstructive airway disease is a major cause for concern. In those with this condition, if they are able to walk 100 meters on a flat surface without stopping and/or if they have an arterial oxygen pressure of 9 kPa (70 mm Hg), they do not normally require supplimentary oxygen for airline travel. Often, it is not so much the cardiopulmonary condition but stress, fear, and excitement which result in problems; thus, emotional factors need also to be seriously considered.

The following conditions are considered contraindications for flying:

- Severe congestive heart failure (note: oxygen is available on request)
- Myocardial infarction within the past 2 to 12 weeks, depending on severity (assessment by cardiologist)
- Psychosis that is obvious; possibly allowable when accompanied and sedated
- Gas trapped in body cavities (see also below, air ambulance), such as in
  - the middle ear due to eustachian tube dysfunction
  - recent middle ear surgery (wait for healing of eardrum)
  - recent inner ear surgery (wait 2 to 8 weeks)
  - pneumothorax: wait until lung has re-expanded plus 10 days
  - mediastinal tumors
  - recent chest surgery (wait 21 days)
  - big intestinal hernias
  - recent abdominal surgery (wait 10+ days)
- Plaster cast, if air is trapped in plaster; split plaster
- Acute contagious diseases of relevance
- Repulsive dermatologic diseases
- Incontinence or other disorders causing bad odor
- Recent surgical wounds that are insufficiently healed
- Recent gastrointestinal bleeding (wait 21 days)
- Serious anemia (< 3 million erythrocytes per mm^3, no preflight transfusion)
- Pregnant women <1 month before delivery, for long-range flights

- Newborns (wait until 48 hours, preferably 2 weeks, as the lungs may not be fully expanded)

Patients with colostomies will have increased gas venting and may require extra bags and dressings. In epilepsy, it may be necessary to increase the drug dose, as excitement, fear, sleep deprivation, hypoglycemia, alcohol intake, and hyperventilation may trigger seizures.

Medical services offered by different airlines have varying criteria for acceptance and refusal of patients, depending on internal regulations and the duration of a flight. It is of utmost importance to complete and submit the Incapacitated Passengers Handling Advice form required by the International Air Transport Association preferably 72 hours before departure. These forms can be obtained from the airline office. The airline office will relay the necessary information to the aircraft personnel and will outline the special requirements to be provided to the passengers (PAX):

- Special diets (about 20 different types, depending on the catering service)
- Special seating (with options for leg rest, adjacent seat for escort)
- Wheelchairs to bring the patient right up to
  - the stairs of the plane (when PAX able to ascend/descend stairs)
  - the ramp (when PAX can walk a few steps, but not up the stairs)
  - the seat in the plane (when PAX is completely immobile)
- Stretcher
- Oxygen (usually intermittent 2 to 4 liters per minute, with option for humidified oxygen)
- Medical/doctor's kit on board, some including a defibrillator
- Ambulance at departure/arrival airports

Note that patients flying without escorts must be able to care for themselves. Some patients may be holders of a Frequent Traveller's Medical Card with a specific number and duration of validity; this is valid on all IATA airlines, and no further formalities are required.

There are only very few limitations for an ambulance flight, since rescussitation and defibrillation are possible even during the flight. The limitations are as follows:

- Gas trapped in body cavities, such as after
  - pneumoencephalography (1 week)
  - vitrectomy with gas inflation
  - pneumothorax, unless in-flight treatment is possible
- Decompression sickness after a diving accident
- Infectious diseases which may be a risk to crew members (the US Air Force has special planes for the evacuation of highly contagious patients)

Fear of Flying

According to surveys using different methods, 1 to 15% of the traveling population experience at least some degree of fear of flying. Among patients with stress disorders, 82% admitted to some degree of anxiety while flying. In the United States, some 15% of adults limit or completely avoid air travel.

Anticipatory anxiety is characterized by unease and somatic symptoms, tending to increase as the event draws closer. The dysphoric arousal tends to settle some time after take-off. Phobic anxiety—most frequently agoraphobia, claustrophobia, or social phobia—is more intense and may lead to panic reactions and often subsequent avoidance of flying. Typically, the attack has a rapid onset; the patients feel that they have lost personal control and are preoccupied with anxiety about what others will think of them. Fear of heights is not really associated with flight phobia; one might find the former even in airline pilots.

Contributing factors to flight phobia are recent stress and an anxious, obsessional, depressive, or immature personality, inactivity and quietness during the flight also may play a part. Lack of information or knowledge is a major cause for fear in infrequent or novice passengers, e.g., fear experienced when strange new noises are heard before landing. There are two basic treatments, which may be combined. Some airlines offer therapeutic courses to persons suffering from fear of flying, by providing information about aircraft on the ground and all the noises made by an aircraft during a flight; a short demonstration flight during which the captain is particularly careful to explain all his moves and also environmental factors is also part of the course. Cognitive and behavioral therapies may also be useful. Many passengers get relief from anticipatory anxiety or slight to moderate phobic anxiety by administration of alcohol or tranquillizers before and during the flight.

Scuba Diving

Scuba diving requires physical and emotional aptitude, and usually divers need to present a certificate stating that they are fit to dive, at least for the training course. Such medical evaluation should contain examinations for factors listed in Table 8.

Table 8 Evaluation of the Aptitude for Diving: The Most Frequent Problems*

Evaluation	Risks	Contraindications
Ear / Nose / Throat		
Ear wax, other obstruction of ear canal	Rupture of tympanic membrane	(Treatment before aptitude is granted)
Ear canal with exostosis, – atresia	Barotrauma of middle ear	Occlusion
External otitis	Barotrauma in case of occlusion	If tympanic membrane not visualized
Perforation of tympanic membrane	Disorientation, vomiting	Perforation
Scarring of tympanic membrane	Rupture of tympanic membrane	Large, thin scars
Hearing loss	Aggravation, deafness	Unilateral deafness
Septal deviation	Barotrauma of middle ear and sinuses	Negative Valsalva's maneuver

Table 8 Continued

Evaluation	Risks	Contraindications
Rhinitis, sinusitis	Barotrauma of middle ear and sinuses	Negative Valsalva's maneuver
Eustachian tube blockage	Barotrauma of middle ear	Negative Valsalva's maneuver
Vertigo	Disorientation, vomiting	Most cases, depending on history
Disorders of lips, mouth, and tongue	Poor bite on regulator mouthpiece	Depending on function
Eyes		
Conjunctivitis	Superinfection	If persistent
Cataract surgery, recent	Wound dehiscence (cornea is slow to heal)	At least 12 months
Loss of one eye, absolute hemianopia	Difficulties in orientation	4 months
Visual field defects	Poor contact with buddies	Depending on case, experience
Errors of refraction, reduced visual acuity	Inability to check instruments, disorientation	Hyperopia with > 4 D coorection required
Bronchopulmonary		
Asthma	Rupture of alveoli and pneumothorax, exhaustion	$FEV_1/VC < 0.7$
Acute bronchitis	Rupture of alveoli, aspiration due to cough	Acute bronchitis
Pneumothorax	Recurrence, tension pneumothorax, air embolism	At least 3 months
Cardiovascular		
Ischemic heart disease	(Re-)infarction, arrhythmia, syncope	Angina, even treated
Arrhythmia	Dyspnea, exhaustion, syncope	Depending on case
Hypertension	None, if well controlled	Uncontrolled hypertension
Hypotension	None	None
Nervous system		
Seizure disorder	Seizure, loss of consciousness, drowning	< 5 y free from seizures and off medication
History of decompression sickness (DCS)	Recurrence	Panic reactions

Table 8 Continued

Evaluation	Risks	Contraindications
Psychiatry		
Hyperventilation syndrome	Muscle spasms, vasoconstriction, loss of consciousness	Recurrent episodes
Panic reactions	Uncontrolled reactions, emergency ascent, DCS	Panic reactions
Personality disorders, psychosis	Uncontrolled reactions, may endanger team members	Usual, depending on case
Drug dependence (drug abuse incl. alcoholism)	As above, additionally withdrawal symptoms	Usual, depending on case
Various		
Endocrine disorders, e.g., diabetes	Impaired consciousness	Depending on case
Peptic ulcer disease, gastroesophageal reflux	Dyspepsia, nausea	Acute ulcer, subjective symptoms
Intestinal adhesions	Intestinal barotrauma	Recurrent symptoms
Hernia	Incarceration, aggravation when lifting weight	Should be repaired before diving
Urolithiasis, cholelithiasis (gallstones)	Colic may cause panic reaction, emergency ascent	Subacute, depending on case
Benign prostatic hyperplasia	Acute urinary retention	Recurrent urinary retention
Arthrosis and other rheumatic disorders	Impaired control of body, poor physical fitness, pain	Depending on case
Obesity	DCS due to impaired metabolism of lipid-rich tissues	Persons with BMI $\geq$ 30 to be warned of DCS, if BMI > 35 critically assess for exercise tolerance
Pregnancy	Congenital abnormalities, miscarriage, DCS	Discourage travel
Medication	Side effects	Depending on case

*For rare conditions see specialized literature.

PART 2

INFECTIOUS HEALTH RISKS
AND THEIR PREVENTION

ANTHRAX

Anthrax outbreaks occur occasionally during the summer in central Asia (Uzbekistan, Russian Federation, etc.) among those who have consumed the meat from diseased animals. Several cases of cutaneous anthrax have been documented in travelers returning from Haiti, and in personnel working with materials imported from Pakistan. In Germany in the 1970s, 4 out of 29 individuals diagnosed with anthrax had traveled abroad. Particularly at risk are those who had purchased handicrafts made from animal products such as skin, hair, or wool contaminated with *Bacillus anthracis*. An inactivated vaccine, available primarily for armed forces personnel, is administered subcutaneously (SC) in three doses at 2-week intervals, with three further doses at 6, 12, and 18 months, providing a 93% reduction in disease occurence. Boosters are required annually. Mild local reactions to the vaccine occur in 30% of cases, and systemic reactions are rare ($<0.2\%$).

Anthrax is not considered a travel-related disease requiring immunization. Travelers should avoid contact with souvenirs which may be contaminated.

ARENAVIRAL HEMORRHAGIC FEVERS

Argentine, Bolivian, Venezuelan, and Brazilian hemorrhagic fevers are caused by Arenaviruses, as is Lassa fever. Rodents are the hosts. Infection occurs through inhalation or ingestion of contaminated excreta or by entrance of the etiologic agent through the skin or mucous membranes. Most of these infections take their name from the areas where they are prevalent. Lassa fever, named after the town in Nigeria where the fever was first reported, occurs in West and Central Africa (e.g., Liberia, Sierra Leone, and Nigeria). The incubation period for Lassa fever is 3 to 16 days, and 7 to 14 days for the other hemorrhagic fevers. The illness begins with chills and fever accompanied by malaise, weakness, headache, myalgia, and upper gastrointestinal symptoms including anorexia, nausea, and vomiting. Lassa fever is marked by purulent pharyngitis and aphthous ulcers. Other early signs of these fevers are conjunctivitis, skin rash, and facial edema. Before the end of the first week, dehydration, hypotension, bradycardia, and hemorrhage may be seen. Bleeding from the nose and gums, gastrointestinal tract, and urinary tract or uterus is particularly common with the hemorrhagic fevers and less frequent in Lassa fever. Neurologic signs are commonly found in the Bolivian form of hemorrhagic fever. Leukopenia and thrombocytopenia are common during the early phase of these fevers. The acute phase lasts between 1 and 2 weeks. In fatal cases, uremia and hypovolemic shock usually occur after the first week of illness.

Diagnosis can be made by isolating the virus from the blood, cerebrospinal fluid, throat washings, or other body fluids. Serologic approaches (e.g., immunofluorescence) are generally employed. Treatment is supportive, involving replacement of electrolyte and fluid deficiencies and administration of plasma expanders in the early stages of the disease, taking care to avoid pulmonary edema. Specific virus-immune human plasma may be administered to treat Argentine hemorrhagic fever, and phase three trials of a live attenuated vaccine are underway at the time of this publication. Ribavirin given early in the course of Lassa fever is beneficial.

BOTULISM

Botulism is usually a paralytic disease resulting from ingestion of a neurotoxin produced by one of a number of *Clostridium botulinum* types (A, B, E, F, or G). The toxin is destroyed by boiling liquids for 5 to 10 minutes or heating food for 30 minutes at 80°C. Travelers usually contract botulism from eating improperly canned foods in which heat-resistant spores of *C. botulinum* have germinated and multiplied. The customary incubation period for botulism is 1 day but may range from a few hours to a week or slightly longer. The patient usually experiences nausea, vomiting, and general weakness. Autonomic dysfunction may occur, causing dryness of the mouth, ileus, constipation, diarrhea, urinary retention, and hypotension. The hallmarks of the disease are neurologic impairments including double or blurred vision, ptosis, dysphonia, dysarthria, and dysphagia in the early stages and weakness of the peripheral and respiratory muscles as the disease progresses. The patient is usually alert, conscious, and without fever. Dilated pupils in an alert patient suggests botulism, as does generalized muscle weakness without sensory loss. Treatment includes respiratory support, purging of the intestine with lavage, purgatives, and saline enemas, and administration of a trivalent antitoxin. The latter is an equine-derived material directed against *C. botulinum* types A, B, and E, and is available from CDC.

Half of each dose of antitoxin may be given intravenously and half intramuscularly or the full dose intravenously. Hypersensitivity to equine-derived antiserum (urticaria or angioedema) occurs in one-fifth of patients, and anaphylaxis may occur in a smaller number. Specific human immune globulin may be available in small quantities in some countries. The armed forces of some countries have access to a vaccine.

BRUCELLOSIS

Brucellosis is a worldwide infection most commonly found in the developing regions. The specific microorganism responsible for human infection depends upon its animal host: cattle host, *Brucella abortus*; goats and sheep, *B. melitensis*; pigs, *B. suis;* and dogs, *B. canis*. The organism passes from its animal host to humans through inhalation of infected aerosols, direct contact with infected animals, or ingesting unpasteurized milk or cheese. The disease is characterized by fever and systemic signs and symptoms, such as chills, myalgias, and headache, with an insidious onset. Relapse following treatment is common. Diagnosis is usually confirmed in a patient with a compatible illness by demonstrating an elevated titer of specific antibodies in serum samples. Brucellosis should always be considered when diagnosing a patient with febrile illness who has traveled to a developing region or southern Europe, particularly if there has been contact with animals or ingestion of unpasteurized milk or cheese. Diagnosis is made by recovery of organisms from blood cultures or by serologic study. Brucellosis is treated with an antimicrobial agent, including doxycycline (200 mg/d) plus rifampin (600 to 900 mg/d) (or streptomycin with doxycycline), trimethoprim/sulfamethoxazole (160/800 mg twice a day [b.i.d.]) or a fluoroquinolone (e.g., ofloxacin 400 mg b.i.d. orally [PO]) for 6 weeks.

CHOLERA

Infectious Agent

Vibrio cholerae is a motile, curved, gram-negative bacterium of the family *Vibrionaceae*. It has a single polar flagellum. Two serogroups, O1 and O139 ("Bengal") have been implicated in human cholera epidemics. Among serogroup O1 there are the classic and El Tor biotypes and the Inaba and Ogawa serotypes. Strains expressing both Inaba and Ogawa serotypes are classified as serotype Hikojima. The principal virulent component of *V. cholerae* is an enterotoxin composed of a central A subunit and five B subunits arranged in circular form. Nontoxigenic O1 strains and non-O1/O139 strains can cause diarrhea and sepsis but not epidemics.

Most laboratories in the developed nations do not routinely test for *V. cholerae* in diarrheal stool samples, and such a test must be explicitly requested if cholera is suspected.

Transmission

Cholera infection is spread through oral contact with fecal matter. Humans are the only known natural hosts. For a previously healthy person to become infected, contact with more than 10^5 cholera bacteria is usually required.

Global Epidemiology

Cholera is linked to poverty. It often occurs when overcrowding is accompanied by poor sanitation and untreated drinking water. Cholera is spread mainly through contaminated drinking water, other beverages, ice, ice cream, locally grown vegetables, raw fish, and shellfish. Food and beverages sold by street vendors are particularly suspect.

Cholera occurs throughout the developing world (Figure 18). In 1994, 384,403 cases of cholera with 10,692 deaths were

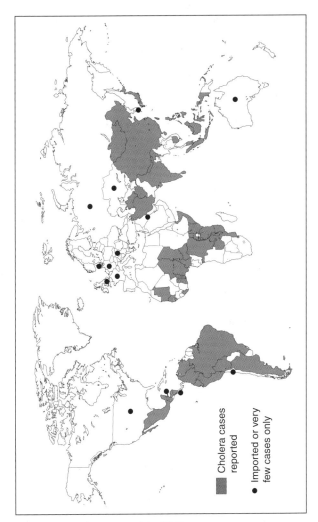

Figure 18   Countries/areas reporting cholera (1997).

reported, a case fatality rate of 2.8%. The World Health Organization Weekly Epidemiological Record regularly identifies jurisdictions where infections have been documented.

Currently, the El Tor biotype predominates, except in Bangladesh, where the classic biotype has reappeared. After its detection there in 1992, strain O139 caused major epidemics in both Bangladesh and Calcutta the following year. Although O139 continues to be detected in southeast Asia, it has not yet resulted in an eighth cholera pandemic, as was initially feared.

Risk for Travelers

There are about 100 cases of imported cholera reported to the WHO each year. This figure, however, is deceptive since many travelers are treated and cured while abroad, many are cured without diagnosis, and many are oligosymptomatic or asymptomatic.

Retrospective surveys reviewed cases of cholera imported to the United States from 1961 to 1980 and 1965 to 1991, and to Europe and North America from 1975 to 1981. All three surveys concluded that the rate of importation of cholera from an endemic to a developed country was usually less than one case per 100,000 travelers. Many had acquired cholera in North Africa or in Turkey despite the fact that these countries had, at the time, reported no or very few cases of cholera to the WHO. Recent data identify Mexico as a country where the infection is frequently acquired. Risk factors for cholera infection in the endemic areas were consumption of sea food (particularly raw), unboiled water, and food and beverages from street vendors. The *V. cholerae* strains are becoming resistant to antimicrobial treatment.

The Center for Disease Control recently reviewed the problem of cholera in the United States. While there were an average of five cases per year in the U.S. between 1965 and 1991, the number of reported cases jumped to 53 per year between 1992 and 1994. Ninety-six percent of these were travel related.

This included 86 residents of the U.S. traveling to cholera-endemic areas and 65 foreign residents visiting the U.S. from cholera-endemic areas. In six cases, cholera was contracted in the U.S. either from local sea food (two cases) or from exotic food imported from cholera-endemic areas.

There is evidence that the incidence rate of cholera is increasing, at least under specific circumstances. A retrospective analysis of all cases of cholera reported to national surveillance centers in the developed countries in 1991 found an attack rate of 13.1 per 100,000 (mean duration of stay less than 2 weeks) in 38 cases of cholera imported from Bali to Japan. According to Japanese quarantine officers and other local experts, this is likely a low estimate since despite tight surveillance at Japanese airports, some returning travelers do not report diarrheal illness. Similarly, the only follow-up study to date observed a rather high incidence rate of five cases per 1000 U.S. government employees in Lima in the first 3 years of the epidemic (1991 to 1993). More than 90% of cases of cholera imported from Asia were *V. cholerae* Ogawa El Tor infections, while in the majority of cases, cholera contracted in Latin America was of the Inaba serotype, El Tor biotype. Importation of O139 infections to Denmark and the U.S. have been reported.

Clinical Picture

Vibrio cholerae infections may lead to a broad spectrum of clinical illnesses. In El Tor infections, for each symptomatic case, up to 50 asymptomatic or mildly symptomatic cases indistinguishable from other diarrheal causes occur. The proportion of a typical clinical picture in classic biotype infections is one to five.

Severe watery diarrhea is experienced in less than 5% of cases, often accompanied by vomiting due to acidosis, without nausea, abdominal pain, or fever. Up to 1 liter per hour of stool is produced in the first day, becoming colorless, odorless, and flecked with mucus; these are often described as "rice-water stools." Dehydration (cholera gravis) results, leading to a loss of body weight of more than 10% within the first 24 hours. Patients may die within 2 hours from circulatory collapse if no treatment is provided. More commonly, diarrhea from *V. cholerae* infections leads to shock accompanied by drowsiness or unconsciousness in 4 to 12 hours, and death in 18 hours to several days. Bicarbonate losses lead to acidosis as well as hypovolemia. Hypokalemia produces cardiac arrhythmia, renal failure, and leg cramps. Hypoglycemia may cause seizures in children with cholera.

The case fatality rate of cholera is currently low. It was 0.9% in the Latin American epidemic of 1991 to 1994. Case fatality rates of 1 to 2% have been noted among surveyed travelers.

Incubation

The incubation period in cholera ranges from several hours to 5 to 7 days.

Communicability

Patients may be infective 3 days prior to the onset of symptoms. They are usually noninfective after 2 to 3 weeks but occasionally become persistent carriers. In the developed countries, no secondary outbreaks could be attributed to the several hundred patients with imported cholera in 1990 to 1993. The secondary infection rate may reach 17% from household contacts in the developing countries.

Susceptibility/Resistance

Adults, particularly those over 65 years of age, are more often affected than children. Persons with the "O" blood group are more likely to develop symptoms and experience severe illness. Hypochlorhydria apparently also predisposes to the development of symptomatic illness where an infective dose of 10^4 organisms causes diarrhea in 90% of such individuals and a dose of 10^3 causes diarrhea in 50%. Japanese tourists demonstrate an elevated attack rate, possibly due to the prevalence of atrophic gastritis among the population. Atrophic gastritis is also common among Peruvians, particularly young people of the lowest socioeconomic level. This may be partly due to infection with *Helicobacter pylori*. The role of H_2-receptor antagonists in predisposition to cholera remains unclear.

Infection with *V. cholerae* results in production of antibodies to both subunits of the enterotoxin. Resistance to reinfection is of limited duration, lasting longest against the homologous biotype. Infection with the classic biotype confers better protection against El Tor biotypes than vice versa.

Minimized Exposure in Travelers

Basic sanitation and public health procedures are essential to fighting cholera. The state of Ceara, Brazil, reduced the number of cholera cases from 20,000 in 1994 to 35 in 1995 by such measures.

Travelers could virtually avoid cholera by being careful about what they eat and drink. The majority of tourists and business people, however, do not avoid local culinary temptations. Travelers should avoid raw or undercooked sea food and tap water in areas with endemic cholera.

Chemoprophylaxis

Antibiotics for prophylaxis of traveler's diarrhea may provide some protection against cholera. Antimicrobial prophylaxis for cholera has been considered only for closed situations where a group may have had common exposure, such as on board a ship.

Immunoprophylaxis by Cholera Vaccines

Three different cholera vaccines are currently available or will become available in the future. The two oral vaccines are superior in terms of efficacy and tolerance to the older and soon obsolete parenteral vaccine (Table 9).

Table 9 Synopsis of Cholera Vaccines

Characteristics	"Traditional"	CVD 103 HgR	WC/rBS
Application (mode)	Parenteral	Oral	Oral
Number of doses	2 (1 sufficient for legal purpose)	1 2 (1 for booster)	2
Antigen	Whole cell, inactivated	Live attenuated, genetically manipulated V. cholerae 01. Produces only b-subunits	Whole cell, inactivated V. cholerae 01 plus recombinant b-subunit cholera toxin
Number of organisms	8×10^9	5×10^8	10^{11} WC, 1mg rBS
Buffer	None	Yes	Yes
Efficacy rate	50%	Challenge 62–100%, field <20% (prevents mainly serious illness)	Field efficacy of 85%
Beginning of efficacy	6 days after second dose	8 days after single dose	7 days after second dose
Efficacy against ETEC	No	No	Yes (52%)
Duration of protection	Less than 3 months	6 months	78% after one year in subjects over 5 years old
Adverse events	Frequent pain, swelling, occasional fever, rarely life-threatening	Few, mainly from buffer	Few, mainly from buffer
Contraindication	Pregnancy	Children <2 years. Pregnancy	None known
Special requirements	None	No food or drink −1h/+1h before/after ingestion	No food or drink −1h/+1h before/after ingestion
Interaction	With yellow fever vaccine	Antibiotics	None known

Oral Cholera Vaccine (CVD 103-HgR)

Immunology and Pharmacology

Viability: live attenuated, lyophilized

Dosage and antigenic form: 2 to 10×10^8 viable colony-forming units (CFU) of genetically manipulated *V. cholerae* O1 from the classic Inaba 569B strain, plus 20 to 100×10^8 nonviable *V. cholerae* CVD 103-HgR

Adjuvants: none

Preservative: buffer—sodium bicarbonate 2.4 to 2.9 g, ascorbic acid

Allergens/Excipiens: sucrose, lactose, aspartame, casein, ascorbic acid

Mechanism: induction of specific local and circulating vibriocidal as well as antitoxin antibodies

Administration

Schedule: single dose, one sachet each with buffer and lyophilized vaccine to be mixed with 1 dL unchlorinated water, stirred, and ingested immediately. No food and beverages for 1 hour before and after vaccination.

Booster: so far undetermined; manufacturer indicates after 6 months

Route: oral

Storage: Store at 2 to 8°C (35 to 46°F).

Availability: Switzerland (Orochol Berna®, Swiss Serum and Vaccine Institute), Canada (Mutacol Berna® Products), various developing countries

Protection

Onset: 8 days after the single dose

Efficacy: according to challenge data, 62 to 100% but in an Indonesia field trial, < 20%. Prevents primarily serious illness in both biotypes Inaba and Ogawa infections but only against cholera O1-serogroup. No protection against O139 (Bengal) serogroup.

Duration: 6 months, possibly more

Contraindications

Absolute: immunodeficient persons

Relative: previous adverse reactions to the vaccine, any acute illness, diarrhea, or vomiting. Phenylketonuria, as the vaccine is sweetened with aspartame

Children: children under 2 years (lack of data)

Pregnant women: contraindicated (lack of data)

Lactating women: according to the manufacturer, not contraindicated. It is not known if cholera vaccine or corresponding antibodies are excreted into human breast milk. Problems in humans have not been documented.

Immunodeficient persons: contraindicated

Adverse Reactions

Few, mainly from buffer, e.g., belching, nausea, vomiting rarely. Mild diarrhea in 2% of cases, occasional abdominal cramps. No serious adverse reactions documented

Interactions

Antibiotics and some antimalarials may inactivate the vaccine if taken simultaneously. The manufacturer recommends delaying CVD 103-HgR until 3 days after the last dose of oral typhoid Ty21a vaccine.

Oral Cholera Vaccine: Whole Cell, Recombinant B-Subunit (WC/rBS)

Immunology and Pharmacology

Viability: inactivated

Dosage and antigenic form: 10^{11} whole cell inactivated *V. cholerae* 01 representing the classic Inaba and Ogawa serotypes and El Tor biotypes, plus 1 mg recombinant B-subunit cholera toxin

Adjuvants: buffer

Preservative: none

Allergens/Excipiens: none

Mechanism: induction of specific IgA and IgG circulating vibriocidal as well as antitoxin antibodies

Administration

Schedule: two oral doses administered with a 1- or 2- to 6-week interval. Recipients should not eat or drink 1 hour before or 1 hour after ingesting the vaccine.

Booster: so far undetermined, probably indicated after 1 year

Route: oral

Storage: Store at 2 to 8°C (35 to 46°F). Discard frozen vaccine.

Availability: Sweden, Norway (Dukoral, SBL Vaccin), several Latin American countries

Protection

Onset: 7 days after the second dose

Efficacy: field efficacy of 85% but only against cholera O1-serogroup, none against O139 (Bengal) serogroup. So far not assessed in nonimmunes

Also, some (52%) efficacy against enterotoxigenic *Escherichia coli* has been documented.

Duration: 78% after 1 year in subjects over 5 years

Contraindications

Absolute: none

Relative: previous adverse reactions to the vaccine, any acute illness, diarrhea, or vomiting

Children: no lower age limit

Pregnant women: not contraindicated, based on the nature of the vaccine and the oral route

Lactating women: according to the manufacturer not contraindicated. It is not known if cholera vaccine or corresponding antibodies are present in human breast milk. Problems in humans have not been documented.

Immunodeficient persons: not contraindicated. Persons receiving immunosuppressive therapy or having other immunodeficiencies may experience a diminished antibody response to active immunization.

Adverse Reactions

Few, mainly from buffer, e.g., belching, abdominal discomfort, vomiting rarely. No serious adverse reactions have been documented.

Interactions

Food and beverages 1 hour each before and after vaccine ingestion. Uncertainty about interaction with other oral vaccines. Immunosuppressant drugs and radiation therapy may result in an insufficient response to immunization.

Parenteral Cholera Vaccine

Immunology and Pharmacology

Viability: inactivated

  Dosage and antigenic form: 8×10^9 whole bacteria of O1 serogroup, Ogawa and Inaba serotypes, El Tor biotype

  Adjuvants: none

  Preservative: 0.4 to 0.5% phenol

  Allergens/Excipiens: none

  Mechanism: induction of specific circulating vibriocidal antibodies primarily of the IgM type

Administration

Schedule: primary immunizing series: 2 doses 1 to 4 or more weeks apart, followed by a booster dose every 6 months

  Persons 5 years of age or older may receive 0.2 mL of vaccine ID per dose. By SC or IM injection, persons 6 months to 4 years receive 0.2 mL per dose, 6 to 10 years 0.3 mL, and older than 10 years 0.5 mL per dose.

  A single dose of 0.1 mL ID is sufficient in the rare cases when vaccination is required by the destination country. A two-dose series is suggested only for special high risk groups.

  Booster: after 6 months, single dose. Never repeat primary series.

  Route: ID, SC, or IM. The volume varies according to administration chosen (see above).

Site: IM preferably in deltoid muscle. ID over deltoid

Storage: Store at 2 to 8°C (35 to 46°F). Discard frozen vaccine.

Availability: previously worldwide, withdrawn from registration where oral vaccines are available

Protection

Onset: data not provided. Induction of protective antibody titers probably occurs within 2 weeks after the second dose.

Efficacy: about 50% effective in reducing disease incidence for 3 to 6 months but only against cholera O1-serogroup, none against O139 (Bengal) serogroup. Protection in humans correlates to acquisition of circulating vibrocidal antibody. No documentation is available on efficacy in nonimmunes. Does not prevent inapparent infection and excretion of bacteria

Duration: probably less than 3 months, maximum 6 months

Adverse Reactions

Local reactions persisting for several days occur in most recipients. They consist of erythema, induration, and pain and swelling at the injection site. Side effects may occur 3 to 14 days after the injection. Persistent loss of pigmentation may occur after ID administration. Recipients frequently develop malaise, headache, and mild to moderate temperature elevations for several days, occasionally lasting up to 10 days. Anaphylactic and other systemic reactions occur rarely. Life-threatening complications have been described after the application of combined cholera-TAB vaccine.

Contraindications

Absolute: persons with previous severe systemic or allergic reactions to parenteral cholera vaccine

Relative: any acute illness

Children: not contraindicated but no studies have been conducted in children under 6 months old, therefore not recommended for this age group

Pregnant women: category C. Use only if absolutely needed. It is not known if cholera vaccine or corresponding antibodies cross the placenta. Generally, most IgG passage across the placenta occurs during the third trimester. One case of abortion related to parenteral cholera vaccine has been documented in the literature.

Lactating women: It is not known if cholera vaccine or corresponding antibodies are excreted in human breast milk. Problems in humans have not been documented.

Immunodeficient persons: not contraindicated. Persons receiving immunosuppressive therapy or having other immunodeficiencies may experience a diminished antibody response to active immunization.

Interactions

Administration of cholera and yellow fever vaccines within 3 weeks of one another results in diminished antibody response to each vaccine but this is not of practical relevance. Simultaneous application of parenteral cholera vaccine and poliovirus type 1 vaccine reduces seroconversion to poliovirus type 1. Separate doses by 1 month, if possible. Immunosuppressant drugs and radiation therapy may result in an insufficient response to immunization. Patients receiving anticoagulants should be given the vaccine SC or ID.

Recommendations for Vaccine Use

Persons following the usual tourist routes are at virtually no risk of *V. cholerae* O1 infection, unless they break the most fundamental rules of food and beverage hygiene.

Vaccination against cholera cannot prevent importation of the disease. The World Health Assembly therefore amended the International Health Regulations in 1973 so that cholera vaccination is no longer required of any traveler. Currently, no country requires proof of cholera vaccination from travelers arriving from nonendemic countries. Several rarely visited countries, however, and local authorities in some countries, still request proof of vaccination from travelers who have passed through endemic areas in the past 5 days (see Appendix C). In these cases, cholera vaccination should be given at least 6 days prior to entry and recorded in the International Certificate of Vaccinations.

In view of the minimal risk of cholera to prudent travelers, immunization is of questionable benefit and, according to the CDC, "almost never recommended." Preference is given to either of the oral vaccines, following the WHO view that "the traditional parenteral cholera vaccine conveys an incomplete, unreliable protection of short duration and its use, therefore, is not recommended." Cholera immunization is suggested only for special high-risk individuals who live and work in highly endemic areas under inadequate sanitary conditions, such as refugee camps. A two-parenteral-dose series may be given in such circumstances when neither of the more effective and less reactogenic oral vaccines is available.

Self-Treatment Abroad

Not applicable, as travelers will not know their precise diagnosis.

Principles of Therapy

Cholera patients require immediate therapy. Rapid rehydration is crucial to prevent death and should never be withheld until laboratory confirmation is obtained. Depending on the degree of dehydration, oral rehydration with WHO oral rehydration solutions may be sufficient. Patients who have lost more than 10% of their body weight or are experiencing severe vomiting, lethargy, or an inability to drink should be treated with intravenous fluid and electrolyte replacement until the oral medication can be taken.

Antibiotics will decrease the duration of illness. Tetracycline and doxycycline are recommended. If the strains are resistant, erythromycin, co-trimoxazole, quinolones, etc., may be used. Oral administration is usually feasible as vomiting subsides soon after initiation of rehydration.

Community Control Measures

Current International Health Regulations (IHR) (see page 57, Appendix A) require reports on any case of cholera. Isolation of patients is not necessary but cleanliness (enteric precautions) should be practiced around the patient, whether or not they are hospitalized. Feces can be directly discharged in sewers without preliminary disinfection.

Some countries trace contacts of imported cholera. Observation of persons who shared food and beverages with a cholera patient is recommended for 5 days from last exposure. Household members may be given chemoprophylaxis for 3 days with doxycycline or tetracycline if there is likelihood of secondary transmission.

DENGUE

Infectious Agent

The causative agents of dengue fever are four RNA viruses of the *Flaviviridae* family (single-stranded, nonsegmented RNA viruses). Two genotypes for dengue virus type 1 have been characterized, five for type 2, four for type 3, and two for type 4.

Transmission

The infection is spread through the bite of the *Aedes aegypti* mosquito and others of the same genus. They bite mainly in the morning and early evening. In areas such as southeast Asia, there is a jungle cycle of dengue, with monkeys serving as a reservoir.

Global Epidemiology

Dengue viruses are spread throughout the regions where *A. aegypti* are found—tropic and subtropic areas between 30 degrees north and 20 degrees south latitude. The principal geographic areas include the Caribbean, Central America, Mexico, Australia, the South Pacific, southeast Asia, and Hawaii (Figure 19). Transmission occurs at altitudes below 2000 feet during the rainy seasons. Sustained cold weather will interrupt transmission by destroying the mosquito vector. Viremic humans represent the reservoir of infection, aside from the monkeys mentioned above, which explains why most cases occur in crowded, urban areas. Mosquitoes remain infectious for life and a single mosquito can infect many humans. Vertical transmission in *Aedes* mosquitoes has been documented.

Risk for Travelers

Rates of occurrence of dengue among travelers visiting endemic areas depends upon the intensity of local infection but well-

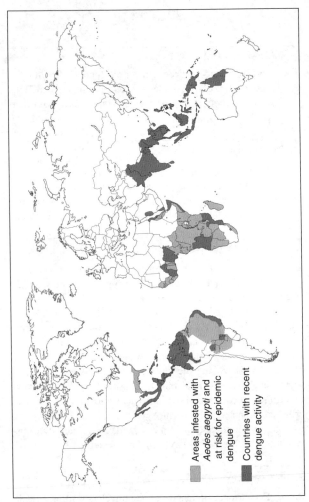

Figure 19 Geographical distribution of dengue viruses and their primary mosquito vector, *Aedes aegypti,* in 1995.

kept tourist accommodations away from crowded habitations may result in below-average risk. In southeast Asia, an attack rate exceeding 300 per 100,000 has been observed among German travelers, with the Island of Kopangan in Thailand having a particularly elevated incidence rate according to anecdotal reports. Risk of acquiring dengue is highest immediately after sunrise and before sunset.

Clinical Picture

Dengue or "breakbone fever" in previously nonimmune persons typically begins with fever lasting 1 to 5 days. Most cases are characterized by mild muscle aches, back pain, frontal or retro-orbital headache, pharyngitis, arthralgia, rhinitis, and cough. Bradycardia may occur. Scleral and pharyngeal redness are commonly found. Transient generalized macular rash that blanches under pressure is common early in the illness; petechiae may be seen later. Biphasic febrile illness may occur. On resolution, the rash may desquamate.

Dengue hemorrhagic fever (DHF) is characterized by fever, platelet count $< 100,000/mm^3$, hemorrhagic manifestations, and evidence of increased vascular permeability, e.g., pleural or abdominal effusions. This occurs mainly in previously exposed children but has repeatedly been observed in travelers.

Dengue shock syndrome (DSS) is DHF plus narrow pulse pressure, hypotension, and shock. It is often associated with a case fatality rate exceeding 40%.

Incubation

The incubation period for dengue usually ranges from 4 to 7 (minimum 3 to maximum 14) days after being bitten by a mosquito harboring the virus.

Communicability

The infection is spread from viremic local persons to susceptible individuals through the bite of an *Aedes* mosquito. Direct person-to-person transmission does not occur.

Susceptibility/Resistance

Most travelers visiting endemic areas are susceptible to dengue. Prior infection confers resistance to infection although children even with a history of prior infection are susceptible to DHF and DSS.

Minimizing Exposure

Avoiding mosquito bites is the best prevention against dengue in endemic areas. Frequent use of insect repellent during day and night is essential. Other mosquito avoidance measures should be practiced as well (see Part 1 and "Malaria" later).

Chemoprophylaxis

None available.

Immunoprophylaxis

Live and attenuated dengue vaccines are under development. None is currently available.

Self-Treatment Abroad

Self-diagnosis test kits as for malaria are marketed in various countries. Treatment for dengue, whether self-treatment while in an endemic area or medical treatment at home, is supportive. Antipyretic/analgesic drugs (not aspirin, as it has anticoagulant properties, or nonsteroidal anti-inflammatory agents) should be used to keep the body temperature from reaching high levels and to provide symptomatic pain relief. Fluids and electrolytes should be taken to ensure adequate hydration.

Principles of Therapy

See "Self-Treatment Abroad" section above. Dengue diagnosis is confirmed by virus isolation or serologic tests. Recent dengue infection is indicated by the presence of IgM antibodies.

Community Control Measures

Since currently there is no treatment and no immunoprophylactic agent available for dengue infection, community control measures relate to insect vector control. Ultra-low-volume aerial spray of organophosphate insecticides such as malathion may reduce the mosquito population and hence the dengue reservoir during epidemic periods.

Other Arboviral Diseases

Four agents produce illness similar to dengue but without skin rash: sandfly fever, Rift Valley fever (discussed later), Ross River fever, and Colorado tick fever. Sandfly fever occurs in the Mediterranean area, the Middle East, Russia, and India. Ross River fever occurs in eastern Australia and the South Pacific. Colorado tick fever is seen among campers or hunters in western U.S.

DERMATOLOGIC INFECTIONS

Common dermatologic bacterial infections include impetigo, furunculosis, erysipelas, ecthymata, cellulitis, tropical ulcer, erythrasma, intertrigo, pitted keratolysis, cat-scratch disease, and borreliosis. Atypical mycobacterioses such as aquarium granuloma or mycobacterial ulcus (Buruli) can occur. Among the viral infections, herpes, condylomata acuminata and common warts are the most important. Fungi and yeasts include tinea of the type corporis, faciei, barbae, cruris, pedis, manuum, nigra, and unguium; perlèche, *Candida intertrigo*, *Candida paronychia*, and pityriasis versicolor. A variety of parasitic diseases are frequently transmitted, including trichomoniasis, cutaneous leishmaniasis, and creeping eruption. Epizootic infestation is possible through pediculosis (see also Part 3).

DIPHTHERIA

Infectious Agent

Corynebacterium diphtheriae strains are classified based on severity of illness produced: gravis (serious), mitis (mild), or intermedius biotype. All may produce toxins but it is mostly the toxigenic strains that produce lesions. Nontoxigenic strains have been associated with infective endocarditis.

Transmission

Diphtheria is transmitted through contact with a patient, an asymptomatic carrier, or occasionally contaminated materials or raw milk.

Global Epidemiology

Although it can occur throughout the world, diphtheria has to a large extent been eliminated by immunization programs. It should be noted, however, that in many countries more than 40% of adults lack protective levels of circulating antitoxin. In temperate zones, the disease most often occurs in the colder months among nonimmunized children but may also appear in adults who have not received booster doses of vaccine. From 1992 to 1997 there has been an epidemic of diphtheria throughout the New Independent States of the former Soviet Union.

Risk for Travelers

Several cases have been reported of travelers importing the infection from the New Independent States of the former Soviet Union to Northern and Western Europe, and at least one died in Russia. Cutaneous diphtheria may be imported after visits to tropical regions. Of 23 cases diagnosed in Switzerland from 1990 to 1994, 11 were imported, mainly from Southeast

Asia, India, and East Africa. Many of these patients were intravenous drug users with poor personal hygiene.

Clinical Picture

Diphtheria is an acute bacterial disease characterized by pseudomembranous pharyngitis (patches of gray-white membrane), often accompanied by lymphadenopathy, a bull neck, and/or serosanguinous nasal discharge. The infection may involve the tonsils, pharynx, larynx, nose, and occasionally other mucous membranes or the skin. Complications after 1 to 6 weeks include neurologic problems and myocarditis. The case fatality rate is 5 to 10%.

Cutaneous diphtheria with open sores may occur as a primary or secondary infection in the tropics. There is usually no systemic toxicity, and postdiphtheric complications, such as myocarditis or polyneuritis, are rare.

Incubation

The incubation period is 2 to 5 days, occasionally longer.

Communicability

Communicability extends usually no longer than 2 weeks but chronic carriers may shed the agent for more than 6 months. Effective antibiotic therapy promptly terminates organism shedding.

Susceptibility/Resistance

Prolonged active immunity to classic diphtheria can be induced by the toxoid but immunized persons may still contract cutaneous diphtheria. Recovery from a clinical attack does not always result in lasting immunity. Inapparent infection, however, often results in immunity.

Minimized Exposure in Travelers

Only by immunization.

Chemoprophylaxis

Penicillin IM as a single dose or erythromycin for 10 days is recommended for contacts, regardless of their immune status.

Immunoprophylaxis by Diphtheria Vaccine

Immunology and Pharmacology

Viability: inactivated

Dosage and antigenic form: 6 to 25 international units (IU) (pediatric doses, depending on product) or 2 IU (adult dose) toxoid

Adjuvants: aluminium phosphate, hydroxide, or potassium sulfate

Preservative: 0.01% thimerosal

Allergens/Excipiens: not > 0.02% residual-free formaldehyde

Mechanism: induction of protective antitoxin antibodies against diphtheria toxin

Administration

Schedule: for primary immunizing series, three 0.5 mL doses are given 6 to 8 weeks apart at 2, 4, and 6 months of age, a fourth dose at 15 to 24 months, and a fifth at 4 to 7 years. There are slight differences in the various national immunization schedules. Combined vaccines are usually used (with tetanus, pertussis, etc.). Note that in older children (age limit 7 to 12 years, depending on the product) and in adults, a vaccine containing less IU is used.

Booster: after 5 years (but in practice after 10 years, as given with tetanus vaccine)

Route: deeply IM

Site: deltoid

Storage: store at 2 to 8°C (35 to 46°F). Discard frozen vaccine.

Availability: worldwide

Protection

Onset: Immunity begins to develop several weeks after second dose. Total immunity develops after completing the basic series.

Efficacy: > 95%

Duration: 5 to 10 years

Protective level: Antidiphtheria antitoxin levels of 0.01 antitoxin units per mL are generally considered protective although 0.1 units per mL are optimal.

Adverse Reactions

Redness, tenderness, and induration surrounding the injection site; transient fever, malaise, generalized aches and pains; rarely, flushing, generalized urticaria or pruritus, tachycardia, hypotension

Contraindications

Absolute: persons with a previous hypersensitivity reaction to diphtheria vaccine doses, particularly thrombocytopenia or neurologic symptoms, or with known hypersensitivity to any component of the vaccine

Relative: any serious acute illness

Children: Defer first dose to the age of 2 months

Pregnant women: category C. Use only if clearly indicated.

Lactating women: It is not known if diphtheria toxoid or corresponding antibodies are excreted in breast milk. Problems in humans have not been documented. Use if clearly needed.

Immunodeficient persons: Persons receiving immunosuppressive therapy or having other immunodeficiencies may experience diminished antibody response to active immunization. Primary diphtheria immunization should be deferred until treatment is discontinued. An additional dose may be injected at least 1 month after immunosuppressive treatment has ceased. Nonetheless, routine immunization of symptomatic and asymptomatic HIV-infected persons is recommended.

Interactions

Immunosuppressant drugs and radiation therapy may result in an insufficient response to immunization. In patients receiving anticoagulants, administer SC.

Recommendations for Vaccine Use

Immunization against diptheria is routine worldwide. After completion of a primary series, a booster dose should be administered every 10 years for life, usually in conjunction with tetanus immunization.

Since the occurrence of the diphtheria epidemic in the New Independent States of the former Soviet Union, pilgrims to Mecca in Saudi Arabia from these areas have been required to show proof of diphtheria vaccination.

Self-Treatment Abroad

None. Medical consultation is required.

Principles of Therapy

Patients: The antitoxin should be administered as soon as possible if diphtheria is suspected, even before microbiologic confirmation. Erythromycin or penicillin should be given. (In some countries only the equine antitoxin is available.)

Carriers: single dose penicillin IM

Community Control Measures

In most countries, notification of cases to public health authorities is mandatory. Strict isolation is indicated for pharyngeal diphtheria and contact isolation for cutaneous diphtheria. Adults in contact with the disease whose occupation involves handling food, especially milk, should abstain from work until bacteriologic examination establishes they are not carriers.

FILARIASIS

Eight human filarial parasites are transmitted through arthropod bites. They include lymphatic filariasis caused by *Wuchereria bancrofti*, *Brugia malayi*, and *Brugia timori*; *Onchocerca volvulus*, *Loa loa*, *Mansonella perstans*, *Mansonella streptocerca* and *Mansonella ozzardi*. The more important filarial parasites are discussed below.

Lymphatic Filariae

The lymphatic filarial parasite *W. bancrofti* is endemic in Haiti, South America, Africa, the South Pacific, and Southeast Asia (including India and Indonesia). *Brugia malayi* occurs in India, the Philippines, Malaysia, Indonesia, and China. *Brugia timori* is found in Indonesia. Fever is the first clinical manifestation of symptomatic lymphatic filariasis. Asymptomatic infection is common in local populations. In travelers, expatriates, and military personnel, localized inflammatory reactions and lymphangitis of the lower extremities or genitalia more commonly occur, with or without immediate hypersensitivity reactions such as urticaria and eosinophilia. Filarial fever is often associated with localized reactions in episodic fashion. With chronic infection, refractory edema and elephantiasis may occur. Biopsy of affected lymph nodes reveals eosinophils surrounding adult worms and sexually immature parasites. Signs and symptoms do not recur if afflicted individuals leave the endemic area. The presence of microfilariae in the blood provides the diagnosis. Lymphatic filariasis is treated with diethylcarbamazine (DEC) given orally twice a day for 10 to 14 days. Ivermectin given as a single oral dose is a suitable alternative treatment.

Tropical eosinophilia is seen mainly in persons living in an area in which lymphatic filariae are endemic. The clinical manifestations of infection relate to pulmonary reactions to microfilariae such as nocturnal coughing and wheezing. Since the parasites are nocturnal, blood should be obtained between midnight and 4 AM to increase the chances of detection. Antifilarial IgE antibodies may be sought in travelers with a compatible illness. Treatment is with a 2-week course of DEC (Figure 20).

Loiasis

Loa loa infection is seen in Central and West Africa. The insect vector is the deerfly, which deposits larvae in the skin. Adult worms later migrate throughout the subcutaneous tissue including the conjunctivae. Microfilariae can be found in the blood, with a diurnal variation peaking at approximately noon. Migratory angioedema and egg-like swellings over bony prominences ("Calabar swellings") may be found. Immune reactions to antigens released by the migrating worms account for the angioedema accompanying the disease. Swellings resolve over several days but typically recur. Adult worms may be visible during migration through the ocular conjunctivae. Diagnosis is made by demonstrating the presence of microfilariae in blood obtained at midday. Administration of DEC for 3 weeks is the appropriate therapy. Corticosteroids are given for the first 3 days in the presence of neurologic symptoms on initiation of DEC (Figure 21).

Onchocerciasis

Onchocerciasis or "river blindness" is caused by chronic infection by the filarial parasite *O. volvulus*. The infection typically occurs in West and Central Africa, Guatemala, southern Mexico, Venezuela, northwest Brazil, Colombia, Ecuador, Yemen, and Saudi Arabia near the Red Sea. Cutaneous and ocular tissue inflammatory reactions occur in response to the microfilariae. Infiltrates of lymphocytes, histiocytes, eosinophils, and plasma cells are found on biopsy of the involved tissue. Microfilariae are not prevalent in the blood of persons with the infection. Scarring of the cornea from inflammation may lead to

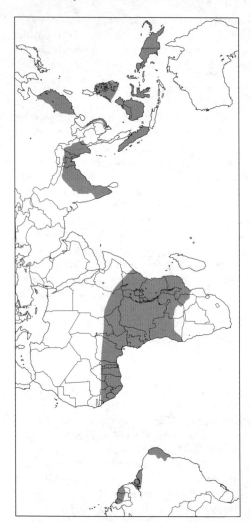

Figure 20   Geographical distribution of human lymphatic filariasis

blindness. Mobile skin nodules are often found. Travelers tend to experience less severe infections than permanent residents in endemic areas. Infected travelers characteristically present with pruritis and an intermittent papular rash, erythema, and edema or thickened skin. Nodules occur occasionally in travelers with onchocerciasis. Diagnosis is made by demonstrating microfilariae in skin biopsies. Typically, multiple skin snips

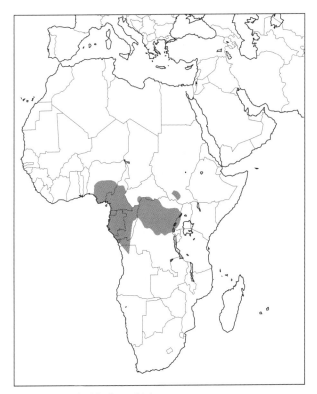

Figure 21 Geographical distribution of *L. loa*

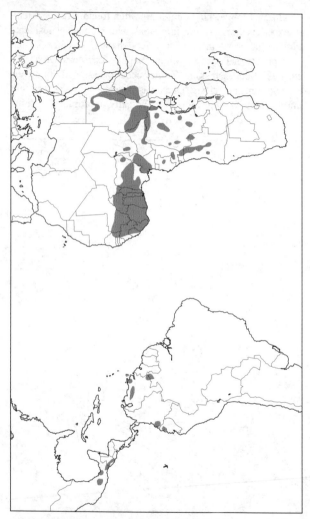

Figure 22 Geographical distribution of onchocerciasis

are examined for microfilariae. Ivermectin is given in a single oral dose (150 µg/kg). The drug has no effect on adult worms, and further treatment may be required (Figure 22).

Dracunculiasis

Dracunculiasis or guinea worm disease is a parasitic infection caused by *Dracunculus medinensis*. The disease is widely distributed in West Africa from Mauritania to Cameroon, in the Nile Valley and eastern equatorial Africa, in the Arabian peninsula, and in India. The infection is acquired when copepods containing the larvae in drinking water are ingested. The larvae develop into adult worms within 12 months; then the fertilized adult females migrate to form a superficial cutaneous blister.

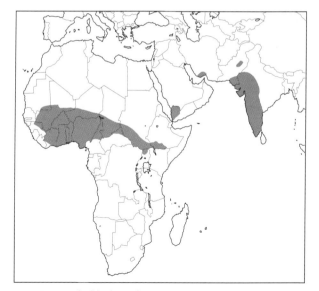

Figure 23   Geographical distribution of guinea worm

Symptoms relate to the local ulcer that forms or to immunologic reactions such as urticaria. Chronic complications may include contracture of extremities. Treatment involves manual extraction of the worm by winding it on a stick, using gentle traction. Patients should also receive the tetanus toxoid. Simple prevention measures such as filtering drinking water through a mesh fiber or boiling it before drinking should be followed (Figure 23).

FILOVIRUS INFECTIONS

Marburg and Ebola viruses are members of the family *Filoviridae*. They are capable of causing the highly fatal African hemorrhagic fever in humans and primates. Marburg virus infection was first identified in Germany and Yugoslavia among handlers of tissue from Ugandan monkeys. Marburg virus is endemic in Africa. Ebola virus infection has been reported in Zaire, Sudan, Kenya, and the Ivory Coast (see Table 10, Figure 24).

Following an incubation period of 3 to 18 days, patients experience headache, myalgias, back pain, and occasionally abdominal discomfort. Nausea, vomiting, and diarrhea accompanied by passage of mucus and blood commonly develop, followed by the appearance of a maculopapular rash on the trunk which then spreads to the extremities. Mental function is compromised, followed by spontaneous bleeding from multiple body sites. Death occurs from the end of the first week to through the second week of illness. Diagnosis is made by identifying the virus in body tissue or by serologic studies. There is no specific treatment. Supportive treatment consists of administration of fluid and electrolytes, blood, platelets, or fresh frozen plasma to control the hemorrhage, and dialysis for renal failure. Heparin has been used against disseminated intravascular coagulation although its value has not been established. Control measures are not available since the spread mechanism has not been confirmed. Nosocomial spread may be prevented by standard infection control measures.

Table 10 Travel-Related Filovirus Infections

Infection	From/To	Travelers	Staff*
Ebola	Ivory Coast/Switzerland	1	5 (–10)
Marburg	Africa/Europe, South Africa	3	32

*laboratory, hospital, and animal-handling staff

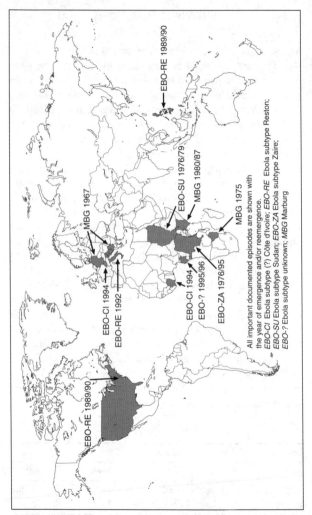

Figure 24 Outbreaks of hemorrhagic fever caused by filoviruses

HANTAVIRUS

Hantaviruses, belonging to the *Bunyaviridae* family, chronically infect various rodents throughout the world. Transmission to humans results from contact with excretion (e.g., urine) from an infected rodent. Different hantaviruses are found in Asia, eastern and western Europe, and North America. In the Asian and European forms, hemorrhagic fever with renal disease or nephropathia epidemica, a milder form of renal disease, are the common manifestations. In North America, hantavirus pulmonary syndrome is found without a significant renal component. Diagnosis is made by detection of a virus-specific antibody, particularly IgM, or by direct virus isolation. The customary procedure for documenting serologic response to infection is by enzyme-linked immunosorbent assay (ELISA) testing. An elevated IgM titer with a compatible clinical illness establishes the diagnosis. The IgG antibodies persist for decades at high titers. Intravenous ribavirin administered for 10 days may have some treatment value, if given early in the disease (up to the 4th day of illness). Supportive treatment is important (Figure 25).

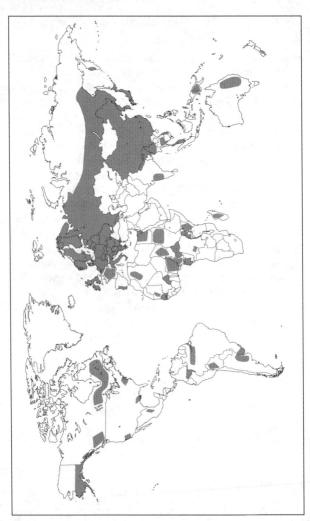

Figure 25 Geographical distribution of hantavirus infections

HEPATITIS

Several distinct hepatic infections are grouped as hepatitides due to their similar clinical presentations and because prior to the 1970s, it was impossible to differentiate the various etiologies, most of them viruses. These include the hepatotrophic viruses hepatitis A, B, C, D (delta), E, and G, and members of the herpes virus group—Coxsackie, dengue, yellow fever, and other agents. Hepatitis can also be a manifestation of *Leptospira*, *Mycobacterium*, *Rickettsia*, hantavirus, and of bacteremia. Mixed infection is impossible.

In all infections, there is a similar acute illness; prodromal symptoms include malaise, fever, headache, and later anorexia, nausea, vomiting, and right upper quadrant pain. Dark urine, light-colored stools, and jaundice may follow. Subclinical forms are common in infants and children whereas in adults, the prognosis gets worse with increasing age. Jaundice can be prolonged, and hepatic coma and death may occur. Chronic illness may be a result of hepatitis B and hepatitis C infections.

HEPATITIS A
(INFECTIOUS HEPATITIS, HA)

Infectious Agent

Hepatitis A virus (HAV), a picornavirus.

Transmission

Person to person transmission usually occurs as a result of fecal-oral contact and occasionally by way of contaminated needles. Outbreaks may be related to contaminated water or ice cubes or foods such as shellfish, lettuce, and strawberries, or other foods contaminated during handling.

Global Epidemiology

Crowded living conditions and poor sanitation result in HA being highly endemic throughout the developing world. Most infections occur at an early age, and almost all children acquire protective immunity, which probably lasts for life. Outbreaks of clinical HA are rare; children usually experience asymptomatic or mild infection. As economic and hygienic conditions improve, exposure gradually shifts to older age groups, in which the proportion of clinical infection increases. In the developed countries, a large proportion of the population remains susceptible to HA despite low endemicity and may acquire it at any age during travel. Figure 26 shows high-, intermediate-, and low-risk countries for hepatitis A infection throughout the world.

Risk for Travelers

In nonimmune travelers, the average incidence rate of HA per month of stay in a high-risk area is 3 per 1000, increasing to 20 per 1000 for those facing unfavorable hygienic conditions (e.g., backpackers, aid workers in remote areas, missionaries). There

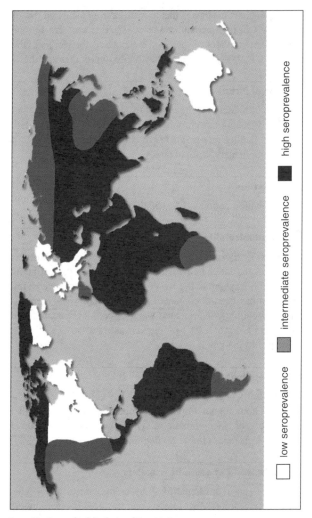

Figure 26 Geographical distribution of Hepatitis A

is no recent data to suggest that tourists have an increased risk of hepatitis A in intermediate-risk areas such as southern Europe while there is evidence that risk is increased for workers who originated in those areas when they return to visit their families.

Clinical Picture

(See the introduction to the hepatitis section.) Fulminant, fatal HA rarely occurs but chronic infection has not been reported. The case fatality rate is < 0.1% in children but exceeds 2% in those more than 40 years of age.

Incubation

The incubation period is 15 to 50 days.

Communicability

Excretion of the virus in the stool, hence communicability, is highest in the latter half of the incubation period, continuing for several days after the onset of jaundice. Prolonged viral excretion has been documented in infants. The virus is inactivated by boiling contaminated water or cooking contaminated food at 85°C for at least 1 minute. Drinking water is also made safe by chlorination.

Susceptibility/Resistance

Susceptibility is general for all previously nonimmune persons. Lifelong homologous immunity results after infection. Higher proportions of asymptomatic to symptomatic cases are seen at younger ages (see "Global Epidemiology" above).

Minimized Exposure in Travelers

Travelers can avoid hepatitis A by being careful about what they eat and drink. Most tourists and business people, however, do not avoid local culinary temptations.

Chemoprophylaxis

None available.

Immunoprophylaxis

Hepatitis A Vaccines

Various hepatitis A vaccines exist in the developed countries:

- Avaxim (Pasteur-Mérieux-Connaught)
- Epaxal (Swiss Serum and Vaccine Institute)
- Havrix (SmithKline Beecham Biologicals)
- Vaqta (Merck & Co.)

All the vaccines have a similar profile and are therefore described under a single heading. There is a live hepatitis A vaccine available in China, which is not discussed here.

Immunology and Pharmacology

Viability: inactivated

Antigenic form: whole virus, strains GBM (Avaxim), RG-SB (Epaxal), HM-175 (Havrix), attenuated CR326F (Vaqta), all cultivated on human MRC-5 diploid cells

Adjuvants: aluminum hydroxyde, except in the virosome-formulated vaccine Epaxal: 5 µg influenza-hemagglutinin, phospholipids

Preservative: Avaxim and Havrix: 2-phenoxyethanol; Epaxal: thimerosal, amino acids, polysorbate 20, traces of neomycin sulfate; Vaqta: none

Allergens: none

Excipiens: various, e.g., formalin traces, proteins

Mechanism: Neutralizing anti-HAV antibodies protect against infection.

Application

Primary schedules and initial booster:

Pediatric:

Epaxal	0, 6 to 12 months, all ages ≥ 1 year (some countries ≥ 5 years)
Havrix 720 EL U	0, 6 to 12 months, ages 2–18 years
Vaqta 25 µg	0, 6 to 18 months, ages 2–17 years

Adult:

Avaxim	0, 6 to 12 months, all ages ≥ 16 years
Epaxal	0, 6 to 12 months, all ages
Havrix 1440 EL U	0, 6 to 12 months, ages ≥ 19 years
Vaqta 50 µg	0, 6 to 18 months, ages ≥ 18 years

Subsequent boosters: undetermined, not needed before 10 years, possibly needed later

Route: IM

Site: deltoid, except in infants, midlateral muscles of the thigh. No gluteal application to avoid suboptimal immune response

Storage: Store at 2 to 8°C (35 to 46°F). Discard frozen vaccine.

Availability: Worldwide there is at least one vaccine available, except in some developing countries.

Protection

Onset: protective antibodies can be demonstrated within 2 weeks in the majority (80 to 98%) of recipients. Almost immediate protection may possibly result from immunization. Havrix was shown to provide protection in postexposure trials in primates. (See recommendations below.)

Efficacy: close to 100%

Duration: 1 year after initial dose, 10 to 30 years after initial booster according to current extrapolations. Possibly no further booster necessary

Protective level: anti-HAV-concentration exceeding 10 to 20 mIU/mL. It is not necessary to test anti-HAV after immunization, as vaccine efficacy is close to 100%, and most commercially available anti-HAV tests do not detect low levels obtained after immunization.

Adverse Reactions

Local reactions occasionally occur, consisting of pain, swelling, or erythema at the injection site. These reactions may persist for several days. Epaxal produces fewer local reactions due to lack of aluminum.

Recipients occasionally develop mild temperature, malaise, or fatigue. These reactions may persist for a few days.

No life-threatening adverse reaction to hepatitis A vaccines has been documented.

Contraindications

Absolute: persons with previous hypersensitivity reaction to hepatitis A vaccine doses or with known hypersensitivity to any component of the vaccine

Relative: any serious acute illness

Children: Safety and efficacy in infants aged less than 1 year has not been established.

Pregnant women: category C. Hepatitis A vaccine and corresponding antibodies cross the placenta. Generally, most IgG passage across the placenta occurs during the third trimester. Problems have not been documented and are unlikely. Use if clearly needed.

Lactating women: It is not known if hepatitis A vaccine or corresponding antibodies are excreted in breast milk. Problems in humans have not been documented and are unlikely. Use if clearly needed.

Immunodeficient persons: Persons receiving immunosuppressive therapy or having other immunodeficiencies may experience diminished antibody response.

Interactions

Immune globulins reduce the antibody titer obtained from vaccination as compared to vaccine alone.

Immune response of hepatitis A vaccine given with other vaccines is not compromised and does not compromise the immune response of the other vaccines.

Immunosuppressant drugs and radiation therapy may compromise the effectiveness of the vaccine.

In patients receiving anticoagulants, give SC.

Immune Globulin (IG)

Immunology and Pharmacology

Viability: inactive

Antigenic form: human immune globulin, unmodified, with varying content of antibodies reflecting the antibody diversity of the donor population

Adjuvants: none

Preservative: usually none, occasionally thimerosal

Allergens/Excipiens: none

Mechanism: induction of passive immunity

Application

Schedule: single dose 1 to 14 days before potential exposure to hepatitis A

Dosage: for travel < 3 months, 0.02 mL/kg body weight; for travel > 3 months, 0.06 mL/kg

Booster: none. If no active hepatitis A vaccine was administered, give same dose every 4 to 6 months.

Route: IM, not IV. Use different injection site than for hepatitis A vaccine.

Site: preferably in the upper outer quadrant of the gluteus muscle, maximum 5 to 10 mL per site to limit pain and discomfort.

Storage: store at 2 to 8°C (35 to 46°F).

Availability: worldwide, however in industrialized countries there is concern about low anti-HAV content. Products with guaranteed titers are sometimes imported from developing countries. Some products have guaranteed titers of 100 IU/mL.

Protection

Onset: immediate

Efficacy: approximately 85%. At least one case of fulminant, fatal hepatitis A has been described despite adequate pre-travel IG application.

Duration: 3 to 5 months, depending on dosage

Adverse Reactions

Local pain and tenderness are frequent. Persons having received IG tend to faint more often afterward than active vaccine recipients. Urticaria and angioedema may occur in rare instances.

Contraindications

Absolute: patients with isolated IgA deficiency, because of the risk of an anaphylactoid reaction. Patients with a history of systemic allergic reactions following the administration of human IG.

Relative: patients with thrombocytopenia and coagulation disorders, considering the IM route and considerable volume injected. Patients receiving anticoagulants may have extensive hematomas after an IG injection.

Children: not contraindicated

Pregnant women: not contraindicated

Lactating women: not contraindicated

Immunodeficient persons: not contraindicated

Interactions

Immunoglobulin may diminish the antibody response to various live vaccines (except yellow fever and oral poliomyelitis vaccines) and to hepatitis A vaccine. Live vaccines should therefore be administered > 14 days before or > 6 weeks after IG application.

Recommendations for Vaccine Use

In view of the considerable risk of hepatitis infection in the developing world, most experts agree that all travelers visiting the following countries should be immunized: Africa; Asia except Japan and Singapore; Latin America; parts of the Caribbean; and remote parts of Eastern Europe (Figure 27 and Table 6). This recommendation is based on the observation that many cases of hepatitis A have been contracted in these regions by travelers with standard tourist itineraries, accommodation, and food consumption behaviors. It, therefore, differs slightly from the endemicity map in Figure 26. The risk is higher for travelers off the beaten track. While Europeans consider it unnecessary to immunize tourists visiting southern Europe, the CDC lists this as an area with intermediate endemicity and recommends immunization for "persons traveling to or working in" this destination.

To eliminate unnecessary immunization, antibodies for hepatitis A virus (anti-HAV IgG) should be tested for in travelers who may have developed lifelong immunity previously by natural infection. This is most likely among those who

- have a history of undetermined hepatitis;
- were raised in a developing country or who lived there for at least 1 year; or
- were born before 1945 in countries of very low endemicity, such as northern and western Europe; or before 1960 in countries of low endemicity (Figure 28).

Such testing may be beneficial only if the cost of screening (laboratory and consultation fee) is considerably less than the cost of immunization, and if testing does not interfere with subsequent receipt of vaccine or immune globulin.

For susceptible persons, hepatitis A vaccine is usually preferable to immune globulin as it grants specific protection for longer duration. In many countries, there is mounting concern that decreasing anti-HAV prevalence may result in an insufficient content of antibodies in immune globulins. There is no indication that immune globulins may transmit hepatitis B virus, hepatitis C virus, human immunodeficiency virus, or as yet undetectable infective agents. Immune globulin may still be considered for travelers who plan only one trip lasting no longer than 5 months, as it is cost beneficial.

There is an ongoing debate as to whether hepatitis A vaccination is immediately protective when the vaccine has not been previously given. The CDC publication "Health Information for International Travel" (1996/1997) recommends that "because

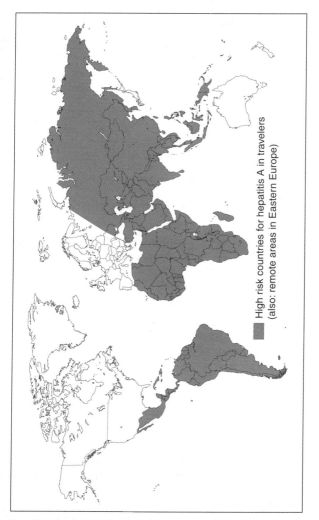

Figure 27 Recommendations for hepatitis A prevention in travelers.

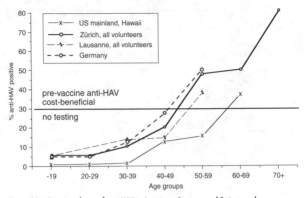

Figure 28   Seroprevalence of anti-HAV in American, German, and Swiss travelers

protection may not be complete until 4 weeks after vaccine administration, persons traveling to high-risk areas less than 4 weeks after the *initial* dose should also be given IG...." In Europe, where Havrix was introduced as of 1992, many doctors decided to strictly give the vaccine because

- postexposure vaccine doses in primates gave good protection;
- there had been no documented case of vaccine failure resulting from this strategy;
- the 4 week limit is defined on the basis of measurable antibodies but protection is likely to occur at an earlier stage;
- IG diminishes the antibody response to the vaccine; and
- many persons disliked the use of blood-derived products for fear of transmission of as yet unknown pathogens.

Giving IG alone in a young person likely to travel again is not recommended as it does not provide long-term protection and does not guarantee protection against fatal, fulminant hepatitis A. The efficacy of the booster dose is undisputed. Even if given later than 12 months after the initial dose, a rapid rise of antibodies from the booster grants immediate protection.

Self-Treatment Abroad

None. Medical consultation required.

Principles of Therapy

Supportive.

Community Control Measures

Notification of authorities in most countries. Enteric precautions during first 2 weeks of illness, such as sanitary disposal of feces, urine, and blood. No quarantine, passive immunization of contacts through IG (0.02 mL per kg of body weight), as soon as possible for all household and sexual contacts. Active immunization of population at risk should be considered.

HEPATITIS B
(SERUM HEPATITIS, HB)

Infectious Agent

Hepatitis B virus (HBV), a hepadnavirus, is the infectious agent for hepatitis B. It consists of a core antigen (HBcAg), surrounded by a surface antigen (HBsAg). The HBsAg is antigenetically heterogenous with four major subtypes: adw, ayw, adr, ayr. The third antigen (HBeAg) is a soluble part of the core and an indirect marker of infectivity. The respective antibodies are anti-HBc, anti-HBs, and anti-HBe.

Transmission

Transmission is parenteral. The HBV is transmitted by percutaneous and permucosal exposure to infective body fluids, with minute doses being sufficient for infection. Razors and toothbrushes have been implicated as occasional vehicles of transmission. Perinatal transmission occurs mainly in hyperendemic areas.

Global Epidemiology

Close to 40% of the world's population has experienced infection with the HBV, and there are an estimated 20 million new infections per year worldwide. Areas of high endemicity are shown in Figure 29. The highest HBsAg seroprevalence rates, reaching 15%, are found in Asia. There are 350 million people worldwide positive for HBsAg and thus potentially infectious.

In areas of high endemicity, infection often occurs in infancy and childhood, often causing chronic rather than apparent infection. In low-endemicity countries, exposure to HBV may be common in groups with high-risk behavior, such as intravenous drug users, heterosexuals with multiple partners, homosexual men, and medical personnel.

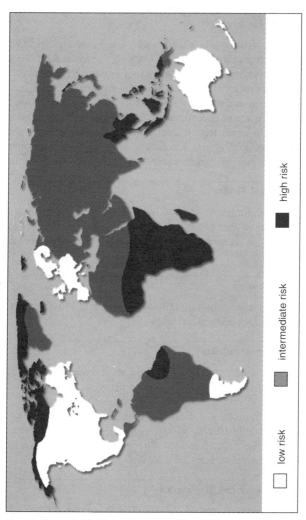

Figure 29   Geographical distribution of hepatitis B

Risk for Travelers

The risk of HB is low in tourists whose stay in an endemic area is of short duration. This may not be so if they break fundamental rules of hygiene (see "Minimized Exposure in Travelers" below) or receive blood transfusions in countries where donated blood is not routinely screened for HBsAg. Among long-term residents of endemic areas, the incidence rate of symptomatic HB ranges from 0.2 per 1000 per month (Africa, Latin America) to 0.6 (Asia). The rates of seroconversion, including also asymptomatic infection, are 0.8 and 2.4, respectively.

Clinical Picture

See introduction to hepatitis section. Fulminant fatal cases with hepatic necrosis and chronic forms potentially leading to cirrhosis or primary hepatocellular carcinoma result in a case fatality rate of 2%.

Incubation

The incubation period for HB ranges from 45 to 180 days, with 60 to 90 days being most common.

Communicability

All people who are HBsAg positive are potentially infectious. Communicability may commence many weeks before the onset of symptoms and persist throughout the acute clinical course. In patients with chronic infection, infectivity persists, particularly in HBeAg-positive persons and to a lesser extent in anti-HBe positive patients. The virus may remain stable on environmental surfaces for more than 7 days.

Susceptibility/Resistance

Susceptibility is general. As described above, the younger the patient, the milder is the clinical course. Protective immunity against all subtypes follows infection if anti-HBs develops and HBsAg is negative. Individuals with Down syndrome, lymphoproliferative disease, HIV infection, and those on hemodialysis are more likely to develop chronic infection.

Minimized Exposure in Travelers

Travelers are advised to abstain from unprotected sex, intravenous drug use, tattooing, piercings, acupuncture, and unnecessary dental or medical treatment where proper sterilization of equipment is suspect. Unscreened whole blood or potentially hazardous blood products should be given only to patients in dire need.

Chemoprophylaxis

None available.

Immunoprophylaxis by Hepatitis B Vaccines

Various hepatitis B vaccines exist in the developed countries:

- Engerix-B (SmithKline Beecham Biologicals)
- GenHevac B (Pasteur Mérieux Connaught)
- Heprecomb (Swiss Serum and Vaccine Institute)
- Recombivax HB (Merck and Co.), other brand names locally

The vaccines have a similar profile and are therefore described under a single heading. Additional vaccines are available particularly in Southeast Asia.

Immunology and Pharmacology

Viability: inactivated

Antigenic form: recombinant purified antigen of hepatitis B virus surface-coat (HBs) protein

Adjuvants: aluminum hydroxide

Preservative: 0.005 to 0.01% thimerosal

Allergens/Excipients: less than 5% yeast protein or plasmid DNA

Mechanism: induction of specific antibodies against hepatitis B virus

Application

Schedule: three doses, with the second dose after 1 month and the third after 6 to 12 months. For travelers, an accelerated schedule has been shown to be effective with doses of 20 µg given at 0, 7, and 21 days or 0, 14, and 28 days but a fourth dose is then required at 12 months.

Dosage: Engerix-B for adults and adolescents > 15 years of age—20 µg in 1 mL

Engerix-B junior for newborns and children up to age 15—10 µg in 0.5 mL

GenHevac B for all age groups—20 µg in 0.5 mL

Heprecomb for adults and adolescents—10 µg in 0.5 mL

Heprecomb for newborns and children to age 10—5 µg in 0.25 mL

Recombivax HB for adults and adolescents > 15 years of age—10 µg in 1 mL

Recombivax HB for newborns and children up to age 15—5 µg in 0.5 mL

Recombivax HB for dialysis patients—40 µg in 1 mL

(Note: The age cut-off at 15 years applies to European countries. Other parts of the world may have other cut-offs.)

Control of antibody response: indicated only in high-risk travelers such as medical personnel. Responders with an anti-HBs ≥ 100 IU/L will have lifelong protection from symptomatic infection. Those with no or low response will require additional doses every 6 to 12 months. Some individuals are known to have seroconverted after more than 10 doses.

Booster: While in most countries boosters now are considered unnecessary (see above), some still recommend a booster after 5 to 10 years.

Route: IM. Intradermal injections of 1/10 dose results in suboptimal antibody titers, probably due to inadequate technique.

Site: deltoid. Infants, anterolateral thigh

Storage: Store at 2 to 8°C (35 to 46°F). Discard frozen vaccine.

Availability: Worldwide, there is at least one product available. Plasma-derived vaccines are predominant in the developing countries and recombinant vaccines in the developed countries.

Protection

Onset: Seventy to 80% of recipients are protected after the second dose and over 95% after the third dose.

Efficacy: 96 to 99% seroconversion among infants, children, and adolescents; 94 to 98% seroconversion among adults 20 to 39 years of age; 89% seroconversion in adults ≥ 40 years of age 1 to 2 months after third dose.

Duration: lifelong for symptomatic infection in responders. Booster vaccinations would be warranted in certain situations, such as in immunocompromised hosts.

Protective level: Anti-HBs titer of ≥ 100 IU/L is considered protective.

Adverse Reactions

Adverse reactions are similar for the various hepatitis B vaccines. Local reactions (17 to 22%) may involve pain, swelling, tenderness, pruritus, induration, ecchymosis, warmth, nodule formation, or erythema at the injection site.

Systemic complaints (10 to 15%) include fatigue, weakness, headache, fever > 37.5°C (100°F), malaise, nausea, diarrhea, and dizziness. Fewer than 1% of recipients may experience sweating, achiness, chills, tingling, pharyngitis, upper respiratory tract infection, abnormal liver function, thrombocytopenia, eczema, purpura, tachycardia or palpitations, erythema multiforme by temporal association, hypertension, anorexia, abdominal pain or cramps, constipation, flushing, vomiting, paresthesia, rash, angioedema, urticaria, arthralgia, arthritis, myalgia, back pain, lymphadenopathy, hypotension, anaphylaxis, bronchospasm, or Guillain-Barré syndrome. Many of these events may simply have been temporally associated with immunization. A slight, but not significant, increase in the relative risk of first attacks or relapse of demyelating diseases, mainly multiple sclerosis, has been described in France and the U.K. after hepatitis B vaccination. The illness must, however, have been pre-existing as it takes years for clinical features to develop.

Transient positive HBsAg reactions have been described (Abbott's ELISA and neutralization tests) after administration of Engerix B.

Contraindications

Absolute: persons with a previous hypersensitivity reaction to hepatitis B vaccine doses

Relative: persons with a history of hypersensitivity to yeast or other vaccine components, or any serious acute illness

Children: not contraindicated. Hepatitis B vaccine is tolerated well and highly immunogenic in newborns, infants, and children. Maternal antibodies do not interfere with pediatric immunogenicity.

Pregnant women: category C. It is not known if hepatitis B vaccine or corresponding antibodies cross the placenta. Generally, most IgG passage across the placenta occurs during the third trimester. Use if clearly needed.

Lactating women: It is not known if hepatitis B vaccine or corresponding antibodies are excreted in breast milk. Problems in humans have not been documented. Use if clearly needed.

Immunodeficient persons: Persons receiving immunosuppressive therapy or having other immunodeficiencies may experience a diminished antibody response. Response may be impaired in HIV-positive persons. Dialysis patients and other immunocompromized persons should receive 40 µg doses.

Interactions

Immune response of hepatitis B vaccines given with other vaccines is not compromised and does not compromise immune responses of other vaccines. In one study, the concomitant application of yellow fever vaccine resulted in a lower antibody titer than expected for yellow fever. It should not be concluded from this that the vaccines should be separated by at least 1 month.

Immunosuppressant drugs and radiation therapy may produce an insufficient response to immunization.

In patients receiving anticoagulants, give subcutaneously.

Recommendations for Vaccine Use

Hepatitis B immunization has recently become routine in many countries so that most infants or adolescents are immunized. Planned travel may offer the opportunity to vaccinate those not vaccinated previously.

Since the risk of hepatitis B transmission in the average tourist is low, immunization is recommended only for risk groups visiting high and intermediate HBsAg prevalence areas. These groups include health care professionals and those whose stay will be 3 months (WHO: 6 months) or longer.

Some doctors recommend immunization for those whose behavior places them at risk (see Minimized Exposure above). Although protection against hepatitis B is indicated in such circumstances, immunization may give a false sense of security against other infections, including HIV.

Self-Treatment Abroad

None. Medical consultation required.

Principles of Therapy

Usually none. Alpha interferon in some patients with chronic hepatitis B

Community Control Measures

Notification is mandatory in many countries. Universal precautions should be taken to prevent exposure to contaminated blood and body fluids. No quarantine. Contacts should be immunized with hepatitis B immunoglobulin and/or hepatitis B vaccine.

HEPATITIS C

Hepatitis C (HC) is a parenterally transmitted infection, with hepacavirus as the infectious agent. It has historically been associated with transfusion but may also be transmitted by exposure to contaminated needles or syringes. It occurs worldwide, with prevalence rates of 0.5 to >10% (Figure 30). Like hepatitis B, the infection may progress to chronic hepatitis, cirrhosis, and hepatocellular carcinoma. Transmission from mother to child is uncommon, and spread through sexual or household contact is low. Immune globulin from unscreened donors may reduce the risk of sexually transmitted HC infection.

Hepatitis C has not been associated with travel. There is no vaccine commercially available. Patients with chronic hepatitis C who acquire hepatitis A infection have a substantial risk of fulminant hepatitis (41%) and death (35%). Hepatitis A vaccination is strongly recommended for chronic HC patients traveling to high- or intermediate-risk areas; it should, in fact, be considered for *all* HC patients.

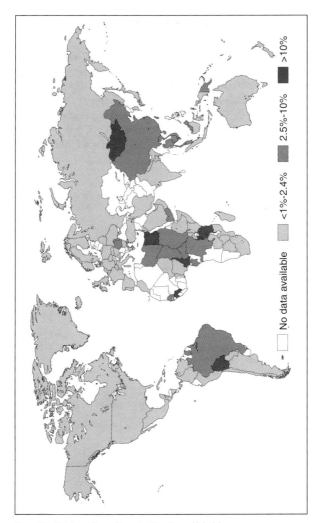

Figure 30 Global prevalence of hepatitis C based on published data

DELTA HEPATITIS

Delta hepatitis (HD) is caused by a defective RNA virus that can only replicate in the presence of the HB virus. It occurs most often in the Mediterranean region and South America and may result in a more serious clinical course for those with acute or chronic HB infection. Hepatitis D has not been identified as a pathogen associated with travel.

Immunization against HB will protect against viral hepatitis D.

HEPATITIS E

Infectious Agent

The hepatitis E virus (HEV) has not been conclusively classified. It is most likely either a calicivirus or related to a rubellavirus.

Transmission

As with hepatitis A, outbreaks are related to contaminated water. Transmission through fecal-oral contact is less likely as secondary household cases are uncommon. Sexual transmission is possible as young adults have a high incidence rate. Hepatitis E (HE) may be a zoonosis since it can often be linked to swine HEV.

Global Epidemiology

Hepatitis E has been associated with waterborne epidemics mainly in Asia, specifically India and Nepal, but has been detected in all regions with inadequate sanitation. The attack rate is highest among young adults.

Risk for Travelers

Many cases of HE have been associated with travel, particularly to Nepal but the mechanism remains to be determined by further study of HE among travelers and immigrants.

Clinical Picture

The clinical course resembles that of HA, with a large proportion of anicteric infections, their severity increasing with age. There is no evidence of a chronic form. Case fatality rate is 3% but a rate of 20% has been noted in pregnant women.

Incubation

The incubation period is 15 to 64 days.

Communicability

The period of communicability is unknown but persists for at least 2 weeks after the onset of jaundice.

Susceptibility/Resistance

Susceptibility is unknown. More icteric cases occur with increasing age.

Minimized Exposure in Travelers

Travelers should avoid drinking tap water. Like all enterically transmitted infections, travelers can minimize risk by avoiding potentially contaminated food and liquids.

Chemoprophylaxis

None available.

Immunoprophylaxis

None commercially available, though several candidates are being tested. The IG prepared from plasma collected in non-HE-endemic areas does not grant protection, whereas IG rich in hepatitis E antibodies may possibly offer protection.

Self-Treatment Abroad

None. Medical consultation required.

Principles of Therapy

Supportive.

Community Control Measures

See "Hepatitis A."

HEPATITIS G (HG)

The HG virus, a flavi-like virus, is transmitted parenterally through blood, blood products, and intravenous drug use. Hepatitis G infection is likely to be associated with progressive liver disease. Among children who have received multiple transfusions, there are marked variations in seroprevalence. The highest rates are reported in Egypt (24%) and Indonesia (32%) whereas the rate drops to 1 to 3% in the developed nations. This infection has not been associated with travel.

HUMAN IMMUNODEFICIENCY VIRUS

Infectious Agent

Human immunodeficiency virus (HIV) is a lentivirus among the retrovirus family. Two types have been identified, HIV-1 and HIV-2, the latter being less pathogenic.

Transmission

Transmitted like hepatitis B, through contact with semen and vaginal secretions during sexual activity and through exposure to contaminated blood on needles, syringes, etc. Transfusions also carry a risk. Tissue used in transplants may transmit HIV. Saliva, tears, urine, and bronchial secretions do not conclusively result in transmission, even with lower doses of HIV detected in these fluids. Transmission from mother to child is possible during or shortly after birth, and also by breastfeeding.

There is no risk of transmission from casual contact at home, at work, or socially. Insects do not transmit HIV.

Global Epidemiology

HIV infection occurs throughout the world. It is estimated that over 8 million cases of acquired immunodeficiency syndrome (AIDS) have occurred since the beginning of the epidemic and that about 23 million men, women (43% of cases), and children are currently infected with HIV. The seroprevalence per 100,000 in 1994 was high in many countries of Africa (except for the Mediterranean countries), with rates of 500 to over 15,000 in Botswana, Zambia, and Zimbabwe. In some of the Caribbean islands and several Central American countries (Guyana, Surinam) rates of 500 to 4000 were found. Thailand, Cambodia, and Myanmar showed rates of 1300 to 1900. Extremely low rates (<1) are observed in some of the New Independent States, the DPR of Korea, and Afghanistan.

The highest proportion of HIV infections worldwide is attributable to heterosexual intercourse rather than the commonly thought of risk factors—intercourse with homosexual or bisexual men, shared needles and/or syringes, or blood transfusions.

The HIV epidemic is a global problem of ever-increasing significance. There are an estimated 8500 new infections daily.

Risk for Travelers

Since travelers, like the rest of the population, also engage in unprotected casual sex, HIV infection remains a primary concern for travel health professionals. Estimating the number of sexual exposures during a given length of stay, the proportion with condom use, and assuming a risk of infection of 1 per 500 through sexual intercourse with an infected person, it can be extrapolated that among 100,000 male travelers having sex abroad, 19 will become infected if HIV prevalence among female partners is 1%. One hundred and ninety-three will become infected at a prevalence of 10%, and 576 will become infected at a prevalence of 30%. In various European countries, a previous trip abroad has been found to be the most important risk factor in new HIV infections among heterosexuals.

Transmission rates from casual, unprotected sex far outweigh those from blood transfusions as transfusion abroad is rarely needed and as many centers now screen blood to be transfused.

Clinical Picture

HIV infection often manifests itself with a flu-like illness that resolves spontaneously. The infected person then remains without symptoms for up to 15 years or more. The proportion of persons not developing further symptoms is increasing with current antiviral therapy. Persons who gradually develop symptoms often experience fever, enlargement of lymph nodes, oropharyngeal or vulvovaginal candidiasis, oral hairy leukoplakia, herpes zoster, and peripheral neuropathy. In AIDS, various serious opportunistic infections such as Kaposi's sarcoma and various lymphomas are possible symptoms as are loss of appetite, loss of weight, fatigue, and dementia. The CD4+ T-lymphocyte counts may gradually fall to <200 cells/μL. The disease is called "slim disease" in East Africa because of profound wasting. The ultimate fatal outcome is often due to an opportunistic infection.

Incubation

Variable, usually 1 to 3 months to detection of antibodies.

Communicability

Presumed to start early after infection and persist for life.

Susceptibility/Resistance

Susceptibility is presumed to be general. Presence of other sexually transmitted diseases (STDs), particularly those with ulcerations, increases susceptibility. No postinfective immunity has been observed.

Minimized Exposure in Travelers

Information about HIV risk and prevention should be provided to those travelers likely to engage in casual sex—persons traveling alone or in groups of the same sex, persons who are stressed or lonely, and those who will be away a long time. The following elements are essential:

- Knowledge of the facts
- Awareness of the implications of the risks and consequences
- Motivation to sustain a certain standard of behavior
- Skill to negotiate the conduct of sexual relations
- Support from family, colleagues, and community

While a mutually monogamous sexual relationship with a noninfected partner is safe, condoms should be used for all other sexual intercourse. Note that condoms drastically reduce but do not eliminate the risk of infection. Intravenous drug use involving shared needles or syringes represents particularly high-risk behavior.

Transfusions of unscreened blood should be accepted only if medically essential.

Chemoprophylaxis

None before exposure. Postexposure prophylaxis is possible under specific circumstances.

Immunoprophylaxis

None available so far. Various candidate vaccines are being tested.

Self-Treatment Abroad

None. Medical consultation required.

Principles of Therapy

Antiviral prophylaxis and a therapy for complications.

Community Control Measures

Notification is mandatory in many countries. No isolation, but universal precautions should be taken.

INFLUENZA

Infectious Agent

Influenza A viruses are classified on the basis of two surface antigens: hemagglutinin (H, with three subtypes pathogenic in humans, except for the exceptional H5N1 cases [1998] in Hong Kong) and neuraminidase (N, with two subtypes). There is continuous and substantial antigenic variation, most frequently originating in China. Influenza B viruses are more stable. New variants due to minor antigenic drift result in small or intermediate epidemics. More substantial shifts may lead to major epidemics or pandemics when no immunity to distantly related, previously occurring subtypes exists.

Transmission

Transmission is airborne, particularly in enclosed spaces. Influenza can also be spread by direct contact, as the virus persists for hours, particularly in cold and low-humidity environments.

Global Epidemiology

Influenza occurs worldwide in the winter or early spring. In the northern hemisphere, transmission is highest from November to March. In the southern hemisphere, most activity occurs from April to September. Influenza can occur throughout the year in the tropics.

Risk for Travelers

Influenza is not considered a classic travel-associated infection although the risk of exposure may be considerable, depending on season and destination. Flu-like symptoms were reported by 72% of the passengers aboard a plane in 1977 that had a 3-hour ground delay and inoperative ventilation. Although many anecdotal reports mention the onset of influenza during or after individual and group travel, the potential risk factors have not been formally evaluated.

Clinical Picture

Influenza is characterized by abrupt onset of fever, myalgia, sore throat, and nonproductive cough. It should not be confused with the common cold. Pneumonia is the most frequent serious complication.

Incubation

One to 3 days.

Communicability

Communicability extends 3 to 5 days from clinical onset in adults and up to 7 days in small children.

Susceptibility/Resistance

There is universal susceptibility of nonimmune persons to new subtypes. Infection results in resistance to that specific virus.

Minimized Exposure in Travelers

Immunization, possibly reduced exposure in first-class compared to economy air travel, avoidance of crowds as far as possible.

Chemoprophylaxis

Amantadine hydrochloride, 200 mg/d.

Immunoprophylaxis

The antigenic characteristics of new circulating strains are selected for planning for new vaccines each year. With 6-month intervals, WHO (and some national) expert groups determine which antigens should be included in the northern and southern hemisphere vaccines.

In the developed countries, there are a wide variety of trivalent influenza vaccines offering protection against type A and B infections, all based on current WHO recommendations. Although differing in their antigenic form, they all have a similar profile and are described here under one heading.

Immunology and Pharmacology

Viability: inactivated

Antigenic form: split or whole-virus—whole-virion, subvirion, purified subvirion antigen, purified surface antigen. Usually three antigens, 15 µg each in 0.5 mL.

Strains: revised annually for the northern and southern hemispheres. Usually three strains named for the location, sequence number, and year of their isolation are selected in the spring for the northern hemisphere. That year's vaccine is then released in the autumn. Vice versa for the southern hemisphere

Adjuvants: none, except in Inflexal Berna V (liposomes)

Preservative: 0.01% thimerosal, except in Inflexal Berna V (none)

Allergens/Excipiens: residual egg proteins/0.05% gelatin, glycol p-iso-octylphenyl ether, polysorbate-80, tri(n)butylphosphate, not >0.02% residual-free formaldehyde, in some vaccines polymyxin B, gentamicin, neomycin, propiolactone

Mechanism: induction of specific active immunity against influenza viruses

Application

Schedule and dosage: There are slight variations among national and product recommendations. Consult the package insert. The usual procedure is:

Children 6 to 12 months (depending on vaccine) to 6 years—2 doses of split or subunit vaccine only (0.25 mL)

Children 6 to 12 years of age—one dose of split or subunit vaccine only (0.5 mL)

Children >12 years and adults—one dose of any vaccine (0.5 mL)

When two doses are given, they should be at least 1 month apart. Give the second dose before December 1 (northern hemisphere), if possible.

Booster: Because of changing antigenicity of prevalent viral strains and waning immunity, persons at risk of influenza should be given a booster dose annually.

Route: IM or jet injection, some vaccines also SC

Site: Use the deltoid muscle for adults and older children. For infants and young children, the anterolateral thigh is preferred.

Storage: Store at 2 to 8°C (35 to 46°F). Discard frozen vaccine.

Availability: worldwide. There are a multitude of products marketed.

Protection

Onset: 2 to 4 weeks after application

Efficacy: Vaccination will reduce influenza incidence by approximately 70% but is less effective in elderly recipients. The vaccine is ineffective against common cold viruses. Influenza vaccine is more effective at preventing mortality and hospitalization than at preventing morbidity.

Duration: declines gradually from 4 months following the immunization

Protective level: Hemagglutination inhibition (HI) antibody titers ≥1:40 correlate with clinical protection.

Adverse Reactions

Side effects of influenza vaccine are generally inconsequential in adults and occur at low frequency but may be more common in pediatric recipients, in whom only subunit or split-virus vaccines should be used.

Up to two-thirds of recipients experience soreness around the vaccination site for 2 days.

Fever, malaise, myalgia, and other systemic symptoms occur infrequently and usually affect persons with no prior exposure to the antigens in the vaccine (such as young children).

These effects usually begin 6 to 12 hours after vaccination and persist for 1 to 2 days. Immediate, probably allergic reactions such as hives, angioedema, allergic asthma, or systemic anaphylaxis occur extremely rarely following influenza vaccination.

Contraindications

Absolute: persons with an anaphylactoid or other immediate reactions (e.g., hives, difficulty breathing, hypotension) to previous influenza vaccine doses. Do not vaccinate persons with a severe egg allergy.

Relative: any serious acute illness or unstable neurologic disorders. In multiple sclerosis, uncertainty exists as there is an elevated risk of exacerbation 6 months after vaccination. Evidence for effectiveness in this group is lacking.

Children: not contraindicated. Children and teenagers (6 months to 18 years) receiving long-term aspirin therapy should be vaccinated as they are at risk of developing Reye's syndrome after influenza infection.

Pregnant women: category C. Vaccinating after the first trimester can minimize hypothetical risk of teratogenicity. However, do not delay vaccination of pregnant women with high-risk conditions who will still be in the first trimester when the influenza season begins. It is not known if influenza vaccine or corresponding antibodies cross the placenta. Generally, most IgG passage across the placenta occurs during the third trimester. Use only if clearly needed.

Lactating women: It is not known if influenza vaccine or corresponding antibodies are excreted in breast milk. Problems in humans have not been documented. Use if clearly needed.

Immunodeficient persons: Persons receiving immunosuppressive therapy or having other immunodeficiencies may experience a diminished antibody response to active immunization. Chemoprophylaxis of influenza A with amantadine may be indicated in such persons. Vaccination of persons infected with HIV is a prudent measure and will result in protective antibody levels in many recipients. However, antibody response to vaccine may be low in persons with advanced HIV-related illnesses. Booster doses have not improved the immune response in these individuals.

Interactions

Pneumococcal and influenza vaccines may safely and effectively be administrated simultaneously at separate injection sites. There is no indication that influenza vaccine should not be given simultaneously with any other travel vaccine.

Immunosuppressant drugs and radiation therapy may result in an insufficient response to immunization.

In patients receiving anticoagulants, give SC. Several patients treated with warfarin have shown prolonged prothrombin time after influenza vaccination.

Phenytoin plasma concentrations sometimes rise or fall after influenza vaccinations, and carbamazepine and phenobarbital levels sometimes rise.

Influenza vaccination may lead to false-positive HIV serologic tests when particularly sensitive screening tests (ELISA, PERT for reverse transcriptase epitopes, etc) are used. The latter is related to EAV-0, an avian retrovirus remaining in residual egg proteins.

Recommendations for Vaccine Use

The risk of exposure to influenza during foreign travel varies, depending on season and destination.

Influenza immunization is routinely recommended for persons aged >65 years and for those with pre-existing medical conditions which may increase complications. This recommendation is particularly valid for travelers. Travelers may elect to be immunized against influenza in order to avoid contracting it abroad.

Self-Treatment Abroad

Supportive. Amantadine if prescribed before departure.

Principles of Therapy

Supportive. Consider amantadine.

Community Control Measures

None that relate to travel medicine.

JAPANESE ENCEPHALITIS

Infectious Agent

The Japanese encephalitis (JE) virus is a flavivirus.

Transmission

Japanese encephalitis is an arboviral infection transmitted by various *Culex* mosquitoes. In an endemic area, usually < 1–3% of the mosquitoes are infected. This vector feeds on various animal hosts and humans. The vector becomes infective by feeding on viremic swine and various wild birds. Agricultural regions, mainly rice fields, present the highest risk of transmission.

Global Epidemiology

Japanese encephalitis occurs only in Asia (Figure 31). In temperate regions transmission is limited to summer and fall. Transmission occurs predominantly in rural areas, and children are at greatest risk of infection. Risk of JE for travelers depends on destination, season, duration of travel, and activities. Although roughly 50,000 cases are reported annually with an incidence rate reaching 10 per 10,000, the risk of JE for short-term travelers and long-term residents residing in urban centers is extremely low.

Risk for Travelers

From 1978 to 1992, only 24 cases of JE have been diagnosed worldwide among travelers. Of these, six were American soldiers. Rates of JE infection of 1 to 21 per 100,000 per week have been observed in military personnel. The rate of infection seems to be less than 0.1 per 100,000 in tourists and business people.

Clinical Picture

Most infections (99.5%) are asymptomatic. Patients who develop clinical illness have a case fatality rate of 30%, and survivors experience neuropsychiatric sequelae in 50% of cases. The clinical course becomes more serious with age.

Incubation

The incubation period is usually 5 to 15 days.

Communicability

The virus is not transmitted from person to person.

Susceptibility/Resistance

Susceptibility is highest in infancy and old age. Homologous immunity occurs after infection.

Minimized Exposure in Travelers

Personal protective measures against mosquito bites in endemic areas.

Chemoprophylaxis

None available.

Immunoprophylaxis by Japanese Encephalitis Vaccine

Immunology and Pharmacology

Viability: inactive

　Antigenic form: mouse-brain-derived inactivated, whole virus, Nakayama-NIH strain, or Beijing 1 strain

　Adjuvants: none

　Preservative: 0.007% thimerosal within the lyophilized powder

　Allergens/Excipiens: <50 µg mouse serum protein. No myelin basic protein can be detected at the lower threshold of the

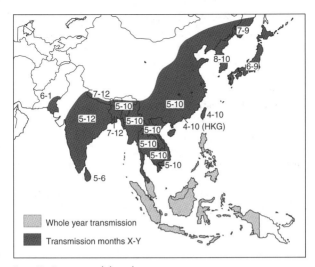

Figure 31 Japanese encephalitis endemic areas

assay (<2 ng/mL) per 500 microgram gelatin, <100 microgram formaldehyde

Mechanism: induction of protective antibodies

Application

Schedule: reconstitute the contents of single and multidose vials with 1.3 mL and 11 mL of diluent, respectively. Three doses of 1 mL for adults and children >3 years of age, normally on days 0, 7, and 30 for optimal immunogenicity. For children <3 years of age, give 0.5 mL each dose. Give the third dose on day 14 in urgent situations. Optimally, administer the third dose at least 10 days before arrival in endemic areas to allow protective antibody titers to develop. Residents of endemic areas may receive a schedule with only two doses separated by 7 days, as pre-existing exposure to flaviviruses may contribute to the immune response. Short-term travelers may receive a similar schedule.

Booster: A booster dose appropriate to the age group may be given 24 to 48 months after the first dose. In the absence of clear data, a definite recommendation on booster intervals cannot be made.

Route: SC

Site: over deltoid

Storage: Store powder at 2 to 8°C (35 to 46°F). Do not freeze the reconstituted suspension. Protect from direct sunlight. Contact manufacturer regarding prolonged exposure to room temperature or elevated or freezing temperatures. Shipping data are not available. Refrigerate and use as soon as possible after reconstitution, preferably with 8 hours.

Availability: available in many countries as JE-Vax (Biken) distributed by Pasteur-Mérieux Connaught. In Japan, the Japanese Encephalitis Vaccine "Seiken" is licensed and imported to a few European countries from Delta Seiken, Tokyo. Note that dosage is different from JE-Vax. In China, a cell-culture-derived inactivated vaccine is used so far, soon to be replaced by a cell-culture-derived live vaccinea.

Protection

Onset: 10 days after two doses, after the third dose in persons ≥ 60 years of age

Efficacy: 78% after two doses, 99% after three doses

Duration: uncertain, but a substantial proportion of antibody is lost 6 months after two doses. Subsequent to a three-dose schedule, antibodies persist for at least 24 months, and possibly up to 4 years

Protective level: based on challenge experiments in passively protected mice, neutralizing antibody levels ≥ 1:10 protected a 10^5 LD$_{50}$ dose, which is the viral dose thought to be transmitted by infected mosquitoes.

Adverse Reactions

Overall, 20% of vaccine recipients experience mild to moderate local side effects in the area of the injection, such as tenderness, redness, or swelling.

Systemic effects such as fever, headache, malaise, rash, chills, dizziness, muscle pain, nausea, vomiting, or abdominal pain may occur in 5 to 10% of cases. Hives and facial swelling were reported in 0.2% and 0.1% of vaccinees, respectively. Although JE vaccine is reactogenic, rates of serious allergic reactions (e.g., generalized urticaria, angioedema) are moderate (1 to 104 per 10,000). This may have been associated with a specific Biken vaccine lot. Two fatal cases of anaphylaxis have been recorded in the Republic of Korea. Persons with certain allergic histories are more likely to react adversely to vaccination. Vaccine recipients should be observed for 30 minutes and warned about delayed allergic reactions.

Several cases of encephalitis have been associated with JE vaccination, two of them fatal. Anecdotally, sudden death, in a patient who also received plague vaccine, and cases of Guillain-Barré syndrome have been reported but association with JE vaccine is questionable.

Contraindications

Absolute: persons with hypersensitivity to any component of the vaccine, or who experienced urticaria or angioedema after a previous dose of JE vaccine. There is no indication that prophylactic antihistamines or steroids prevent allergic reactions related to the vaccine.

Relative: any acute illness, history of urticaria, multiple allergies, chronic cardiac, hepatic, or renal disorders, generalized malignancies, diabetes

Children: Safety and efficacy of JE vaccine in children < 1 year of age have not been established.

Pregnant women: category C. It is not known if JE vaccine or corresponding antibodies cross the placenta. Generally, most IgG passage across the placenta occurs during the third trimester. Japanese encephalitis infection acquired during the first or second trimesters of pregnancy may cause intrauterine infection and fetal death. Infections during the third trimester have not been associated with adverse outcomes in newborns.

Use only if the woman must travel and the risk of infection clearly outweighs the risk of adverse reaction to vaccine.

Lactating women: It is not known if JE vaccine or corresponding antibodies are excreted in breast milk. Problems in humans have not been documented.

Immunodeficient persons: Persons receiving immunosuppressive therapy or having other immunodeficiencies may experience diminished response to active immunization. They may remain susceptible to JE despite immunization.

Interactions

Immunosuppressant drugs and radiation therapy may cause an insufficient response to immunization.

Simultaneous application of JE vaccine with diphtheria-tetanus vaccines and with hepatitis A and B vaccines is apparently safe and immunogenic. No published data exist on concurrent use with other vaccines.

Recommendations for Vaccine Use

Risk to short-term tourists and business travelers is very low, even outside the urban areas. The vaccine has a considerable potential for adverse effects.

The vaccination is recommended for persons residing for longer than 1 month in rural areas where JE is endemic or epidemic (see Figure 31). Travelers should protect themselves against mosquito bites especially during the evening and night in rural areas.

Advice for Self-Treatment Abroad

None. Medical consultation required.

Principles of Therapy

No specific treatment.

Community Control Measures

Notification is mandatory in many countries. No isolation or quarantine required.

LEGIONELLOSIS

Infectious Agent

Bacteria of the *Legionella* genus, of which there are 35 species. The main infectious agent in legionellosis (also known as legionnaires' disease) is *L. pneumophila*, serogroup 1.

Transmission

Transmission is likely airborne. The organism may survive for months in warm water, air-conditioning cooling towers, humidifiers, jacuzzi-type baths, decorative fountains, etc. Immersion in a river has been associated with legionellosis.

Global Epidemiology

Worldwide distribution. Sporadic cases and outbreaks are more common in summer and autumn.

Risk for Travelers

There have been many anecdotal cases and documented outbreaks of the disease. An attack rate of <0.1 per 100,000 has been found among Europeans visiting France, 0.1 to 1.0 in visits to Spain, Greece, and Italy, and 0.7 and 2.0 in two separate years in visits to Turkey.

Clinical Picture

Pneumonia develops after an initial phase of anorexia, malaise, myalgia, headache, and rapidly rising fever.

Incubation

Two to 10 days, with 5 to 6 days most common.

Communicability

Legionellosis is not directly transmitted from person to person.

Susceptibility/Resistance

Attack rates of 0.1 to 5% are seen in the population at risk but unrecognized infections are common. Risk factors include age (most patients >50 years old), gender (male to female incidence ratio is 2.5 to 1), smoking, history of diabetes, chronic illness.

Minimizing Exposure in Travelers

Some experts recommend staying out of the bathroom for the first minute after turning on the warm water for showers.

Chemoprophylaxis

Not applicable.

Immunoprophylaxis

None available.

Self-Treatment Abroad

None. Patient should be treated by a physician.

Principles of Therapy

Antibiotics, e.g., macrolides, possibly quinolones.

Community Control Measures

Hot water temperatures above 60°C inactivate the bacilli. This is rarely done in hotels, however, because of cost and risk of burns.

LEISHMANIASIS

Infectious Agent

Leishmania parasites are protozoal pathogens found in many regions of the developing world. There are two morphologically different forms: intracellular amastigotes seen in humans and animals, and extracellular promastigotes found in the intestine of the sandfly.

Transmission

Female sandflies are the vectors of disease transmission. Sandflies are found in poorly constructed housing and in forested regions. Insect saliva increases promastigote infectivity. The reservoir for cutaneous or mucosal leishmaniasis is often forest rodents. Humans become infected when visiting forested areas. Elsewhere, dogs, other animals, and humans serve as reservoirs.

Global Epidemiology

Visceral leishmaniasis or kala-azar is endemic in the Middle East, Central and South America, India, Bangladesh, and Africa (Figure 32). Specific *Leishmania* are categorized depending on geographic occurrence, for example, *L. aethiopica, L. mexicana, L. peruviana, L. braziliensis*. Cutaneous leishmaniasis is more widespread than the visceral or mucosal form (Figure 33).

Risk for Travelers

Visceral leishmaniasis is occasionally contracted by visitors to endemic areas. U.S. military personnel participating in Operation Desert Storm developed classic visceral disease. Cutaneous and mucosal involvement ("oriental sore") is the more common form.

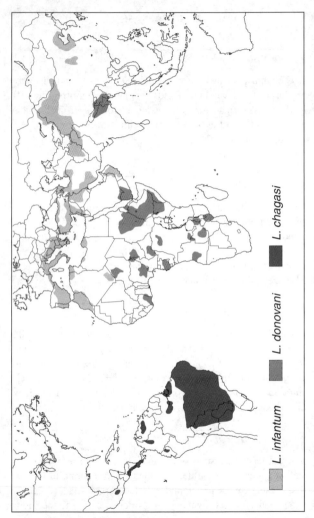

Figure 32   The distribution of visceral leishmaniasis

Clinical Picture

The onset of visceral disease is insidious, leading to a chronic course with fever, malaise, anorexia, weight loss, and often abdominal swelling resulting from hepatosplenomegaly. In the cutaneous form, a single or multiple lesion develops from the initial erythematous papule at the site of inoculation by the sandfly. The nodule then ulcerates. Satellite lesions may then be seen. Cutaneous leishmaniasis may last months or years before healing. Regional adenopathy and systemic symptoms may develop.

Incubation

The incubation period for the visceral disease ranges from 3 to 8 months, and several weeks to months for the cutaneous form.

Communicability

The infection is not communicable from person to person.

Susceptibility/Resistance

Leishmanial infection may stimulate a protective T-cell immune response. Humoral antibodies to the parasite develop following infection but do not appear to be protective.

Minimizing Exposure in Travelers

Travelers should use an insect repellent containing DEET and wear permethrin treated clothing to minimize exposure to infected sandflies. Sleeping areas should be enclosed by a fine mesh netting.

Chemoprophylaxis

Not applicable.

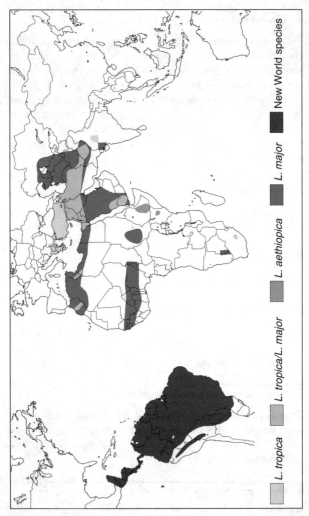

Figure 33 The distribution of cutaneous leishmaniasis

Immunoprophylaxis

Not applicable.

Advise for Self-Treatment Abroad

Not applicable.

Principles of Therapy

Treatment is with one of the pentavalent antimonials—stibogluconate sodium (Pentostam) or meglumine antimoniate (Glucantime). The dose should be 20 mg/kg/d of antimony for 28 days (visceral or mucocutaneous disease) or 10 to 20 days (cutaneous disease). Amphotericin B also appears to be effective.

Community Control Measures

Not applicable.

LEPROSY

Leprosy is a chronic bacterial infection involving the skin and peripheral nerves. It occurs worldwide. Clinical illness is determined in part by host immune response to the organism. No immune response indicates the lepromatous form of the disease. An immune response suggests the tuberculoid form. There are also intermediate forms. Prolonged intense exposure is required for transmission, therefore travelers are at low risk. The organism is particularly common in Asia, Africa, Central and South America, and the South Pacific, with tropical areas posing the highest risk. The causative agent is *Mycobacterium leprae*, and diagnosis is made by culturing the organism from infected tissue. The presence of acid-fast bacilli upon staining provides presumptive diagnosis in an individual showing compatible symptoms. Susceptible strains are treated with dapsone 100 mg/d plus rifampin 600 mg/d for 1 to 2 years. Dapsone is replaced by clofazimine for treating resistant strains.

LEPTOSPIROSIS

Leptospirosis is a spirochetal infection acquired on exposure to contaminated urine of wild and domestic mammals. The illness may take an acute febrile form or a hemorrhagic form associated with jaundice, renal failure, and aseptic meningitis. Leptospirosis is endemic throughout the world. Tropical countries show the highest rates of endemicity due to humidity and heat. Infection can occur throughout the year in endemic areas. The organism enters through breaks in mucous membranes or in the skin. Direct contact with infected animal urine places the individual at risk, as does swimming or bathing in contaminated water.

The incubation period of the disease ranges from 2 days to 3 weeks, with an average of 7 to 12 days. Infections may be asymptomatic or range to Weil's syndrome, which is characterized by fever, jaundice, renal failure, neurologic disorders, and hemorrhage. Conjunctival suffusion is common in the acute form. Skin rash may be seen on the trunk and occasionally the extremities. Frank meningitis is common in the acute form of the disease. Leptospirosis in its classic form is a biphasic disease with a leptospiremic phase followed by a noninfectious immune phase. The infection is diagnosed by demonstration of a fourfold rise in antileptospira antibodies in paired serum samples. Antimicrobial therapy may be of benefit, if initiated within the first 4 days of clinical illness. Intravenous penicillin is generally considered the treatment of choice. Short-course corticosteroids may help control the bleeding and hemorrhaging caused by thrombocytopenia.

Risk can be minimized by immunizing domestic animals, controlling their access to human water supply, and eliminating rodent and other hosts. Travelers should avoid swamps and ponds that may have been contaminated by animal urine. Clothing that prevents contact with surface water should be worn. In contaminated areas weekly chemoprophylaxis with 200 mg of doxycycline may prevent the infection. Vaccines are currently available for human use.

LYME BORRELIOSIS

Lyme disease is a tickborne disease caused by *Borrelia burgdorferi*. The disease occurs in the summer in endemic areas in the U.S., Europe, and Asia. It is characterized in the early stages by an expanding skin lesion often with central clearing (erythema migrans), followed weeks to months later by joint, cardiac, or neurologic manifestations. Early skin manifestations are often associated with nonspecific musculoskeletal complaints such as fever, chills, malaise, myalgias, and headache. Some patients show clinical evidence of meningeal involvement. Central nervous system manifestations may occur within weeks to months after the onset of the illness, including meningitis, encephalitis, etc. Bell's palsy may occur in the same period without other neurologic findings, as can cardiac involvement including AV block and myopericarditis. Arthritis may develop up to 2 years after onset, involving one or two large joints at a time. This form of the illness may persist to resemble rheumatoid arthritis with pannus formation and erosion of bone and cartilage in 10% of patients. Lyme disease is diagnosed only when the characteristic clinical picture presents itself. The organism has rarely been isolated from the blood early in the disease. Serologic diagnosis is generally the most effective way to confirm the infection. Treatment is with antimicrobials including amoxicillin, penicillin, doxycycline, or ceftriaxone for 14 to 28 days, depending on the clinical picture.

A vaccine consisting of recombinant *B. burgdorferi* outer surface lipoprotein A (LYMErix™) has been introduced on the American market after having proved to be effective against strains in five different states in the U.S. This vaccine, however, is unlikely to be effective against the European strains. Three doses will be administered, the first two 1 month apart, and the booster dose at 12 months.

MALARIA

Infectious Agent

Malaria is a protozoal infection caused by four species of the genus *Plasmodium:P. falciparum, P. vivax, P. ovale*, and *P. malariae*.

Transmission

These plasmodia are transmitted by the bite of an infected female *Anopheles* mosquito (Figure 34). Among 400 *Anopheles* species, some 80 will transmit malaria in different parts of the world, 45 of which are considered important vectors. *Anopheles* requires water for its early development, which can be found in rice fields, foot prints, lakes, etc. The water may be fresh or salty, running or stagnant. The active flight range of an adult female is limited to about one mile but passive dispersal by strong seasonal winds may transport *Anopheles* far from their place of origin. Transmission peaks at midnight for these nocturnal mosquitoes in Asia and Latin America and about 10 PM in Africa. Younger, uninfected mosquitoes may commence feeding at sunset. *Anopheles* will feed during the day only if unusually hungry. Following a latency period, the infected mosquito may

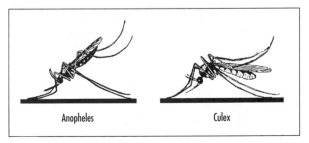

Anopheles   Culex

Figure 34   Anopheles and culex mosquitoes

inject plasmodial sporozoites from its salivary glands into the bloodstream of a human while feeding.

Global Epidemiology

Malaria transmission occurs in most tropic and subtropic countries (Figure 29). Roughly 40% of the world's population lives in areas afflicted with endemic malaria. There are more than 400 million new cases of malaria annually, resulting in 1.5 to 3 million deaths, mainly in infants and children but also often in pregnant women. Mortality is related to the distribution of *P. falciparum*, which is predominant in tropical Africa, eastern Asia, the South Pacific, and the Amazon Basin. The malaria situation is worsening in many areas of the world.

While malaria is also transmitted in most urban centers in Africa, this is not the case for cities in Latin America and Southeast Asia, nor for many tourist destinations in endemic regions (Figure 35). Risk of malaria transmission decreases at altitudes over 1500 meters but may occur at altitudes up to 3000 metres in hotter areas. Transmission is highest at the end of the rainy season.

Risk for Travelers

More than 10,000 cases of malaria are imported to nonendemic countries annually. This is considered a low estimate due to lack of reporting and inadequate reporting systems. There are an additional unknown number of cases treated abroad. The risk depends on the area: the degree of endemicity, the predominant *Plasmodium* species, distribution of resistance, season, type of area visited (urban or rural), type of accommodation (air-conditioned or screened indoor versus outdoor), and most importantly on duration of exposure, preventive measures taken, and individual behavior.

The risk for nonimmune travelers varies enormously between countries and even within a country. Risk is highest in some Pacific islands, Papua New Guinea, and tropical Africa.

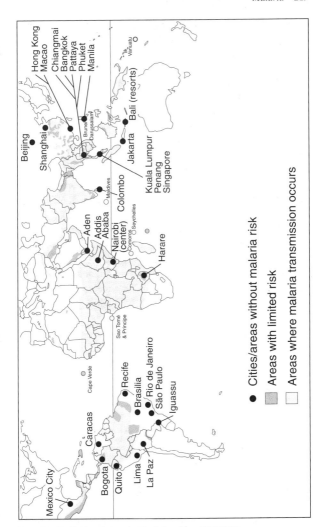

Figure 35 Worldwide malaria endemicity (adapted from WHO 1997)

For travelers with no chemoprophylaxis, the risk of symptomatic malaria infection is estimated to be 2.4% per month of stay in West Africa and 1.5% in East Africa (Figure 36). The incidence rate of malaria cases imported from West Africa varies from less than 200 cases per 100,000 travelers in Senegal and Gabon, 200 to 399 from Burkina Faso, Ivory Coast, and Cameroon, and 400 to more than 700 from Togo, Mali, Guinea, Benin, Congo-Zaire, and the Central African Republic.

Recent seroepidemiologic surveys using *P. falciparum* circumsporozoite antibodies indicate a high rate of infection in travelers returning from sub-Saharan Africa. Antibodies were detected in the sera of more than 20% of travelers who had visited Kenya for 2 to 16 weeks, with individual travelers at a 8.7 times greater risk (48.8%) compared to those on package tours (5.6%). There is intermediate risk on the Indian subcontinent. There is low risk of transmission in frequently visited tourist destinations in Latin America and Southeast Asia (see Figure 35), but some areas of Brazil, India, and Thailand (see Appendix C) have a considerable risk. Differing meteorologic conditions may cause annual and seasonal fluctuations.

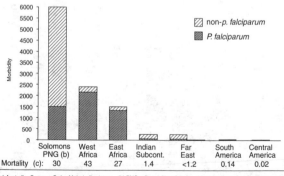

(a) Australia, German, Swiss Malaria Registers   (b) PNG = Papua New Guinea   (c) assuming a case fatality rate of 2%

Figure 36   Morbidity and mortality in 100,000 nonimmune travelers exposed for 1 month **without** chemoprophylaxis (a).

There have been rare cases of malaria contracted by nontravelers living near international airports ("airport malaria"), by passengers aboard a plane touching down at an airport in an endemic area ("runway malaria"). Additionally, "harbor," "taxi," and "luggage malaria" have been anecdotally described. Malaria may also be transmitted by infected blood, placing intravenous drug users, laboratory staff, and recipients of transfusions and transplants at risk.

Clinical Picture

Initial malaria symptoms may be mild, particularly in travelers who use chemoprophylaxis. There is usually fever and possibly headache, myalgias (muscular pain), vomiting, diarrhea, and cough. Malaria may be subjectively indistinguishable from influenza. Clinical symptoms such as fever are caused principally by the rupture of large numbers of erythrocytic schizonts in the erythrocytic cycle. Symptoms may or may not occur with classic periodicity. In the most serious forms, such as malaria tropica resulting from *Plasmodium falciparum* infection, complications may occur 24 hours after onset of symptoms or later. These include cerebral malaria with initial signs of confusion, drowsiness, and disorientation, followed by coma, or anemia, pulmonary edema, circulatory failure, renal failure, jaundice, acidosis, hemorrhages, etc. Infected red blood cells deform and rosette (become sticky) before rupturing, which results in capillary clotting and some of the complications described. Immunologic responses, changes in regional blood flow, and biochemical systemic complications also occur. The case fatality rate for *P. falciparum* infections in the developed countries ranges from 0.5 to 7%. It is close to zero for malaria caused by other *Plasmodium* species.

Incubation

Sporozoites infect hepatocytes in the human liver and develop and multiply. After a minimum incubation period of 6 days, asexual parasites are released from the liver to invade red blood cells where they grow and multiply cyclically (see Figure 14).

The incubation period ranges from 6 to 14 days for *P. falciparum* and from 7 to 30 days for the other species. There may be an incubation period exceeding 1 year for *P. ovale*.

Communicability

Untreated or inadequately treated patients can be a source of infection for 1 year or longer.

Susceptibility/Resistance

Susceptibility is general except for reduced susceptibility in those with certain genetic traits such as sickle cell trait or the absence of Duffy factor in the erythrocytes. There is no complete immunity after infection but a semi-immunity as observed in the native population, or in long-term residents with continuous exposure to parasites, may persist for approximately 1 year. Those leaving endemic areas lose their semi-immunity and become susceptible to malarial infection again. Some immunologic memory is, however, retained, which can reduce the severity of symptoms should the individual become infected.

Minimized Exposure in Travelers

Personal protection measures against mosquito bites as described in Part 1.

Chemoprophylaxis

Atovaquone/Proguanil (see also proguanil section below)

Pharmacology

Description: Atovaquone, formerly known as 566C80 or BW566C, is a novel hydroxynaphthoquinone used in a fixed-dose combination with the dihydrofolate antagonist proguanil. Available in tablet form as Malarone®, each containing 250 mg atovaquone and 100 mg proguanil hydrochloride.

Mode of action: Atovaquone affects mitochondrial electron transport leading to reduced pyrimidine nucleotide pools and decreased nucleic acid synthesis. Atovaquone is a schizontocide. Additional causal prophylactic activity was recently confirmed in volunteers challenged with *P. falciparum* malaria. Proguanil has a slow erythrocytic action but is highly effective against the pre-erythrocytic forms and has sporontocidal effects on *P. falciparum*. It is less active against *P. vivax*.

Pharmacokinetics: Atovaquone is highly lipophilic with relatively poor oral bioavailability. The drug should be administered with food for increased absorption and bioavailability. In the plasma, atovaquone is highly protein bound (>99%) and has a lengthy elimination half-life (50 to 70 hours). Excretion is almost exclusively (>90 %) through the feces.

Administration

Dosage: one standard tablet daily for adults, starting at least 24 hours prior to arrival in the endemic area (preferably 1 week in advance, to evaluate tolerance). To date, children's doses ranging from 3.1 to 5.7 mg/kg body weight have been effective. Prophylactic medication can be discontinued 1 week after leaving the endemic area.

Availability: The drug is currently approved for malaria treatment only but has been submitted for registration as a prophylactic agent in some countries. Registered in some European and Asian countries as Malarone®.

Protection

Efficacy: Limited data available. Early clinical treatment studies using atovaquone monotherapy showed high rates of recrudescence. Its use in combination with proguanil resulted in dramatic improvements in cure rates. In a 10-week prophylactic trial, the combination was 100% effective against *P. falciparum* malaria in semi-immune Kenyans. A recent randomized, double-blind, placebo-controlled cohort study showed 100% protective efficacy against *P. falciparum* malaria in Gabonese school children.

Causal prophylaxis: yes

Adverse Reactions

Adverse reactions occurring can be attributed to the constituents or their combination. Proguanil has the reputation of being a very safe drug at standard chemoprophylactic doses. Mouth ulceration has been reported and mild epigastric discomfort may occur. To date, atovaquone has been well tolerated. The most common adverse reactions to atovaquone include gastrointestinal disturbances, headache, anorexia, diarrhea, and coughing. In the chemoprophylactic studies performed to date, the drug combination was well tolerated. Serious adverse events include anaphylactic reaction, seizures in persons with a history of seizures, and hemolysis in a G-6P-D-deficient individual.

Contraindications and Precautions

Absolute: The combination is contraindicated in persons with known hypersensitivity to atovaquone, proguanil, or any component of the formulation. The chemoprophylactic role of this combination in nonimmune travelers has not yet been established.

Relative: Patients with a history of seizures or with G-6-PD deficiency should not receive this agent.

Interactions

Concomitant administration of metoclopramide or rifampicin leads to significantly reduced plasma concentrations of atovaquone. Atovaquone reductions are also caused by paracetamol, benzodiazepines, acyclovir, opiates, cephalosporins, antidiarrhea agents, and laxatives. Vaccination with oral live typhoid or cholera vaccines should be completed 3 days before the first antimalarial dose.

Pregnant women: category B. Ther is no evidence of teratogenicity in laboratory animals but there have been no controlled clinical studies.

Lactating women: It is not known if atovaquone is excreted in breast milk. The combination cannot currently be recommended for breastfeeding mothers.

Recommendations for Use

Currently recommended for the treatment of resistant *P. falciparum* malaria. May soon be used for chemoprophylaxis

Future prospects: The combination is promising. Further studies of its chemosuppressive activity and tolerance in non-immune travelers are required.

Azithromycin

Pharmacology

Description: semi-synthetic derivative of erythromycin with methyl-substituted nitrogen in the macrolide ring

Mode of action: inhibition of protein synthesis on 70S ribosomes. Azithromycin is a blood schizontocide and has been shown to have partial causal prophylactic activity in the human challenge model.

Pharmacokinetics: The drug is well absorbed with 37% bioavailability after oral administration. Food may reduce the bioavailability of the suspension or sachet forms but this is not clinically significant. Maximum plasma concentration is reached 2 to 3 hours after administration. Azithromycin has 10 to 100 times greater bioavailabilty in tissue than in serum. Protein binding is approximately 52% and the drug is highly concentrated in the liver. Azithromycin has a half-life of 56 to 70 hours. Excretion is predominantly in the form of unchanged drug in the feces (88%) or urine (6 to 12%). Terminal plasma half-life ranges from 2 to 4 days.

Administration

Dosage: The dose for adults is 250 mg/d. Azithromycin can be administered with food. No data are available on pediatric doses for malaria chemoprophylaxis.

Availability: available as Zithromax in capsule form (250 mg), suspension (5 mL containing 200 mg), and in powder sachets (100 mg, 200 mg, 300 mg, 400 mg, and 500 mg).

Protection

Efficacy: Azithromycin had a causal prophylactic efficacy superior to doxycycline in rodents but only partial causal prophylactic efficacy in humans. One study has shown 100% efficacy for the regimen of 250 mg/d for 28 days after challenge, indicating that the combined causal and suppressive clinical efficacy of azithromycin is high. An efficacy trial in western Kenya showed 84% efficacy for azithromycin 250 mg/d versus 92% efficacy for doxycycline 100 mg/d.

Adverse Reactions

Diarrhea (2 to 7%), abdominal pain (2 to 5%), nausea (1 to 5%), vomiting up to 2%, allergic reactions (<1%), and vaginitis (up to 2%).

Contraindications and Precautions

Absolute: Azithromycin is contraindicated in persons with known hypersensitivity to the drug or other macrolide antibiotics or adjuvants in the formulation and in patients receiving ergot alkaloids. Patients with liver or kidney insufficiency require dosage adjustments. Patients with severe hepatic disease should not receive the drug. Rare serious allergic reactions have been observed, as with erythromycin and other macrolides. Superinfection with resistant microorganisms is a possibility in all antibiotic treatment. Pseudomembranous colitis is possible in patients with diarrhea.

Interactions

Azithromycin should not be administered concomitantly with ergotamine or antacids. Serum concentrations of cyclosporin and digoxin should be monitored when administered with azithromycin. Like other macrolide antibiotics, azithromycin can potentially affect the cytochrome P450 system. No statistically significant interactions were observed however, in pharmacokinetic studies with concomitant administration of theophylline, carbamazepine, methylprednisolone, terfenadine, or zidovudine.

Vaccination with live bacterial vaccines, such as oral live typhoid and cholera vaccines, should be completed at least 3 days before the first prophylactic dose of azithromycin.

Pregnant women: Azithromycin is category B, with no evidence of teratogenicity in laboratory animals but no well-controlled clinical studies. It may be used during pregnancy if clearly required and if safer options are contraindicated.

Lactating women: No studies are available regarding excretion of azithromycin in breast milk.

Recommendations for Use

Azithromycin presents an alternative option for children traveling to high-risk areas when chloroquine, mefloquine, or doxycycline are contraindicated. Pediatric dosage guidelines are required.

Future perspectives: niche drug for target groups, such as pregnant women and young children, when other alternatives are contraindicated. The main disadvantage is the prohibitive cost of the extended prophylactic regimen.

Chloroquine

Pharmacology

Description: Chloroquine is chemically classified as a 4-aminoquinoline. Preparations are available as phosphate, sulfate, and hydrochloride salts.

Mode of action: potent blood schizontocide. Highly active against the erythrocytic forms of sensitive strains of all four species of malaria. Gametocidal against *P. vivax, P. malariae,* and *P. ovale.* Activity is probably due to the inhibition of the polymerization of toxic hemin into hemozoin.

Pharmacokinetics: Oral bioavailability is approximately 90%. Peak plasma levels of chloroquine and the principal active metabolite desethychloroquine are reached within 1 to 6 hours. Food increases the absorption and bioavailability of the drug. Chloroquine has a large volume of distribution and binds 50 to 65% to plasma proteins. The drug is eliminated in the urine. Elimination half-life is between 6 hours and 10 days. Terminal elimination half-lives of up to 2 months for chloroquine and desethylchloroquine have been reported.

Administration

Dosage should be calculated in terms of the base. Chloroquine base of 100 mg is approximately equivalent to 161 mg of chloroquine phosphate or 136 mg of chloroquine sulfate. The recommended prophylactic regimen is administered either weekly or daily. Pediatric solutions are available.

Weekly: The adult dose of 300 mg is administered once weekly. In infants and children, the weekly dosage is 5 mg/kg of body weight but, regardless of weight, should not exceed the adult dose.

Daily: In some countries (mainly France), 100 mg base daily for adults or 1.5 mg/kg of body weight daily for children is prescribed.

Availability: worldwide. There are many well-known brand names such as Aralen, Avloclor, Bemaphate, Chinamine, Chlorquim, Cidanchin, Delagil, Gontochin, Imagon, Iroquine, Klorokin, Luprochin, Malarex, Matalets, Nivaquine, Nivaquine B, Resochin, Resochine, Resoquine, Sanoquin, Tanakan, Tresochin, and Trochin.

Protection

Efficacy: Due to widespread chloroquine-resistant *P. falciparum* (CRPF), chloroquine alone as a malaria prophylactic is limited to Central America, Haiti, the Dominican Republic, and the Near East. The effectiveness of the drug exceeds 95% in these areas. Chloroquine is active against other forms of plasmodia, with the exception of some resistant *P. vivax* strains in Papua New Guinea, Southeast Asia (Indonesia and Myanmar), and possibly Brazil. In areas with considerable risk of CRPF, chloroquine in combination with proguanil or an alternative chemoprophylaxis such as mefloquine should be used.

Causal prophylaxis: none

Adverse Reactions

Usually well tolerated at standard chemoprophylactic doses.

Side-effects include transient headache, gastrointestinal disturbances such as nausea, vomiting, diarrhea, abdominal cramps, pruritus, and macular, urticarial, and purpuric skin lesions. Itching of the palms, soles, and scalp is common in users with darker pigmentation.

Less frequent adverse events include loss of hair, bleaching of hair pigment, pigmentation of mucous membranes, tinnitus, hearing loss and deafness, photosensitivity, and neuromyopathy. Rare blood disorders including aplastic anemia, agranulocytosis, thrombocytopenia, and neutropenia may occur. Hemolysis has been described in a few patients with G-6-PD deficiency.

Severe reactions include rare psychotic episodes, convulsions, hypotension, cardiovascular collapse, electrocardiographic (ECG) changes, double vision, and difficulty in focusing. Corneal and retinal damage may occur, usually with prolonged usage or high dosages as used in rheumatology. Pigmented deposits and opacities in the cornea are often reversible if the drug is withdrawn early enough but retinal damage with macular lesions, defects of color vision, pigmentation, optic nerve atrophy, scotomas, field defects, and blindness are usually irreversible.

Those using chloroquine long term should have ophthalmologic checks every 6 months, particularly when the total cumulative dose exceeds 100 g. Changes may occur after the drug is withdrawn.

Contraindications and Precautions

Absolute: Use of chloroquine is contraindicated in persons with known hypersensitivity to 4-aminoquinoline compounds or a deficiency of G-6-PD. Also contraindicated in persons with pre-existing retinopathy, diseases of the central nervous system, myasthenia gravis, or disorders of the blood producing organs. Chloroquine should not be taken by persons with a history of epilepsy, psychosis, or retinopathy.

Caution is necessary in administering the drug to patients with hepatic disease, alcoholism, impaired renal function (dosage reduction may be required in patients with kidney impairments), porphyria, or psoriasis.

Chloroquine is toxic if the recommended dose is exceeded. Vomiting should be induced immediately if an overdose occurs. Admission to an intensive care unit may be indicated.

Pregnant women: category C. Although some adverse fetal effects have been reported, chloroquine can be used freely in pregnancy, either alone or in combination with proguanil.

Lactating women: The drug is excreted in breast milk but not in sufficient quantities to harm or protect the infant against malaria.

Interactions

Concomitant use with proguanil increases the incidence of mouth ulcers.

Cimetidine inhibits the metabolism of chloroquine and may cause elevated levels of the drug in the plasma.

Administration of live bacterial vaccines, such as oral live typhoid vaccines, should be completed at least 3 days before the first prophylactic dose of chloroquine. Chloroquine can suppress the antibody response to intradermal primary pre-exposure rabies vaccine, which should therefore be administered intramuscularly.

Concurrent administration of chloroquine with drugs capable of inducing blood disorders, such as gold salts, should be avoided. Other possible interactions can occur with monoamine oxidase (MAO) inhibitors, digoxin, and corticosteriods. The activity of methotrexate and other folic acid antagonists is increased by chloroquine use.

Recommendations for Use

Chloroquine is the drug of choice in areas without CRPF as it is cheap and comparatively well tolerated. See proguanil section below for the recommendation of the combination with proguanil.

Doxycycline

Pharmacology

Description: base doxycycline monohydrate. A 100 mg base is approximately equivalent to 115 mg doxycycline hydrochloride. Administered in tablets or capsules as the hydrochloride or in syrup and suspension as calcium chelate or monohydrate.

Mode of action: slow but effective blood schizontocide of *P. vivax* and multidrug-resistant strains of *P. falciparum*. Weak activity against the pre-erythrocytic stages of *P. falciparum*

Pharmacokinetics: Doxycycline is highly lipophilic. After oral administration the drug is almost fully absorbed and peak plasma levels are achieved within 2 hours. Thereafter, the drug is strongly bound to plasma proteins (90%). The half-life of doxycycline ranges from 15 hours after a single dose to 22 hours after repeated doses. Doxycycline is not significantly metabolized and is eliminated from the body in feces and urine. There is no significant accumulation of the drug in patients with reduced kidney function. Unlike other tetracyclines, concomitant administration of food or milk does not significantly decrease absorption of doxycycline.

Administration

Dosage: The dosage for malaria chemoprophylaxis in adults and children over 12 years is 100 mg base daily. Daily doses of 50 mg doxycycline are probably inadequate against *P. falciparum*. The potential for using a combination 50 mg daily doxycycline combined with a weekly chloroquine dose against *P. vivax* appears limited due to compliance and emergence of chloroquine-resistant *P. vivax* malaria. Exceptionally, children aged 8 to 12 may receive 1.5 mg/kg daily.

Doxycycline should be taken with plenty of liquid to avoid esophagitis.

Availability: worldwide under many brand names, including Vibramycin®, Doxyclin®, Biociclina®, Doxacin®, and Nordox®

Protection

Efficacy: Limited data are available regarding the efficacy of doxycycline for malaria chemoprophylaxis in nonimmune travelers. In areas of multidrug resistance such as the Thai-Cambodian border provinces of Tak and Trat, doxycycline is considered to be the most effective chemoprophylactic agent available. In Somalia, most malaria cases occurred in persons who missed at least one dose of medication.

Causal prophylaxis: some causal activity. However, a recent challenge has shown that the agent's causal prophylaxis is inadequate against *P. falciparum* malaria.

Adverse Reactions

Side effects are reported by some 20% of users, and 6% discontinue medication due to perceived adverse effects. Gastrointestinal symptoms such as nausea, vomiting, and diarrhea are reported as well as dizziness, headache, and skin rash. Overgrowth of resistant coliform organisms such as *Proteus* species, *Pseudomonas* species, and *Campylobacter enteritis* may occur and should be considered in persons with diarrhea who have been taking doxycycline. Reported diarrhea should also be distinguished from pseudomembranous colitis due to superinfection with *Clostridium difficile*.

Use of doxycycline may result in overgrowth of nonsusceptible organisms such as fungi. Oral candidiasis, vulvovaginitis, and pruritus in the anogenital region may result due to proliferation of *Candida albicans*. Photosensitivity of the skin has frequently been reported.

Permanent brown discoloration of teeth in children under 8 years of age has been observed. Blood disorders have been reported occasionally. Hepatotoxicity, nephrotoxicity, erythema multiforme, intracranial hypertension, and lupus erythematosus have been associated with the use of tetracyclines.

Contraindications and Precautions

Absolute: The drug is contraindicated in persons who have shown previous hypersensitivity to any of the tetracyclines.

The use of tetracyclines during periods of tooth development may cause permanent staining of the teeth and should be avoided in pregnant women and children under 8 years of age.

Caution: Doxycyline users should be advised to use an effective sunscreen due to increased photosensitivity. The drug should be discontinued at the first sign of skin erythema. Doxycycline should not be taken before lying down as there is a theoretical danger of esophagitis associated with the drug.

Interactions

Concomitant administration of preparations containing aluminium, iron, calcium, or magnesium reduces absorption of doxycycline.

Vaccination with live bacterial vaccines such as oral live typhoid and cholera vaccines should be completed at least 3 days before the first prophylactic dose of doxycycline.

The mean half-life of doxycycline is reduced by concomitant use of alcohol, phenobarbitone, phenytoin, or carbamazepine. Reduced dosages of anticoagulants may be necessary due to reduced plasma prothrombin activity. There are reports suggesting reduced activity of oral contraceptives during doxycycline intake. Fatal nephrotoxicity has been reported with concomitant use of methoxyflurane.

Pregnant women: contraindicated in pregnancy due to interference with fetal bone and teeth formation. Evidence of embryotoxicity has been noted in animals treated early in pregnancy.

Lactating women: The drug is readily excreted in breast milk.

Recommendations for Use

Recommended as an alternative chemoprophylactic regimen in areas with considerable risk of CRPF when mefloquine is contraindicated. Doxycycline is the prophylactic drug of choice in areas of multidrug resistance such as the Thai-Burmese and Thai-Cambodian borders (see Figure 31).

For this reason, the use of doxycycline is currently increasing due to a lack of alternatives for these areas. Further tolerability and efficacy data are required for civilian travelers, particularly women.

Mefloquine

Pharmacology

Description: Mefloquine is a 4-quinolone methanol derivative structurally related to quinine. It is used clinically as a 50:50 racemic mixture of the erythroisomers. The commercial form is available as mefloquine hydrochloride in oral preparations only.

Mode of action: Mefloquine is a potent, long-acting blood schizontocide that targets trophozoites and schizonts in particular and is effective against all malarial species. It is ineffective against mature gametocytes and intrahepatic stages. There is some evidence for sporontocidal activity. The exact mechanism is unclear but the most plausible hypothesis points to hemoglobin degradation. Mefloquine is thought to compete with the complexing protein for heme binding. The resulting drug-heme complex is toxic to malarial parasites.

Pharmacokinetics: There is significant variation among individuals. Bioavailability of the tablet formulation is approximately 89%. Food increases the rate and extent of absorption, causing a 40% increase in bioavailability. The mean peak concentration in whole blood or plasma is reached in a mean time of 17.6 hours after a single dose. Mefloquine is distributed in the tissues, with extensive binding to plasma proteins (98.2%) and high lipid solubility. The mean volume of distribution is 20 L/kg, and the drug is cleared slowly from the body, resulting in a long terminal half-life of about 18 days. Studies in animals have shown that the drug is excreted primarily in the bile and feces. Carboxylic acid is the main metabolite, the concentrations of which exceed those of the parent compound by a factor of three to four. This metabolite is devoid of antimalarial activity. The pharmacokinetics of mefloquine are highly stereospecific but its potential to cause adverse events does not appear to depend on the stereochemistry of the enantiomers or the concentration of the carboxylic acid metabolite.

Administration

Mefloquine has a bitter, slightly burned taste and should be taken after food to maximize bioavailability and thus optimize prophylactic efficacy. The food-enhanced drug absorption has been attributed to stimulated gastric acid secretion and delayed gastric emptying, enhanced intestinal motility, and increased bile flow. The tablets should be swallowed whole but can be divided and mixed with milk or jam for small children or those with difficulties swallowing.

Dosage: The U.S. mefloquine tablet formulation contains 250 mg hydrochloride which is equivalent to 228 mg base whereas elsewhere the tablets contain 250 mg base.

The recommended adult dose for chemoprophylaxis in adults >45 kg is 250 mg base weekly as a single dose, translating to 228 mg base in the U.S. There is some concern that heavy individuals may require more than one 250 mg tablet weekly to attain the required protective plasma concentration within the required time frame. This issue needs clarification.

Adults weighing <45 kg and children weighing >5 kg should take a single weekly dose of 5 mg/kg. Prophylactic use in children younger than 3 months or weighing less than 5 kg has not been documented.

In the U.K. and several other countries, mefloquine is not recommended for children <2 years of age or <15 kg, as originally recommended. This limitation was waived, however, by the manufacturer, WHO, CDC, and in various other countries in the mid-1990s.

Travelers with last-minute bookings who are unable to take a first dose 5 days or more prior to departure may require a loading dose to attain levels of prophylactic efficacy. This consists of one 250 mg tablet daily for 3 days followed by the usual weekly dosage.

Good tolerability has been shown during use over 3 years and more. The original 3-month restriction for use no longer applies.

Mefloquine intake may be begun 2 to 4 weeks before travel if the prescriber feels tolerance is questionable in a patient or if the compatibility of coadministered medications requires monitoring.

Availability: available worldwide as Lariam®. Mephaquine® is also widely available but has a bioequivalence approximately 80% that of Lariam®.

Protection

Onset: first day with loading dose (see above). Otherwise after 5 to 7 days

Efficacy: Mefloquine is effective against *P. falciparum* strains resistant to other antimalarials. The minimal inhibitory chemosuppressive plasma concentration of mefloquine is estimated at 600 µg/L. Resistance to mefloquine increases with time and an efficacy of only 30% has been reported in the Thai provinces of Trat and Tak. Mefloquine resistance is also slowly developing in other areas of Southeast Asia, the Amazon Basin, and endemic areas of central and West Africa. There are sporadic pockets of resistance in endemic regions of East Africa, however, the effectiveness probably still exceeds 90% at tourist destinations. Failure of mefloquine prophylaxis despite proven adequate drug concentrations has been documented in four West African countries.

Mefloquine is fairly effective against other *Plasmodium* species, primarily *P. vivax*, although clusters of resistance have been reported along the Omo River and other regions in Ethiopia.

Causal prophylaxis: none

Adverse Reactions

High rates of perceived adverse reactions (24 to 90%) are reported by all population groups, as is the case with the other malaria chemoprophylactics. The most frequent reactions to mefloquine are dizziness, nausea, and vomiting. Other reported reactions include muscle weakness and cramps, myalgia, arthralgia, fatigue, asthenia, malaise, fever, chills, and loss of appetite. Laboratory abnormalities including transient elevation of transaminases, leukopenia or leukocytosis, and thrombocytopenia have also been reported.

Dermatologic reactions occur in 1 to 11% of recipients, including rash, exanthema, urticaria, pruritus, and hair loss. Skin photosensitivity among American troops in Somalia was significantly lower for mefloquine users than for doxycycline users. Several studies suggest mefloquine causes fewer dermatologic reactions than other antimalarials.

Neurologic reactions include vertigo, disturbed balance, headache, sleep disturbances, nightmares, and, less frequently, auditory and visual disturbances. Psychiatric events such as neurosis, affective disorders, hallucinations, delusions, paranoia, anxiety, agitation, and suicidal ideation have also been observed. Isolated cases of encephalopathy have been known to result from taking mefloquine.

The frequency of serious adverse central nervous system (CNS) reactions to mefloquine is 1 in 607 in a British study, 1 in 10,000 to 13,000 among European travelers, and 1 in 20,000 in Canadians surveyed. Reactions included seizures, disorientation, and toxic encephalopathy. Rare severe cutaneous adverse reactions have been reported, including erythema multiforme and Stevens-Johnson syndrome.

Persons with a personal or family history of neurologic or psychiatric disorders appear to be at higher risk for such events. Women appear to have significantly more CNS events compared to men, which may reflect higher mg/kg dosing for women. Persons receiving the standard weekly mefloquine regimen, with or without adverse events, however, show similar levels of mefloquine and its carboxylic acid metabolite. Other reports suggest that concurrent alcohol and/or drug abuse may play a role in those events. Reported cardiovascular events include circulatory disturbances, tachycardia, bradycardia, irregular pulse, extrasystoles, and other transient alterations in cardiac conduction.

Events attributable to mefloquine may occur up to several weeks after the last dose due to the long half-life of the drug but most adverse events occur early on in prophylaxis and approximately 75% are apparent by the third dose.

Contraindications and Precautions

Mefloquine is contraindicated in persons with a history of hypersensitivity to mefloquine or related substances such as quinine. Those with epilepsy or psychiatric disorders should not be given this drug.

The WHO and various national expert groups advise persons involved in tasks requiring fine coordination and spatial discrimination to avoid using mefloquine prophylaxis. Recent studies, however, have shown no impact on fine coordination in healthy subjects experiencing no adverse events.

Users experiencing anxiety, depression, confusion, or uneasiness during mefloquine prophylaxis should discontinue the regimen and seek medical advice. If symptoms are slight, a biweekly dosage of 125 mg may be considered.

Interactions

Mefloquine and related substances (e.g., quinine, halofantrine) should not be used concomitantly or consecutively due to an increased risk of cardiotoxicity—a life-threatening prolongation of the corrected QT interval—and convulsions.

Concomitant use of mefloquine with antiarrhythmic agents, beta-adrenergic blocking agents, calcium channel blockers, antihistamines including H1-blocking agents, and phenothiazines could theoretically contribute to the prolongation of the QTc interval but this does not constitute a contraindication.

Vaccination with oral live typhoid or cholera vaccines should be completed at least 3 days before the first dose of mefloquine.

Both slight increase and decrease of the effects of anticoagulants have been noted, but not to an extent that concomitant use would be contraindicated.

Pregnant women: category C. Studies of mefloquine prophylaxis during the second and third trimesters have shown no evidence of elevated maternal or fetal toxicity. The potential for teratogenicity in the first trimester requires further clarifi-

Table 11 Mefloquine and Survival

Risk in 14 Million Users in Africa, according to ROCHE files

No fatality associated with convincing evidence
14 probably / possibly associated cases

Benefit per 1,000,000 Users in Africa (assuming average 2 week duration)

Risk of Malaria (conservative estimate)	Infection (P.f.)		Death (CFR 1%)	
• without chemoprophylaxis	5000		50	
• with mefloquine (efficacy 90%)	500	△ 4500	5	△ 45
• with CQ + PG (efficacy 75%)	1250	△ 750	12	△ 7

CQ = chloroquine, PG = proguanil

cation and mefloquine should only be used during this period
if benefits outweigh potential risks. Women of childbearing
age should avoid conception during mefloquine prophylaxis
and for 3 months thereafter. However, termination is not indicated if pregnancy occurs in this time frame.

Lactating women: Mefloquine is excreted in breast milk.
No adverse effects have been observed in breast-fed infants.

Recommendations for Use
Mefloquine prophylaxis is recommended by the WHO and several European and North American expert groups for travelers
visiting high-risk areas with CRPF. British experts concerned
about the agent's tolerability recommend the combination
chloroquine/proguanil rather than mefloquine for short-term
tourists visiting Gambia and East Africa in low transmission
season. Risks and benefits of the agent are shown in Table 11.

Proguanil

Pharmacology
Description: available as proguanil hydrochloride. Tablets contain 100 mg hydrochloride which equals 87 mg base. Dosage is
expressed in terms of the hydrochloride. Chlorproguanil, a long-
acting analogue of proguanil, has also been extensively used.

Mode of action: Both proguanil and chlorproguanil are pro-drugs whose activity is due to the action of the metabolites cycloguanil and chlorcycloguanil, respectively. The drug is a dihydrofolate reductase inhibitor which acts by interfering with the folic-folinic acid systems. The main effect occurs at the time of nuclear division. The drug is a slow-acting blood schizontocide which acts on the erythrocytic forms of all malaria parasites. It is highly effective against the primary exo-erythrocytic (hepatic) forms and is therefore an effective causal prophylactic. It also interferes with malaria transmission through sporontocidal effects against *P. falciparum*. It is less active against *P. vivax*.

Pharmacokinetics: Proguanil is only available in oral for-mulations. It is rapidly absorbed, and peak plasma concentra-tions are reached in approximately 4 hours. Peak plasma levels of about 140 ng/mL are attained after a single oral dose of 200 mg proguanil hydrochloride. Proguanil is metabolized to cycloguanil and 4-chlorophenylbiguanide. The active triazine metabolite cycloguanil reaches a maximum serum concentra-tion of 75 ng/mL after 5 hours. Plasma protein binding of proguanil is approximately 75%, and high concentrations occur in the erythrocytes. Blood concentrations decline rapidly and proguanil is excreted largely unchanged (60%) in the urine with about 30% as the metabolite cycloguanil and 10% as chlorophenylbiguanide. The elimination half-life of proguanil is 11 to 20 hours, and concentrations fall to an undetectable level a week after administration. Proguanil is metabolized in the liver to cycloguanil by the cytochrome P-450 system. There is considerable variation in individual ability to convert the prodrug to the active metabolite. About 3% of Caucasians are considered to be poor metabolizers of proguanil, and in some subpopulations in Kenya, the proportion is estimated to be as high as 35%. The prophylactic efficacy of the drug is therefore limited for certain groups due to inadequate circulat-ing concentrations of the active metabolite.

Administration

Dosage: The adult dosage is usually 200 mg daily when combined with chloroquine (or 100 mg if in combination with atovaquone) and should be taken with water after meals. Several different dosage regimens are used for children but the WHO recommends 3 mg/kg daily in combination with chloroquine. Tablets can be crushed and mixed with milk, honey, or jam.

Use of proguanil alone is not recommended. The current British guidelines indicate as the only exception to that rule that proguanil alone (200 mg/d) can be used in areas without chloroquine resistance when that drug is contraindicated, as in epilepsy.

In some countries, Savarine®, a new combination tablet containing 100 mg chloroquine base and 200 mg proguanil hydrochloride combined in a single tablet taken daily is available. This should increase acceptability of and compliance with the combined chloroquine/proguanil regimen.

Malarone®, a fixed combination containing 250 mg atovaquone and 100 mg proguanil is so far registered for malaria therapy only, except in Denmark where it can be used for prophylaxis as well.

Availability: Proguanil is available in many countries (except the U.S.) usually as Paludrine®. Combinations available as above

Protection

Efficacy: Proguanil-resistant *P. falciparum* is widespread, which limits the drug's usefulness in some areas. Cross-resistance occurs with other antimalarials. Studies of proguanil chemoprophylaxis in Southeast Asia have shown poor efficacy for proguanil monoprophylaxis. There is improved protection with combination proguanil sulfonamide regimens although a proguanil/dapsone combination on the Thai-Cambodian border resulted in unacceptably high infection rates. There is a high degree of proguanil resistance in Papua New Guinea and Southeast Asia. In East Africa, poor protective efficacy with 100 mg proguanil daily was experienced in 1984 but an increase to 200 mg daily resulted in a protective efficacy of 91%, which led the manufacturer to increase the recommended dosage to that amount. Recent publications estimate a protective efficacy in West Africa of only 50% for chloroquine alone (300 mg weekly or 100 mg daily) compared to 66 to 78% for the chloroquine/ proguanil combination regimen. Studies in Kenyan school children showed varying protective efficacy ranging from 36 to 77%. Dutch travelers to East, Central, and southern Africa in a more recent randomized study showed no significant difference in the number of prophylaxis failures with three different proguanil regimens: 200 mg/d proguanil monoprophylaxis, 300 mg/ week chloroquine with 100 mg/d proguanil, and 300 mg/week chloroquine with 200 mg/d proguanil.

Causal prophylaxis: yes. Proguanil is effective against pre-erythrocytic forms of *P. falciparum.*

Adverse Reactions
Proguanil is considered a very safe antimalarial drug. Mouth ulcers in up to 25% of cases may occur, and some experts believe the addition of chloroquine exacerbates this tendency. Abdominal discomfort and nausea are also frequently reported. Other reactions include hair loss and scaling, and a significant drop in neutrophils. Users of the chloroquine plus proguanil regimen experienced a 30% incidence rate of adverse events in a retrospective study of returning travelers, compared to an incidence of approximately 17% in users of monochloroquine regimens. Most of these events were minor.

Serious adverse events with the combination regimen are estimated to occur in 1 out of 10,000 users.

Contraindications and Precautions
There is no known absolute contraindication for proguanil. Dosage adjustments are necessary in patients with acute kidney failure.

Pregnant women: category B. Proguanil has been used safely for over 40 years without any association with teratogenicity. Most experience has been with the older 100 mg daily regimen.

Lactating women: Both proguanil and its metabolite are excreted in breast milk.

Interactions

Use with chloroquine may increase the incidence of mouth ulcers. Vaccination with live oral typhoid or cholera vaccines should be completed at least 3 days before commencing chemoprophylaxis with proguanil combinations.

Recommendations for Use

Use in combination with chloroquine in areas where CRPF is a risk (other than Southeast Asia) and more effective regimens are contraindicated. British experts recommend the combination for U.K. tourists visiting east African coastal resorts for 2 weeks or less whereas other expert groups prefer mefloquine. In the future, proguanil will most likely be used with atovaquone. Use of proguanil monoprophylaxis is rarely indicated.

Obsolete or Withdrawn Agents

Maloprim® (a combination of dapsone and pyrimethamine) is sometimes used as a chemoprophylactic drug especially among British and Australian travelers. Potentially fatal agranulocytosis has been associated with this regimen.

Other regimens previously used in malaria chemoprophylaxis include amodiaquine, which was frequently associated with agranulocytosis, mepacrine, and sulfonamide-pyrimethamine combinations (Metakelfin® and Fansidar®), which frequently caused serious adverse cutaneous reactions.

Immunoprophylaxis

Various candidate vaccines are being investigated but none expected to be ready for travel health protection before 2005.

Self-Treatment Abroad

Most travelers are able to obtain prompt medical attention when malaria is suspected. Stand-by emergency treatment (SBET) is an option when malaria symptoms (fever, chills, headache, malaise) occur and medical attention cannot be obtained within 24 hours. Travel health professionals prescribing antimalarials for self-administration must instruct the traveler on the following:

- Recognition of malaria symptoms
- The importance of first seeking medical attention if symptoms occur no earlier than 7 days after reaching the endemic area
- The fact that SBET is a temporary measure and that medical evaluation is imperative as soon as possible

Stand-by emergency treatment should be provided to travelers using agents of limited prophylactic efficacy such as chloroquine with or without proguanil for travel to areas where plasmodia are resistant to chloroquine. Travelers with no chemoprophylaxis visiting low-risk areas can also be provided with SBET, as should those making very short, often repeated visits into malarious areas (e.g., airline crews). While the travel medicine expert should strongly recommend chemoprophylaxis for travelers visiting high-risk areas, the traveler sometimes refuses this option. They may have had a previous adverse reaction, the cost of the drug may be prohibitive, or their planned stay may be long term. These individuals should be provided with SBET. Choice and dosages of SBET are given below.

Drugs

Antifolate/Sulfa Drug Combinations: Fansidar®, Fansimef®, Metakelfin®

Pharmacology
Description: Each standard Fansidar® tablet contains 500 mg sulfadoxine and 25 mg pyrimethamine (SDX/PYR). Fansimef®, rarely used and thus not described in detail, additionally contains 250 mg mefloquine. Metakelfin® contains the combination sulfalene/pyrimethamine.

Mode of action: The components in SDX/PYR are synergistic, and activity is due to the sequential blockade of two enzymes involved in the biosynthesis of folinic acid within the parasites. Sulfadoxine is active against asexual blood forms of *P. falciparum,* and pyrimethamine acts against the erythrocytic stage *of P. falciparum* and to a lesser extent against *P. ovale, P. vivax* and *P. malariae.* The compound also inhibits sporogeny in the mosquito.

Pharmacokinetics: Both components in SDX/PYR are absorbed orally and are excreted mainly by the kidney. After oral administration, peak plasma levels of sulfadoxine and pyrimethamine are achieved within 4 to 5 hours. Both drugs are bound to plasma proteins (approximately 90%).The mean plasma elimination half-life for each agent is 7 to 9 days and 4 days, respectively.

Administration

Dosage: The adult dose (for individuals weighing more than 45 kg) is a single administration of three tablets which should be swallowed without chewing and taken with ample fluids after a meal.

Childrens' doses are shown below:

Weight (kg)	No. of Fansidar® tablets (single dose)
5–6	0.25
7–10	0.5
11–14	0.75
15–18	1
19–29	1.5
30–39	2
40–49	2.5
50+	3

Availability: Fansidar® is the most widely used of the antifolate/sulfa drug combinations and available almost worldwide. Metakelfin® and Fansimef® are available only in a few countries, and production may be discontinued.

Protection

There is increasing prevalence of parasites resistant to antifolate and sulfa drug combinations particularly in Southeast Asia and in South America. In Southeast Asia, the cure rate has declined to such an extent that PYR/SDX is of little practical value. Decreased efficacy has been reported from Rwanda, and failure of emergency self-treatment with Fansidar® has been reported in visitors to East Africa. In Kenya and Tanzania, the response has diminished to a rate of approximately 60%. SDX/PYR remains effective in most other parts of Africa (especially West Africa) and in southern Asia.

Adverse Reactions

The combination therapy is generally well tolerated at prescribed doses, and few data are available regarding the tolerability of a single dose therapy. Possible adverse events attributable to either the sulfonamide or pyrimethamine component include gastrointestinal symptoms such as glossitis, and stomatitis, nausea, vomiting, liver injury including hepatic failure, diarrhea, and pancreatitis. Hematologic reactions have also been reported. CNS reactions include headache, peripheral neuritis, depression, convulsions, vertigo, insomnia, and tinnitus. There is little information on the frequency of occurrence of such reactions in a therapy setting. Other miscellaneous reactions include fever, chills, and hypersensitivity pneumonitis. Among skin reactions, generalised skin rashes, pruritus, urticaria, photosensitization, and hair loss have been described. These reactions are normally mild and resolve spontaneously. The most important associated adverse events are the severe, life-threatening cutaneous reactions (erythema multiforme, Stevens-Johnson syndrome, Lyell-syndrome or toxic epidermal necrolysis) which are mainly associated with prophylactic dosing. Few data are available on the incidence of severe cutaneous adverse reactions following a single-therapy dose but the risk is estimated to be 40-fold lower compared with weekly dosing where the reported incidence ranges from 1/5,000–

10,000 users with fatality rates of 1/11,000–50,000 respectively. A single case of severe cutaneous adverse reaction has been associated with the drug after SBT.

Contraindications and Precautions

Absolute: Use of Fansidar® is contraindicated in persons allergic to sulfonamides or with a known hypersensitivity to pyrimethamine or any components of the formulation. Repeated use of Fansidar® is contraindicated in persons with severe blood, kidney or liver diseases. The agent should not be used in infants aged less than 2 months.

Pregnancy: category C. Extensive use of sulfonamide combinations has shown no clear incidence of congenital abnormalities in exposed women although there have been reports of minor musculoskeletal congenital abnormalities. A risk-benefit analysis is recommended as sulfonamides cross the placenta and may cause kernicterus although there is no evidence in the literature to support this hypothetical risk.

Lactation: Sulfadoxine is secreted in breast milk.

Interactions

Concomitant use of chloroquine may increase the incidence and severity of adverse reactions. Fansidar® potentiates antifolic drugs such as sulfonamides and trimethoprim-sulfamethoxazole combinations and also the action of warfarin and thiopentone.

Recommendations for Use

Indicated as SBT agent only for the treatment of uncomplicated chloroquine-resistant *P. falciparum* malaria in areas where there is no widespread resistance against the agent, such as in West Africa.

Artemisinin (Qinghaosu) and Derivatives: Artemether, Artesunate, Arteether (see also co-artemether below)

Pharmacology

Description: These compounds are derived from the leaves of the Chinese traditional herb *Artemisia annua* which has been used as a treatment for fever in China for over 2,000 years. The antimalarial properties of the qinghaosu compounds were rediscovered in 1971. Artemisinin is available as capsules or in suppository form. Artesunate is formulated in tablets or used parenterally for severe malaria. Artemether and arte-ether are oil soluble ethers suitable for intramuscular injection. Artemether is also formulated for oral administration.

Mode of action: Chemically, these compounds are sesquiterpine lactones which contain an endoperoxide linkage, which is essential for their antimalarial activity. Artemisinin has been shown to be a schizontocide but the exact mechanism of action of this drug and its more potent derivatives is poorly understood. Studies have shown that this group of drug compounds give faster parasite and fever clearance than any other antimalarial drugs. One property of the artemisinins which is of great importance is their gametocidal effect, which could result in reduced transmission.

Pharmacokinetics: The compounds bind strongly to plasma proteins and red blood cells. In vivo, the derivatives of artemisinin are converted to the biologically active metabolite, dihydroartemisinin which reaches peak plasma levels in about 3 hours. Current data suggest a short half-life for artesunate (minutes) and longer half-lives (hours) for the oil soluble derivatives. Metabolites of dihydroartemisinin are excreted in the urine.

Administration

Currently not recommended by the WHO for self-treatment of malaria. Oral preparations of artemisinin and derivatives are, however, widely available in Asia and Africa but their optimal use needs clarification. A possible combination with a long acting schizontocide such as mefloquine would provide the initial fast artemisinin response coupled with the prolonged action of mefloquine to clear residual parasites. The national authorities in Thailand recommend a first-line treatment of mefloquine plus artesunate or artemether as first-line treatment in areas with highly mefloquine-resistant malaria.

Dosage: for the treatment of uncomplicated malaria in adults and children > 6 months:

Artesunate (oral)	
Day 1	5 mg/kg as a single dose
Day 2	2.5 mg/kg as a single dose
	+ mefloquine 15-25 mg base/kg
Day 3	2.5 mg/kg as a single dose
Artemisinin (oral)	
Day 1	25mg/kg as a single dose
Day2	12.5mg/kg as a single dose
	+ mefloquine 15-25 mg base /kg
Day3	12.5 mg/kg as a single dose

Availability: Artemether solutions for injection are available as Paluther® and Artenam®. Oral preparations for uncomplicated malaria are available in Asia.

Efficacy

Several studies have confirmed the accelerated parasite clearence and rapid defervescent action of this group of agents against *P. falciparum* and have shown a more rapid therapeutic response with the artemisinin group than with the combination drugs which included quinine and mefloquine. A recurring and major problem with artemisinin and derivatives is the high recrudescence rate (45 to 100%) which occurs within 1 month after treatment. This problem can be reduced by combining a short course of artemisinin with a longer-acting antimalarial such as mefloquine. Resistance to these drugs can be induced in animal models, and treatment failures have been reported. Recent in vitro sensitivity tests indicated that isolates of *P. falciparum* from the Chinese Hainan and Yunnan provinces were resistant to this group of drugs. Use of these agents should be tightly controlled to minimize the potential for the development of resistance.

Adverse Reactions

This is considered to be a very safe group of drugs. Treatment of several thousand patients has failed to reveal any significant toxicity. Mild transient gastrointestinal symptoms, headache, and dizziness have been reported. Several studies have reported a drug-induced fever. Cardiotoxicity and dose-related decreases in reticulocyte counts have been observed as have transient reductions in neutrophil counts. High doses produce neurotoxicity in large animals, and this is the main reason why regulatory authorities in the developed countries hesitate to approve these compounds.

Contraindications and Precautions

There are no known contraindications.

Pregnancy: Qinghaosu compounds can cause rodent fetal resorption even at relatively low doses. Experience in humans is limited.

Lactation: No data available regarding secretion in breast milk.

Interactions

There are no known interactions.

Recommendations for Use

Use of these valuable compounds must be controlled. They cannot be recommended in the developed countries because they are not licensed. When used, however, as advised by medical professionals in the developing countries, they appear very promising for safe and rapid treatment of malaria, particularly in sequential combination with a slower-onset, longer-acting antimalarial such as mefloquine.

Atovaquone / proguanil

(For "Pharmacology," "Contraindications and Precautions," "Adverse Events," and "Interactions," refer to section on "Chemoprophylaxis.")

Administration

The combination therapy with 250 mg atovaquone and 100 mg proguanil (Malarone®) has been approved in several countries for the treatment of acute, uncomplicated *P. falciparum* infection in adults and children weighing more than 10 kg. The therapy dose of Malarone® is divided over 3 days. The daily dose should be taken at the same time each day with a meal or a glass of milk.

Weight (kg)	Day 1	Day 2	Day 3
11–20 kg	1 tablet	1 tablet	1 tablet
21–30 kg	2 tablets	2 tablets	2 tablets
31–40 kg	3 tablets	3 tablets	3 tablets
> 40 kg	4 tablets	4 tablets	4 tablets
Adult	4 tablets	4 tablets	4 tablets

Chloroquine

(For "Pharmacology," "Contraindications and Precautions," "Adverse Events," and "Interactions," refer to section on "Chemoprophylaxis.")

Administration

The total dose for the treatment of uncomplicated, chloroquine-sensitive malaria is 25 mg base/kg over 3 days. The following treatment schedule is suggested by the WHO:

Weight kg	Age	Number of Tablets (100 mg base) Day 1	Day 2	Day 3	Number of Tablets (150 mg base) Day 1	Day 2	Day 3
5–6	< 4 mo	0.5	0.5	0.5	0.5	0.25	0.25
7–10	4–11mo	1	1	0.5	0.5	0.5	0.5
11–14	1–2 y	1.5	1.5	0.5	1	1	0.5
15–18	3–4 y	2	2	0.5	1	1	1
19–24	5–7 y	2.5	2.5	1	1.5	1.5	1
25–35	8–10 y	3.5	3.5	2	2.5	2.5	1
36–50	11–13 y	5	5	2.5	3	3	2
50+	14+ y	6	6	3	4	4	2

Tablets for children can be crushed and added to jam or yogurt to disguise the bitter taste.

Efficacy

Chloroquine remains the drug of choice for the treatment of susceptible malaria; however, only *P. malariae* and *P. ovale* remain fully sensitive to the drug. The use of this drug as an agent for emergency self-treatment is currently limited due to widespread chloroquine-resistant *P. falciparum* (CRPF) and *P. vivax*.

Adverse Reactions

The standard treatment dosage is comparatively well tolerated. Minor events include gastrointestinal symptoms, dizziness, and visual disturbances. Itching, rash, and psoriasis may occur. Rare neuropsychiatric reactions have been reported, including epileptic seizures.

Recommendations for Use

Indicated for the treatment of malaria caused by chloroquine-susceptible plasmodia. Chloroquine can be provided for stand-by treatment to travellers with destinations in Hispaniola, in Central America, Egypt, and the Near East.

Co-artemether

Pharmacology

Description: Coartemether (formerly CGP56697) is an orally administered fixed combination of 20 mg artemether, the methyl ether of dihydoartemisinin and 120 mg lumefantrine (formerly benflumetol), a novel aryl amino alcohol. This combination was developed in the 1970s in China by the Academy of Military Medical Sciences, Beijing, and is now produced by Novartis Pharma AG, Switzerland.

Mode of action: This new treatment agent has effective schizontoicidal and gametocytocidal activity against *P. falciparum*. Potentiation between artemether and lumefantrin was detected in combination experiments, and it is proposed that use of the combination should reduce the speed of development of resistance.

Pharmacokinetics: Artemether is rapidly absorbed, and there is improved bioavailability after postprandial administration. A broad inter- and intraindividual variability of the plasma concentrations of both components has been observed. Artemether is rapidly metabolized into the active dehydroartemisinin. While artemether has a brief half-life of 2 hours, that of lumefantrin is 2–3 days in healthy volunteers and 4-6 days in patients.

Administration

Currently not recommended by the WHO or by any national expert group for self-treatment of malaria, as the agent has only been introduced in early 1999.

Dosage: in nonimmune adults, 4 tablets each at 0, 8, 24, 36, 48, 60 hours, 24 tablets total. In semi-immune adults, a course of 16 tablets at 0, 8, 24, 48 hours is sufficient in areas without multiresistant *P. falciparum.* In children, the recommended dosage is:

- 10–15 kg: 1 tablet each at 0, 8, 24, 36, 48, 60 hours, 6 tablets total
- 15–25 kg: 2 tablets each at 0, 8, 24, 36, 48, 60 hours, 12 tablets total
- 25–35 kg: 3 tablets each at 0, 8, 24, 36, 48, 60 hours, 18 tablets total

Availability: Riamet® available in Switzerland since January 1999.

Efficacy

Dose-finding studies indicate usually good efficacy with a four-dose regimen, except in an area of multidrug resistance in Thailand but six dose regimens were highly effective there. A randomised controlled trial of coartemether versus pyrimethamine/sulfadoxine showed that coartemether is safe in African children with acute, uncomplicated falciparum malaria, that it clears parasites more rapidly than the comparator, and that it results in fewer gametocyte carriers. In mixed infections with *P. vivax,* additional therapy with 8-aminoquinoline is indicated, to eliminate exoerythrocyte forms of the parasites.

Adverse Reactions

Frequent adverse events (≥10%) include headache, dizziness,

insomnia, abdominal pain, and anorexia. Less frequent (1 to 10%) were palpitations, prolongation of QTc without any clinical symptoms (7%), diarrhea, nausea and vomiting, pruritus, exanthema, arthralgia and myalgia, and rarely (<1%) cough. A slight elevation of ALT has been observed. Due to tiredness and asthenia, the ability to drive a car or to handle machines may be impaired.

Contraindications and Precautions

Relative contraindications in serious renal or hepatic insufficiency, known congenital QT-prolongation or conditions which may result in QT prolongation, such as specific cardiac conditions, hypokalemia, hypomagnesemia, for medication see below in "Interactions." Contraindicated also in severe malaria, as bioavailability, mainly of lumefantrin, may be insufficient.

Pregnancy: category C, no data available.

Lactation: contraindicated

Interactions

There are no known interactions but Riamet® should not be used concomitantly with halofantrin, quinine, antiarrhythmic agents (classes IA, III), H_1-blockers such as terfenadin or astemizol. In contrast, no interaction with mefloquine has been noted.

Recommendations for use

Novel option for treatment of uncomplicated malaria caused by *P. falciparum*. The role of this new agent in travel medicine, particularly for self-therapy of malaria, remains to be determined.

Mefloquine

(For "Pharmacology," "Contraindications and Precautions," "Adverse Events," and "Interactions," refer to section on "Chemoprophylaxis.")

Administration

The treatment schedule for mefloquine depends on the extent of mefloquine resistance in a particular area. A single dose of 15 mg base/kg is recommended in areas with little or no resistance to the agent. A higher, split dose of 25 mg/kg is recommended in areas with significant mefloquine resistance, such as the Thai border provinces of Trat and Tak. The split dose is administered as a first dose of 15 mg base/kg on day 1 followed by a second dose of 10 mg base/kg, 6 to 24 hours later. The table below shows the recommended WHO dosages. Tablets for children can be crushed and added to jam or yogurt to disguise the bitter taste.

Number of tablets

Weight (kg)	Age	Single dose (15 mg base/kg)	Split dose (25mg base/kg)	
			First dose (15 mg base/kg)	Second dose (10 mg base/kg)
< 5	< 3 mo	NR	NR	NR
5–6	3 mo	0.25	0.25	0.25
7–8	4–7 mo	0.5	0.5	0.25
9–12	8–23 mo	0.75	0.75	0.5
13–16	2–3 mo	1	1	0.5
17–24	4–7 mo	1.5	1.5	1
25–35	8–10 y	2	2	1.5
36–50	11–13 y	3	3	2
51–59	14–15 y	3.5	3.5	2
60 +	15+ y	4	4	2

NR = not recommended

Adverse Reactions

The rate of adverse events in higher doses used for treatment are markedly elevated as compared to the ones in prophylaxis. There is an incidence of 30 to 50% of severe nausea and dizziness, but use of the split dosage reduces the incidence of dose-related adverse events, especially vomiting. Serious adverse events, particularly neuropsychiatric events, show a higher incidence after treatment (1 of 216) than after prophylactic use of the drug. The mechanism for serious neurotoxicity is unknown but may be dose related although serious adverse events have also occurred at relatively low plasma mefloquine concentrations. Because mefloquine has a long and variable half-life of up to 33 days, treatment with mefloquine or quinine in persons who are using mefloquine prophylaxis should only be performed under close medical supervision.

Recommendations for Use

Indicated for the treatment of uncomplicated malaria caused by CRPF. Mefloquine can be provided for stand-by treatment to travelers with destinations in South and Southeast Asia, or in South America. When the destination is in tropical Africa, mefloquine is hardly ever indicated as an SBET drug, as in case of a mefloquine chemoprophylaxis failure, the drug would be of limited value. Exceptions may be travelers using the less effective chloroquine plus proguanil chemoprophylaxis, or in travelers using no chemoprophylaxis (e.g., very short trips as in airline crews, long-term residents, or refusal of chemoprophylaxis).

Quinine

Pharmacology

Description: Quinine is the main cinchona alkaloid and has been used for more than 300 years in the therapy of malaria. Quinidine is a stereoisomer of quinine. Available as the quinine salts, most commonly quinine hydrochloride, quinine dihydrochloride, and quinine sulfate. Each 10 mg salt contains approximately 8 mg quinine base. Quinine is most valuable in the treatment of severe falciparum malaria, when it must be administered parenterally. This section is concerned with the treatment of uncomplicated malaria only.

Mode of action: Quinine is a highly active blood schizontocide and is also gametocyticidal against *P. vivax*, *P. ovale,* and *P. malariae*.

Pharmacokinetics: Good oral bioavailability and peak plasma levels are achieved within 1 to 3 hours. Quinine is metabolized in the liver and excreted as the parent drug (20%) or its metabolites in the urine. The mean elimination half-life varies from approximately 11 hours (healthy volunteers) to 16 hours (uncomplicated malaria patients).

Administration

The WHO recommends the following dosages:

- for areas where parasites are sensitive to quinine: 8 mg base/kg orally 3 times daily for 7 days
- for areas with a high degree of quinine resistance: 8 mg base/kg orally 3 times daily for 7 days plus doxycycline 100 mg salt daily for 7 days (contraindicated in children aged < 8 years and in pregnant women) or tetracycline 250 mg salt 4 times daily for 7 days (contraindicated in children < 8 years and in pregnant women)

Availability: worldwide. Numerous preparations containing quinine salts are marketed.

Efficacy

Resistance to quinine is developing in some parts of the world, especially in Southeast Asia (mainly Vietnam and Thailand), where quinine is administered in a 7-day course with tetracycline. Despite the two-pronged approach, increasing recrudescence rates and decreased in vitro sensitivity have been noted. In a stand-by treatment setting, the probable success of a complex combination regimen therapy over a prolonged period of 7 days is questionable due to projected poor compliance. Rather, this treatment option is for malaria treatment under a physician's supervision.

Adverse Reactions

The adverse events associated with this agent are collectively known as "cinchonism," which consists of high-tone deafness, tinnitus, nausea, vomiting, dizziness, malaise, and vision disturbances. Other potential adverse reactions include hypoglycemia in persons with a high level of *P. falciparum* parasitemia. CNS and cardiovascular reactions have been reported especially in cases of of overdose. Other less frequent adverse events include skin reactions (e.g., erythema multiforme), asthma, agranulocytosis, thrombocytopenia, hemolysis, and liver damage.

Contraindications and precautions

Absolute: Hypersensitivity to the drug and in the presence of hemoglobinuria during malaria or in persons with optic neuritis or myasthenia gravis.

Relative: Caution in required in patients with atrial fibrillation or other heart disease. Quinine should not be combined with digoxin and should only be given with caution to persons who have been taking mefloquine prophylaxis or to persons who have received mefloquine therapy in the preceeding 2 weeks due to possible cardiovascular toxicity. Quinine has been associated with hemolysis in persons with a G-6-PD deficiency.Caution is advised with diabetics and in persons with impaired liver function.

Pregnancy/Lactation: Quinine can stimulate uterine contractions and may cause abortion at high doses. Quinine is, however, considered a safe agent for the treatment of malaria in pregnant women who should, if at all possible, seek prompt medical attention for all febrile episodes. Quinine is secreted in breast milk.

Interactions

Interactions have been reported for digoxin, cimetidine, and mefloquine (see above).

Recommendations for Use

May be used to treat chloroquine resistant malaria but compliance and tolerability are delimiting factors for SBET (see above).

Obsolete Therapeutic Agents

Halofantrine (Halfan) is a phenanthrene methanol antimalarial, which is available in tablet form (250 mg) and as an oral suspension (20 mg/mL). Clinical trials have repeatedly established the efficacy of this agent against chloroquine-sensitive and chloroquine-resistant *P. falciparum*. Originally considered to be a very safe drug, a disadvantage was the agent's poor and erratic absorption. Mainly, however, the cardiotoxic potential of halofantrine has been established; sudden deaths have been associated with the therapeutic use of this drug, which led to the issue of the WHO statement "halofantrine is no longer recommended for stand-by treatment following reports that it can result in prolongation of the QTc intervals and ventricular dysrhythmias in susceptible individuals. These changes can be accentuated if halofantrine is taken with other antimalarial drugs that can decrease myocardial conduction." An ECG with normal QTc interval prior to departure apparently does not preclude the risk of a fatal adverse event with this drug.

Future Prospects

Pyronaridine, a blood schizontocide, is highly effective against multiresistant strains. Pharmacokinetic data indicate poor bioavailability. This drug has yet to be registered outside China.

Chlorproguanil/dapsone is a synergistic, low-cost combination, which has been shown to be effective against pyrimethamine/sulfadoxine-resistant *P. falciparum* in healthy human volunteers.

Agents in early clinical development include tafenoquine (formerly etoquine, WR 238605), also desferioxamine (an iron-chelating agent) and calcium antagonists including verapamil and promazine.

Agents in preclinical development include inhibitors of phospholipid metabolism and protease inhibitors which have blocked in vitro parasite development and cured malaria infected mice.

Principles of Therapy

The mainstay of malaria therapy is speed. The patient should be made aware of symptoms to minimize "patient delay," and the consulted medical professional should promptly conduct diagnostic tests (not confusing malaria with influenza) to minimize "doctor delay." Therapy should be given according to the circumstances, availability of drugs, and instructions in the specific country. Details of management are not discussed here as it should be conducted by a specialist in tropical medicine or infectious diseases after a definite species diagnosis has been established.

Community Control Measures

Notification to Authorities

Required in most countries.

Isolation/Quarantine

None.

Contacts

Travel partners should also be examined as they are often infected.

Measles

Infectious Agent

Measles is caused by the measles virus, a member of the genus *Morbillivirus* of the family *Paramyxoviridae*.

Transmission

Measles is transmitted by droplet spread and occasionally by freshly soiled articles.

Global Epidemiology

Measles occurs throughout the world but has become rare in the Americas due to vaccination campaigns. Only 2106 cases were confirmed in Europe in 1996 but there was a resurgence in 1997 with 88,485 cases reported, 27,635 of them confirmed. Overall, 44 million cases were reported to WHO in 1995.

Risk for Travelers

In the U.S., approximately 100 measles cases were imported annually from 1980 to 1985, accounting for 0.7 to 6.9% of the annual number of reported measles cases. Secondary spread of infection occurred in approximately 20% of these. Roughly 43% of reported cases were epidemiologically linked to exposure to an imported case. The importation rate varied from one to three cases per million travelers when the destination had been Europe or Mexico to > 30 per million when travelers had been to India or the Philippines. Cases in non-U.S. citizens were considered non-preventable. Among the rest, 44% had not been vaccinated and 28% occurred in children younger than the recommended age for vaccination or in people with a history of adequate vaccination. There have been reports of suspected transmission of measles during international and domestic flights.

Clinical Picture

Measles initially causes fever, conjunctivitis, coryza, and Koplik's spots. These initial symptoms are followed in 3 to 5 days by a red blotchy rash, beginning in the face. Complications include otitis media, pneumonia, croup, diarrhea, and encephalitis, more often observed in infants and adults than in children and more often in malnourished individuals. The case fatality rate is 0.3% in the developed nations and usually 3% in the developing countries but it may reach 30% in some localities.

Incubation

There is an incubation period of 7 to 18 days before the onset of fever. The rash develops a few days later.

Communicability

The communicable period extends from slightly before the beginning of prodromal symptoms until 4 days after the appearance of the rash.

Susceptibility/Resistance

General susceptibility. Permanent immunity occurs after illness.

Minimized Exposure in Travelers

Immunization.

Chemoprophylaxis

None.

Immunoprophylaxis by Measles Vaccine

Immunology and Pharmacology
Viability: live, attenuated

Antigenic form: whole virus strains—Edmonston-Enders, Edmonston-Zagreb EZ19. Schwarz strains usually used, minimum 1000 $TCID_{50}$

Adjuvants: none

Preservative: none

Allergens/Excipiens: variable, some with residual egg or human proteins, 25 µg neomycin per dose. Sorbitol and hydrolized gelatine added as stabilizer

Mechanism: induction of a modified measles infection in susceptible persons. Antibodies induced by this infection protect against subsequent infection.

Application

Schedule: 0.5 mL SC preferably at 12 to 15 months of age. Usually, a combined measles, mumps, rubella (MMR) vaccine is used. In nonimmune adults, one single dose is sufficient.

Booster: A second dose is recommended in many countries at age 4 to 7 or 11 to 15 years. Routine revaccination with MMR is recommended.

Route: SC

Site: preferably over deltoid

Storage: Store at 2 to 8°C (35 to 46°F). Freezing does not harm the vaccine but may crack the diluent vials. Store the diluent at room temperature or in the refrigerator. The vaccine should be transported at 10°C (50°F) or cooler and protected from light. The vaccine powder can tolerate 7 days at room temperature. Reconstitued vaccine can tolerate 8 hours in the refrigerator.

Availability: Many products are available worldwide.

Protection

Onset: 2 to 6 weeks

Efficacy: Induces neutralizing antibodies in at least 97% of suspectible children. Seroconversion is somewhat less in adults. Disease incidence is typically reduced by 95% in family and classroom cohorts.

Possibly, attenuated rubella vaccine given within 72 hours after exposure to natural measles virus will prevent illness. There is no contraindication to vaccinating children already exposed to natural measles.

Duration: Antibody levels persist 10 years or longer in most recipients, with possible lifelong protection granted.

Protective level: Specific measles neutralizing antibody titer of $\geq 1:8$ is considered immune.

Adverse Reactions

Burning or stinging of short duration at the injection site is frequently reported. Local pain, induration, and erythema may also occur at the injection site.

Symptoms similar to those following natural measles infection may occur, such as mild regional lymphadenopathy, urticaria, rash, malaise, sore throat, fever, headache, dizziness, nausea, vomiting, diarrhea, polyneuritis, and arthralgia or arthritis (usually transient and rarely chronic). Reactions are usually mild and transient. Moderate fever occurs occasionally, high fever ($> 39.4°C$ [$103°F$]) less commonly.

Erythema multiforme has been reported rarely, as has optic neuritis. Isolated cases of polyneuropathy, including Guillain-Barré syndrome, have been reported after immunization with vaccines containing measles. Encephalitis and other nervous-system reactions have occurred very rarely in subjects given this vaccine but no causal relationship has been established.

Contraindications

Absolute: persons with known hypersensitivity to the vaccine or any of its components. Persons with a history of anaphylactoid or other immediate reactions following egg ingestion for the vaccines with traces of egg protein (see below)

Relative: any acute illness

Children: safe and effective for children ≥ 12 months of age. Vaccination is not recommended for children < 12 months of age since remaining maternal measles-neutralizing antibodies may interfere with the immune response.

Pregnant women: contraindicated. Postpubertal women should be advised to avoid pregnancy for 3 months on theoretical grounds.

Lactating women: The vaccine-strain virus is secreted in

milk and may be transmitted to infants who are breast-fed. In the infants with serologic evidence of measles infection, none exhibited severe symptoms.

Immunodeficient persons: Do not use in immunodeficient persons, including persons with immune deficiencies, whether due to genetic disease, malignant neoplasm, or drug or radiation therapy. Routine immunization of asymptomatic HIV-infected persons with MMR is recommended.

Interactions

To avoid hypothetical concerns over antigenic competition, administer measles vaccine simultaneously with other live vaccines or 1 month apart. Routine immunizations may be given concurrently.

Measles vaccination may lead to false positive HIV serologic tests when particularly sensitive assays (e.g., PERT) are used. This is related to the presence of EAV–0, an avian retrovirus remaining in residual egg proteins of most measles vaccines.

Recommendations for Vaccine Use

Children are routinely immunized against measles throughout the world, usually with the preferred combined measles, mumps, rubella (MMR) vaccine administered at age 12 to 15 months. In many countries, a second dose is given at 4 to 12 years.

In view of the increased risk of infection in the developing countries resulting from complications in malnourished local populations, the age limit for children traveling there should be lowered to 6 months for preferably a single measles antigen vaccine dose. Children vaccinated before their first birthday must be revaccinated as per standard recommendations, ideally at 12 to 15 months and upon starting school. Infants under 6 months are usually protected by maternal antibodies.

For admission to schools in the U.S. it is usually compulsory to provide proof of immunization against measles, or natural immunity. Recently, the CDC also recommended administration of MMR to all crew members of cruise ships lacking documented immunity to rubella.

Self-Treatment Abroad

Supportive.

Principles of Therapy

No specific treatment.

Community Control Measures

Notification is mandatory in some countries. Isolation is not practical in the community at large but if possible, contact with nonimmunes should be avoided for 4 days after the appearance of rash. Quarantine is not practical. Immunization of contacts may provide protection if given within 72 hours of exposure. Specific IG may be used within 6 days of exposure (plus vaccine 6 months later) in contacts who have a high risk of complications, such as infants < 1 year of age, pregnant women, or immunocompromized persons.

MENINGOCOCCAL MENINGITIS
(MENINGOCOCCAL DISEASE)

Infectious Agent

There are 13 serogroups of the infections agent *Neisseria meningitidis*, the most important being A, B, C, Y, and W-135.

Transmission

Person-to-person transmission proceeds by aerosol from the nose or pharynx of patients (particularly when coughing) or asymptomatic carriers.

Global Epidemiology

The worldwide incidence of meningococcal meningitis probably exceeds 100,000 cases per year. The majority of these occur in the Lapeyssonie meningitis belt in sub-Saharan Africa (Figure 37), mainly during the dry season from December to June. Sporadic outbreaks may occur anywhere, particularly when people are living in close quarters. From 1996 to 1997, serogroup A was predominant in Africa and in South Asia (with a few C) and serogroups B and C in Europe, the Americas, and Australia whereas all serogroups were found in the rest of Asia.

Risk for Travelers

The incidence of meningococcal meningitis is usually very low in travelers except during the Hajj pilgrimage to Mecca in Saudi Arabia due to overcrowding. Several cases have also occurred during trekkings in Nepal when tourists slept in crowded huts. During and after the Hajj pilgrimage of 1987, 77 per million pilgrims had meningococcal meningitis. The incidence rate of meningococcal disease in other travelers has been estimated to be 1 per 3 million per month of stay, with a

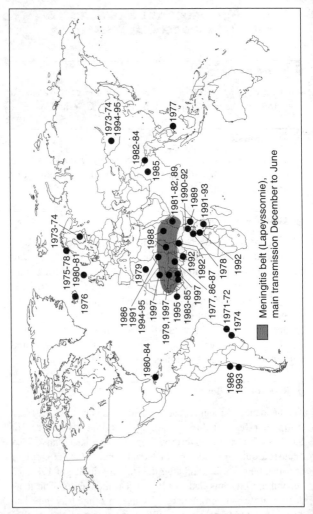

Figure 37 Major outbreaks of meningococcal meningitis, 1971–1997

substantial proportion of infections having occurred outside hyperendemic regions.

Clinical Picture

Symptoms include sudden onset of fever, intense headache, vomiting, and frequently the appearance of a rash. Subsequently delirium and coma may occur. Other clinical syndromes include pneumonia, bacteremia, and sepsis. Without therapy, the case fatality rate exceeds 50%. With modern treatment, it has dropped to 5 to 15%.

In countries with endemicity, up to 25% of the population are asymptomatic carriers of *N. meningitidis* in their nasopharynx. Only a small minority among those infected will develop symptomatic disease after transmission of droplets from person to person.

Incubation

The incubation period is 3 to 4 days and rarely 2 to 10 days.

Communicability

Communicability persists until no meningococci are present in the discharge from the nose and mouth, which is the case within 24 hours following initiation of adequate antimicrobial treatment.

Susceptibility/Resistance

Susceptibility to the clinical disease is low and decreases with age. Asplenic patients are susceptible to bacteremic illness. Group-specific immunity follows even subclinical infections for an unknown duration.

Minimized Exposure in Travelers

Immunization and avoidance of crowded situations.

Chemoprophylaxis

Possible with various agents, e.g., rifampicin, ceftriaxone, ciprofloxacin.

Immunoprophylaxis by Meningococcal Polysaccharide Vaccines

Immunology and Pharmacology

Viability: inactivated

Antigenic form: capsular polysaccharide fragments, groups A, C, in some vaccines also Y, and W-135—50 µg each. The B-group vaccine is being tested in various countries.

Adjuvants: none

Preservative: 0.01% thimerosal in some vaccines

Allergens/Excipiens: none / 2.5 to 5 mg lactose per 0.5 mL

Mechanism: induction of protective bactericidal antibodies

Application

Schedule: 0.5 mL as a single dose. Some manufacturers recommend a second dose in small children < 18 months of age.

Booster: Revaccination may be indicated, particularly in children at high risk who were first immunized at <4 years of age. Revaccinate such children after 2 or 3 years if they remain at high risk. Subsequent doses will reinstate the primary immune response but not evoke an accelerated booster.

Route: SC or jet injection. Some also IM

Site: over deltoid

Storage: Store at 2 to 8°C (35 to 46°F); discard if frozen. Powder can tolerate 12 weeks at 37°C (98.6°F) and 6 to 8 weeks at 45°C (113°F). Shipping data are not provided. Some vaccines must be reconstituted gently. Use the single-dose vial within 24 hours after reconstitution. Refrigerate the multidose vial after reconstitution and discard within 5 days. In many countries, reconstituted A + C vaccines are marketed.

Availability: Various vaccines are marketed worldwide either against groups A and C or A, C, Y, and W-135. No group B vaccine is yet commercially available, except in Cuba.

Protection

Onset: 7 to 14 days

Efficacy: Group A vaccine reduces disease incidence by 85 to 95% and group C vaccine by 75 to 90%. Clinical protection from the Y and W-135 strains has not been directly determined. Immunogenicity has been demonstrated in adults and children >2 years of age. Meningococcal vaccine is not likely to be effective in infants and very young children because of insufficient immunogenicity at this age. The vaccine is not effective against serogroup B, the most common form of meningococcal infection in the developed countries. Results are inconclusive as to whether meningococcal polysaccharide vaccines show a lasting effect on carriage.

Vaccination does not substitute for chemoprophylaxis in individuals exposed to meningococcal disease because of the delay in developing protective antibody titers. However, the meningococcal polysaccharide vaccine has been effective against serogroup C meningococcal disease in a community outbreak.

Duration: Antibodies against group A and C polysaccharides decline markedly over the first 3 years following vaccination. The decline is more rapid in infants and young children than in adults, particularly with respect to group C. In a group of children >4 years of age 3 years after vaccination, efficacy declined from >90 to 67%.

Protective level: 3 to 5 years. Probably only 2 years in young children.

Adverse Reactions

Reactions to vaccination are generally mild and infrequent, consisting of localized erythema lasting 1 to 2 days. Up to 2% of young children develop fever transiently after vaccination.

Contraindications

Absolute: none

Relative: any acute illness

Children: not recommended for children under 2 years of age because they are unlikely to develop an adequate antibody response (see above for schedule). Serogroup A polysaccharide vaccine induces antibody in some children as young as 3 months of age although a response comparable to that seen in adults is not achieved until 4 or 5 years of age.

Pregnant women: category C. The manufacturer recommends that this vaccine not be used in pregnant women, especially in the first trimester, on theoretical grounds. It is not known if the meningococcal vaccine or corresponding antibodies cross the placenta. Generally, most IgG passage across the placenta occurs during the third trimester. Use only if clearly needed.

Lactating women: It is not known if the meningococcal vaccine or corresponding antibodies are excreted in breast milk. Problems in humans have not been documented.

Immunodeficient persons: Persons receiving immunosuppressive therapy or those with other immunodeficiencies may have diminished response to active immunization. Nevertheless, this vaccine is indicated for asplenic patients.

Interactions

Meningococcal vaccine efficacy was slightly suppressed following measles vaccination in one study. If possible, these vaccines should be separated by 1 month for optimal response.

Immunosuppressant drugs and radiation therapy may result in an insufficient response to immunization.

Recommendations for Vaccine Use

Vaccination is required for pilgrims visiting Mecca in Saudi Arabia for the Hajj.

Vaccination is indicated for travelers to regions with current meningococcal disease epidemics caused by a vaccine preventable subgroup, usually A or C in the developing countries.

There is continued hyperendemicity and frequent epidemics of serogroup A or C meningococcal disease during the dry season (December through June) in the sub-Saharan meningitis belt (Lapeyssone, see Figure 37). Vaccination is recommended for those traveling there, particularly if close and prolonged contact with the indigenous population is anticipated. The CDC also recommends immunization of travelers to Kenya, Tanzania, Burundi, Nepal, Mongolia, and the Delhi area in India whereas most European expert groups consider this unneccessary, provided no new outbreaks have been reported.

Self-Treatment Abroad

None. Medical consultation is urgently required.

Principles of Therapy

Parenteral penicillin (resistances in Africa and Spain), ampicillin, or chloramphenicol are to be given rapidly.

Community Control Measures

Notification is mandatory in most countries. The patient should be placed in respiratory isolation for 24 hours following start of antimicrobial therapy. No quarantine is required. Intimate contacts should be actively traced for prophylactic administration of an effective antimicrobial agent.

MONKEYPOX

Monkeypox virus infection was identified in central and West Africa during the smallpox eradication program. The infection is spread from chimpanzees, other species of monkeys, and squirrels. Squirrels are probably the most important reservoir for this virus. Human infections usually occur sporadically, and children are most frequently affected, particularly in rural areas where there is greater contact with animals. With decreasing immunity to smallpox resulting from decreasing use of vaccine, the incidence of monkeypox infection seems to increase as illustrated by an epidemic in remote parts of Congo-Zaire in 1997. The infection is systemic, producing a generalized rash. Diagnosis is made based on serologic testing. There is no known therapy for this infection.

PLAGUE

Infectious Agent

Yersinia pestis is the bacterium that causes plague.

Transmission

Plague is an acute bacterial illness transmitted to humans by the bites of infected fleas, direct contact with infected animals (rodents, cats), or transmission of infected droplets between persons.

Global Epidemiology

Plague occurs infrequently on all continents except Europe, Australia, and the Antarctic (Figure 38). Worldwide, an average of 1200 cases and 120 deaths per year were reported to WHO between 1980 and 1994; however, there is considerable under-reporting. The WHO Weekly Epidemiological Record regularly reports infected areas. The plague epidemic of 1994 in India was extensively covered by the media which resulted in some hysteria in the developed countries. However, the epidemic was due to a large extent not to plague but to various other infections. Such inadequacies in diagnosis mostly result from limited laboratory facilities.

Risk for Travelers

Plague is extremely rare among international travelers. Since 1970, only a single case has been reported, in an American researcher who was investigating rats in Bolivia. Plague has occasionally been associated with recreational activities in California.

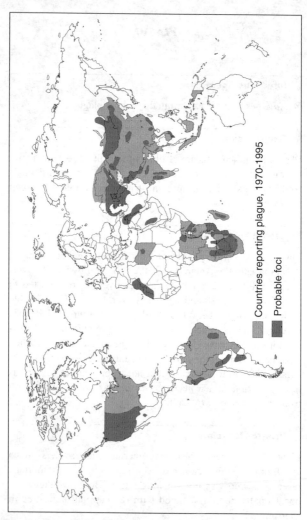

Figure 38 Geographical distribution of natural foci of plague

Clinical Picture

More than 80% of *Yersinia pestis* infections result in bubonic plague. Initial signs include unspecific fever, headache, myalgia, nausea, sore throat, followed by lymphadenitis usually in the inguinal drainage area of the site of the flea bite. Progress to septicemic plague is possible, resulting in meningitis, shock, and disseminated intravascular coagulation. Primary septicemic plague without detectable lymphadenopathy is rare (10% of all cases). Secondary pneumonic plague may result in the uncommon but most dangerous primary pneumonic plague (10% of all cases) by direct person-to-person transfer. The case fatality rate in untreated bubonic plague exceeds 50%, and reaches 100% in primary pneumonic plague. The prognosis is far better with timely antimicrobial therapy.

Incubation

The incubation period is 1 to 7 days and possibly slightly longer in immunized persons.

Communicability

Communicability is most feared in pneumonic plague but pus from suppurating buboes may rarely result in person-to-person transmission of bubonic plague.

Susceptibility/Resistance

General susceptibility with limited immunity after recovery.

Minimized Exposure in Travelers

Travelers should avoid overcrowded areas during outbreaks.

Chemoprophylaxis

Tetracycline 15 to 30 mg/kg or chloramphenicol, 30 mg/kg daily in four divided doses for 1 week once exposure ceases.

Immunoprophylaxis by Plague Vaccine

Immunology and Pharmacology

Viability: inactivated

Antigenic form: whole bacterium *Y. pestis*

Adjuvants: none

Preservative: 0.5% phenol

Allergens/Excipients: peptones and peptides of soy and casein, beef proteins/yeast extract, agar, formaldehyde

Mechanism: Antibodies against capsular fraction 1 (F1) antigen are thought to be key in protection but other factors may play a role.

Application

Schedule: three doses in a primary series

Children: not recommended as insufficient data are available

Adults: 1 mL on day 0, 0.2 mL day 30 to 90, 0.2 mL 3 to 6 months after second dose

Booster: at 1 to 2 year intervals if risk persists

Route: IM

Site: deltoid region

Storage: Store at 2 to 8°C (35 to 46°F); discard if frozen. Product can tolerate 15 days at room temperature.

Availability: available in the United States (generic, Greer Laboratories) and in several other countries.

Protection

Onset: protective titers 2 weeks following second dose in 90% of recipients

Efficacy: 90% reduction in the incidence of bubonic plague after the second dose. Efficacy against pneumonic plague is unknown. Vaccination will often limit the severity of infection but not completely prevent it.

Duration: 6 to 12 months

Protective level: PHA titer > 1:128

Adverse Reactions

Mild local reactions frequently follow primary immunization, with increasing incidence and severity following repeated dose. These include erythema, induration, and edema, which usually subside after 2 days. Sterile abscess can occasionally occur.

Systemic effects in 10% of cases include malaise, headache, lymphadenopathy, fever, and exceptionally arthralgia, myalgia, and vomiting for several days. Anaphylactic shock, tachycardia, urticaria, asthma, and hypotension occur on rare occasions.

Contraindications

Absolute: persons with a previous severe adverse reaction to the vaccine

Relative: any acute illness

Children: relative contraindication due to lack of data. Early empiric recommendations indicate giving 20% of adult dose in infants, 40% in children 1 to 4 years of age, and 60% in children 5 to 10 years of age.

Pregnant women: category C. Use only if clearly needed.

Lactating women: It is not known if plague vaccine or corresponding antibodies are excreted in breast milk. Problems in humans have not been documented.

Immunodeficient persons: Persons receiving immunosuppressive therapy or those with other immunodeficiencies may have diminished antibody response to active immunization.

Interactions

Plague vaccine should not be administered with parenteral typhoid (TAB) or cholera vaccines because of the risk of accentuated adverse reactions.

Immunosuppressant drugs and radiation therapy may result in an insufficient response to immunization. Give SC to patients receiving anticoagulants.

Recommendations for Vaccine Use

Plague is not a health problem in international travel since there has been only one imported case reported in the past decades, which occurred in a professional investigating rodents. The vaccine is rarely to be recommended to travelers, and in most countries, no vaccine is commercially available. Immunization is not required by any country as a condition for entry.

The CDC states that "selective vaccination may be considered for persons who will have direct contact with wild or commensal rodents or other animals in plague-epizootic areas and for persons who will reside or work in plague-endemic rural areas (see Figure 38) where avoidance of rodents and fleas is difficult."

Self-Treatment Abroad

None. Medical consultation is required.

Principles of Therapy

Streptomycin or other antimicrobial agents.

Community Control Measures

Notification is mandatory according to International Health Regulations. Patients should be isolated, and contacts should receive chemoprophylaxis and be placed under surveillance.

Poliomyelitis ("Polio")

Infectious Agent

The infection is caused by types 1, 2, or 3 of the poliovirus, all of which can cause paralysis. Type 1 has most often been associated with epidemics or paralysis.

Transmission

The virus is usually transmitted through oral contact with feces but where sanitation is good, pharyngeal spread becomes more important. Food and beverages contaminated by feces have occasionally been implicated.

Global Epidemiology

The WHO adopted the goal of global poliomyelitis eradication in 1988 by vaccination campaigns. In the Americas, the last patient with isolation of wild poliovirus was diagnosed in Peru in 1991, and 3 years later, this continent was certified free of indigenous wild poliovirus. The number of polio patients is rapidly declining on the other continents as well. In 1997, just 5119 cases of polio were confirmed worldwide (Figure 39). Of these, most cases occurred in India (2262), Pakistan (920), Indonesia (463), and Chad and Nigeria (>300 each). In 1998, 3228 confirmed wild polio cases were reported in these countries. In the European region, only Turkey and Tadjikistan reported a few cases.

Risk for Travelers

While it was estimated that from 1975 to 1984 one in 100,000 travelers would be infected by poliovirus and that one in 3,000,000 would be paralyzed, the risk currently is minimal. In the developed nations, poliomyelitis is occasionally diagnosed in immigrants. Two travelers imported polio to Germany in

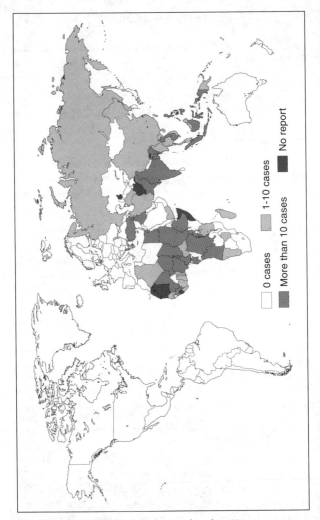

Figure 39   Global reported incidence of indigenous poliomyelitis, 1996

1991, one returning from Egypt and one from India. Until complete eradication is achieved, vaccination remains important for travelers visiting endemic countries. Infected travelers may shed the virus while visiting areas where polio had previously been eradicated, which may lead to a resurgence of endemicity.

Clinical Picture

Poliovirus infection occurs primarily in the gastrointestinal tract, spreads to regional lymph nodes, and in a minority of cases to the nervous system to cause flaccid paralysis in less than 1% of all infections. Infections may be accompanied by fever and occasionally by headache, vomiting, and muscle pain. Poliomyelitis, in many languages known as "infantile paralysis," is not limited to children. It may cause an even higher rate of paralysis and death in adults; the oldest patient to have been diagnosed with a travel-acquired polio infection was over 80 years of age.

Incubation

The incubation period for polio is 3 to 35 days, usually 7 to 14 days.

Communicability

Communicability extends from 36 hours up to 6 weeks after exposure but rarely beyond that.

Susceptibility/Resistance

Susceptibility is common but paralysis rarely occurs. Lifelong type-specific immunity results from clinical and subclinical infection.

Minimized Exposure in Travelers

Travelers should be immunized.

Chemoprophylaxis

None.

▌ Immunoprophylaxis by Poliovirus Vaccines

Two fundamentally different vaccines are available, each with its advantages and disadvantages.

Inactivated Poliomyelitis Vaccine (IPV, Salk)

Immunology and Pharmacology

Viability: inactivated

Antigenic form: whole viruses: serotypes 1 (Mahoney strain), 2 (MEF-1 strain), 3 (Saukett strain). Enhanced inactivated poliomyelitis vaccine (e-IPV, Salk) is a more potent formulation.

Adjuvants: none

Preservative: 0.5% 2-phenoxyethanol, <0.02% formaldehyde

Allergens/Excipiens: <5 µg neomycin, 200 µg streptomycin, or polymyxin B, each per 0.5 mL / none

Mechanism: Induces protective antipoliovirus antibodies, reducing pharyngeal excretion of poliovirus after exposure to the wild virus

Application

Schedule: A primary series consists of three 0.5 mL doses.

Children: Separate the first two doses by at least 4 weeks, but preferably 8 weeks; they are commonly given at 2 and 4 months of age. Give the third dose at least 6 months (but preferably 12 months) after the second dose, commonly at 15 months of age. Give all children who received a primary series of e-IPV or a combination of e-IPV and oral poliomyelitis vaccine (OPV) a booster dose of OPV or e-IPV before they enter school unless the third dose of the primary series was administered on or after the fourth birthday.

Adults: For nonvaccinated adults at increased risk of exposure to poliovirus, give a primary series of e-IPV—two doses given at a 1- to 2-month interval with a third dose given 6 to 12 months later. If <3 months but >2 months remain before protection is needed, give three doses of e-IPV at least 1 month apart. Likewise, if only 1 or 2 months remain, give 2 doses of e-IPV 1 month apart.

Give at least one dose of OPV or e-IPV to adults at increased risk of exposure who have had at least one dose of OPV that is equal to three doses of conventional IPV (available before 1988; in some countries still the only available Salk vaccine), or a combination of conventional e-IPV and OPV totaling an equivalent of three doses. Give any additional doses needed to complete a primary series if time permits. Adults who have completed a primary series with any poliovirus vaccine and who are at increased risk of exposure to poliovirus should be given a single dose of either OPV or e-IPV.

To complete a series of primary and booster doses, a total of four doses is required. Give incompletely immunized children and adolescents sufficient additional doses to reach this number.

Booster: The need to routinely administer additional doses is not apparent except for exposed persons such as travelers to endemic areas, who should receive booster doses every 10 years.

Route: SC

Site: in the deltoid region. In infants and children the preferred site is the anterolateral thigh.

Storage: Store at 2°to 8°C (35°to 46°F); do not freeze. Contact manufacturer regarding prolonged exposure to room temperature or elevated or freezing temperatures.

Availability: available in the developed countries and many others.

Protection

Onset: Antibodies develop within 1 to 2 weeks following several doses.

Efficacy: 97.5 to 100% seroconversion to each type after two doses. This e-IPV formulation is more potent and more consistently immunogenic than previous IPV formulations. Cases of existing or incubating poliomyelitis cannot be modified or prevented by e-IPV.

Duration: many years, precise duration still uncertain

Protective level: 1:4

Adverse Reactions

IPV/e-IPV administration may result in erythema, induration, and pain at the injection site. Body temperatures at 39°C (102°F) or higher were reported in up to 38% of e-IPV vaccinees. No paralytic reactions to e-IPV are known to have occurred.

Contraindications

Absolute: persons with a history of hypersensitivity to any component of the vaccine

   Relative: any acute illness

   Children: e-IPV is safe and effective in children as young as 6 weeks of age although OPV is the preferred immunizing agent for most persons until age 18.

   Pregnant women: category C. It is not known if e-IPV or corresponding antibodies cross the placenta. Generally, most IgG passage across the placenta occurs during the third trimester. Use only if clearly needed.

   Lactating women: It is not known if e-IPV or corresponding antibodies are excreted in breast milk. Problems in humans have not been documented.

   Immunodeficient persons: e-IPV is the preferred product for polio immunization of persons who reside with an immunodeficient person. Use of e-IPV in children infected with the HIV virus outweighs the theoretical risk of adverse immunologic effects. Persons receiving immunosupressive therapy or with other immunodeficiencies may experience diminished antibody response to active immunization with e-IPV.

Interactions

Use of routine pediatric vaccines and travel vaccines does not interfere with e-IPV. All immunosuppressant drugs and radiation therapy may cause an insufficient response to immunization.

Oral Poliomyelitis Vaccine (OPV, Sabin)
Immunology and Pharmacology

Viability: live, attenuated

   Antigenic form: whole viruses, Sabin strains 1, 2, 3

Adjuvants: none

Preservative: none

Allergens/Excipiens: <25 µg neomycin per dose, 25 µg strep-tomycin per dose, calf serum / Sorbitol, phenol red, polygeline

Mechanism: The OPV administration simulates natural infection, inducing active mucosal and systemic immunity.

Application

Children: A primary series consists of three doses, starting optimally at 6 to 12 weeks of age. Separate the first two doses by at least 6 weeks, but preferably 8 weeks; they are commonly given at 2 and 4 months of age. Give the third dose at least 8 months, but preferably 12 months, after the second dose, commonly at 18 months of age. An optional additional dose of OPV may be given at 6 months of age in areas where poliomyelitis disease is endemic. Give older children (up to 18 years of age) two OPV doses, not <6 weeks and preferably 8 weeks apart, followed by a third dose 6 to 12 months after the second dose. Children entering elementary school who have completed the primary series should be given a single follow-up dose of OPV. All others should complete the primary series. This fourth dose is not required in those who received the third primary dose on or after their fourth birthday. The multiple doses of OPV in the primary series are not administered as boosters but to ensure that immunity to all three types of virus has been achieved.

Adults: The e-IPV or, where unavailable, IPV is preferred for the primary series as adults are slightly more likely to develop OPV-induced poliomyelitis than children.

Booster: The need for routine additional doses of poliovirus vaccine has not been determined, except in exposed persons such as travelers to endemic areas, in whom booster doses should be administered every 10 years.

In some countries, e-IPV is preferred if persons older than 18 years of age need additional vaccine.

Route: oral

Storage: Store in a freezer. After thawing, use vaccine within 30 days. Vaccine is not stable at room temperature. Do not expose to more than 10 freeze-thaw cycles, with none exceeding 8°C (46°F). If the cumulative period of thaw is >24 hours, use the vaccine within 30 days. During this time, it must be stored at between 2°C to 8°C (35° to 46°F). The vaccine is shipped at –18°C (0°F) or colder in insulated containers with dry ice.

Availability: worldwide

Protection

Onset: Antibodies develop within 1 to 2 weeks following several doses.

Efficacy: >95% of children studied 5 years after immunization had protective antibodies against all three types of poliovirus. Type-specific neutralizing antibodies will be induced in at least 90% of susceptible persons. The OPV is not effective in modifying or preventing cases of existing or incubating poliomyelitis.

Duration: The vaccine is effective for many years; however, symptomatic poliomyelitis has occurred in travelers who had completed their primary OPV series and had the last dose at least 17 years prior to infection.

Protective level: 1:4

Adverse Reactions

Poliovirus is shed for 6 to 8 weeks in vaccinees' stools and by the pharyngeal route.

Some report tiredness or fever.

According to U.S. data, paralysis associated with polio vaccine occurs with a frequency of one case per 2.6 million OPV doses distributed. Of 105 cases of paralytic poliomyelitis recorded from 1973 to 1984 (in this period, 274.1 million OPV doses were distributed), 35 cases occurred in vaccine recipients, 50 in household and nonhousehold contacts of vaccinees, 14 in immunodeficient recipients or contacts, and 6 in persons with no history of vaccine exposure.

Contraindications

Absolute: immunosuppressed patients or their household contacts. Use e-IPV in these cases.

Relative: any acute illness, diarrhea, or vomiting

Children: not contraindicated; administer at 2, 4, and 15 or 18 months of age, and at 4 to 6 years of age. An additional dose at 6 months of age is usually recommended.

Pregnant women: category C. Use OPV in pregnancy if exposure is imminent and immediate protection is required.

Lactating women: Breast-feeding does not generally interfere with successful immunization of infants, despite IgA antibody secretion in breast milk. In certain tropical endemic areas where the infant may be vaccinated at birth, the manufacturer suggests the OPV series be completed when the infant reaches 2 months of age.

Immunodeficient persons: Do not use in immunodeficient persons, including persons with congenital or acquired immune deficiencies, whether due to genetic disease, medication, or radiation therapy. Avoid use in HIV-positive persons, whether symptomatic or asymptomatic. Use IPV or e-IPV if available.

Interactions

There is no evidence of interaction between routine or travel-related vaccines (including oral Ty21a) and OPV, except that the seroconversion rate to an experimental oral rotavirus vaccine was reduced.

Recommendations for Vaccine Use

Polio immunization is routine worldwide. After completion of a primary series, a booster dose should be administered every 10 years to travelers going to countries where transmission of wild polio virus is still a risk (Figure 39).

There is no international unanimity as to whether oral (OPV) or inactivated (IPV) vaccine is preferable. Travel health professionals should follow the recommendations valid in their country. In general, there is a trend toward IPV (or e-IPV where available) out of concern about paralytic poliomyelitis following OPV use.

Table 12 Advantags and Disadvantages of IPV and OPV

	IPV	OPV
Administration	Injection possibly combined with other pediatric vaccines	Oral, easy, cheaper
Cold chain	Less temperature sensitive	Cold chain needed
Effectiveness	Better in young infants in tropical areas	Serological response less in very young infants
Immunity, onset	≥ 2 doses needed	Rapid
Intestinal resistance	Low	High
Herd immunity	Limited	Yes
Vaccine related paralysis	None	Yes, rare — in recipients and contacts
Immunocompromised	Can be used	Contraindicated

Advantages and disadvantages of both vaccines are shown in Table 12.

Self-Treatment Abroad

None. Medical consultation is required.

Principles of Therapy

No specific treatment.

Community Control Measures

Notification is mandatory in most countries. Enteric precautions should be taken in hospitals. No quarantine, immunization of contacts, and tracing the source of infection are required.

RABIES

Infectious Agent

The rabies virus belongs to the genus *Lyssavirus* and occurs primarily in the animals as listed below.

Transmission

Humans contract rabies by being bitten or occasionally scratched by an infected animal. The rabies virus is introduced into wounds or through mucous membranes. Airborne infection is rare but has been contracted in caves from infected bats and recreated in laboratory settings. Person-to-person transmission has never been documented although saliva may contain the virus. Rabies has occurred after corneal transplant from a donor with an undiagnosed fatal CNS disease.

Global Epidemiology

Rabies occurs throughout the world with several exceptions (Figure 40). There are an estimated 40,000 to 60,000 human deaths per year from rabies (15,000 to 35,000 in India), mostly in the developing countries where transmission by dog bites in urban areas is common. Fox rabies predominates in Europe, usually transmitted in rural areas. Bat rabies cases have been reported in Europe (Denmark, Holland, Germany, Spain), Africa, Asia, and the Americas. Rabies in North America primarily involves raccoons, skunks, foxes, coyotes, wolves, and occasionally dogs and cats. It is likely that over one million persons receive postexposure prophylaxis annually around the world.

Risk for Travelers

The risk of rabies and subsequent death for travelers is unknown but many anecdotal cases have been reported, particularly after

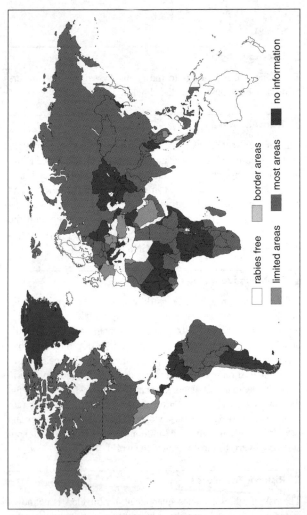

Figure 40   Geographical distribution of rabies in individual countries 1992

exposure in India and Southeast Asia. The annual incidence of animal bites in expatriates is approximately 2%, according to two studies, with most of the animals potentially infected. The number of these individuals receiving postexposure rabies vaccination is unknown.

Clinical Picture

Initial rabies symptoms include a sense of apprehension, headache, fever, malaise, and indefinite sensory changes in the area of the wound. These are followed by excitability, aerophobia, later hydrophobia due to spasms of the swallowing muscles, delirium, and convulsions. Death occurs after several days due to respiratory paralysis. Case fatality rate is close to 100% in patients who develop symptoms.

Incubation

The incubation period is usually 3 to 8 weeks but may be as short as 4 days or as long as 7 years, depending on the severity of the wound and its distance from the brain.

Communicability

Dogs and cats are infective 3 to 14 days before the onset of clinical signs and throughout the course of the clinical disease.

Susceptibility/Resistance

Some natural resistance has been demonstrated in Iran, where in spite of not being treated, only 40% among those bitten by rabid animals developed the disease.

Minimized Exposure in Travelers

Travelers should avoid contact with animals that are not known to be immunized against rabies. Travelers should be made aware which animals are most likely to transmit rabies in the host country (usually dogs) and that no animal bite can be ignored with respect to the possibility of rabies transmission.

Chemoprophylaxis

None.

Pre-exposure Immunoprophylaxis by Rabies Vaccine

Various rabies vaccines exist in the developed countries. These include

- human diploid cell vaccines (HDCV—Chiron-Behring, Pasteur Mérieux Connaught), strain Pitman-Moore, cultivated on human cells WI38 or MRC5;
- purified chick embryo vaccine (PCEV—Chiron-Behring);
- purified duck embryo vaccine (PDEV—Swiss Serum and Vaccine Institute);
- rabies vaccine absorbed (RVA—Michigan Department of Public Health, also distributed by SmithKline Beecham), Kissling/MDPH strain. RVA is available only in the U.S. and is not recognized by WHO as modern tissue culture vaccine;
- vero cell rabies vaccine (PVRV—Pasteur Mérieux Connaught);
- chromatography purified rabies vaccine (CPRV, purified vero cell—Pasteur Mérieux Connaught) marketing pending in many countries.

These vaccines have a similar profile and are described under separate headings below. Additional vaccines that are more reactogenic and less immunogenic are available, particularly in the developing countries.

Immunology and Pharmacology

Viability: inactivated

   Antigenic form: whole virus

   Adjuvants: none

   Preservative: 0.1 mg thimerosal or none

Allergens/Excipiens: Lyssavac N—none; Rabies Pasteur Mérieux Connaught—Neomycin < 150 µg, human serum albumin < 100 mg/mL dose; Lyssavac N—20 µg phenol red; Rabies Pasteur Mérieux Connaught 3 µg phenol red

Mechanism: induction of neutralizing antibody, cellular immunity, and perhaps interferon

Application

Pre-exposure prophylaxis: three doses (each 1 mL, except PVRV 0.5 mL) IM on days 0, 7, and 21 to 28. Also, 0.1 or 0.2 mL ID is adequate for HDCV if the proper technique is used (not SC).

Postexposure prophylaxis: See below.

Booster: Persons at extremely high risk, such as those who work with live rabies virus in research laboratories in vaccine production, conducting diagnostic tests for serum rabies antibody titers, should check their titers every 6 months. Booster vaccine doses should be given as required to maintain an adequate titer. Booster dosage is a single 1 mL IM injection every 2 years (or 0.1 mL ID, although not recommended by WHO). Alternatively, serum rabies antibody titers can be determined every 2 years and a booster dose given if the titer is insufficient.

Travelers do not require routine assessment after completion of primary pre-exposure immunization but where risk is considerable, boosters may be given every 3 years.

Route: IM. Travelers to endemic areas may receive ID vaccine (applicable for HDCV) if the three-dose series can be completed 30 days or more before departure. Otherwise, give the vaccine IM.

Site: The deltoid area is the only acceptable site for rabies vaccination of adults and older children (IM and ID). In younger children, use the anterolateral thigh. Never administer the rabies vaccine in the gluteal area.

Storage: Store at 2 to 8°C (35 to 46°F). Do not freeze.

Availability: Rabies vaccines are available worldwide. In the developing countries, some embassies (Sweden, Canada)

have the vaccine. Travelers should contact their embassy first if they require rabies vaccine while abroad. In the developing countries, often only suboptimal vaccines are available.

Protection

Onset: Antibodies appear 7 days after IM injection and peak within 30 to 60 days. Adequate titers usually develop within 2 weeks after the third pre-exposure dose. Antibody kinetics following ID injection presumably are comparable.

Efficacy: essentially 100%. Note that pre-exposure immunization does not eliminate the need for prompt postexposure prophylaxis if bitten by a rabid animal. Immunization only eliminates the need for rabies immune globulin (RIG) and reduces the number of vaccine injections required.

Duration: Antibodies persist for at least 1 and usually 3 years.

Protective level: Two alternate definitions are used for minimally acceptable antibody titers in vaccinees. The CDC considers a 1:5 titer by rapid fluorescent focus inhibition test (RFFIT) to indicate an adequate response to pre-exposure vaccination. The WHO specifies an antibody titer of 0.5 IU/mL (comparable to a dilution titer of 1:25) as adequate for postexposure vaccination.

Adverse Reactions

Rabies vaccination can cause transient pain, erythema, swelling, or itching at the injection site in 25% of cases (up to 70% occasionally). These reactions can be treated with simple analgesics. Mild systemic reactions including headache, nausea, abdominal pain, muscle aches, and dizziness are seen in 8 to 20% of cases.

In general, ID administration results in fewer adverse reactions, except for a slight increase in transient local reactions. Serum-sickness-like reactions occur 2 to 21 days after injection in <1 to 6% of those receiving HDCV doses. These reactions may result from albumin in the vaccine formula rendered allergenic during manufacturing by beta-propiolactone.

Contraindications

Absolute: previous hypersensitivity reactions to components of pre-exposure prophylaxis vaccine. None in postexposure prophylaxis

Relative: any acute illness (pre-exposure prophylaxis)

Children: not contraindicated; pediatric dosage is the same as for adults. Safety and efficacy for children are established.

Pregnant women: category C. It is not known if rabies vaccine or corresponding antibodies cross the placenta. Generally, most IgG passage across the placenta occurs during the third trimester. Use only if clearly needed.

Lactating women: It is not known if rabies vaccine or corresponding antibodies are excreted in breast milk. Problems in humans have not been documented.

Immunodeficient persons: Immunosuppression and immunodeficiency may interfere with development of active rabies immunity and may predispose the patient to develop the disease following exposure. Immunosuppressive agents should not be administered during postexposure therapy unless essential for treatment of other conditions.

Interactions

Simultaneous administration of RIG may slightly delay the antibody response to rabies vaccine. Recommendations for postexposure prophylaxis must be followed closely.

Chloroquine may suppress the immune response to low-dose ID HDCV. Complete pre-exposure vaccination should be done 1 to 2 months before chloroquine administration. Other travel-related vaccines may be administered simultaneously.

Immunosuppressant drugs and radiation therapy may cause an insufficient response to immunization.

In all IM administration, caution is indicated in patients receiving anticoagulants.

Recommendations for Vaccine Use

Pre-exposure prophylaxis should be considered for prolonged stays (> 1 [WHO] to 3 months depending on the available recommendations) in countries where rabies is endemic. Veterinarians, animal handlers, field biologists, spelunkers, and certain laboratory workers are known to be at high risk. Anecdotal reports suggest that children, teenagers, and young adults riding a bicycle are at greater risk since they more often come in contact with animals.

Pre-exposure prophylaxis does not eliminate the need for additional therapy after a rabies exposure. It simplifies postexposure treatment, however, as RIG is not required and the number of doses of vaccine required is reduced. Vaccines produced in the developing countries may have an elevated risk of adverse reactions and lower efficacy.

Self-Treatment Abroad and Postexposure Prophylaxis

Bites and wounds received from animals should be cleaned and flushed immediately with soap and water. Apply either ethanol (70%) or tincture or aqueous solution of iodine or povidone iodine. The need for postexposure immunization must be decided by a physician taking into account

- the animal species involved;
- circumstances of bite (unprovoked?) or other exposure (touching, licking, etc.);
- immunization status of the animal;
- whether the animal should be kept under observation for 10 days (postexposure prophylaxis required immediately if animal develops symptoms) or sacrificed for appropriate laboratory evaluation;
- presence of rabies in the region;
- that persons not previously (or incompletely) immunized with high-risk exposure should be given RIG, 20 IU/kg body weight; if possible one-half should be infiltrated at the bite site and the remainder IM. They should receive a total of five doses of vaccine (HDCV, PDEV, or RVA) IM (e.g., deltoid area) on days 0, 3, 7, 14, and 28 to 35. Vaccination should commence as soon as possible;

- that persons previously immunized with a complete pre- or postexposure course (or who have received >0.5 IU/mL rabies neutralizing antibody previously) should receive two doses of vaccine, one each on days 0 and 3. The third dose of vaccine should be given on day 7 if the previous dose was given more than 3 years ago. No RIG is required.

Principles of Therapy

Supportive.

Community Control Measures

Rabies is a notifiable disease in most countries. Danger of transmission from saliva and respiratory secretions requires the patient to be isolated from contacts. Immunization of contacts is necessary only if they have open wounds or mucous membrane exposure. Check whether other persons may have been exposed.

Respiratory Tract Infections

Most upper respiratory tract infections are caused by viruses and are uncomplicated. Recognition of group A streptococcal infection is important to prevent of poststreptococcal complications, particularly acute rheumatic fever. Streptococcal pharyngitis is suggested by the presence of enlarged anterior cervical lymph nodes, inflamed tonsils with exudates, fever, and pain on swallowing.

Infectious Agents

While there are regional differences in endemic pathogens, the similarity of pathogens found in all regions of the world is more impressive than the differences in distribution. There are many causes of acute respiratory tract infection. Most of these are not identified in patients with acute illness. The common pathogens in acute upper respiratory tract infection include

- viruses—rhinoviruses, adenoviruses, coronaviruses, enteroviruses, Epstein-Barr virus, influenza, parainfluenza, respiratory syncytial virus;
- bacteria—group A, C, and G streptococci; *Mycoplasma* and *Chlamydia.*

The important causes of lower respiratory tract infection include adenoviruses, enteroviruses, influenza viruses, parainfluenza viruses, respiratory syncytial virus, *Chlamydia, Haemophilus influenzae, Legionella pneumophila, Mycobacterium tuberculosis, Mycoplasma,* and *Streptococcus pneumoniae.*

Transmission

Virtually all the infectious agents are spread by the airborne route in large droplets or droplet nuclei or by direct contact. Recirculated air in aircrafts may be particularly risky for airborne spread of these agents.

Global Epidemiology

Respiratory tract infections occur worldwide. Occurrence rates are higher during dry winter seasons and in China, northern Europe, and North America.

Risk for Travelers

Acquisition of an upper respiratory tract infection during international travel is a common problem. This is especially true for travel in China and other regions during dry, cool periods. Respiratory tract infection is the most common illness among travelers to the developed regions and is second in importance to diarrhea among travelers to the developing tropical areas.

Group travelers acquire acute respiratory tract infection in a range between 1 and 88%, depending on the group. The average incidence for all travelers ranges from 6 to 12%.

Clinical Picture

Patients with acute respiratory tract infection present with runny nose, nonproductive cough, sore throat, headache, malaise, and muscle aches and pains. In acute streptococcal pharyngitis, patients experience abrupt onset of sore throat with pain on swallowing, tender swollen anterior cervical lymph nodes, pharyngeal and tonsilar inflammation occasionally with patchy exudates. Laryngitis is common in those with viral respiratory tract infection. Uncomplicated illness lasts between 3 and 7 days. Lower respiratory tract infection typically presents with sudden onset of fever, chills, productive cough, and systemic symptoms including myalgias. Lower respiratory tract infection may progress and have a more serious outcome. These cases, therefore, require emergency evaluation and therapy.

Incubation

The incubation period for most respiratory tract infections is short, between 12 and 72 hours.

Communicability

Many of the viral agents causing upper respiratory tract infection are highly communicable to susceptible (previously unexposed) persons in close proximity to infected individuals. Recirculated air in aircrafts may facilitate the spread of respiratory pathogens including viruses and *M. tuberculosis.* Bacterial pathogens, including *Legionella,* are not normally highly communicable.

Susceptibility/Resistance

Previous exposure to viral respiratory pathogens with resulting infection induces protective immunity in most persons. The many agents present in the environment explain repeated bouts of infection. Cigarette smokers, particularly those older than 50 years of age, are at increased risk for certain pathogens such as *Legionella* and *S. pneumoniae.*

Minimizing Exposure in Travelers

Patients at high risk for health problems, such as those with diabetes mellitus and cardiopulmonary disease, should avoid large groups of people during viral seasons (e.g., winter when the disease is prevalent). Prolonged air travel, particularly in winter months, and travel to northern China may be inadvisable for these persons. The only other practical way to prevent exposure to respiratory tract infections is to practice frequent handwashing when in contact with other persons.

Chemoprophylaxis

For the most part, this is not applicable. Antimicrobials (e.g., rifampin) may be used short term for prevention of meningococcal infection when exposed to an active case.

Immunoprophylaxis

Immunization with diphtheria toxoid is important to prevent diphtheria in international travelers. Pneumococcal and influenza vaccines should be given before travel to those at high risk (see respective sections).

Self-Treatment Abroad

Travelers with upper respiratory tract infection can usually treat symptoms themselves. Acetaminophen can be taken for relief of headache and sore throat, nose drops can be used short term (<48 hours) to relieve severe nasal congestion, (particularly if flying), antitussives may relieve dry cough with no fever, and interrupting sleep and consuming adequate fluids will ensure adequate hydration. Complications of respiratory tract infection should be looked for, including group A streptococcal pharyngitis, adenitis, epiglottitis, pneumonia, mastoiditis, otitis media, periorbital cellulitis, retropharyngeal or peritonsillar abscess, sinusitis, and bronchitis. If complications occur, local medical attention should be sought so the patient can be evaluated and considered for antibacterial or other therapy. Fluoroquinolones, which a traveler may have for possible diarrheal disease, may not be appropriate for therapy of bacterial infection of the respiratory tract since they may not be active against some of the *Streptococcus* strains.

Principles of Therapy

As mentioned above, symptomatic treatment and consumption of fluids should be undertaken for acute upper respiratory tract infection, and antimicrobial therapy should be reserved for group A *Streptococcus* infection and lower respiratory tract infection.

Community Control Measures

For the most part community control measures are not practical to control the broad array of respiratory pathogens. Decontamination of industrial cooling water and proper disinfection of spas and hot tubs in recreational areas will minimize *Legionella* infection.

Notification of authorities, isolation, quarantine, and contact study are not applicable, except for *Legionella* in some countries.

RICKETTSIAL INFECTIONS

Rickettsial infections are transmitted to humans by various insect vectors including ticks, mites, lice, and fleas or by aerosol from animals and animal products. They may be classified by cause of infection as follows:

- *Rickettsia*—spotted fever group, typhus group, and the scrub typhus group
- *Coxiella*
- *Ehrlichia*

The relevance of rickettsial infections for travelers is undetermined since many imported cases likely remain undiagnosed. Serologic surveys among travelers show that this group of diseases is underdiagnosed.

Skin rash is common in rickettsial infection although it may be faint or not present in ehrlichiosis and is not present in Q fever. Epidemic typhus, Brill-Zinsser disease, flying squirrel-associated typhus, and scrub typhus are more prevalent worldwide than other rickettsial infections. In *Rickettsia* and *Ehrlichia* rickettsial infections, the illnesses are clinically similar although skin rash is prominent only in the former. Diagnosis is made by serology, and treatment is with antirickettsial drugs. Adults are treated primarily with doxycycline although chloramphenicol is also used. Typhus vaccine was available in the U.S. from 1941 to 1981. Rocky Mountain spotted fever vaccine is also no longer available.

RIFT VALLEY FEVER

This arboviral infection is caused by the Rift Valley fever virus. It is transmitted by various mosquitoes or through close contact with animals, most often sheep and goats, and less frequently horses and camels. Slaughter and consumption of sick animals, or drinking unpasteurized milk can also lead to the disease. Incubation time is 2 to 4 days, and infectivity persists for 4 to 6 days. Epidemics occur mainly after heavy rainfall and flooding, such as occurred in Kenya and Somalia in 1997 and 1998. Symptoms resemble those of flu or dengue, and nausea and vomiting may occur. Late manifestations of a hemorrhagic fever may occur, mainly in malnourished populations, with a 1 to 3 week delay. Prevention includes protection against mosquito bites, avoidance of unpasteurized milk, and avoidance of sick animals and their products. Animals may be immunized. Inactivated and live human vaccine candidates are under study.

SCHISTOSOMIASIS

Infectious Agent

Schistosomiasis is caused by a number of species of schistosomes differing in infectivity and geographic location. These include *Schistosoma haematobium, S. mansoni, S. japonicum, S. intercalatum, S. mekongi, S. bovis, S. mattheei*, and a number of avian schistosomes.

Transmission

Ova of the parasites are introduced into aquatic environments through the urine and feces of infected persons in endemic areas. Miracidia are released within a few hours and are picked up by the snail, which is intermediate host. They multiply in the snail and transform into cercariae, the form which is infective to humans. The cercariae emerge from the snail, attach to the skin of the host, and penetrate within a few minutes. The worms emerge in the liver as well as the portal venous system. Adult schistosome worms may live inside a human for decades.

Global Epidemiology

Chronic schistosomiasis is one of the most ubiquitous infectious diseases. There are more than 200 million infected persons around the world, resulting in widespread morbidity and mortality. Schistosomiasis is endemic in Africa (with many reports from the Omo River region in Ethiopia), Asia, South America, and certain Caribbean islands (Figures 41 and 42). Transmission occurs in areas where susceptible snails are found, and urine and feces are not disposed of in a sanitary manner.

Risk for Travelers

Even a minimal exposure to fresh water in an endemic area poses a risk for the traveler; therefore, bathing, swimming,

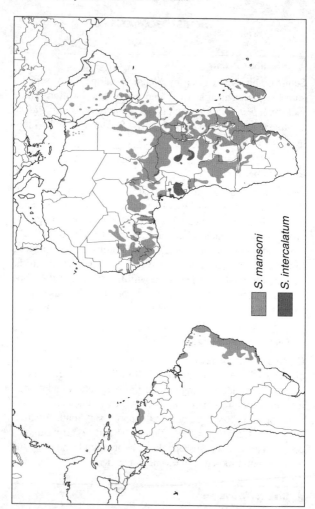

Figure 41 Global distribution of schistosomiasis due to *Schistosoma mansoni* and *S. intercalatum*, 1985

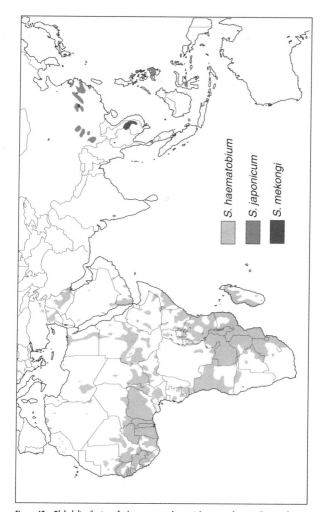

Figure 42   Global distribution of schistosomiasis due to *Schistosoma haematobium* and *S. japonicum*, 1985

boating, or rafting are risk activities in these areas. Risk is highest along lake margins and in slow-moving bodies of water such as irrigation ditches and flooded paddy fields. Infection may be acquired in poorly maintained swimming pools or in brackish water near salt water sources.

Clinical Picture

There are three syndromes in schistosomiasis. These include
- cercarial dermatitis or "swimmer's itch," which may follow cutaneous infection with any of the schistosomes, but most commonly with avian and other nonhuman schistosomes;
- acute schistosomiasis (Katayama fever), which is a serum-sickness-like disorder occurring in previously unexposed persons. Fever, headache, abdominal pain, and hepatosplenomegaly are found, often in association with eosinophilia;
- chronic schistosomiasis, which is associated with deposition of eggs in tissue and local granuloma formation. Eosinophilia occurs in approximately half these patients.

Incubation

The incubation period of acute schistosomiasis is 2 to 9 weeks after exposure. Manifestations occurring after a prolonged incubation will develop slowly.

Communicability

Schistosomiasis is not transmitted from person to person.

Susceptibility/Resistance

Children become susceptible when they come in contact with local water sources. The incidence of infection increases with age, peaking between 10 and 20 years of age. Intensity of infection, rather than incidence, appears to decrease with age thereafter, suggesting that partial immunity occurs with repeated exposure.

Minimizing Exposure in Travelers

Travelers should be advised to avoid freshwater bodies in endemic areas and to dry themselves off by rubbing vigorously with a towel immediately after coming in contact with water.

Chemoprophylaxis

Not applicable.

Immunoprophylaxis

Research work on an antischistosome vaccine is underway.

Self-Treatment Abroad

Schistosomiasis should be treated by a physician.

Principles of Therapy

The diagnosis of schistosomiasis is based on the clinical picture and identification of parasite eggs in fecal samples or biopsy material. Eosinophilia is often present and serologic evidence of infection is also frequently useful in making the diagnosis. Antischistosomal treatment (praziquantel) is effective, if given early in the disease and may prevent further damage by the parasite, if given later.

Community Control Measures

Community programs designed to prevent exposure to bodies of fresh water in endemic areas are of some value. Effective control programs are often centered around diminishing the reservoir of the parasite by building of privies, avoiding use of human excreta as a fertilizer, improved sewage disposal, and widespread chemotherapy of active cases. Molluscacides aimed at reducing the population of the intermediary snail are of limited value.

SEXUALLY TRANSMITTED DISEASES

Infectious Agents

The list of STD pathogens is long, and the resulting clinical infectious diseases are varied. In this section, we will consider the more important STD agents, including the following:

- *Neisseria gonorrhoeae* (gonorrhea)
- *Chlamydia trachomatis* (genital chlamydia infection and lymphogranuloma venereum)
- *Haemophilus ducreyi* (chancroid)
- *Calymmatobacterium inguinale* (donovanosis)
- *Treponema pallidum* (syphilis)
- human papillomavirus (genital warts)
- herpes simplex (herpes)
- hepatitis B and C (see also sections on hepatitis B and C)
- human immunodeficiency virus (HIV 1, 2; see also section on HIV)
- scabies
- lice
- *Trichomonas vaginalis*

Transmission

Transmission occurs when a susceptible person is exposed to an infected person. Tourists may have sexual contact with local persons or with prostitutes, who are at high risk for STD. The STD infections transmitted by blood may also be acquired by contact with nonsterile IV needles, infected lancets, or contaminated surgical instruments. Risk of HIV infection is higher in travelers with other STD infections.

Global Epidemiology

While data are incomplete on the occurrence of STDs in populations, up to 200 million STDs occur per year throughout the world. Roughly 80% of the infections occur in the developing world. Up to one-third of the world's population has an STD or carry a transmissible STD pathogen. Syphilis, gonorrhea, *C. trachomatis,* and herpes simplex are worldwide pathogens. Chancroid and donovanosis are diseases of the tropic and subtropic regions. Penicillinase-producing *N. gonorrhoeae* may be seen worldwide but are not commonly contracted during international travel.

Risk for Travelers

Tourists may be the source of STDs or may acquire an infective organism during travel. Many seek "sun, sand, and sex" during international travel, having left their inhibitions at home. Alcohol consumption often leads to unprotected intercourse with unfamiliar contacts. Condom use is increasing but unprotected sex still occurs frequently among international travelers (see also Part 1).

Clinical Picture

Sexually transmitted diseases vary in their clinical presentation including genital discharge or ulceration, conjunctivitis, uveitis, proctitis, symptoms of pelvic inflammatory disease, hepatitis, skin rash, arthritis, and urethritis. The syphilitic chancre is characteristically nontender and indurated with a clean base. Significant pain with ulceration is more characteristic of chancroid or herpes genitalis. Genital ulceration beginning as vesicles suggests herpes genitalis. Chancroid ulcers vary in size and have ragged and necrotic borders. Crusted lesions of the genital tract appear as healing genital herpes and scabies. Intensely pruritic genital lesions are seen in scabies. Clinical appearance of specific STDs vary. Laboratory tests are required to make a diagnosis.

Incubation

The various STDs have different incubation periods as follows:

- *N. gonorrhoeae:* 3 to 10 days
- *C. trachomatis:* 2 days to 4 weeks
- *H. ducreyi:* 4 to 14 days
- *C. inguinale:* 6 weeks to 1 year
- *T. pallidum:* 1 to 10 weeks
- Human papillomavirus: 1 month to 1.5 years
- Herpes simplex: 4 to 10 days
- HIV 1 and 2: 2 weeks to 10 years

Communicability

Most STD pathogens are fragile and incapable of survival for any significant periods of time outside the infected host but they are highly communicable through sexual contact or by transfusion of blood products.

Susceptibility/Resistance

Virtually all uninfected persons are susceptible to the wide array of STDs.

Minimizing Exposure in Travelers

Education of travelers in the prevention of STDs is part of standard pretravel counseling. If abstinence from sexual contact during trips is not likely, condom use must be stressed as an absolute necessity. Travelers should take a supply of condoms with them since they may be of poor quality or unavailable in many destinations (see Part 1).

Chemoprophylaxis

While chemoprophylaxis is feasible for a limited number of STDs (e.g., gonorrhea), it is not practical or advised.

Immunoprophylaxis

There is no vaccine available for STDs, with the exception of hepatitis B vaccines.

Self-Treatment Abroad

Travelers who develop a symptomatic STD should seek medical attention when symptoms develop. Self-treatment of STDs is not advised.

Principles of Therapy

Ceftraxone is recommended for gonorrhea and *H. ducreyi* infection. Doxycycline or azithromycin may be used for *C. trachomatis* infection. Penicillin is used to treat syphilis, acyclovir for herpes, and metronidazole for *Trichomonas vaginalis*. The threat of HIV transmission is reduced by treatment of STDs since STDs (particularly, ulcerative processes) facilitate the spread of HIV.

Community Control Measures

Contact tracing and treatment of active STD cases are important in reducing the occurrence of STDs, including HIV infection.

SMALLPOX

Smallpox has been eradicated. The last known cases occurred in 1977 in Somalia and in 1978 in a laboratory incident in the U.K. Smallpox vaccination may be dangerous both for vaccinees and contacts because of risk of generalized vaccinia and eczema vaccination or vaccinia gangrenosa for the vaccinee.

TETANUS

Infectious Agent

Clostridium tetani, the tetanus bacillus, is found in the intestines of animals and humans, where it is harmless.

Transmission

Tetanus spores in soil contaminated with feces may enter the body through wounds. The wounds may have been unnoticed or untreated; in 20% of cases the source of tetanus entry is unknown.

Global Epidemiology

Tetanus occurs worldwide (Figure 43) but is uncommon in the developed nations. In the developing countries, infants and young children are most often affected. In the developed countries, tetanus occurs most often in persons over 60 years of age who have neglected booster vaccine doses and have lost immunity. The disease is more common in rural areas where contact with animal (mainly horse) excreta is more likely.

Risk for Travelers

Worldwide there has been only one single case of tetanus reported in a traveler, a German returning from Spain.

Clinical Picture

Initial symptoms include rigidity in the abdomen and region of the injury and painful muscular contractions in the masseter, neck muscles, and later in the trunk muscles. Generalized spasms then occur, followed by risus sardonicus (sardonic smile) and opisthotonos. Death most often results from spasms of the thoracic mus-

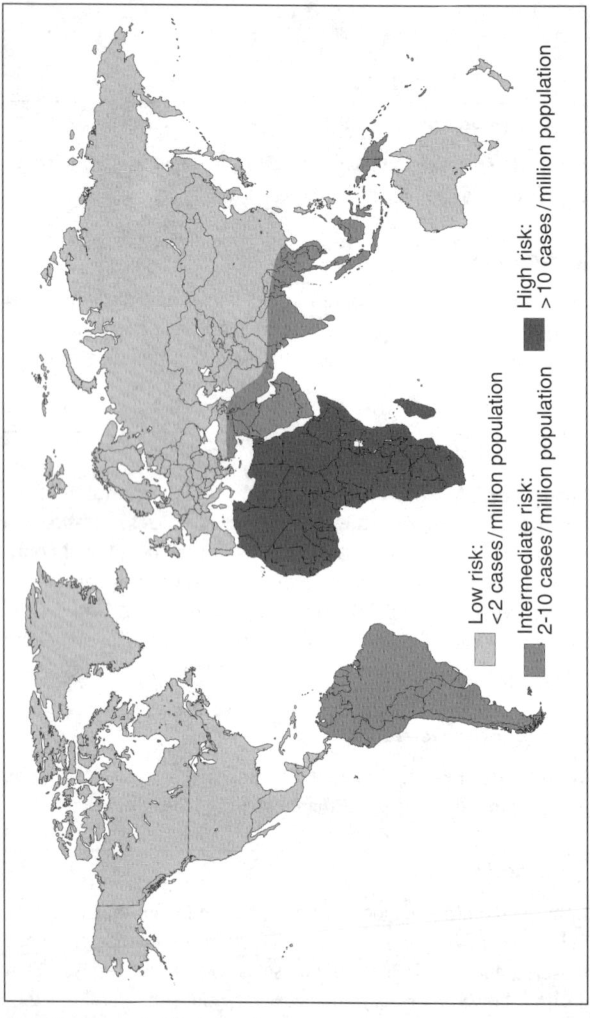

Figure 43   Geographical distribution of tetanus

cles, if untreated. Case fatality rates range from 10 to 20%, depending on the quality of treatment received in intensive care.

Incubation

The incubation period can be from 1 day to several months (3 to 21 days most commonly), depending on the nature, extent, and location of the wound.

Communicability

There is no direct transmission from person to person.

Susceptibility/Resistance

There is general susceptibility to tetanus. Immunity by tetanus toxoid lasts for at least 10 years after full immunization. Recovery from tetanus may not result in immunity.

Minimized Exposure in Travelers

Immunization should be kept up to date. If this is not possible for some reason (perhaps refused), the traveler should be educated about the necessity of prophylaxis after injury.

Chemoprophylaxis

None.

Immunoprophylaxis by Tetanus Toxoid Vaccine

Immunology and Pharmacology
Viability: inactivated

Antigenic form: toxoid. Note that in children polyvalent vaccines and in adults diphtheria-tetanus vaccines are preferred to tetanus toxoid alone.

Adjuvants: aluminum phosphate, potassium sulfate, or hydroxide

Preservative: 0.01% thimerosal

Allergens/Excipiens: none; not >0.02% residual-free formaldehyde

Mechanism: induction of protective antitoxin antibodies against tetanus toxin

Application

Schedule: The primary immunizing series usually consists of three doses. For children, the series begins at 6 to 8 weeks of age with two 0.5 mL doses given 4 to 8 weeks apart, and a third 0.5 mL dose given 6 to 12 months later. The same series is followed for adults. When immunization with tetanus toxoid begins in the first year of life (usually as combined vaccine DTwP), the primary series consists of three 0.5 mL doses 4 to 8 weeks apart followed by a fourth reinforcing 0.5 mL dose 6 to 12 months after the third dose.

Booster: 0.5 mL after 10 years is routine.

Postexposure prophylaxis: See below.

Route: deeply IM

Site: deltoid; use anterolateral thigh in infants and small children.

Storage: Store at 2 to 8°C (35 to 46°F). Discard frozen vaccine.

Availability: worldwide

Protection

Onset: after third dose

Efficacy: >99%

Duration: approximately 10 years

Protective level: Specific antitoxin levels of >0.01 units per mL are generally regarded as protective.

Adverse Reactions

Erythema, induration, pain, tenderness, and warmth and edema surrounding the injection site occur for several days in 30 to 50% of cases. There may be a palpable nodule at the injection site for several weeks.

Transient low-grade fever, chills, malaise, generalized aches and pains, headaches, and flushing may occur. Temperatures $>38°C$ ($>100°F$) following tetanus and diptheria toxoid (Td) injection are unusual. Patients occasionally experience generalized urticaria or pruritus, tachycardia, anaphylaxis, hypotension, or neurologic complications.

Interaction between the injected antigen and high levels of pre-existing tetanus antibody from prior booster doses seems to be the most likely cause of severe Arthus-type local reactions.

Combined Td vaccine causes slightly higher rates of local and systemic adverse reactions than tetanus toxoid vaccine but none that are incapacitating.

Contraindications

Absolute: persons with a history of serious (particularly neurologic) adverse reactions to the vaccine

Relative: any acute illness. Persons with previous severe adverse reactions to the vaccine should not be given even emergency doses of tetanus toxoid more frequently than every 10 years. Many of these persons will have generated great quantities of antitoxins during reactions, and levels >0.01 antitoxin units per mL may persist for decades. Antitoxin levels can be measured.

If the patient's tolerance of tetanus toxoid is in doubt and an emergency booster dose is required, test with a small dose (0.05 to 0.1 mL) SC. The balance of the full 0.5 mL dose can be given 12 hours later if no reaction occurs. If a marked reaction does occur, further toxoid injections need not be administered at that time since reducing the dose of tetanus toxoid does not proportionately reduce its effectiveness.

Children: Tetanus toxoid is effective and safe for children as young as 2 months. Nevertheless, trivalent DTwP or DTaP is the preferred immunizing agent for most children until age 7 to 12, depending on national regulations. The preferred immunizing agent for most adults and older children is Td.

Pregnant women: category C. Use only if clearly needed. The Td is preferred.

Lactating women: It is not known if tetanus toxoid or corresponding antibodies are excreted in breast milk. Problems in humans have not been documented.

Immunodeficient persons: Persons receiving immunosuppressive therapy or having other immunodeficiencies may experience diminished antibody response to active immunization. For this reason, primary tetanus immunization should be deferred until treatment is discontinued, or an additional dose should be injected 1 month after immunosuppressive treatment has ceased. Routine immunization of symptomatic and asymptomatic HIV-infected persons is recommended.

Interactions

Like all inactivated vaccines, administration of tetanus toxoid to persons receiving immunosuppressant drugs, including high-dose corticosteroids, or radiation therapy may result in an insufficient response to immunization.

Give SQ to persons receiving anticoagulant therapy.

No interactions with other travel-related vaccines have been documented.

Recommendations for Vaccine Use

This is a routine immunization worldwide. After completion of a primary series, a booster dose should be administered every 10 years for life, usually together with diphtheria immunization.

Self-Treatment Abroad and Postexposure Prophylaxis

All wounds should be cleaned and immediately flushed with soap and water.

Apply ethanol (70%) tincture or aqueous solution of iodine, or povidone iodine.

The need for postexposure immunization must be determined by a physician, taking into account the risk of contamination and the immunization status of the patient (Table 13):

Postexposure treatment depends on the nature of the wound. For clean minor wounds, the patient who has previously received < 3 doses of absorbed tetanus toxoid or whose vaccine status is unknown should be given a tetanus-diphtheria vaccine dose with no tetanus immune globulin (TIG). If they have previously received three doses of absorbed tetanus toxoid, they should be given a tetanus-diphtheria booster dose if > 10 years have elapsed since the last dose of tetanus toxoid (no TIG).

Wounds possibly contaminated with dirt, feces, soil, and saliva, puncture wounds, avulsions, and wounds resulting from crushing, missiles, burns, or frostbite, should be treated as follows:

- If the patient has previously received < 3 doses of absorbed tetanus toxoid or their vaccine status is unknown, a tetanus-diphtheria vaccine dose should be given along with TIG 250 IU IM

Table 13 Summarized Recommendations for the Use of Tetanus Prophylaxis in Routine Wound Management. Advisory Committee on Immunizations Practices (ACIP), 1991

History of Absorbed Tetanus Toxoid	Clean, Minor Wounds		All Other Wounds*	
	Td[†]	TIG[§]	Td	TIG
Unknown or <3 doses	Yes	No	Yes	No
≥ 3 doses[¶]	No**	No	No[††]	No

*Such as, but not limited to, wounds contaminated with dirt, feces, soil, or saliva; puncture wounds; avulsions; and wounds resulting from missiles, crushing, burns, or frostbite.

†For children aged <7 years the diphtheria and tetanus toxoids and acellular pertussis vaccines (DTaP) or the diphtheria and tetanus toxoids and whole-cell perutssis vaccines (DTP) — or pediatric diphtheria and tetanus toxoids (DT), if pertussis vaccine is contraindicated — is preferred to tetanus toxoid (TT) alone. For persons aged ≥7 years, the tetanus and diphtheria toxoids (Td) for adults is preferred to TT alone.

§TIG = tetanus immune globulin.

¶If only three doses of *fluid* toxoid have been received, a fourth dose of toxoid — preferably an absorbed toxoid — should be administered.

**Yes, if >10 years have elapsed since the last dose.

††Yes, if >5 years have elapsed since the last dose. More frequent boosters are not needed and can accentuate side effects.

- If the patient has previously received three doses of absorbed tetanus toxoid, they should be given a tetanus-diphtheria booster dose if >5 years have elapsed since the last dose of tetanus toxoid (no TIG).

In general, if emergency tetanus prophylaxis is indicated some time between the third primary dose and the booster dose, give a 0.5 mL dose. If given before 6 months have elapsed, count it as a primary dose. If given after 6 months, regard it as a reinforcing dose.

Principles of Therapy

Tetanus immune globulin is used for therapy or, if unavailable, tetanus antitoxin. Metronidazole and active immunization are administered. Supportive care should be given.

Community Control Measures

Notification is required in most countries. No other measures are necessary.

TICKBORNE ENCEPHALITIS
(SPRING-SUMMER ENCEPHALITIS)

Infectious Agent

The tickborne encephalitis (TBE) virus is found in rural Europe closely related to the Russian spring-summer encephalitis virus (RSSE, also called TBE, Far Eastern subtype) transmitted by other ticks in vast areas of Asian Russia. The vaccine protects against both infections.

Transmission

Tickborne encephalitis is spread by ticks (mainly *Ixodes ricinus*), which are most active from April to August in forests, fields, or pastures. The infection is occasionally acquired from unpasteurized dairy products.

Global Epidemiology

This infection occurs in large parts of rural Europe (Figure 44). Transmission seems to be highest in parts of the Baltic States, Austria, the Czech Republic, Hungary, and Russia. Tickborne encephalitis rarely occurs at altitudes above 1000 m or in urban areas. The main period of transmission is April to October but during warm winters patients may be infected in almost any month, particularly in the southern endemic regions. Risk of infection is highest in areas favoring the establishment of a virus cycle, such as forests and areas containing shrubs and bushes.

Risk for Travelers

Almost none, unless hiking or camping in forested areas or pastures in endemic areas. Imported cases of TBE have been observed in Australia, Austria, Canada, Germany (average 18 per year), Italy, Sweden, the United States, and the United Kingdom. The risk per week in Austria is estimated to be 1 per 77,500.

Clinical Picture

Usually, 1 to 2% of ticks harbor the TBE virus. Occasionally, up to 10% of ticks may be infected. Infection is symptomatic

Figure 44   Distribution of TBE in Europe

in 10% of patients, who develop flu-like symptoms, with a second phase of febrile illness developing in 10% of cases. This second phase is associated with encephalitis, which may result in paralysis with subsequent sequelae or death. Prognosis is worse with increasing age.

Incubation

The incubation period ranges from 2 to 28 days (usually 10), followed by an interval with no symptoms for 4 to 10 days.

Communicability

No person-to-person transmission occurs.

Susceptibility/Resistance

Inapparent infections are common, particularly in children, among whom the overt disease is rare. Long-term homologous immunity follows infection.

Minimized Exposure in Travelers

Travelers should wear clothing covering as much skin as possible when walking in endemic areas.

Chemoprophylaxis

None.

Immunoprophylaxis by TBE Vaccine

Immunology and Pharmacology
Viability: inactivated
  Antigenic form: purified whole virus
  Adjuvants: aluminum hydroxide
  Preservative: thimerosal 0.01%

Allergens/Excipiens: human albumin 0.5 mg/0.5mL; formaldehyde <0.01 mg/0.5 mL

Mechanism: induction of active immunity against the causative virus

Application

Schedule: three 0.5 mL doses at 0, 1 to 3, and 9 to 12 months. Accelerated schedules are being investigated. The second dose can be given as soon as 2 weeks after the first dose. To achieve immunity before the beginning of tick activity, the first two doses should be given during winter months. If departure to an endemic region is imminent, specific immune globulin in a single dose will offer protection for at least 1 month.

Booster: recommended 3 years after the primary series or last booster

Route: IM

Site: deltoid

Storage: Store at 2 to 8°C (35 to 46°F). Discard frozen vaccine.

Availability: available in many European countries as Encepur (Chiron-Behring), or FSME-Immun Inject (Immuno AG)

Protection

Onset: following the second injection

Efficacy: over 90% of vaccine recipients are protected against TBE for 1 year after the second dose. Efficacy increases to 97% for the year following the third dose. The TBE vaccine is also effective against Russian/Asian strains, as the determining protein E is at least 94% congruent with the European strain.

Duration: 3 years

Protective level: unknown

Adverse Reactions

Erythema and swelling around the injection site may occur, as may swelling of regional lymph glands. Systemic reaction such as fatigue, limb pain, headache, fever >38°C (100°F), vomiting, or temporary rash occasionally occur. Neuritis is seen very rarely.

Contraindications

Absolute: persons with a history of serious, adverse reactions to the vaccine

Relative: any acute illness

Children: none. Usually unnecessary in first year of life

Pregnant women: category C. Use only if clearly needed.

Lactating women: It is not known if the vaccine or corresponding antibodies are excreted in breast milk. Problems in humans have not been documented.

Immunodeficient persons: Persons receiving immunosuppressive therapy or having other immunodeficiencies may experience diminished antibody response to active immunization.

Interactions

Like all inactivated vaccines, TBE vaccine administered to persons receiving immunosuppressant drugs, including high-dose corticosteroids, or radiation therapy may result in an insufficient response to immunization.

Administer SQ to persons receiving anticoagulant therapy.

Interactions with other travel-related vaccines have not been documented.

Recommendations for Vaccine Use

This vaccine is recommended only for travelers (particularly adults) who are planning outdoor activities in rural areas of endemic regions.

Self-Treatment Abroad

The tick should be removed as soon as possible by pulling slowly and constantly with forceps, taking care to remove the tick whole. Do not use oil, varnish, or other substances to suffocate the tick as this may prompt ejection of more infectious material into the body.

Postexposure prophylaxis with tickborne immune globulin may be beneficial, if given within 48 hours but this is questionable.

Principles of Therapy

Supportive.

Community Control Measures

None.

TRAVELERS' DIARRHEA

Infectious Agents

Travelers' diarrhea can be caused by a number of bacterial agents. Enterotoxigenic *Escherichia coli* (ETEC) is the most important in the developing world. Between 5 and 50% of diarrhea cases in high-risk areas are caused by ETEC (Figure 45, Table 14).

Invasive *E. coli* occasionally causes travelers' diarrhea, as does HEp-2 cell adherent *E. coli* generally referred to as enteroaggregative or enteroadherent *E. coli*. The invasive bacterial pathogens *Salmonella*, *Shigella,* and *Campylobacter jejuni* account for 5 to 30% of cases contracted in high-risk areas. When ETEC rates drop in Mexico and Morocco during the drier seasons, *C. jejuni* becomes more important. In Thailand, *C. jejuni* and *Aeromonas* are major causes of travelers' diarrhea. *Plesiomonas shigelloides* is an occasional cause often associated with seafood consumption, as is noncholera *Vibrios* (Figure 46). *Vibrio cholerae* 01 causes diarrhea (cholera) very rarely. Viral agents are important causes of gastroenteritis in travelers, particularly children. The parasitic pathogens are not common causes of travelers' diarrhea although they are found more often among travelers to Nepal (especially *Cyclospora*), St. Petersburg (*Giardia* and *Cryptosporidium*), and to mountainous areas of North America (*Giardia*). *Entamoeba histolytica* is an occasional cause of travelers' diarrhea, especially among those who live close to the local population such as volunteers and missionaries. Parasitic agents are suspected in returning travelers with persistent diarrhea since most cases of bacterial and viral infection are self-limiting or respond to antibacterial therapy.

Transmission

Food and, to a lesser degree, water are the principal sources of enteric infection for travelers in high-risk areas. Food and bever-

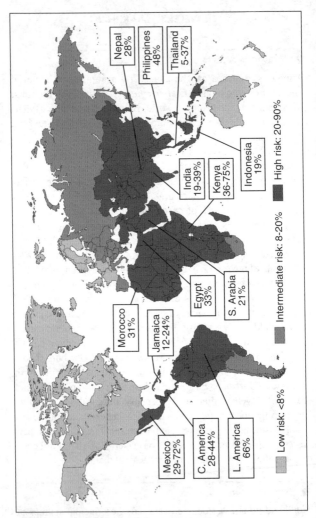

Figure 45   Proportion of ETEC as a cause of travelers' diarrhoea

Table 14 Etiologic Agents Causing Travelers' Diarrhea among Persons from Developed Countries Visiting High-Risk Areas

Etiologic Agent	Frequency –Range (%)	Comment
Enterotoxigenic E. coli (ETEC)	5–50	The most common travelers' diarrhea pathogen worldwide; seasonal pattern in some semitropical regions
Enteroinvasive E. coli (EIEC)	0–6	Variable importance
Adherent/Aggregative E. coli (EAEC)	?–10	Uncertain importance
Salmonella spp	2–7	Variable importance
Shigella spp	2–15	Variable importance
Campylobacter jejuni	3–50	Variable importance; seasonal pattern in some semitropical regions: important in Thailand
Aeromaonas and Plesiomonas	3–15	Important in some tropical areas such as Thailand
Vibrio cholerae 01	.005	Rare cause of potentially life threatening diarrhea
Non-cholera Vibrios	0–3	Occasional cause of seafood associated diarrhea in coastal areas
Rotavirus and Small	5–15	Comcause of gastroenteritis with vomiting as the primary clinical symptom
Giardia lamblia	0–5	Common among travelers to Russia or to recreational waters in proximity to wildlife
Cryptosporidium	0–5	Common among travelers to Russia
E. histolytica	<1	Ameobiasis occurs in persons who are living close to a local population living under poor hygienic conditions
Cyclospora	0–5	Particularly important among travelers to Nepal

ages are categorized based on potential for contamination by diarrhea-causing microbes in Figure 9. The most dangerous food items are those containing moisture and are served at room temperature or have been kept that way for some time. The safest foods and beverages are those served steaming hot. Most diarrhea-causing enteropathogens are inactivated at temperatures above 60°C. Other generally safe foods are those served with no liquid added, such as breads, syrups, and jellies, and items with low pH such as citrus fruits. Bottled carbonated beverages are considered safe. Ice cubes and tap water should always be considered contaminated, whether in a hotel or elsewhere.

Global Epidemiology

Diarrhea often occurs in international travelers. The frequency of the resultant illness depends on the countries of origin and destination (Table 15).

The world may be divided into three levels of risk for diarrhea based on degree of hygiene. The low-risk areas include northwestern Europe, the United States and Canada, Australia, New Zealand, and Japan. High-risk areas include Latin America, most of Asia, and North, West, and East Africa. Intermediate or moderate-risk areas include the northern Mediterranean countries and the Middle East (although Turkey is considered high-risk in some studies), China, and Russia, the other countries of the former Soviet Union, and South Africa.

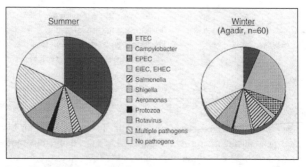

Figure 46   Etiology of travelers' diarrhea

Table 15 Risk of Acquiring Diarrhea among Travelers According to Host Country and Country Visited

Country of Origin	Country to be Visited		
	Low	Intermediate	High
Low	2–4%	10–20%	20–90%
Intermediate	2–4%	Uncertain	8–18%
High	2–4%	N/A	8–18%

Risk for Travelers

Enteric infection and diarrheal diseases are the most commonly reported medical complaint among travelers from the developed countries to tropic and semitropic areas. The incidence of diarrhea among persons from low-risk areas visiting other low-risk areas is approximately 2 to 4%, 5 to 19 for travel to intermediate-risk areas, and 20 to 40% for travel to high-risk areas. In select groups (e.g., Nile cruises), the rate may be as high as 90% per week. The 2 to 4% rate above for persons visiting low-risk areas is also applicable to travelers from high or intermediate-risk areas.

These background rates of illness probably relate to dependence on public eating establishments for most travelers, stress, and differences in behavior (e.g., increased consumption of alcohol). These rates are based on published studies, which are few in number except for travel from low-risk to high- and intermediate-risk regions.

Clinical Picture

Enteric infections vary widely in severity, from subclinical or self-limiting and mild diarrhea to cholera-like potentially fatal diarrhea accompanied by dehydration, febrile dysentery, or enteric (typhoid-like) fever. Travelers' diarrhea typically develops during the first week after arrival. The illness may be divided into three groups based on severity, each with different recommendations for treatment. In mild diarrhea, normal activities can be carried out. In moderate diarrhea, activities are limited but the person is able to function. In severe diarrhea, the person is incapacited and usually confined to bed.

The specific clinical enteric syndromes and etiology of enteric infection in international travelers vary widely as is shown in Table 16.

The symptoms, to some extent, suggest the etiology. When vomiting is the primary symptom, the patient has gastroenteritis, generally due to preformed toxins in foods or to viral agents. The preformed toxins are produced by *Staphylococcus aureus* or *Bacillus cereus*. The viral pathogens that produce gastroenteritis include rotavirus, or the small, round, structured viruses such as Norwalk virus or astrovirus. When the upper intestinal process leads to watery diarrhea with or without vomiting, any of the known bacterial, viral, or parasitic enteropathogens may be responsible. Fever and passage of bloody stools, frequently containing mucus, indicate dysenteric illness due to one of a variety of pathogens. The most common

Table 16 Clinical Syndromes caused by Enteric Pathogens

Clinical Enteric Syndrome	Etiologic Agent to Consider
Gastroenteritis with vomiting as the predominant symptom	Rotavirus or small round structured viruses (e.g. Norwalk or astrovirus)
Watery diarrhea with or without vomiting	Any bacterial, viral or protozoal pathogen
Febrile dysentery	*Shigella* ssp or *C. jejuni* likely; other possibilities invasive *E. coli*, *Salmonella* spp, *Aeromonas* spp, non-cholera *Vibrios*, *Entamoeba histolytica*
Persistent diarrhea (duration ≥ 14 days)	Bacterial enteropathogens, *Giarida*, *Cryptosporidium*, *Cyclospora*, small bowel bacterial overgrowth syndrome, lactase deficiency, brainerd dearrhea
Typhoid (enteric) fever	*Salmonella typhi*, *S. paratyphi*, other *Salmonella* spp

enteric pathogens are *Shigella* and *Campylobacter*. Other enteric pathogens less frequently causing dysenteric disease in the traveler include invasive *E. coli, Salmonella, Aeromonas,* noncholera *Vibrios,* and *Entamoeba histolytica.*

Approximately 2% of travelers' diarrhea lasts longer than 2 weeks. This persistent diarrhea may be caused by a bacterial enteropathogen, by a parasitic pathogen such as *Giardia, Cryptosporidium, Cyclospora,* or *Microsporidium,* by small bowel bacterial overgrowth, by lactase deficiency, or by an idiopathic form of chronic diarrhea classified as Brainerd diarrhea. Typhoid fever is unusual in travelers (see below).

Incubation

One to several days depending on the pathogenic agent.

Communicability

Person-to-person spread is possible with poor hygienic practices.

Susceptibility/Resistance

Persons from low-risk areas are particularly susceptible to enteric infection in moderate- and high-risk areas. Persons from intermediate- and high-risk areas visiting other high-risk areas experience lower rates of illness compared to persons from low-risk areas. This suggests that they have had prior exposure to the prevalent microbes.

Risk factors for acquiring travelers' diarrhea are multiple (see Table 17). Young children who eat at the table and young adults appear to be at higher risk than adults. Young infants who eat only carefully prepared formula or who are breastfed should be at reduced risk. High rates of illness were found in this group in one study, however, attributable to the infants crawling in a contaminated environment and frequently putting their hands in their mouth. Adventure travelers or those living close to the local population, such as volunteers and missionar-

Table 17 Established Risk Factors Predisposing to Travelers' Diarrhea

Risk Factor	Comment
Age	Rates are highest for infants exposed to contaminated environment and young children eating from the table and among young adults
Type of travel	Adventure travelers and persons living close to the local population are at greater risk
Beverage and food restrictions	Persons who do not exercise care in the food and beverages they consume have higher rates
Genetics	Although a poorly studied area, certain people seem more susceptible to illness based on genetic factors
Hypochlorhydria and Achlorhydria	Low gastric acidity whether induced by prior surgery or proton pump inhibitor predisposes to travelers' diarrhea
Prior travel to high risk regions	Previous travel to high risk areas within the past six months is associated with a reduced rate of travelers' diarrhea

ies, have higher rates of illness compared to those staying in the better hotels. Certain persons appear to have reduced rates of enteric infection based on genetic factors. Studies have shown that some animal populations have an absence of receptors for attachment of enterotoxigenic *Escherichia coli*, the principal cause of travelers' diarrhea. Similar differences probably exist in human populations on a genetic basis. Persons with blood type O are predisposed to cholera and experience a more severe case. They also appear to have an increased susceptibility to *Shigella* infection.

Stomach acidity is an important defense against enteric infectious disease agents, particularly bacterial enteropathogens. Persons with hypochlorhydria or achlorhydria based on genetic or nutritional factors, those who have had prior gastric surgery, or those taking proton pump inhibitors such as omeprazole are at greater risk of acquiring travelers' diarrhea. Nocturnal users of H_2 receptor antagonists do not appear to be at increased risk. Travel to high-risk areas within 6 months after traveling to the same or another high-risk area seems to afford some protection against the illness. This suggests that prior exposure to prevalent agents results in protective immunity.

Minimized Exposure in Travelers

Travelers consuming low-risk foods and beverages reduce their risk of contracting travelers' diarrhea (see Figure 9).

Chemoprophylaxis

While effective in reducing the frequency of diarrhea during visits to high-risk areas, chemoprophylaxis should not be recommended for most travelers. The pros and cons of chemoprophylaxis are outlined in Table 18. Bismuth subsalicylate (BSS) is 65% effective in eliminating travelers' diarrhea, probably through the antimicrobial effects of bismuth. The BSS causes minor side effects including blackening of the tongue and stools, and mild tinnitus in a small percentage of users. There are no major side effects of BSS when used as a prophylactic agent although it is not recommended for use in patients with abnormal intestinal tracts, such as AIDS patients or those

Table 18 Protection, Minor and Major Side Effects of Conventional Therapy for Resultant Diarrhea in Patients Using or not Using Chemoprophylaxis to Prevent Travelers' Diarrhea

Use of Chemoprophylaxis	Protection Rate	Number Ill per 100	Minor Side Effects	Major Side Effects	Treatment of Diarrhea
None	0%	40	0%	0%	Conventional*
BSS	65%	14	Common**	0%	Conventional*
Quinolone (for adults)	90%	4	3%[†]	.01[††]	Uncertain

*Antibacterial agent plus Loperamide (see Table 22)

**Black tongues, black stools, tinnitus

[†]Skin rash, vaginal yeast infection, insomnia, irritability, headache

[††]Anaphylaxis, antibiotic-associated colitis, aplastic anemia, superinfection

with inflammatory bowel disease, as bismuth absorption may lead to bismuth encephalopathy.

Antibacterial agents, particularly one of the newer fluoro-quinolones, are more effective prophylactics than BSS, preventing diarrrhea in roughly 90% of cases. These drugs occasionally produce minimal but objectionable side effects, including insomnia, irritability, headache, skin rash, or fungal vaginitis. In very rare instances, travelers taking a fluoroquinolone as a prophylactic (<0.01%) may experience a major side effect that could be life threatening, such as anaphylaxis, aplastic anemia, antibiotic-associated (*Clostridium deficile*) colitis. Antibacterial chemoprophylaxis makes therapy difficult when diarrhea does develop. For example, if diarrhea develops under quinolone prophylaxis, the illness is not likely to respond to treatment with that class of drugs. Symptomatic drugs (BSS or loperamide) should be used for this illness. It is not known whether those rare cases of diarrhea, likely stemming from quinolone-resistant causes, would occur without prophylaxis or if they are caused by the chemoprophylactic drug, either directly or by selecting out that enteropathogen.

Preventive medication may be considered if the traveler strongly requests it or if they have a predisposing condition such as immunodeficiency (AIDS), advanced malignancy, organ transplantation, inflammatory bowel disease, regular use of proton pump inhibitors of gastric acid, or insulin-dependent diabetes mellitus. Prophylaxis may also be an option if the nature of the trip does not allow for an illness which may be rendered short term (6 to 10 hours) by self-treatment. Table 19 outlines the recommended approach for prophylaxis for travelers according to category.

Chemoprophylaxis dosage is shown in Table 20. For BSS, two tablets are taken with meals and at bedtime (8 tablets per day). For adults opting for quinolone treatment, norfloxacin 400 mg, ciprofloxacin 500 mg, or ofloxacin 300 mg are taken once a day. In each case, the drug is begun the first day the traveler is in the high-risk area and is continued for approxi-

**Table 19 Recommended Approach to Chemoprophylaxis for Travelers'
According to Indication for Disease Prevention**

Patient Category	Prophylaxis Recommended
Most travelers to high risk areas	No prophylaxis
Traveler requests prophylaxis	BSS prophylaxis
Travelers with underlying medical problem (see text)	
Traveler's itinerary will not allow a 6–10 hour illness	Quinolone prophylaxis

*Prophylaxis is used for trips less than or equal to 14 days

mately 2 days after return. Chemoprophylaxis is not advised
for trips to high-risk areas lasting longer than 14 days due to
the cost of the drug in prolonged prophylaxis, increased risk of
adverse reactions, and interference with natural immunity.

Immunoprophylaxis

Vaccines are currently being developed to help prevent travelers' diarrhea. Poor hygienic standards in high-risk destinations
remain a constant problem, and the fact that natural immunity
tends to develop as persons remain in these areas makes
prospects for vaccines promising. The organisms being targeted include ETEC, *V. cholerae* 01, *C. jejuni*, *S. typhi*, *Shigella*
species, and rotavirus (Table 21).

**Table 20 Prophylactic Regimens Preventing Travelers' Diarrhea for Trips
of 14 Days or Less**

Drug Used in Prophylaxis	Dosing Regimen
Bismuth subsalicylate	Two 265 mg tablets chewed well with meals and at bedtime (eight tablets/d) during stay in high risk area and for two days after leaving area
Norfloxacin (NF), Ciprofloxacin (CF), Ofloxacin (OF)	NF 400 mg, CF 500 mg, or OF 300 mg once a day during stay in high risk area and for two days after leaving area

There have been a number of approaches taken to develop an immunizing agent against ETEC, which is considered the most important target because of its prominent role in causing travelers' diarrhea and the immunity that results from long-term exposure. Developed immunity has been linked to the colonization factor antigen (CFA) fimbriae produced by the organism, one or more of the toxins produced, and the lipopolysaccharide

Table 21   Available Enteric Vaccines in Those in the Planning Stages

Enteric Vaccine	Status

ETEC
   rBS-CFA ETEC
   LT/ST Toxoids
   Attenuated *E. coli*
   CFSs/Attenuated *S. typhi* or Shigellas
	The rBS-CFA ETEC vaccine is in advanced field testing. The other vaccine candidates are in early development.

Vibrio cholerae 01 and 0139
   rBS-WC (01)
   BS-WC 01/0139
   CVD 103 HgR (01, Classical)
   CVD 111 (01, El Tor)
   CVD 112 (0139)
	These vaccine candidates are in advanced field testing. CVD 103 HgR and rBS/WC vaccines are both marketed in some European countries.

Campylobacter jejuni	These vaccine candidates are in early development
Salmonella typhi Oral Live Ty21a Vaccine Vi Antigen Vaccine	The two vaccines are commercially available
Shigella spp *Shigella* Antigens in an Avirulent Carrier Bacterium or Attenuated *Shigella* Mutants, O-Polysaccharide-Crrier Protein Conjugate or Ribosomal Vaccine	These vaccine candidates are in early development
Rotavirus Atenuated Animal or Reassortant Animal-Human or Reassortant Human Vaccine Strain	Introduced 1999

of the organism. Vaccines being developed for ETEC include both inactivated antigens and live-administered attenuated strains given orally. The first and currently most promising vaccine against ETEC is a mixture of killed *E. coli* expressing CFAs and CS fimbrial components given with recombinant cholera B (binding) subunit (rBS). This vaccine prepared by SBL Vaccine, Stockholm, has been shown to be safe and immunogenic. Field trials in travelers are currently being conducted. Other laboratories are working on the development of toxoids with or without CFAs, attenuated nontoxigenic *E. coli* expressing colonization fimbriae, or attenuated *Salmonella, Shigella,* or *V. cholerae* live vectors expressing ETEC antigens. If an ETEC vaccine is 80% effective in preventing ETEC diarrhea in travelers to high-risk areas and if ETEC explains 30% of the diarrhea in the area, the vaccine would be expected to prevent 24% of cases occurring without immunization.

There is also great interest in developing safe and effective vaccines against *V. cholerae* 01 and *Salmonella typhi* because of the danger of contracting cholera and typhoid fever, respectively, in endemic areas (see details in respective sections).

Immunity against *C. jejuni* occurs with age. Potential vaccine candidates against the organism are currently being investigated by a number of laboratories.

Efforts are also underway to develop an effective vaccine against prevalent serotypes of *Shigella*. Orally administered attenuated bacteria containing *Shigella* antigens or attenuated *Shigella* chromosomal genes and attenuated *Shigella* strains (e.g., auxotrophic strains and others with altered chromosomal regions that control virulence and other plasmid mutations), have been or are being evaluated, as are ribosomal vaccines and O-specific LPS linked to a carrier protein.

Vaccines against rotavirus gastroenteritis have been licensed, an important initiative, considering the role of rotavirus in causing fatal disease among infants in the developing countries. Animal strains of rotavirus showing reduced pathogenicity for humans have been employed with some success. The leading vaccine candidates are derived from calves and rhesus monkeys. Reassortant animal-human or reassortant human strains are currently licensed for use. The role of the newly introduced rotavirus vaccine in travel health has not yet been defined but the vaccine is recommended for unimmunized infants and young children who will be residing in countries with high rates of rotavirus gastroenteritis.

Self-Treatment Abroad

Travelers to high-risk areas should be given antidiarrheal medication to treat the illness if it occurs (Table 22). The two types of therapy for adults are

- symptomatic treatment with either bismuth subsalicylate or loperamide;
- antibacterial treatment.

Designating the severity of illness (see above) determines self-therapy (Table 23). Symptomatic therapy is given for mild to moderate illness and antibacterial therapy is given for moderate to severe diarrhea, or any cases showing signs of bacterial invasion of the mucosa (fever or blood in stool).

Table 22 Self-Therapy of Travelers' Diarrhea

Therapeutic Agent	Dosage
Bismuth subsalicylate	Two 262 mg tablets chewed well or if liquid 2 tablespoons taken every $1/2$ hour for 8 doses. May be repeated on day 2
Loperamide	4 mg (2 tablets) initially followed by 2 mg (1 tablet) after each unformed stool passed. Not to exceed 8 mg (4 tablets) per day for over-the-counter dosage or 16 mg (8 tablets) per day for prescription dose
Quinolone: Norfloxacin (NF), ciprofloxacin (CF), or ofloxacin (OF)	NF 400 mg, CF 500 mg, or OF 300 mg b.i.d. for 1 to 3 days, depending on severity

Table 23 Management of Travelers' Diarrhea Based on Clinical Symptoms*

Mild diarrhea (i.e., normal activities can be continued)		Moderate to severe diarrhea (i.e., activities limited to patient disabled)	
Number of unformed stools passed per 24 hours		Fever (38.5°C body temperature) or passage of bloody stools	Other cases
1 or 2	≥ 3		
No other therapy	Symptomatic therapy (see Table 22)	Antimicrobial therapy (see Table 22)	Antimicrobial plus symptomatic therapy (see Table 22)

*All patients should receive oral fluids and electrolytes such as diluted fruit juice, soft drinks, or soups and broth with saltine crackers.

Particularly in infants, children, and in senior travelers, it is paramount to avoid dehydration by administering oral rehydration therapy (ORT) with oral rehydration solutions (ORS). This is effective because glucose-coupled sodium results in absorp-

Table 24 Oral Rehydration Solutions and Alternative Solutions

Product	CHO G/L	Na mEq/L	CHO/Na ratio	K mEq/L	Base HCO3	mOSM/L(a)
Oral Rehydration Solutions — recommended						
ORS (WHO)	25	90	1:2	20	30	310
Pedalyte	25	45	3:1	20	30	270
Other Fluids — not recommended for patients with high risk of dehydration (b)						
Cola (a)	50–150	2	350	0.1	13	550
Juice	100–150	3	250	20	0	700
Broth	0	250	—	5	0	250
Gatorade	45	20	13	3	3	330
Tea	0	0	—	0	0	5

(a) more than 310 mOSM/L may cause osmotic diarrhea

(b) combination thereof may be adequate for adult travelers without high risk

(c) contains caffeine which increases intestinal motility

tion of water by the small intestine during the course of infection. Although ORT is highly effective for combating dehydration and its consequences, it does not diminish the amount or duration of diarrhea, which leads to a lack of confidence in the treatment, particularly in mothers and in rushed travelers. A more recently developed cereal-based generation of ORS has advantages over glucose-based brands in speeding recovery, at least in cholera. In contrast, administering solutions that contain too much sugar creates an osmotic density in the intestine that draws fluid into the intestinal lumen.

The amount of ORT is 5% of body weight in mild, 6 to 9% in moderate, and 10% in severe dehydration to be administered within 4 to 6 hours. Oral rehydration should be administered in small quantities at regular intervals. Plain water and food may also be given to minimize the monotony and the nausea or vomiting induced by ORS. After rehydration, the ongoing losses through stool or vomiting are corrected, and maintenance solutions with smaller amounts of sodium (40 to 50 mEq per liter), e.g., Infalyte, Lytren, Pedialyte, or Resol, can be used. Oral rehydration therapy should be replaced by intravenous therapy only in rare cases of incessant vomiting, with signs of dehydration either reappearing or worsening, or in unconsciousness.

Although normal aciduric bacteria in the human intestine inhibit the growth of certain bacterial pathogens, *Lactobacillus, Bifidobacterium, Saccharomyces boulardii* and *Streptococcus faecium* have shown limited or no beneficial effect in the treatment of acute diarrhea. Charcoal, kaolin, and other agents can bind and inactivate bacterial toxins but results of clinical use have been disappointing. Moreover, some of these agents interfered with the beneficial effect of tetracycline.

A reduction of food consumption is frequently observed due to anorexia. However, except for milk and dairy products in the initial 24 to 48 hours, food should not be deliberately withheld during the diarrheal episode because at least some macronutrients are still absorbed; moreover, children who ate some food showed better and sustained weight gain than children who did not eat. After recovery, extra nourishment should be encouraged.

Principles of Therapy

See "Self-treatment" section above.

TRYPANOSOMIASIS

American Trypanosomiasis (Chagas' Disease)

The American form of trypanosomiasis is caused by the protozoan parasite, *Trypanosoma cruzi*. Bloodsucking reduviid insects, having fed on infected humans or animals, spread the infection to a susceptible host. The organism and associated insect vector are widely distributed, from Mexico and Central America as far south as central Argentina and Chile (Figure 47). The vector is characteristically found in cracks and holes in poorly constructed housing. The disease is therefore a public health problem among the rural poor living in substandard conditions. International visitors may become infected when they live under similar conditions, as may be the case for medical volunteers or missionaries. Infection may be acquired from a chronically infected blood donor during a blood transfusion. The typical traveler to endemic areas does not become exposed to the insect vector and parasite.

In acute disease, a local inflammatory lesion (chagoma) may be seen at the site of entry of the parasite less than 1 week following the insect bite. Periorbital swelling may be seen if the infection occurs by the conjunctival route. Further symptoms include fever, generalized adenopathy, skin rash, and hepatosplenomegaly. Myocarditis and meningoencephalitis may also occur in the acute phase. Symptoms subside within several weeks in most cases. Chronic infection may cause arrhythmias, cardiomegaly, or right-sided congestive heart failure. Megadisease of the esophagus or colon is a secondary manifestation of chronic infection.

Diagnosis is made by identifying motile trypanosomes upon direct microsopic examination of anticoagulated blood or from a buffy coat preparation. Serologic techniques and zenodiagnosis techniques may be used for acute infection. Chronic

Chagas' disease is diagnosed by serologic procedures. Treatment is with nifurtimox or benznidazole. Chronic heart disease is treated with conventional supportive and antiarrhythmic drugs. Adequate housing, public education about the disease, home use of insecticides, and serologic testing of blood in endemic areas will help prevent spread of the infection.

Figure 47 Distribution of vectors of *T. cruzi*

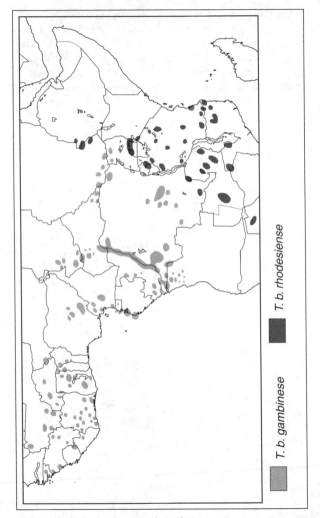

Figure 48   Distribution of trypanosomiasis foci in Africa

African Trypanosomiasis

African trypanosomiasis, commonly known as African sleeping sickness, is an acute and chronic infection caused by *Trypanosoma brucei rhodesiense* (seen in East Africa from Ethiopia to eastern Uganda and south to Botswana) or *T. brucei gambiense* (seen in West and Central Africa) (Figure 48). The organism is spread to humans by the bite of the tsetse fly. Travelers to East Africa on safari, hunting, or fishing trips are at low risk but several cases have been imported, mainly to Europe. The Gambian or West African form is a chronic illness involving the central nervous system. Several days after receiving a tsetse fly bite, a nodule or chancre appears with erythema and swelling. Clinical symptoms present in 1 to 2 weeks and consist of fever, headache, weakness, and adenopathy. After months to years, meningoencephalitis may develop. The East African form is a more rapidly progressive disease with acute neurologic symptoms and occasionally cardiac failure. Early onset of fever, headache, and malaise without adenopathy are followed by altered mental status. Without treatment the East African form may lead to death. Diagnosis is made based on clinical suspicion, likelihood of exposure to insect vector, and demonstration of trypanosomes in blood, bone marrow, centrifuged cerebrospinal fluid, or other biologic tissue. Central nervous system disease is confirmed by lumbar puncture. The customary treatment for the disease, suramin, does not penetrate the blood-brain barrier and is inadequate treatment for neurologic disease. Pleocytosis and increased cerebrospinal fluid protein as well as the presence of trypanosomes in spinal fluid, indicate central nervous system involvement. Serologic tests are available. Suramin administered early before neurologic involvement is an effective treatment. Melarsoprol is required once the central nervous system is involved.

TUBERCULOSIS

Infectious Agent

Mycobacterium tuberculosis, and occasionally *M. africanum,*
M. bovis, and other mycobacteria are the infectious agents
responsible for tuberculosis (TB).

Transmission

Tuberculosis mycobacteria are usually transmitted aerogenical-
ly from person to person.

Global Epidemiology

Tuberculosis is a worldwide problem (Figure 49). Its incidence
tends to be higher where people live closely together, such as
in slums in the developing countries. The disease is making a
resurgence, however, in the developed countries among population groups with a high seroprevalence of HIV and among
immigrants.

Risk for Travelers

It was assumed for many years that to become infected with
TB, a person would have to be exposed for months to a patient
coughing out *Mycobacterium tuberculosis* organisms from their
lungs. Recent evidence shows, however, that TB may be transmitted during a flight or during extended train and bus travel.
Nevertheless, the risk of acquiring TB during travel is very low.

Clinical Picture

There are many clinical forms of TB. The initial infection usually remains unnoticed but after tuberculin test, purified protein derivative (PPD) sensitivity appears within a few weeks.
After a latency lasting months, years, or even decades (less in

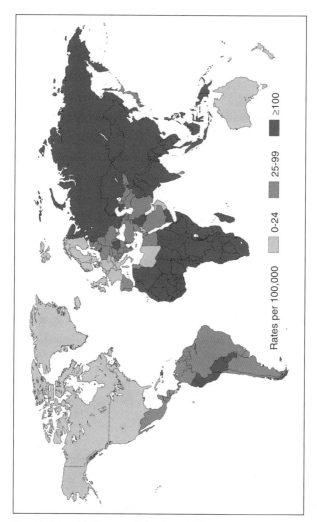

Figure 49 Estimated incidence rates of tuberculosis in 1997

those infected by HIV), there is a risk of reactivation to pulmonary or extrapulmonary tuberculosis, nearly every organ being potentially involved in the latter. With early and adequate treatment, the prognosis is good.

Incubation

The incubation period, from exposure to the infective agent until development of a significant tuberculin reaction or primary infection, is 4 to 12 weeks.

Communicability

Communicability persists for as long as tubercle bacilli are being discharged in the sputum, up to several weeks following initiation of effective chemotherapy. While 12 months used to be the mean exposure time to become infected, a few hours in an airplane seem to be sufficient, probably due to restricted ventilation and a dry environment, which result in a neglibible settling tendency of droplet nuclei.

Susceptibility/Resistance

Risk of infection is related to degree of exposure and previous contact with *M. tuberculosis*. Genetic and other host factors do not appear to influence susceptibility. Risk of developing the disease varies with age, with highest risk in children < 3 years and lowest risk in later childhood. There is a marked increase in tuberculosis among those with HIV infection and other types of immunosuppression. *Mycobacterium tuberculosis* infection induces a degree of resistance but re-infection may occur, particularly with changes in host immunity. Reactivation of long-latent infection may occur.

Minimized Exposure in Travelers

Avoid infectious contacts.

▌ Chemoprophylaxis

None before exposure.

▌ Immunoprophylaxis

Tuberculosis vaccine is made from the bacille Calmette-Guérin (BCG) strain of *M. bovis*.

Immunology and Pharmacology

Viability: live, attenuated

    Antigenic form: whole bacterium

    Adjuvants: none

    Preservative: none

    Allergens/Excipiens: lactose/none

    Mechanism: induction of cell-mediated immunity. Uncertainty exists about the protective effect of antitubercular antibodies.

Application

Schedule/Dosage: different recommendations for different countries

* 0.1 mL intradermally, or
* percutaneous in infants and children, using BCG with 10 times higher strength. Drop 0.2 to 0.3 mL (children < 1 year—half dose) onto cleansed surface of skin, tense skin, and administer percutaneously with instrument provided, e.g., multiple puncture disc. No dressing is required but the site should be kept dry for 24 hours. In countries with high endemicity, the repeat vaccination is administered after > 3 months if the person remains negative to a 5–TU tuberculin skin test. In other countries, no control test is recommended.

    Booster: no routine boosters recommended in persons who had a positive PPD

    Route: percutaneous, ID for some products in some countries

    Site: deltoid region

    Storage: Store powder at 2 to 8°C (35 to 46°F). Protect from light. Lyophilized material can be frozen.

    Availability: worldwide

Protection

Onset: PPD conversion within 8 to 14 weeks

Efficacy: 0 to 80% with lower rates closer to the equator. The BCG vaccine probably confers protection against serious forms of tuberculosis, such as meningeal or miliary forms. It probably does not prevent infection but may possibly reduce transmission.

Duration: long-lasting, although tuberculin reactivity gradually diminishes

Protective level: unknown

Normal and Adverse Reactions

Normal reactions consist of a small red papule appearing at the vaccination site within 2 to 6 weeks. It may reach a diameter of 3 mm within 4 to 6 weeks, after which it will scale and slowly disappear, leaving a small scar. In persons prone to keloid formation, a larger scar may persist. Note that in >90% of vaccinees tuberculin reactivity is induced.

Severe or prolonged ulceration occurs in 1 to 10% of cases. Self-inoculation at other body sites may occur.

Mild systemic reactions may include flu-like symptoms, fever, fatigue, anorexia, myalgia, or neuralgia, usually lasting a few days. Lymphadenitis may persist for several weeks. Abdominal pain, diarrhea, anemia, leukopenia, coagulopathy, and pneumonitis have been reported following TB vaccination.

Anaphylaxis, osteomyelitis (1 per million), disseminated BCG (0.1 to 1 per million), and death have also followed vaccination.

Contraindications

Absolute: immunodeficiency, history of hypersensitivity or other serious adverse reactions, positive PPD

Relative: any acute illness

Children: safely used

Pregnant women: It is not known if BCG vaccine or corresponding antibodies cross the placenta. Avoid use.

Lactating women: It is not known if BCG vaccine or corresponding antibodies are excreted in breast milk. Problems in humans have not been documented.

Immunodeficient persons: Avoid use. Do not immunize HIV-positive, asymptomatic persons.

Interactions

Immunosuppressant drugs and radiation therapy may result in an insufficient response to immunization or in disseminated BCG infection. Simultaneous application of BCG vaccine with oral polio vaccine is safe and immunogenic. No published data exist on concurrent use with other vaccines.

Recommendations for Vaccine Use

There is no agreement on the indication of BCG. The WHO recommends it "for children and young adults expected to make an extended stay in an area of high tuberculosis endemicity." The CDC does not recommend vaccination but rather suggests a tuberculin skin test before departure if there will be prolonged exposure to potentially infective patients. Those who test tuberculin negative should have a repeat test upon return whereas those who test positive are unlikely to become infected. If necessary (e.g., tuberculin test conversion), tuberculosis can be successfully treated with multiple medications.

Live virus vaccines may interfere with tuberculin testing results; both should be done on the same day or 4 to 6 weeks apart. An HIV-positive person may have an impaired response to this test; thus, the travel health professional should inquire about possible HIV infection.

Self-Treatment Abroad

None. Medical consultation is required for assessment (tuberculin testing by the Mantoux method with PPD) followed by treatment, if necessary.

Principles of Therapy

Antimicrobial therapy.

Community Control Measures

Notification is mandatory in many countries. Treatment of active cases of tuberculosis decreases the reservoir of *M. tuberculosis*. Active case finding should be conducted among contacts, and patients with sputum-positive pulmonary tuberculosis should be isolated. Quarantine is not required. Preventive treatment of close contacts should be considered.

TYPHOID FEVER

The Greek word *typhos* means fog or mist. When bacteriologic assessment was not yet available, a variety of acute diseases characterized by fever and confusion were named "typhus," including enteric fever (applied not only to typhoid but also to paratyphoid fevers), relapsing fever, epidemic or classic typhus, and brucellosis.

Infectious Agent

Typhoid fever is caused by *Salmonella typhi* whereas the clinically similar paratyphoid fevers and enteric fevers including paratyphoid A, B, and C, *S. cholerae suis*, and *S. dublin*, are caused occasionally by other *Salmonella* species. These often take a milder course. Part of the Enterobacteriaceae family, the genus *Salmonella* includes flagellated, non-spore-bearing gram-negative bacilli, which usually are able to ferment glucose but not urea, lactose, or saccharose. There are various subspecies within a species, differentiated by DNA structure and biochemical properties. These are divided into serotypes (serovars) based on their somatic (O) and flagellar (H) antigens. A cell wall lipopolysaccharide virulence (Vi) antigen, often associated with virulence, is found in *S. typhi*, *S. paratyphi C*, and occasionally in other enterobacterial organisms. On the basis of antigen characteristics, Kauffmann and White have classified more than 2000 serotypes of nontyphoid *S. enteritidis*. *Salmonella typhi* belongs to group D, having O-antigens 9, 12, Vi, and H-antigen d. At present, more than 100 types can be distinguished by phage typing.

Boiling immediately destroys *S. typhi* by removing the thermolabile Vi antigen.

Transmission

Salmonella typhi is unique among the *Salmonella* species in having humans as its only natural hosts and reservoir. Characteristically, food or beverages contaminated with feces from an *S. typhi* carrier are ingested. Direct fecal-oral contact may result in infection, though less commonly. The risk increases when sewage seeps into wells, or river water is used without appropriate treatment. Fruit watered with contaminated river water, vegetables fertilized by night-soil, milk and milk products contaminated by workers' hands, and, in some countries, shellfish harvested from contaminated coastal waters, have all been associated with typhoid. Canned food and bottled water are usually safe but have been contaminated through faulty processes. Typhoid fever occasionally results from laboratory contamination when workers are not sufficiently careful.

Epidemics originating from water contamination are particularly explosive, partly because a water source may serve a large population and partly because water dilutes gastric acid which inactivates pathogenic agents. Additionally, water and beverages remain in the stomach only very briefly. Transmission by food, however, is associated with larger inocula and higher attack rates. It should be noted that typhoid fever often has a high incidence in high socioeconomic neighbourhoods, where salads or other uncooked dishes are eaten more often, either at home or in restaurants.

Global Epidemiology

The incidence of typhoid fever increased with urbanization before the advent of modern sanitation. Epidemics have often occurred due to war (e.g., Berlin from 1945 to 1946) but have rarely broken out after natural catastrophies.

It is estimated that the worldwide annual incidence of typhoid is 16.6 million cases, with 580,000 deaths. Typhoid fever is endemic in all the developing countries, where children 5 to 19 years old are the most affected. Typhoid incidence rates have dropped markedly during the 1990s in parts of South America, where sanitary facilities were developed and sewage properly restored after the cholera epidemic.

Some low endemicity remains in southern and eastern Europe. Elsewhere in Europe, and in North America, Australia, and New Zealand, typhoid fever is now almost exclusively an imported infection. Annual incidence rates of selected regions are listed in Figure 50.

Typhoid rates are related to the quality of sewage disposal and water treatment in a given area and the number of typhoid carriers in that area. Water quality improvements reduce typhoid incidence but not dysentery, as the latter is a low inoculum disease more frequently a result of person-to-person contact than contamination of water supply. Secondary spread of *S. typhi* is unusual but sporadic infections occur in the developed countries as a result of unrecognized chronic excretors of *S. typhi* contaminating the food they are preparing. This most often happens in households but may also occur in public restaurants. "Typhoid Mary," an immigrant cook from Europe who was a carrier, spread typhoid fever among upper-class families in New York, causing illness in 54 people and three deaths.

Risk for Travelers

Studies assessing the risk of typhoid for travelers to various destinations are summarized in Table 25, although some of the data are over 20 years old. The summary is still valid, however, as the attack rate per trip to most destinations varies little over time.

Most studies show particularly high attack rates among visitors to the Indian subcontinent (India, Pakistan, and Bangladesh), some parts of South America (mainly Peru), and West Africa (Senegal). The rate in these areas exceeds 10 cases per 100,000 visitors, compared to 4 to 10 per 100,000 in North Africa (Egypt, Morocco) and Haiti. Lower rates were observed at other destinations. In southern Europe, mainly persons visiting their families in their native villages in Italy were affected, but hardly ever other tourists.

Only two of the studies also include data on incidence rate per period of time. India and Pakistan had the highest rates at

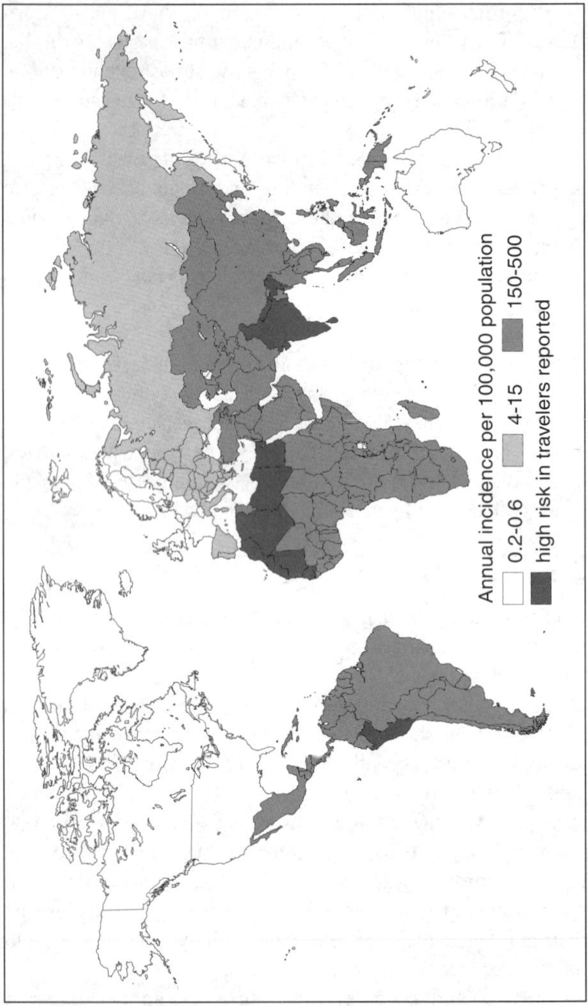

Figure 50   Annual incidence of typhoid fever in various parts of the world

Table 25 Attack Rate of Typhoid Fever per 100,000 International Journeys

Study	Mathieu	Schottenhaml	Ryan	Taylor	Steffen
Period	1980–90	1984–87	1982–84	1977–79	1974–81
Origin	New York	Switzerland	USA	USA	Switzerland
Typhoid Cases	315	183	NA	561	227
Destination					
Asia					
Near East	NA	NA	0.9	1.4	4.0
Turkey	NA	2.0	NA	NA	8.0
Pakistan	NA	0.0	10.1	48.1	NA
India	8.0	43.1	11.8	31.8	30.0*
Far East	NA	NA	0.5	0.6	0.5*
China	NA	3.4	NA	NA	NA
Thailand	NA	0.7	0.5	NA	NA
Philippines	NA	0.0	3.7	NA	NA
Indonesia	NA	3.7	NA	NA	NA
Africa					
North Africa	NA	4.0*	0.5	9.4	4.0
Egypt	NA	5.8	1.3	NA	NA
Tropical Africa	NA	NA	0.7	1.2	NA
West Africa	NA	26.4	NA	NA	8.0
East Africa	NA	0.0	NA	NA	2.0
Americas					
Mexico	1.1	0.0	2.0	2.9	1.6
Caribbean	NA	0.0	NA	NA	1.0
Haiti	3.5	0.0	4.2	2.9	NA
Domin. Rep.	1.3	0.0	NA	NA	NA
other	NA	0.0	0.3	0.6	NA
Central America	NA	4.0	0.8	1.3	NA
South Amercia	NA	NA	NA	2.5	2.2
Peru	50.7	0.0	17.4	NA	NA
Ecuador	7.9	0.0	NA	NA	NA
Brazil	NA	3.8	NA	NA	NA
other	NA	0.0	3.6	NA	NA
Europe					
S. Europe	NA	0.2	0.1	0.7	0.7
E. Europe	NA	0.0	0.3	NA	NA
N./W. Europe	NA	0.0	0.1	<0.1	<0.1

NA, no data available; *unpublished data

10 case per 100,000 per week of stay. Rates ranging from 2 to 10 per 100,000 per week of stay were shown in Iran, North and West Africa, Mexico, and Haiti in one study. These rates are all underestimates as a number of infections are not reported or diagnosed, being successfully treated with antibiotics or treated abroad. The latter appears, from anecdotes, to be particularly true for young people traveling on a limited budget for several months on the Indian subcontinent.

Outbreaks have occasionally been documented, such as in 1991 among a group of 15 students and teachers visiting Haiti, among whom six became symptomatic while no asymptomatic infection could be detected. Outbreaks have been reported among tour groups staying at one or several hotels in the Mediterranean (e.g., on the Greek island of Kos, 1983). To our knowledge, no typhoid outbreaks due to airline catering have been documented since the 1970s.

Clinical Picture

Clinical features range from not apparent to fatal, depending on the number of ingested organisms. In healthy volunteers, 10^9 viable bacteria induced disease in 95% while 10^3 only rarely did so. That single cases typically occur in families suggests exposure to low doses in nature. The Vi-antigen-positive strains cause illness more frequently than do non-Vi variants. The Vi envelope antigen protects the organism from antibodies directed at the complex cell wall O antigen, allowing the organism to escape opsonization and phagocytosis. According to seroepidemiologic studies, at least seven subclinical infections occur for every clinical case.

Typhoid fever shows an insidious onset with rising intermittent fever, headache, nonproductive cough, malaise, lassitude, insomnia, nightmares, and anorexia. Constipation occurs more often than diarrhea in adults and older children.

In the second week of untreated illness, the patient has a sustained fever and looks toxic. Often a relative bradycardia, dicrotic pulse, and hepatosplenomegaly in a distended abdomen are found. Hepatomegaly can be documented in one-third of cases, and jaundice will be found in one-third of these. Respiratory symptoms may predominate early in typhoid fever, and patchy pneumonia may occasionally be documented. In some patients, the illness looks like a primary pulmonary process. Patients frequently have abdominal complaints, including constipation, diarrhea, pain, and ileus or abdominal tenderness. Segmental ileus is frequently found in acute typhoid. Dilated loops of small bowel filled with air and fluid may be felt by deep palpation of the abdomen.

Rose spots 2 to 4 mm in diameter (pink papules which fade on pressure) may be observed on the trunk of Caucasian patients in 25 to 50% of cases.

The third week of untreated typhoid is characterized by further aggravation with persisting high fever, a toxic clinical picture, and a delirious, confused state. The patient becomes weak and has rapid breathing and a feeble pulse. The abdomen is distended and the bowel sounds decreased or absent. Diarrhea resembling "pea soup" is common.

Ulceration of Peyer's patches resulting in intestinal hemorrhage or perforation with peritonitis will begin in the second week of illness, particularly in untreated cases. Perforation is the most serious complication of typhoid fever and occurs in approximately 2% of cases. It is not related to clinical severity of the illness. Hemorrhage occurs in approximately 4% of patients, accompanied by edema of Peyer's patches with subsequent necrosis. The bleeding may be massive and include hematochezia or melena. Corticosteroids do not predispose the patient to hemorrhage. Provided that medical evaluation and, on rare occasions, blood transfusions are available, hemorrhage does not worsen the overall prognosis for typhoid fever.

Toxemia, myocarditis, and pneumonia resulting from typhoid fever may also lead to death. Other complications include hepatitis, cholecystitis, meningitis, polyneuritis, osteomyelitis, disseminated intravascular coagulation, hemolytic-uremic syndrome, glomerulitis, acute pancreatitis, thrombocytopenia, Reiter's syndrome, and polymyositis.

Untreated, the usual duration for a case of average severity is 4 weeks, with the fourth week showing general improvement. Gastrointestinal complications may still occur. Relapses occur in 5 to 12% of untreated cases, which were slightly more common (10 to 20%) following antibiotic treatment in the prequinolone era. Relapse usually takes place about 1 week after therapy is discontinued but has been observed as late as 70 days thereafter. The severity of relapses is inversely related to the severity of primary illness but is usually milder and of shorter duration than the initial illness. Rarely, second and third relapses may occur.

The case fatality rate in the preantibiotic era was 10 to 20% but has been reduced to less than 1% with appropriate therapy, particularly in a well-nourished population. The case fatality rate is higher in older patients as their symptoms are often less characteristic, and diagnosis may be delayed.

Incubation

The usual incubation period for typhoid fever is 1 to 2 weeks, with a range of 3 days to 3 months following ingestion of contaminated food or liquids. The incubation period is inversely related to the ingested bacterial dose.

Communicability

Bacilli appear in the excreta usually from the first week until convalescence. Roughly 10% of untreated typhoid fever patients discharge bacilli for 3 months after the onset of symptoms, and 2 to 5% become chronic carriers. Carriers are typically women with gall bladder disease, who excrete up to 10^{11} organisms/gram in their stool. Organisms are found in gall bladder stones or scarred foci in the intrahepatic biliary system. Persisting urinary carriage is rare except in patients with coexistent urinary tract pathology, such as schistosomiasis. Nontyphoid *Salmonella* carriers rarely carry the disease as long as 1 year.

Susceptibility/Resistance

Children are at higher risk for typhoid fever than adults because they are prone to fecal-oral infections. Like other salmonellae, *S. typhi* is relatively sensitive to the action of gastric acid. Hypochlorhydria resulting from age, disease, gastric surgery, or medication may mean a lower dose of pathogenic agents is necessary to cause symptomatic infection. Normal bacterial flora of the intestine have a protective effect, and antibiotics depleting them may have an effect on the inoculum necessary to cause symptoms.

Relative immunity following recovery from typhoid fever is inadequate to protect against subsequent ingestion of large numbers of *S.typhi*.

The flora of the intestine also have a protective effect, and antibiotics depleting them in a smaller inoculum may be necessary to cause symptoms.

Diagnosis

Typhoid fever should be considered a possible diagnosis in any case of fever of unknown origin accompanied by bradycardia and leukopenia. Nonspecific laboratory findings may include initial leukocytosis followed by leukopenia with neutropenia, normocytic anemia, thrombocytopenia, slightly elevated hepatic transaminases, and mild proteinuria.

According to the CDC, a confirmed case of typhoid shows "a clinically compatible illness that is laboratory confirmed" while a probable case shows a "clinically compatible illness that is epidemiologically linked to a confirmed case in an outbreak." The laboratory criterion referred to for establishment of a diagnosis is "isolation of *S.typhi* from blood, stool, or other clinical specimen."

Diagnosis thus depends on isolation of the typhoid organism. Blood cultures are usually performed and are positive in 80% of untreated patients during the first week. This rate declines rapidly over the course of the illness. Culture of bone-marrow aspirate has been shown to give a recovery rate of 90 to 95% as it is less influenced by antecedant antimicrobial therapy than are blood cultures. *Salmonella typhi* may also be isolated from rose spots (60% positive) and much less frequently from stools and urine. Isolation from stool and urine provides strong evidence of typhoid fever only when there is a characteristic clinical picture since the individual being tested may be a chronic carrier.

The traditional Widal agglutination test measures antibodies against H and O antigens of *S.typhi*. It provides some support for the diagnosis of typhoid if there is a fourfold rise in the titer of antibody to the O antigen. H antibodies appear shortly after O antibodies but persist longer than just a few months. Rising or high O antibody titers thus generally indicate acute infection while a raised H antibody helps identify the type of enteric fever. The Widal test, however, can be misleading. Raised antibodies may result from typhoid immunization, or earlier infection with salmonellae or other gram-negative bacteria sharing common antigens. High Vi capsular antibody is suggestive of a carrier state but there can be high rates of false positives and false negatives. According to the CDC, serologic evidence alone is not sufficient for diagnosis.

Minimized Exposure in Travelers

Safe drinking water and sanitary disposal of human feces and urine are essential for prevention of typhoid fever. Adequate handwashing facilities are required, particularly for handlers of food. Sufficient toilet paper supplies, insect screens, and use of insecticides will all help minimize risk. Sanitary improvements in many parts of the developing world have been hampered, however, by economic conditions and civil unrest.

Whenever travelers are uncertain about sanitary practices—and they should be almost anywhere in the developing world—they should select only freshly cooked food that is served at temperatures of at least 60°C. Fruit that can be peeled by the traveler, bread, and cookies are safe, as are hot tea and coffee, freshly pressed fruit juice, and carbonated bottled water. Otherwise, water can be boiled or chemically treated. Many travelers, unfortunately, often do not take such precautions.

Chemoprophylaxis

Although no chemoprophylaxis is specifically recommended for typhoid fever, those using quinolones for preventing travelers' diarrhea will usually be protected from *S.typhi* infection. Chemoprophylaxis of travelers' diarrhea is, however, recommended only for special-risk groups (see Table 19).

Immunoprophylaxis by Typhoid Vaccines

Three different typhoid vaccines are now widely available. The oral and the parenteral Vi-vaccines are clearly superior to the old, soon obsolete, parenteral TAB vaccine with respect to tolerance (Table 26) although according to a recent meta-analysis, the TAB vaccine may be more effective if two doses are given.

Oral Typhoid Vaccine (Ty21a)

Immunology and Pharmacology

Viability: live, attenuated bacteria

Antigenic form: whole bacterium, 2 to 6×10^9 CFU Ty21a gal E mutant strain

Adjuvants: none

Preservative: none

Allergens/Excipients: 100 to 180 mg lactose per capsule / each capsule contains 26 to 130 mg sucrose, 1.4 to 7 mg amino acid mixture, 3.6 to 4.4 ng magnesium stearate, and ascorbic acid

Table 26 Synopsis of Typhoid Vaccines

Characteristics	TAB	Ty21a	Vi
Usage			
Mode of application	Parenteral (s.c., i.m.)	Oral, enteric-coated capsule	Parenteral (i.m.)
Volume	0.5 ml	Capsule	0.5 ml
Number of doses	2	3–4	1
Primary vaccination regimen: day(s)	0/28–42	0/2/4 (in US, Canada: ±6)	0 only
Booster dose	0.1 ml intradermal	Same as primary	Same as primary
Immunologic correlation to protection	Anti-H antigen antibodies in serum	Anti-O-antigen antibodies and T cell response in serum and intestine	Anti-Vi antibodies in serum
Efficacy			
Reported protective efficacy (range)	70 (51–88)%	70 (33–94)%	70 (61–75)%
Onset of protection		Optimal seroconversion: 14 days after last dose	Optimal seroconversion: 14 days after injection
Duration of protection	2–3 years	≥1 yr in European travelers 5 yr in US/Canadian travelers 3–7 yr in endemic country residents	2–3 years

Characteristics	TAB	Ty21a	Vi
Adverse events			
Local	Frequent pain (60%)	Diarrhoea, (0.1 (–20) %)	Usually mild
Systemic	Fever (7–40%)	Fever (<1–5%)	Fever (<1–5%)
Contraindication			
Children (varies by country)	<6–12 months, half dose when <10 years old	Absolute <3months Usually <6 years	<2 years
Pregnancy	Only when needed	Insufficient data	No data available
Nursing	Insufficient data	Insufficient data	No data available
Other	Allergy, past reaction	Users of antimicrobials, antimycotics diarrhoea, gastroenteritis	Past reaction
Simultaneous application with other vaccines	No restriction	No restriction	No restriction
Antimalarials	No restriction	Proguanil, mefloquine PYR/SDX, chloroquin	No restriction
Manufacturers	Many	Swiss Serum and Vaccine Institute Berna (Vivotif®), Behring (Typhoral L® etc.)	Pasteur-Merieux (Typhim Vi®) SB (Typherix®)

Buffer: only in Vivotif L (liquid form)

Mechanism: induction of specific protective antibodies directed against *Salmonella typhi* lipopolysaccharide. This bacterial strain is restricted in its ability to produce complete lipopolysaccharide, which impairs its ability to cause disease but not to induce an immune response.

Application

Schedule: one capsule orally on days 1, 3, 5, and in the U.S. and Canada, additionally on day 7

Booster: same as primary vaccination described above, recommended every year in Europe (unless continuously exposed to *S. typhi*), every 5 years in the U.S. and Canada, based on field trials in endemic countries

Route: oral

Storage: Store at 2 to 8°C (35 to 46°F) prior to use and between doses. If frozen, thaw the capsules before administering. Product can tolerate 48 hours at 25°C (77°F). Advise travelers to store the vaccine in refrigerator until use.

Availability: Available in many countries as Vivotif (Berna) and Typhoral L (Behring).

Protection

Onset: 2 weeks after third dose (Europe), 1 week after fourth dose (U.S. and Canada)

Efficacy: 70% with a range of 33 to 94% in populations continuously exposed to *S. typhi*. Unknown in nonimmunes

Duration: 1 year in European travelers, 5 years in the U.S. and Canadian travelers (see schedule and booster). Every 3 to 7 years for residents of endemic countries

Protective level: unknown

Adverse Reactions. Diarrhea in 0.1 to 20% of vaccinees, usually mild. Fever in 1 to 5%

Contraindications

Absolute: persons with immunodeficiency and children <2 years of age

Relative: persons with acute illness, diarrhea, vomiting, and users of antimicrobial agents and antimalarials (see "Interactions")

Children: The lower age limit for use of Ty21a capsules varies but they are generally not recommended for children <6 years of age as insufficient safety or efficacy data are available for that age group. Use the liquid form, where available.

Pregnant women: category C. Use typhoid vaccine only if clearly needed (i.e., if disease risks exceed vaccination risks). It is not known if typhoid vaccine or corresponding antibodies cross the placenta. Generally, most IgG passage across the placenta occurs during the third trimester.

Lactating women: It is not known if typhoid vaccine or corresponding antibodies are excreted in breast milk. Problems in humans have not been documented.

Immunodeficient persons: Do not give typhoid vaccine capsules to immunocompromised persons, including persons with congenital or acquired immune deficiencies, whether due to genetics, disease, or drug or radiation therapy, regardless of possible benefits from vaccination. This product contains live bacteria. Avoid use in HIV-positive persons. Use the parenteral, inactivated typhoid vaccine instead in these patients.

Interactions

Concomitant application of antimicrobials, antimalarials (mefloquine, pyrimethamine/sulfadoxine), or phenytoin results in reduced antibody response. Simultaneous application of Ty21a vaccine with oral polio vaccine is probably safe and immunogenic although various sources advise against simultaneous use. There is no indication of interactions with other travel vaccines.

Parenteral Typhoid Vaccine (TAB)

Immunology and Pharmacology

Viability: inactivated

Antigenic form: whole bacterium strain Ty2, acetone killed and dried or heat- and phenol-inactivated. The latter probably contains less Vi antigen.

Adjuvants: none
Preservative: 0.5% phenol
Allergens/Excipiens: veal proteins / agar, bactopeptone

Application
Schedule/dosage: two doses 28 to 42 days apart. Adults and children aged 10 years should receive two 0.5 mL doses, children < 10 years of age two 0.25 mL doses. If the two doses cannot be separated by 4 weeks, common practice has been to administer three doses at weekly intervals. No data show this is effective, however.

Booster: every 3 years
Route: SC or IM
Site: deltoid region
Storage: Store at 2 to 8°C (35 to 46°F). Do not freeze. Can tolerate 10 days at room temperature.
Availability: available in some countries but often withdrawn from market where less reactogenic vaccines such as Ty21a or Vi exist

Protection
Onset: presumably within 1 to 2 weeks after second dose
Efficacy: 70% with a range of 51 to 88% in populations continuously exposed to *S. typhi*. Unknown in nonimmunes. Effectiveness of protective immunity appears to be dependent on the size of the bacterial inoculum with which the patient is challenged.

Duration: 2 to 3 years
Protective level: unknown

Adverse Reactions
Frequent considerable local pain in 60% of vaccinees, erythema, and induration persisting 1 to 2 days. Systemic reactions include fever in 7 to 40% of vaccinees, myalgia, malaise, headache in 9 to 30%, and hypotension occasionally. There has been one death reported anecdotally following combined TAB-cholera vaccine

Contraindications

Absolute: persons with previous severe systemic or allergic reaction to the vaccine

Relative: persons with any acute illness or those involved in intense physical activity

Children: <6 months. Reduce dosage volume for children <10 years of age.

Pregnant women: category C. Vaccination is not specifically contraindicated. Use only if clearly indicated.

Lactating women: It is not known if typhoid vaccine or corresponding antibodies are excreted in breast milk. Problems in humans have not been documented.

Immunodeficient persons: Persons receiving immunosuppressive therapy or having other immunodeficiencies may experience diminished antibody response to active immunization.

Interactions

TAB vaccine should not be administered with reactogenic vaccines to avoid the risk of accentuated adverse reactions.

Immunosuppressant drugs and radiation therapy may cause an insufficient response to immunization.

Administer SC to patients receiving anticoagulants.

Parenteral Vi Polysaccharide Typhoid Vaccine

Immunology and Pharmacology

Viability: inactivated

Antigenic form: Vi polysaccharide

Adjuvants: none

Preservative: 0.5% phenol

Allergens/Excipiens: veal / agar, bactopeptone

Storage: Store at 2 to 8°C (35 to 46°F). Do not freeze. Can tolerate 10 days at room temperature

Mechanism: induction of specific protective antibodies

Availability: available in most countries as Typhim Vi (Pasteur Mérieux Connaught). Typherix (SmithKline Beecham) has just been introduced in several countries.

Application

Schedule: single 0.5 mL dose

> *Booster:* after 2 years in the U.S. and 3 years in Europe
>
> *Route:* IM
>
> *Site:* deltoid region

Protection

Onset: optimal after 2 weeks

> *Efficacy:* 70% with a range of 55 to 75% in populations continuously exposed to *S. typhi*. Unknown in nonimmunes
>
> *Duration:* 2 to 3 years
>
> *Protective level:* unknown

Adverse Reactions

Local reactions are usually mild and transient. Erythema occurs in 4 to 11% of vaccinees, induration in 5 to 18%. Systemic reactions include fever in <1 to 5% of vaccinees, malaise, myalgia, nausea, headache, and lymphadenopathy. Occasionally, hypotension and urticaria have been reported.

Contraindications

Absolute: persons with a previous serious reaction to the vaccine

> *Relative:* any acute illness
>
> *Children:* <2 years of age
>
> *Pregnant women:* category C. It is not known if typhoid vaccine or corresponding antibodies cross the placenta. Generally, most IgG passage across the placenta occurs during the third trimester. Use typhoid vaccine only if clearly indicated.
>
> *Lactating women:* It is not known if typhoid vaccine or corresponding antibodies are excreted in breast milk. Problems in humans have not been documented.
>
> *Immunodeficient persons:* Persons receiving immunosuppressive therapy or having other immunodeficiencies may experience diminished antibody response to active immunization.

Interactions

Immunosuppressant drugs and radiation therapy may cause an insufficient response to immunization.

Administer SC to patients receiving anticoagulants.

Recommendations for Vaccine Use

Typhoid vaccination is only recommended for those traveling to the developing countries and may be at risk. Activities placing travelers at risk include

- exposure of at least 1 month;
- travel to remote areas and consumption of local food;
- consumption of food and beverages purchased from street vendors;
- travel to anywhere on the Indian subcontinent or to North or West Africa, except Tunisia.

Self-Treatment Abroad

None. Medical assessment and therapy are required.

Principles of Therapy

Strict enteric precautions should be taken with regard to hospitalized patients to prevent secondary spread. Chloramphenicol (the standard treatment in the developing world), amoxicillin, or for children trimethoprim-sulfamethoxazole, have all shown similar efficacy, each given for 2 weeks. More recently, quinolones and, to a lesser extent, third-generation cephalosporins, the latter particularly for children, have been used as first-line strategies wherever multiresistant typhoid fever repeatedly occurs, such as on the Indian subcontinent and in the Arabian peninsula. In view of increasing resistance and the potential fatality of typhoid fever treated with ineffective drugs, all isolates should be tested for antimicrobial susceptibility. Oral medication is preferred if the patient can swallow. Standard therapy for adults consists of ciprofloxacin 750 mg or ofloxacin 300 to 400 mg given twice daily for 7 to 10 days. Short course quinolone therapy has been effective but is currently not recommended.

Short-term, high-dose corticosteroid (usually dexamethasone) treatment reduces mortality and is routinely given to severely ill patients, particularly when there is CNS involvement. Supportive care should be provided according to the clinical picture.

Carriers often suffer from chronic cholecystitis, frequently with cholelithiasis. Cholecystectomy is usually indicated in these cases although the procedure does not always eradicate infection due to the intrahepatic location of the organisms. Oral quinolones have successfully eliminated carriage in over 75% of cases. Norfloxacin 400 mg b.i.d. or ciprofloxacin 750 mg for 28 days are the standard therapies for typhoid carriers.

Community Control Measures

Notification is mandatory in many countries. Quarantine is not required. Enteric precautions should be followed, and contacts exposed to carriers should be immunized. The source of infection and contacts (e.g., travel groups) should be actively sought out.

YELLOW FEVER

Infectious Agent

Yellow fever (YF) is an arboviral infection of the *Flaviviridae* family, genus *Flavivirus*.

Transmission

Yellow fever is transmitted primarily by the bite of the infected *Aedes aegypti* mosquito and in the forests of South America, mainly by mosquitoes of genus *Haemagogus* and *Sabethes*. Bites may occur throughout the day, with risk highest at sunrise and in late afternoon. These mosquitoes may be found at altitudes as high as 2500 m.

Global Epidemiology

There is both a sylvatic, jungle cycle involving mosquitoes and nonhuman primates and an urban cycle involving *Aedes aegypti* mosquitoes and humans. Urban and jungle YF occur only in parts of Africa and South America (Figures 51 and 52). There is no YF in Asia but the presence of *Aedes* causes concern that it may some day be imported. Jungle YF is an enzootic infection among nonhuman primates in South American forests, occasionally transmitted to humans between January and March. In Africa, transmission occurs during the late rainy and early dry season in savannah habitats. Epidemics may flare up after long intervals. Kenya, for example, was free of reported YF from 1942 to 1992 (see Figure 51). It is true, however, that there is much under-reporting, particularly of oligosymptomatic cases. The WHO estimates that 300,000 yellow fever infections cause 20,000 deaths annually but annually only 1439 cases with 89 to 491 deaths were notified to WHO in 1993 to 1997. The WHO Weekly Epidemiological Record regularly reports about the infected provinces and districts although virus activity may extend beyond officially reported infective zones.

Risk for Travelers

Compulsory or recommended vaccination makes cases of YF rare in travelers. There has been only one case of yellow fever, despite vaccination, in the past 20 years reported in a Spanish traveler. From 1979 to 1981, four unimmunized hunters and travelers, including one long-term resident, acquired YF in West Africa; three of them died. In 1996, an unimmunized

Figure 51   Yellow fever endemic zone in America

tourist from the United States and another from Switzerland acquired YF probably during an excursion in the Manaus region of Brazil. The absence of reported cases among the local population in an endemic area provides no assurance that YF will not be acquired by unimmunized travelers.

Clinical Picture

Severity varies from inapparent or flu-like symptoms to severe hepatitis and hemorrhagic fever. Onset is sudden with fever, headache, muscle pain, and vomiting, followed in 10 to 20% of

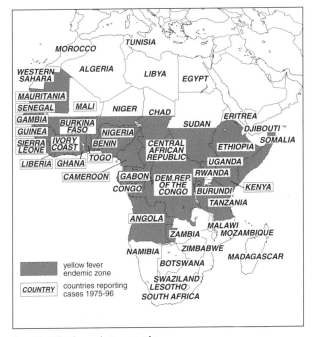

Figure 52   Yellow fever endemic zone in Africa

cases by worsening jaundice. Patients often show hemorrhagic symptoms and liver and renal failure after a very brief remission. The case fatality rate in jaundiced patients is 30 to 50%.

Incubation

The incubation period is 3 to 6 days.

Communicability

Yellow fever can be communicated from patients to mosquitoes for 5 days from shortly before the onset of fever. There is no communicability from person to person or through soiled articles.

Susceptibility/Resistance

Recovery from YF results in lasting immunity. Transient passive immunity occurs for up to 6 months in infants born to immune mothers.

Minimized Exposure in Travelers

Personal protection measures against mosquito bites should be employed throughout the day.

Chemoprophylaxis

None.

Immunoprophylaxis with Yellow Fever Vaccine

Immunology and Pharmacology
Viability: live, attenuated 17D (also known as Rockefeller, Asibi) strain, free of avian leukosis
  Antigenic form: whole virus, 1000 LD_{50} (mouse units)
  Adjuvants: none
  Preservative: only in neomycin and polymyxin

Allergens/Excipiens: residual egg protein. Yellow fever vaccine has more egg protein per dose than do other egg-cultured vaccines. USP requirement—must not contain human serum

Mechanism: induction of protective neutralizing antibodies

Application

Schedule: single injection (0.5 mL) at least 10 days before departure, in accordance with current IHR

Booster: every 10 years in accordance with current IHR. Every 15 years is sufficient for protection.

Route: SC

Site: arm preferably

Storage: depends on the vaccine. For some, -30 to $5°C$ (-22 to $41°F$), preferably $<0°C$ ($32°F$). For others such as Stamaril, 2 to $8°C$ (35 to $46°F$). Check with manufacturer's instructions. The vaccine should be used within 1 to 2 hours when reconstituted, depending on the product.

Availability: available worldwide as Arilvax (Evans, Medeva), Stamaril, Amaril, YF-Vax (Pasteur Mérieux Connaught)

Protection

Onset: 7 days, with an upper limit of 10 days set by current IHR

Efficacy: essentially 100%. There has been one case of YF in an allegedly immunized traveler from Spain.

Duration: 10 years according to IHR, >15 years effectively

Protective level: unknown

Adverse Reactions

Roughly 10% of recipients may experience fever or malaise following immunization, usually appearing 7 to 14 days after administration, with 0.2% being incapacitated. Anaphylaxis may occur. Encephalitis has developed in very young infants. This is usually not severe but deaths have been reported.

Contraindications

Absolute: history of hypersensitivity to vaccine, allergy to egg proteins

Relative: any acute illness, and below

Children: Do not administer to infants <6 (preferably <12) months unless travel to a high-risk area is unavoidable and the child is at risk of encephalitis.

Pregnant women: Avoid unless travel to a high-risk area is unavoidable. It is not known if yellow fever virus or corresponding antibodies cross the placenta. Generally, most IgG passage across the placenta occurs during the third trimester.

Lactating women: It is not known if yellow fever virus or corresponding antibodies are excreted in breast milk. Problems in humans have not been documented.

Immunodeficient persons: Do not use in immunodeficient persons, including persons with congenital or acquired immune deficiencies, whether these are due to genetics, disease, or drug or radiation therapy. The vaccine contains live viruses. Avoid use in asymptomatic HIV-positive persons unless the CD4 count is >400 and travel will be to a current endemic area. Note that poor antibody response has been documented in children infected with HIV. It is unknown whether this increases risk of contracting yellow fever.

Interactions

As with all live viral vaccines, administration to patients receiving immunosuppressant drugs, including steroids, or radiation may predispose patients to disseminated infections or provide insufficient response to immunization.

Concurrent parenteral cholera and yellow fever vaccination impairs the immune response to each vaccine but this probably has little clinical significance. These vaccinations should be separated by ≥3 weeks or administered on the same day if separation is not feasible (not required with other cholera vaccines). Concurrent vaccination against hepatitis B and yellow fever reduced the antibody titer expected from yellow fever vaccine in one study. Separate these vaccinations by 1 month if possible.

Yellow fever vaccination may lead to false positive HIV serologic tests when particularly sensitive assays (PERT, etc.)

are used. This is related to EAV-0, an avian retrovirus in residual egg proteins.

Vaccination Recommendations

Various countries require proof of yellow fever vaccination administered at an approved vaccination center and documented in the International Certificate of Vaccination (see Figure 11) as a condition of entry. While many countries require such proof only from travelers arriving from infected or potentially endemic areas, others require it from all travelers, sometimes from even those in transit. Documented yellow fever vaccination is valid for 10 years starting 10 days after vaccination.

Travelers with contraindications to yellow fever vaccination should obtain a waiver to the above requirements. Additional waivers of requirements obtained from embassies or consulates of the countries to be visited may be useful, as health authorities have occasionally refused medical waivers.

Whether required or not, this vaccination is recommended for all travel outside urban areas in yellow fever endemic zones (see Figure 51).

Self-Treatment Abroad

None.

Principles of Therapy

No specific treatment.

Community Control Measures

Case reporting is universally required by IHR. The patient should be isolated, and adequate blood and body fluid precautions followed. Contacts should receive immunization promptly, wherever there is mosquito activity.

PART 3

NONINFECTIOUS HEALTH RISKS
AND THEIR PREVENTION

ACCIDENTS

Risk Assessment for Travelers

Accident rates among World Bank consultants (see Figure 7) with varying degrees of experience in international travel demonstrate that inexperienced travelers are more at risk. Compared to their nontraveling counterparts, those with one trip had 1.8 more accidents, those with two to three had 1.76 more accidents, and those with 4 had 1.68 more. Inexperienced travelers are unaware of differences in infrastructure and customs, particularly in the developing countries, and are therefore more likely to encounter problems.

Motor Vehicle Injuries

Motor vehicle accidents are the leading cause of death from injury among travelers. Particularly high rates of traffic accidents are reported in many developing countries, as much as 20 times higher than in the developed nations, where the annual mortality rate per million cars varies: most northern European countries, Germany, Switzerland, Canada, Israel, and Japan with rates < 200, most other western European countries, Italy, and the U.S. with rates of 200 to 400, and most southern and eastern European countries with rates > 400 to as high as 700 deaths annually per million cars. Differences are attributable to the extent to which rules are observed, equipment is maintained, roads are under construction, and drivers avoid driving while intoxicated. The consequences of accidents stemming from the above causes are particularly serious in the developing countries. The lack of seat belts results in more serious injuries, poor infrastructure results in inadequate and delayed medical evacuation, and the limited capabilities of regional emergency medical services reduce the chances of survival and quick recovery.

Travelers who rent motorcycles or mopeds are particularly at risk. Among Peace Corps volunteers, 33% of all motor vehicle crash deaths resulted from this mode of transportation. Typical resort destinations such as Bermuda show an accident rate two to five times higher for this mode of transport among tourists older than 40 years, compared to locals of the same age group. At many destinations, helmets are not mandatory, which greatly increases the risk of serious head injury.

Surface Sport and Incidental Injuries

Travelers are frequently injured in sporting activities such as hiking or mountaineering. Senior travelers are prone to falling on hotel premises during the evening or at night because of impaired night vision and because they are in an unfamiliar environment. Balcony falls resulting in spinal cord injury repeatedly occur in countries where the minimum height for balcony guards is lower than at home. These accidents usually occur within the first few days of a vacation, and alcohol plays a part.

Water Sport Injuries

Water sports accidents are very common among travelers. Drowning is a frequent cause of death among travelers of all ages. Unknown currents are often responsible, for example, at Kuta Beach in Bali. Many adult drowning victims are under the influence of alcohol. Increased confidence, impaired risk awareness of hypothermia, hypoglycemia, nausea, and vomiting are associated with swimming while intoxicated. In the Dead Sea, serum electrolyte elevation has been associated with repeated near-drowning incidents, possibly due to the large solute load victims are exposed to.

Surfing has an injury rate of 3.5 per 1000 surfing days, mainly lacerations and soft-tissue injuries and occasionally back, shoulder, and head injuries. Lacerations from rocks, coral, glass, and metal are common in beach sports.

Criminal Injuries

Terrorism and assaults are epidemiologically of less concern than traffic and water sport accidents although the media attention given them is much greater. The terrorist attack against tourists in 1997 in Luxor, Egypt, with over 50 victims, reduced tourism in that country to virtually nil. Cheap packages may gradually bring tourists back after such incidents though the threat may still be there. Many countries now have warning systems in place against terrorist attacks.

▌ Minimized Exposure in Travelers

To avoid traffic accidents, the traveler should avoid the following:

- Moped or motorcycle rental. Helmet should be worn if activity undertaken
- Night-time off-road driving
- Excessive alcohol consumption
- Renting unsafe cars—worn tires, no seat belts, etc.
- Careless driving

  Travelers should use safety equipment, wherever available.

  Prevention of surface sport and incidental injuries varies with the sport. Senior travelers should familiarize themselves with the layout of their hotel or residence during the day, if possible.

  Swimmers must respect yellow or red flags on the beach indicating swimming is dangerous or not allowed. They should ask the local people about river or sea currents.

  To avoid assaults, it is wise to avoid walks or travel in unsafe areas alone at night. Traps such as offers to change money at attractive rates should be avoided. One should not wear expensive jewelry or show large amounts of money, and expatriates should not drive expensive cars or have a predictable routine.

ALTITUDE

Risk Assessment for Travelers

The partial pressure of oxygen decreases as a function of barometric pressure at high altitude, which can lead to hypoxia. The following conditions may be expected with increased altitude:

- High altitude, 1500 to 3500 m (4900 to 11,500 ft)—decreased exercise performance, increased ventilation
- Very high altitude, 3500 to 5500 m (11,500 to 18,000 ft)—hypoxia, altitude sickness
- Extreme altitude, >5500 m (18,000 ft)—severe hypoxia, hypocapnia, progressive deterioration

High and especially very high altitude may lead to acute mountain sickness or its complications (Figure 53). There are individual differences in susceptibility. Those without acclimatization, younger people, and those living at low altitudes are at greatest risk.

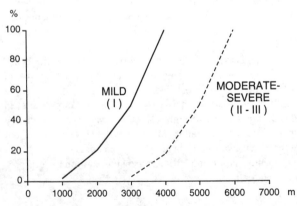

Figure 53 Incidence of acute mountain sickness

█ Clinical Picture

Acute hypoxia sets in after a rapid ascent or accidental decompression in an aircraft. Victims become dizzy, faint, and may become unconscious unless oxygen is given.

Acute mountain sickness (AMS) may develop within 1 to 6 hours of being at high altitudes. It is characterized by bifrontal headache followed by anorexia, nausea and vomiting, and insomnia accompanied by fatigue and lassitude. Patients are often irritable and wish to be left alone. Acute mountain sickness closely resembles an alcohol hangover.

Periodic sleep breathing with apneic phases sometimes exceeding 10 seconds may occur but this is not associated with the severity of AMS.

Life-threatening complications of AMS include high altitude pulmonary edema, cerebral, peripheral, and retinal edema, and thromboembolic problems. Stupor, coma, and death may occur within 8 to 24 hours after the onset of ataxia and changes in mental status.

█ Minimized Exposure in Travelers

Travelers must be made aware of the problems that may be associated with ascent to high altitudes. They should know that AMS may occur and that this may cause complications requiring immediate measures, particularly rapid descent.

Acclimatization for two to three nights at 2500 to 3000 m (8000 to 10,000 ft) helps prevent AMS. One should avoid flying or driving directly to higher altitudes. If this is impossible (e.g., flight to La Paz), overexertion, large meals, and alcohol should be avoided. The ideal rate of ascent varies with the individual.

Vacationers often claim a lack of time for acclimatization. It may be better to limit one's ambitions in such circumstances.

Chemoprophylaxis

Acetazolamide is indicated for those with a past history of AMS and for those anticipating a sudden ascent to >3000 m (10,000 ft). The usual adult dosage is 500 mg extended release per 24 hours (or 5 mg/kg/d in two to three doses) commencing 24 hours before the ascent and continuing for the first 2 days at altitude. Prophylaxis can then be discontinued but therapy with the same agent may be undertaken if symptoms develop. The effectiveness of such prophylaxis in reducing the symptoms of AMS is 75%. Side-effects include tingling in the fingertips, increased urination, and the sensation that carbonated beverages taste flat. Vomiting, drowsiness, and itching occasionally occur.

Acetazolamide is a sulfa drug. Those allergic to this group of drugs may take 4 mg of dexamethasone every 12 hours starting the first day of ascent and continuing for the first 2 days at altitude. Stomach upset may result.

High altitude headaches may be treated with 320 mg of aspirin every 4 hours.

Nifedipine may be considered for persons with a previous history of AMS who have not responded to other agents.

Management Abroad

Headache, the most frequent symptom of mild AMS, may be treated with mild analgesics (aspirin, acetaminophen with or without codeine) but these may be ineffective in moderate AMS. Nausea and vomiting are best treated with prochlorperazine, 5 to 10 mg IM, as this also augments the hypoxic ventilatory response. Short-acting benzodiazepines may be used to prevent frequent wakening but only in healthy subjects as they may cause respiratory depression and decrease oxygenation.

The therapeutic steps indicated in the various stages of AMS and its complications are shown in Table 27. The crucial first step is prompt descent.

Table 27 Management of acute mountain sickness (AMS) and its complications

Mild AMS (headache, nausea, some vomiting, slight breathlessness, insomnia)

    Analgesics: Aspirin® 650 mg or acetaminophen 500-1000 mg, possibly with codein

    Antiemetic: Perchlorperazin 5–10 mg IM (augments also hypoxic ventilatory response)

    Against frequent wakening: Triazolam 0.25 mg or temazepam 15 mg or other short act-
        ing benzodiazepine; not to be used in more severe AMS because of respiratory
        depression

    Acclimatisation can be improved by acetazolamide 125–250 mg twice daily

    Stop ascent, or descend if easily possible

Moderate AMS (headache resistent to analgesics as above, vomiting, dyspnea, lassitude to
the extent of the patient requiring assistance)

    Immediate descent

    Low flow oxygen if available

    Acetazolamide 125-250 mg twice daily

    Dexamethasone 4 mg every 6 hours PO, IM, or IV

    Hyperbaric therapy

Severe AMS with cerebral or pulmonary edema: early recognition is paramount!

    Evacuation or at least immediate descent

    Minimize exertion, keep warm

    Oxygen 2–4 L/min.

    Dexamethasone 8 mg, then 4 mg every 6 hours PO, IM, or IV

    Nifedipine 10 mg PO in pulmonary edema, or 30 mg every 6 hours if no oxygen or
        descent possible

    Furosemide 20–40 mg every 12 hours (potential hypovolemia, incapacitation!)

    Hyperbaric therapy if descent is impossible

ANIMAL BITES AND STINGS

Risk Assessment for Travelers

The incidence of animal bites in human travelers is unknown. Several thousand people are killed annually by mammalian bites and roughly 60,000 by snake bites. Up to 70 shark attacks occur every year in coastal areas. Destination and activity determine the nature of the bite or sting. In addition to mainly soft tissue injuries, bites and stings may transmit infectious diseases, including vectorborne diseases. The bites from venomous animals can be life threatening, and such species are found in most climates and natural settings.

While the risk of being seriously injured by native wildlife is low, the probability of a vacation being ruined by mosquitoes, fleas, ticks, bees, or wasps is high. Awareness, protective clothing, and insect repellents should always be used (see Part 1), and those with a history of allergic reactions should carry their emergency adrenaline syringe. Local information and advice concerning wildlife in the area should always be taken seriously.

Snakes

Venomous snake bite occurrence is highest where dense human and venomous snake populations coexist. This is the case in Southeast Asia, sub-Saharan Africa, and the tropical parts of the Americas. Snakebites are a negligible hazard for tourists engaged in sightseeing or recreation. The risk for those involved in agriculture, engineering projects, or scientific or humanitarian fieldwork is higher but still small.

Scorpions and Spiders

Scorpions are widespread and found in tropic, subtropic, and desert areas. Scorpion bites are a public health concern; mortality is caused mainly by lack of available intensive care support and antivenom.

Spider species have a fairly well-defined geographic distribution although some, such as the black widow, are cosmopolitan. Spiders such as the brown recluse or black widow spiders are not naturally aggressive toward humans and bite only when threatened or trapped. In contrast, the funnel-web spiders of Australia are aggressive and armed with potent venom, making them the most dangerous spiders in the world.

Aquatic Animals

Marine creatures hazardous to humans are found predominantly in tropical oceans. They may envenomate, bite, or puncture.

The coelenterates are a diverse group of invertebrates, including fire corals, jellyfish, and sea anemones which are venomous and potentially dangerous to humans. Severity of envenomation is related to species and season, amount of venom released, and size and age of the victim. Minor contact manifests itself as seabather's eruption ("swimmer's itch" or "sea lice"), a dermatitis caused by jellyfish larvae mainly in the Caribbean. The box jellyfish, found in the shallow waters off Australia's northern coast, is reputed to be the most venomous sea creature, with death occurring within 2 minutes of the sting.

The risk of shark attack is small, provided a discreet distance is kept and waters known to be frequented by sharks are avoided.

▌ Clinical Picture

Mammalian Bites

Tearing, cutting, and crushing injuries may occur in animal bites. Considering the power and weight of many animals, internal organ damage, deep arterial and nerve damage, or multiple fractures are possible, if attacked. Therefore, a complete evaluation is advised in all but the most trivial and isolated of bite injuries.

Snake Bites

Many snakes are not venomous, and even venomous snakes often do not inject venom when they bite. The complexity and diversity of snake venoms are reflected in the wide range of signs and symptoms. The venom's multiple protein and peptide biotoxins produce diverse pathophysiologic effects in humans, such as local tissue and microvascular damage leading to tissue necrosis and hemorrhage. The components best understood are the neurotoxins, found in most elapid and sea snake venoms. These may induce paresthesias, weakness, and paralysis, including that of the respiratory muscles. Venom contacting the eyes from any of the spitting cobras does not produce systemic symptoms but severe eye damage, including blindness, may follow, if untreated. Nearly all snake venoms affect blood coagulation which can result in hemorrhage with hemodynamic consequences. Coagulopathy is a characteristic finding after snake envenomation. Myotoxins cause muscle damage with outpouring of potassium and myoglobin, followed by severe renal and cardiac problems.

Scorpions and Spiders

Scorpion venom is most often a neurotoxin, causing local pain and paresthesia and occasionally somatic skeletal neuromuscular dysfunction and seizures. Other complications include nausea, vomiting, hypertension, tachycardia, and respiratory distress.

Spider venom often serves as a digestive juice, containing a variety of proteolytic substances and often a neurotoxic component to immobilize the victim. In humans, the latter causes severe pain, muscle spasm with nerve dysfunction or hemolysis, and cell necrosis, depending on the species. Spiders such as tarantulas may cause severe irritation of the human skin by hair containing toxins.

Aquatic Animals

Jellyfish envenomation results primarily in skin irritations. There is an immediate stinging sensation accompanied by pain, pruritus, and paresthesia with visible "tentacle prints." These symptoms may progress over several days to local necrosis, ulceration, and secondary infection compounded in severe cases by systemic reactions, including neurologic, cardiovascular, respiratory, and anaphylactic disorders. These may be life threatening for the victim.

Sea urchins or star fish cause immediate pain with edema and possible systemic reactions due to their venom. The embedded spines are difficult to extract and frequently cause secondary infection. Stings by poisonous fish, such as lion fish, scorpion fish, stone fish, or sting rays may cause a variety of severe systemic disorders and even death.

Minimized Exposure in Travelers

Travelers should be made aware of the dangers posed by the local fauna.

Mammalian Bites

Animals rarely attack people without provocation, with the exception of some large carnivores and animals infected by rabies. Restrained or captured animals should be considered high risk. Most wild animals have a strong sense of territoriality, and intrusion can trigger an attack, particularly when the nest or the young are being protected.

Eye contact with dogs should be avoided as it will be interpreted as a threat or challenge. Running away often provokes a chase. When a dog is about to attack, the best reaction is to freeze and turn sideways, leaning away from the dog.

Animal attack is often best avoided by avoiding contact. Entering bear country, one should make enough noise to let the bear know a person is present; constant conversation along the trail is usually sufficient. If fresh signs are seen, the bear may be in the vicinity. Hikers are advised to take an alternative route.

Snake Bites

Snakes are generally afraid of humans, and if given the opportunity, will quickly retreat. Unless confronted at very close range, snakes are unlikely to strike. However, one should avoid known snake habitats, which are generally areas where they seek protection. Hands or feet should not be placed where snakes may be hiding (cracks in rock, etc.) and it is better not to sit on logs or rock piles that may be harboring a snake. Hikers should stay on paths and, if entering an overgrown area, should check questionable obstacles with a stick before proceeding. Adequate protective clothing, especially leather boots and long trousers, should be worn. Extra caution is necessary at night, when most venomous snakes are active.

Scorpions and Spiders

Scorpions and spiders are usually nocturnal and are more active during the warmer season. They hide under rocks, wood, leaves, and clothing, and in holes, corners, shoes, and closets. Clothing, shoes, and camping gear should be carefully checked before being worn. Adequate footwear is important.

Aquatic Animals

Aside from wearing protective clothing such as a "stinger suit" and using a mask or goggles, there is little the swimmers can do to protect themselves from jellyfish stings. If jellyfish are sighted, the swimmer should stay at a distance as the tentacles trail. Even dead jellyfish on the beach can inflict serious stings. Advice from local authorities should always be followed. Partial prophylaxis of seabather's eruption may be provided by washing with soap and water after swimming. Footgear should be worn when walking in shallow waters, especially near tropical reefs. It is wise to shuffle in sandy areas known to be frequented by stingrays to frighten them off. Divers should educate themselves on appropriate behavior toward dangerous or unknown sea creatures. Fingers should not be placed in holes or cracks where sea animals may reside.

▌ Chemoprophylaxis

None.

▌ Management Abroad

The local health professionals are usually experienced with regional animal bites and wounds and should be consulted immediately. It should be noted that some therapies, for instance against jellyfish, may be successful in one place but not in another.

Mammalian Bites

Local treatment of wounds should be initiated immediately (see "Rabies," Part 2). Early cleansing reduces the risk of bacterial infection and effectively kills rabies and other pathogenic agents. The patient should be moved to a hospital as soon as possible where further treatment, including tetanus prophylaxis, can be administered.

Snake Bites

Although snake venom poisoning is a medical emergency, panic with its additional stress reaction must be avoided. The victim should retreat from the snake's range, which is approximately the length of the snake. Killing the snake can be dangerous and may produce another victim. Even the decapitated head of a snake can bite with envenomation for up to 60 minutes.

The bitten extremity should be immobilized to diminish local tissue necrosis and delay systemic absorption of the venom. Physical activity should be reduced to a minimum for the same reason. If prolonged evacuation time is expected, a pressure bandage may be applied to the bitten extremity to occlude lymphatic and venous but not arterial circulation. Medical assistance should be obtained as quickly as possible, which may require transporting the victim on an improvised stretcher. The solitary victim should walk slowly with periodic resting. To maintain renal flow and control intravascular volume, frequent drinking of at least 2 liters of water per 24 hours is recommended. Neither a tourniquet nor incisions in the wound are effective and may result in various complications with no proven benefit. Suction devices to extract venom from the wound cause additional trauma and are not recommended. The use of antivenom in the field should be avoided due to the potential risk of anaphylactic reactions. Antivenom treatment should only be administered in a professional setting.

Scorpions and Spiders

Treatment in the field is supportive. Local pain can be controlled with ice applied for 30 minutes every hour with cloth between the ice and skin. Oral analgesics are useful. The victim should be taken to a medical facility as soon as possible for treatment, especially if symptoms worsen. Antivenom administration is controversial as it is incomplete and can cause allergic reactions.

In the case of a venomous spider bite, the affected limb may be immobilized and pressure wrapped to minimize lymphatic return before adequate medical treatment is received. Within intensive care facilities, victims often can be treated symptomatically. Antivenom may be applied, depending on the spider species and the severity of clinical signs.

Aquatic Animals (Table 28)

Persons stung by jellyfish should leave the water, and the affected skin should be immediately rinsed with *sea* water, not fresh water. A vinegar solution or alcohol (40 to 70%) should then be continuously applied for 30 minutes to inactivate the toxin, which will in most cases relieve the pain. Remaining tentacles should then be scraped from the skin. Local anesthetics may be used but systemic signs are best managed by the nearest medical facility. Antivenom should be administered as soon as possible following envenomation by the box jellyfish.

Table 28 Treatment after injuries due to marine hazards

Hazard	Measures (sequential)
Sponges	Gently dry skin / remove spicules with adhesive tape / vinegar
Coelenterates	Remove cysts by rinsing with sea water (early fresh water would increase envenomation!) / forceful streat of fresh water to dislodge tentacles / remove tentacles with forceps / vinegar or baking soda if unavailable / close observation of children and elderly
Seabather's eruption	Soap and water scrub / papain, powdered or dissolved / for pruritus eruption clamine lotion with 1% menthol
Sea urchins	Nonscalding hot water / remove pedicellariae by applying shaving foam, gentle razor scraping / remove spines if possible, they often brake
Starfish	Nonscalding hot water / remove foreign material /irrigate wound
Bristleworms	Remove spines: dry skin / adhesive tape or facial peel
Cone shells	Pressure immobilization
Octopus	Pressure immobilization
Stingrays	Irrigate with sea water / remove foreign material / nonscalding hot water / anesthetics, surgery often needed / prophylactic antibiotics
Scorpionfish, Lionfish and Stonefish	Nonscalding hot water / debridement / anesthetic / antibiotics
Sea Snakes	Similar to terrestrial snakes: immobilization, etc.

DETAILS:

- vinegar/5% acetic acid: apply for 10–30 minutes four times per day
- nonscalding hot water: up to 45°C or 113oF for 30–90 minutes
- antibiotics: third generation cephalosporins, ciprofloxacin, aminoglycoside, co-trimoxazole

(adapted from Klein JR, Auerbach PS, Textbook of Travel Medicine and Health, 2nd edition, Decker Inc., in press)

The wound from a sea urchin, stingray, or stone fish sting should be soaked in nonscalding hot water (45°C or 113°F) as soon as possible for 30 to 90 minutes to attenuate the thermolabile components of the venom. Surgical exploration is required to remove remaining spines, and systemic symptoms must be treated appropriately. Stonefish antivenom is recommended for serious stings from stone fish or other species of scorpion fish.

Treatment of sea snake bites is similar to that for terrestrial snake bites. Polyvalent or specific sea snake antivenom is available.

DERMATOLOGIC PROBLEMS

Risk Assessment for Travelers and Clinical Picture

Exposure to light may induce photoallergic and phototoxic reactions, polymorphous light eruption, persistent light reaction, hydroa vacciniforme, solar urticaria, actinic reticuloid, or phytophotodermatitis.

Phototoxic Reactions

Phototoxic dermatitis occurs when drug use and sun exposure are combined. The drug molecules absorb energy, which is transmitted to tissue and alters the skin. Phototoxic dermatitis occurs on skin exposed to the sun. Unlike photoallergic dermatitis prior sensitation is not required. Phototoxic dermatitis can occur in any individual, depending on exposure to sunlight and the dose of medication taken. Symptoms are a sunburn type of reaction with erythema in the areas exposed to the sun. Erythema occurs in 5 to 20 hours and worsens within 48 to 96 hours. Sunburn may persist in a netted pattern, that is erythematous and tinged with blue. Nails may also be involved (photo-onycholysis). Drugs most frequently causing phototoxic reactions include tetracycline, sulfonamides, phenothiazines, NSAR, amiodarone, captopril, furosemide, and psoralens.

Phototoxic contact reactions are primarily due to topical agents found in plants such as lime, orange, celery, parsnip, fig, and anise, and in fragrances containing bergamot oil. Furocoumarins in plants may cause erythema, blistering, or bullae on exposed areas (phytophotodermatitits or dermatitis bullosa striata pratensis). Coal tar may cause phototoxic dermatitis with residual hyperpigmentation. Some drugs can provoke both phototoxic and photoallergic reaction, which raises confusion in the use of these terms; "photosensitive" is a more appropriate generic term.

Photoallergic Dermatitis

Photoallergic dermatitis is an eczematous skin reaction caused by concurrent use of a photosensitizing substance and exposure to sunlight. Drugs inducing photoallergy include chloroquine, chlorthiazides, carbamazepine, tolbutamide, chlorpromazine, promazine, amitriptyline, chlorthalidone, indomethacin, piroxicam, and many others. Topical inducers of photoallergy are bithionol, sulfathiazole, salicylanilides, carbanilides, and hexachlorophene.

Clinical symptoms are similar to those of contact dermatitis. Papulovesicular eczematous or exudative dermatitis occurs within 24 to 48 hours, mostly on areas exposed to the sun but also elsewhere on the body.

Polymorph Light Eruption

Polymorph light eruption (PLE) or "sun allergy" occurs mainly when unadapted skin is exposed to strong sunlight. The term PLE describes a group of heterogenous, idiopathic, acquired photodermatoses. They are characterized by delayed abnormal reaction to ultraviolet radiation. Skin lesions which may appear include erythematous macules, papules, plaques, and vesicles, each of which is monomorphous.

See below for sunburn and tumors following chronic UVB exposure.

Dermatologic Side Effects of Prophylactic Medication

Malaria chemoprophylaxis may result in cutaneous adverse reactions, the most severe being erythma multiforme, Stevens-Johnson syndrome, and toxic epidermal necrolysis reported mainly after use of the sulfadoxine-pyrimethamine combination drug Fansidar®. The incidence rate ranges from 1 in 5000 to 1 in 80,000. Chloroquine and mefloquine are also associated with severe cutaneous adverse reactions.

The antibiotics recommended for prophylaxis of traveler's diarrhea, such as sulfamethoxazole, trimethoprim, doxycycline, or quinolones, may also cause adverse dermatologic reactions.

Minimized Exposure in Travelers

Agents used in malaria chemoprophylaxis initiated 1 week prior to departure may be altered should adverse events occur. Travelers should be instructed to contact a doctor abroad should moderate to severe skin reactions occur.

Travelers to the tropics should avoid excessive exposure to the sun. Persons prone to phototoxic or photoallergic reactions should avoid any type of ultraviolet light irradiation and agents which have previously caused phototoxic or photoallergic reactions.

Frostbite is best avoided by wearing warm dry clothing and avoiding smoking and consumption of alcohol as this may result in vasoconstriction and vasodilatation.

Skin infection in tropical climates can be avoided by frequent showers, and wearing cotton clothing. Persons with hyperhydrosis should use baby powder.

Herpes infection is best prevented by applying sunscreens with high sun protection factor (SPF) of at least 20. Kissing people with herpes labialis should be avoided.

Fungus infection of the feet may be avoided by wearing sandals, which helps keep feet dry and clean.

Chemoprophylaxis

Several reports indicate chloroquine, 200 mg base daily, may be partially effective in preventing polymorphous light eruption. Canthaxanthine, a betacarotene, may be of value for patients with abnormal reaction to UVA and visible light (PLE, erythropoietic protoporphyria) however this agent may cause retinal deposits. Antimalarials and carotenes do not protect against sunburn as their spectrum of absorption is not within the UVB zone.

Management Abroad

Phototoxic reactions are treated by stopping the drug and avoiding sunlight, and applying therapy similar to that used in sunburn.

Travelers should be aware that wounds tend to become severely infected in a warm and humid climate. Disinfection and regular wound dressing are essential.

DIVING

Risk Assessment for Travelers

Scuba diving accidents are described in the specialized literature. The main risks involved are decompression sickness, air embolism, panic, and disorientation (e.g., in caves). Despite the large number of scuba divers, fatal incidents are comparatively rare due to the rigorous training courses and regulations implemented worldwide by various international organizations.

Divers frequently experience sinus problems and external otitis following repeated dives. Diving without equipment may be risky as previous hyperventilation can reduce blood carbon dioxide levels, causing diminished breathing stimulus, hypoxia, and unconsciousness. The low partial pressure of the diver's remaining oxygen may fall below a critical point upon surfacing, which may lead to unconsciousness and drowning.

Snorkeling poses few risks except for lacerations and serious sunburn. Snorkeling at depths greater than 50 cm may lead to pulmonary edema.

Clinical Picture

Decompression sickness occurs when a diver surfaces too quickly, causing gases in the blood that would normally be excreted through the lungs to effervesce. This may lead to a wide range of clinical conditions. Decompression problems must be considered in any presenting symptoms after a dive.

Barotrauma may occur when the compression on gases in the middle ear, paranasal sinuses, and teeth, cannot be properly equalized. Even a slight imbalance may result in alternobaric vertigo in a diver, which can be particularly problematic if the water is turbid or dark.

The risk of hypothermia is often underestimated during and following a dive. It is not only uncomfortable but can cause colds and their complications.

Minimized Problems in Travelers

The basic rules of diving safety formulated by various international scuba diving organizations (e.g., PADI, DAN) must be strictly adhered to. Abstinence from alcohol and drugs is essential. The risk of external otitis may be reduced by rinsing the external ear canal with clean water following a dive. (See also Part 1.)

Chemoprophylaxis

There is no official chemoprophylaxis. Some divers use pseudoephedrine HCl, two 3-mg tablets, 30 minutes before a dive to facilitate pressure equalization although there is some concern about reverse blockage. Contraindications include hypertension, heart disease, diabetes, and thyroid disease. There may be some side effects such as dizziness or nervousness.

Management Abroad

Follow the advice of the local emergency service. For serious problems contact the Divers Alert Network (DAN) +1-919-684-8111, or through the website: http://jshaldane.mc.duke.edu

ENVIRONMENT

Risk Assessment for Travelers and Clinical Picture

Changes in climate can cause diseases and other problems directly or indirectly.

Excessive heat and humidity alone or combined with inappropriate activities under such conditions may lead to heat exhaustion due to salt and water losses. Heat stroke and hyperthermia may result. Morbidity and mortality from cardiovascular (including cerebrovascular) accidents are clearly increased after sudden and prolonged exposure to heat. Excessive cold may cause hypothermia, possibly followed by the common cold and its complications, or frostbite.

Food and beverages abroad may harbor pathogenic agents. Food may also be more spicy and cause gastric irritation or gastritis. Fish may contain toxins that are not eliminated by cooking or cleaning.

Dusty roads may increase susceptibility to upper respiratory tract infections, as is frequently observed among travelers in China. Excessive smog, which is often encountered in large cities in the developing countries (e.g., Mexico City, large centers in Southeast Asia) may cause substantial discomfort. Travel on rough roads may aggravate back pain.

Minimized Exposure in Travelers

Acclimatization and avoiding exertion for the first few days in an unfamiliar climate lessens the risk of environmentally induced problems.

Chemoprophylaxis

None.

JET LAG

Jet-lag occurs when long flights across several time zones result in dissociation between environmental time cues and the body's internal clock.

Risk Assessment for Travelers

The severity of the symptoms depends on the number of time zones crossed and individual characteristics such as age, rhythm sensitivity, and motivation. Since the human circadian period is longer than 24 hours (approximately 24.3 hours) in dark isolation, it is easier to adapt to westbound travel by lengthening the period of endogenous rhythms. As many as 94% of long-distance travelers suffer from jet lag, and 45% consider their symptoms severely bothersome. Jet lag and the resulting impairment of physical and mental performance may have serious consequences especially for pilots, business people, athletes, and military personnel. Studies in pilots have shown performance efficiency to decrease by 8.5% after an eastbound flight across eight time zones. Athletes may experience changes in their performance rhythm, and anaerobic power and dynamic strength may be affected for 3 to 4 days.

Clinical Picture

Jet lag is characterized by sleep disturbances, daytime fatigue, reduced mental and physical performance, gastrointestinal problems, and generalized malaise.

Without specific jet lag countermeasures, it takes 4 to 6 days after a transmeridian flight to establish a normal sleep pattern and approximately 4 days until subjects do not feel tired during the day. The resynchronization of endogenous circadian rhythms takes much longer. With a time change of 8 hours, it can take up to 15 days after an eastbound flight and up to 12 days after a westbound flight for complete readjustment.

▌ Nonpharmacologic Measures to Minimize Symptoms

To minimize the effects of jet lag, various nonpharmacological countermeasures have been proposed although only a few of them have been scientifically validated.

Short naps under 4 hours may help compensate for sleep loss and are especially useful for air crew.

The use of timed bright light is a very promising method since the light-dark cycle is the most important factor controlling the body clock. Bright light in the early morning (5 to 11 AM) causes a phase advance in body rhythms while it causes a phase delay in body rhythms in late evening (10 PM to 4 AM). Although under laboratory conditions light is very effective in phase shifting, it is not practical after a transmeridian flight as portable light sources are generally cumbersome and natural light conditions are difficult to control. However, as a supplement to other jet lag treatments (e.g., melatonin) seeking or avoiding light at specific times after an intercontinental flight may help minimize jet lag symptoms. After crossing up to nine time zones in a westward direction self-adjustment to the new light-dark cycle is sufficient. While morning light should be avoided after eastbound flights, evening light should be avoided after trips crossing more than nine time zones in either direction.

Jet lag diets have been proposed based on the fact that carbohydrates induce sleep by facilitating serotonin synthesis and proteins promote alertness by stimulating the synthesis of catecholamines. The effectiveness of this diet is controversial and it seems likely that it is the exact timing of the meals rather than their composition that hastens resynchronization.

Exercise has been shown to be effective in phase-shifting and synchronizing circadian rhythms in rodents. Preliminary studies in humans support the hypothesis that increased physical activity during the habitual rest period alters body rhythms. Since little is known about optimum time and amount of exercise required to counteract jet lag, no specific recommendations can be made.

The following behavioral recommendations may be helpful:

- Get a good night's sleep before the trip.
- Try to sleep at night, during the flight. When the day is much prolonged by westbound flight, try to nap.
- Adopt local time and routines immediately upon arrival (e.g., timing of meals, going to bed).
- Allow plenty of time to sleep and rest in your new location before commencing work or touring activities.

Pharmacologic Prophylaxis and Treatment

Pharmacologic treatment of jet lag symptoms attempts to enhance alertness, promote sleep, and resynchronize the body's clock.

Caffeine is often used to improve alertness and delay the onset of sleep. Amphetamines, with their potentially severe side effects and potential for abuse, are unsuitable for routine use. Modafinil, an O-receptor-agonist, is a new alternative that is as effective as amphetamines in enhancing alertness but causes no impairment of sleep and virtually no side effects. Little is known, however, about chronic use and tolerance of alertness-enhancing drugs and further investigation is required to optimize the dosage regimen.

Short-acting benzodiazepines such as temazepam, triazolam, and lorazepam have been used to minimize sleep loss after transmeridian flights. While they have been effective in reducing sleep problems, there are concerns about their safety. Several studies have reported residual effects, and amnesia may occur. Use of these sleep aids must therefore be carefully considered for those who will be performing complex psychomotor or intellectual tasks the next day (e.g., pilots). Zolpidem, an imidazopyridine, has been suggested to combat insomnia associated with jet lag since it has a short half-life (2.5 hours), no active metabolites, and no residual effects. Amnesia, however, has been reported, particularly with concurrent alcohol abuse.

Timed administration of melatonin is the most promising method of alleviating jet lag. Melatonin is a pineal hormone produced mainly during the dark phase of the day. The presence of specific melatonin receptors in the suprachiasmatic nucleus, where the body clock is located, indicates that melatonin directly modulates the circadian clock. Exogenous melatonin can shift the endogenous circadian system according to a phase-response curve; melatonin given in the afternoon advances the body clock, and melatonin administered in the early morning delays the circadian system. These phase-shifting properties combined with a direct soporific effect make for an effective treatment of jet lag. Irrespective of flight direction, 3 to 5 mg of melatonin should be taken at bedtime (local time), starting the first evening after arrival and continuing for 4 to 6 days. When taken at bedtime, users may benefit additionally from the drug's sleep-inducing properties. When traveling on an eastbound night flight, one dose of melatonin may be taken during the late afternoon to advance the biologic clock and facilitate sleep during the flight. This may, however, reduce alertness prior to the flight, for instance while driving to the airport. For westbound flights, no preflight or in-flight dose is recommended.

MOTION SICKNESS

Risk Assessment for Travelers

Motion sickness (kinetosis) may be experienced in all modes of transportation. It may result from the disruption of the harmony of the balance system's sensors, the price paid for traveling faster than the evolutionary process has equipped us for. It arises from a variety of physical stimuli, mainly changes in acceleration patterns. There is no unanimity on the pathophysiologic origins of motion sickness.

Everyone may suffer from motion sickness of varying degrees. Motion sickness is rare before the age of 2 years and the maximum incidence rate is reached by the age of 12 years. It then declines and by the age of 50 years is rare, at least in commercial aviation. This is explained by a decrease in vestibular afferent information with age. Women are three times more susceptible than men, with the highest risk from 3 days before to 5 days after the onset of menstruation. Predisposing factors are fatigue, alcohol, a variety of drugs, history of migraine, bad odors (e.g., vomit), and emotional condition, with anxiety leading to a higher risk especially in air travel. Acclimatization, as for example in crew members, reduces the tendency to motion sickness but self-selection may also play a role.

Clinical Picture

Symptoms range from mild discomfort to incapacitation, commencing with gasping, drowsiness, lassitude, and inactivity. In moderate forms, malaise, pallor, cold sweats, abdominal discomfort, and nausea are experienced. Cardiovascular symptoms (variations in pulse rate, rise or fall of blood pressure, change in peripheral blood flow) and respiratory symptoms (increased ventilation, shallow breathing, sighing, yawning) may occur as well as a variety of sensations, feelings, and performance changes. Severe forms are characterized by vomiting, which may lead to dehydration. Death occasionally follows.

Minimized Exposure in Travelers

There are many questions surrounding the prevention and treatment of motion sickness. Unanimity exists that there is some adaptation in most passengers during prolonged rough sea conditions. There seems to be no association between sea-sickness and the deck a cabin is located on or whether it has a porthole. The front seat of a car or a seat over the wing in a plane are more stable and therefore reduce risk of motion sickness. Various strategies of questionable benefit have been recommended. These include

- continued visual orientation with the horizon;
- keeping the eyes closed;
- lying down or reclining;
- restricting head and neck movements;
- easing pressure on the neck and abdomen by undoing buttons or belts.

The effectiveness of various traditional methods has never been scientifically demonstrated, such as carrying a horse-chestnut in the left pocket or fixed on a necklace, plugging a piece of cotton into the right ear canal or, if left handed, vice versa, wrist bracelets, and a variety of diets and beverages, including drinking or abstaining from alcohol.

Chemoprophylaxis

Many different agents have been used to prevent motion sickness. All have a limited effectiveness and some side effects, mainly tiredness, sleepiness, dizziness, or dryness in the mouth. Scopolamine has been associated with visual problems, particularly problems in accommodation resulting in falls, par-

Table 29 Chemoprophylactic options against motion sickness

Drugs to be Taken 2 Hours before Exposure	Adult Dose, mg	Common Trade Names	Duration, Hours
Cinnarizine+Domperidon	20 + 15	Touristil	4
Cyclizine	50	Marzine	6-12
Dimenhydrinate	50	Dramamine	8
Dimenhydrinate+Caffeine	50 + 50	Dramamine comp.	8
Ginger root	250	Zintona	4
Meclozine+Caffeine	12.5 + 10	Peremesin	8-12
Phenytoin (rapid onset of efficacy: 15 minutes)	300–1200	Many	24
Promethazine		Phenergan	
theoclate	25		24
hydrochloride	25		18
Drugs to be Taken Longer before Exposure			
Cinnarizine (take 4 hr before)	25 (–150)	Stugeron, Stutgeron	8
Scopolamine (apply 6–8 hr before)	0.5 (patch)	Scopoderm TTS	72

ticularly when the agent contacts the eyes. The effectiveness of commonly prescribed agents does not vary significantly (Table 29) and those which have previously worked for the individual should be recommended.

Management Abroad

Chewing gums containing dimenhydrinate (10 or 20 mg) may bring quick relief in mild cases. For severe cases, a 50 mg injection of promethazine should be considered. Prophylaxis is preferred for those prone to motion sickness.

POISONING

Risk Assessment for Travelers and Clinical Picture

Drug Intoxication

Accidents are common when drug runners smuggle illicit drugs in condoms or plastic containers which they swallow or insert into the rectum or vagina. Condoms may get stuck in the esophagus and lead to obstruction. If such a container leaks or breaks the contents are easily absorbed by the mucosa which, in the case of heroin, results in altered consciousness, myosis, vomiting, constipation, and sphincteric spasms in the bladder and pylorus. Respiratory depression may cause death. Cocaine, which is highly toxic, is rapidly hydrolyzed in the gastrointestinal tract. While the rupture of balloons containing hashish oil or marijuana have resulted in severe intoxication, fatalities have not been recorded.

Fish Poisoning

Various fish carry a variety of toxins. Scombroid is common and occurs worldwide. Fish rich in dark meat, most often mackerel, tuna, mahi-mahi, skipjack, sardines, and anchovies, may cause scombroid poisoning when preserved at temperatures above 15°C. Histidine in the flesh of scombroid fish can then be transformed to histamine by bacteria. Histamine, not destroyed by cooking, and possibly other unidentified factors cause a syndrome resembling an acute allergic reaction within 10 to 90 minutes of ingestion. Flushing, headache, pruritus, urticaria, nausea, diarrhea, occasionally bronchospasm, tachycardia, and hypotension occur. These symptoms usually resolve, even untreated, within 12 hours, and death is uncommon. Sensitization does not occur, and victims may consume the same type of fish later with no ill effect.

Ciguatera is common but limited to coral reef fish such as barracuda, grouper, sea bass, snapper, and jack. The attack rate in the Caribbean has been estimated to be 0.3%, which is similar to that for hepatitis A. Ciguatoxin and various other toxins involved in ciguatera poisoning are produced by sporadic reef algae, which are consumed by herbivorous fish, which are eaten by the carnivorous fish listed above. The toxin accumulates mainly in the viscera and roe. It is harmless to the fish but acts as a sodium channel poison in humans. Heat does not destroy the toxin. Symptoms occur 15 minutes to 24 hours (usually 1 to 6 hours) after ingestion. Gastroenteritis sets in initially, followed by various neurologic symptoms such as paresthesia, pruritus, weakness and paralysis, fasciculations, tremor, seizures, and hallucinations. The reverse sensation of hot and cold is a pathognomonic symptom. Cardiovascular symptoms such as hypotension and bradycardia are less common. There are broad individual differences in susceptibility to the toxins. Ingestion of alcohol or nuts may exacerbate the clinical picture. Symptoms persist for days to months, and the case fatality rate is usually > 1%.

Tetrodotoxin is found in puffer fish and porcupine fish, which are consumed in Japan as the delicacy "fugu," prepared by trained chefs. Ingestion usually causes mild paresthesias and warmth. Initial signs of intoxication occurring within 15 minutes to several hours include nausea and dizziness, which progress to weakness and loss of coordination. By blocking neural sodium conductance, the toxins depress the medullary respiratory center, atrioventricular nodal conduction, and myocardial and skeletal muscle contractility. Symptoms persist for hours to days. Bronchospasm, hypotension, and coma are complications, which produce an overall case fatality rate of 10 to 50%. Most fatalities involve amateur cooks. Fugu consumed in restaurants is likely safe.

Food Poisoning

Bacterial toxins formed in foods before they are ingested may lead to a variety of symptoms. (See "Travelers' Diarrhea" for toxins produced in the patient after ingestion.)

Staphylococcus aureus causes an acute illness characterized by abdominal pain, nausea often with vomiting, possibly diarrhea, and hypotension with an onset 2 to 6 hours after consuming contaminated protein-rich foods. Low-grade fever and headache are observed in a minority of patients. The symptoms persist for 24 to 48 hours. The toxin usually originates in a cook with an infected finger or nasopharynx or in milk from a cow with mastitis. Contaminated food items may have been inadequately refrigerated as the toxin is heat stable. This form of food poisoning may occur anywhere; in the early 1970s, there was an outbreak aboard a long-distance flight.

Clostridium perfringens causes an acute illness with abdominal cramps and watery diarrhea 7 to 16 hours after consumption of contaminated meat or poultry. Nausea and fever are less frequent symptoms. The illness usually persists for no longer than 24 hours. The toxin usually develops in food that is slowly cooled or kept warm on a steam table.

Bacillus cereus may produce two different syndromes. The first, caused by ingestion of a preformed toxin, is identical to *S. aureus* food poisoning, with vomiting and abdominal pain occurring 1 to 6 hours after eating contaminated food. The second syndrome resembles *C. perfringens* foodborne disease, with enterotoxin release leading to watery diarrhea 8 to 16 hours after consuming contaminated food. Fried rice is often the vehicle for *B. cereus* foodborne disease. Other foods may also be the source.

Clostridium botulinum toxins are the cause for rare but life-threatening botulism. After an incubation period of 12 to 36 hours (occasionally 2 hours to 8 days), weakness and dizziness occur, followed by blurred vision, diplopia, photophobia, and descending paralysis leading to dysarthria, dysphagia, and respiratory failure in severe cases. Early anticholinergic symptoms including a dry mouth and sore throat with a variety of gastrointestinal symptoms are also possible. This is a rare disease in travelers but several cases have been reported, usually following consumption of home-canned food and in some instances industrially produced food items.

Lead Poisoning

Lead-glazed ceramic crockery is purchased as souvenirs in various countries in southern Europe and the developing world. The lead poisoning which may result presents a poorly defined clinical picture with stomach pain, vomiting, loss of appetite, and neurologic symptoms.

Plant Poisoning

Travelers who venture away from the usual tourist destinations may be offered local products made from toxic plants, or ingest ones that resemble nontoxic plants at home. Mushroom poisoning is a common problem. Herbal teas may be contaminated with anticholinergic compounds, hallucinogens, hepatotoxins, and heavy metals.

Shellfish Poisoning

In addition to the many infections that can be transmitted by shellfish (e.g., hepatitis A, Norwalk virus, *V. parahaemolyticus*), paralytic shellfish poisoning (PSP), neurologic (NSP), diarrheal (DSP), and amnestic shellfish poisoning (ASP) may also result. Shellfish poisoning is rare compared to fish poisoning although outbreaks have been reported in various parts of the world. It is caused by saxitoxins and other toxins produced by sporadically occurring algae, which shellfish feed upon. The toxins then become concentrated in the shellfish. Symptoms occur within minutes to 3 hours after ingestion. The most serious form is PSP, characterized by paresthesias, vomiting, diarrhea, and dysequilibrium. Fatality resulting from respiratory arrest occurs in approximately 25% of cases. However, NSP and DSP have a milder course without fatalities; ASP leads to gastroenteritis, headaches, loss of short-term memory, and occasionally to seizures and coma. The case fatality rate for ASP is 3%.

Minimized Exposure in Travelers

Adequate preservation will help prevent food, fish, and shellfish poisoning. Raw items must look and smell fresh.

Fish with an ammonia smell or a peppery or metallic taste may cause scombroid poisoning and should not be consumed. Carnivorous reef fish heavier than 3 kg should not be eaten as they may have accumulated large quantities of ciguatera toxins. Viscera of tropical marine fish and moray eels should be discarded for the same reason. Several "stick" or "paddle" tests based on an immunoassay that can detect ciguatoxins in fish are not yet widely available.

Regulatory authorities routinely test for shellfish toxins. Shellfish harvested outside regular commercial channels or during a red tide should be avoided.

Chemoprophylaxis

None.

Management Abroad

Medical treatment should be sought in cases of food, fish, or shellfish poisoning. Antihistamines are useful in scombroid poisoning while treatment of other fish poisoning is mainly supportive.

PSYCHIATRIC PROBLEMS

Risk Assessment for Travelers

Psychological disorder rates among World Bank consultants with varying degrees of experience in international travel demonstrate that inexperienced travelers are more at risk. Compared to their nontraveling counterparts, those with one trip were 2.1 times more likely to have psychological disorders while traveling and those with two or more trips were 3.1 times more likely (see Figure 7).

The extent of psychiatric problems is underestimated in many cases as diagnosis is made by nonpsychiatrists. At the Hospital of Tropical Diseases in London, 2% of all patients were thought to have a psychiatric disorder when a physician made the assessment. This rate rose to 32% when the same assessment was made by a psychiatrist who found an additional 18% with personality disorders that could lead to breakdown. The most frequent psychiatric diagnoses included depression, manic depression, psychosomatic syndrome, anxiety, and alcoholism.

Many persons use travel or work abroad as an escape. Some seek adventure or a more interesting life while some look for a higher salary or social status. Others wish to get away from family, restrictions, and boredom. Some think they will find "the land of milk and honey." Patients with schizophrenia, manic depression, or other psychiatric diseases may believe their illness will be less obvious in an exotic society. Persecution hallucinations may induce patients with chronic psychoses to flee their home. Megalomaniac paranoids may feel an urge to tell politicians or organizations abroad about their ideas. Schizophrenics may be found wandering aimlessly in airports. Finally, some travel to commit suicide in anonymity.

Travel is semantically linked to the French word for work, "travail." To carry luggage, line up, clear formalities, and cope with an unknown language and culture, all means work and stress. This leads to exhaustion, particularly when exacerbated by delays, jet lag, or an inhospitable climate. Increased muscle tonus, headaches, insomnia, aggression, anxiety, and sometimes substance abuse may result. Trips of short duration may turn out to be bad experiences for travelers who lack coping skills.

Expatriates experience additional stresses. Moving to another country, which happens every few years in some professions such as the diplomatic corps, means saying goodbye to friends and adjusting to a new culture and neighborhood. Pre-existing depression tends to become more pronounced during travel; the only conditions which tend to improve are stresses related to feuds with neighbors.

The individual responsible for the move, usually male, tends to underplay the dissatisfaction expressed by other family members, which may cause conflict. In expatriates, mental breakdown may result, particularly when neurosis or other personality problems come into play.

Clinical Picture

The nature of the breakdown suffered depends on personality, surroundings, and cultural attitudes to illness. Many individuals panic, refusing to be left alone for fear of attempting suicide. Most cannot work. The "incubation period" in expatriates varies, with male employees tending to break down within the first 9 months and spouses in 9 months to 4 years.

Drug or alcohol abuse may be a problem among expatriates attempting to cope with the above stresses, especially where drugs are available at low cost.

Minimized Exposure in Travelers

Individuals who will serve abroad for long periods should undergo psychological screening. They should also be educated as to what to expect and to be aware of their own response to stress.

Chemoprophylaxis

None.

Management Abroad

Psychiatric problems are sometimes the reason for evacuation of expatriates, though this is not common. Language and cultural differences abroad make psychiatric therapy difficult.

ULTRAVIOLET RAYS

Ultraviolet rays from the sun (UVA 320–400 nm and UVB 280–320 nm) can cause severe, incapacitating sunburn and other damage, particularly in lighter-skinned persons who are unused to the sun. The first days are particularly dangerous. In the summer, UVB is intense, especially at mid-day. Window glass will block UVB but not UVA.

There is public confusion over the use of multiple UV indices. International organizations recommended a Global Solar UV Index in 1995, which has been endorsed by the WHO. The Global Solar UV Index is an estimate of maximum skin-damaging UV rays measured over a period of 10 to 30 minutes at solar noon. The higher the UV index, the less time it takes for damage to occur. In Europe, the maximum summer UV index is usually no more than 8 but can be higher at beach resorts. Close to the equator, index values may reach 20. Index values are categorized as low (1–2), moderate (3–4), high (5–6), very high (7–8), and extreme (≥9).

▎ Risk Assessment for Travelers

Many tour guides will confirm that at beach destinations sunburn is the most frequent or among the most frequent of incapacitating health problems experienced by their clients. Risk of skin cancer, including malignant melanoma, is greatest with UVB. The eye may be damaged, causing "snow blindness" or, in the long term, cataracts.

Erythema is much less likely to be caused by UVA but photoaging of the skin may be greater with UVA as its skin penetration is higher.

Systemic lupus erythematosus may be triggered by UVB. Various drugs such as oral contraceptives, tetracyclines, sulfas, oral hypoglycemics (sulfonylureas), diuretics, tricyclic antidepressants, isotretinoin, and nonsteroidal anti-inflammatory agents may increase sensitivity to sunlight, particularly to UVA. Risk ultimately depends on exposure.

Clinical Picture

Erythema is noticeable 2 to 6 hours after exposure, peaks at 20 to 24 hours, and fades within 5 days. Note that a "healthy tan" is an oxymoron, as skin tan is a cutaneous response to ultraviolet injury.

Minimized Exposure in Travelers

Skin type I always burns and never tans, type IV rarely burns and always tans, and types V and VI which are moderately or heavily pigmented, rarely burn. Skin type should not be equated with racial pigmentation; a very light-skinned person may just tan while some dark-skinned person may burn readily.

Tightly-knit, dark-colored, dry fabrics are best for blocking UV rays. Snorkelers should wear a T-shirt as UV rays may penetrate several centimeters of clear water. Chemical sunscreens which absorb UV rays or physical screens which reflect or scatter them should be used. The chemical screens are invisible and usually preferred whereas physical sunscreens resist being washed off. The latter are preferred by lifeguards and ski instructors and should be recommended to patients with photosensitivities. The most widely accepted rating of sunscreens is based on the sun protection factor (SPF), which is the ratio of minimum erythema-creating dose (MED) of protected skin to MED of unprotected skin.

The product with an SPF of 15 allows the traveler exposure to the sun with no burn for 15 times longer than with no screen. Most sunscreens labeled waterproof contain fat. They will wash off during swimming or other watersports.

There is a common misconception that sunscreens promote tanning, when, in fact, they simply prevent burning. Sufficient sunscreen (2 mg per cm^2) must be applied. For most tropical destinations or ski resorts, an SPF of 15 to 20 is sufficient though type I skins require a higher SPF. Note that repellents may reduce sunscreen effectiveness.

Tans confer some protection against sunburn but no more than an SPF equivalent of 4.

Chemoprophylaxis

Oral photoprotection has been largely ineffective with the exception of beta-carotene for erythropoietic protoporphyria, chloroquine for lupus erythematosus, and psoralens for poly-morphous light eruption. Corticosteroids are not a prophylaxis for sun exposure.

Management Abroad

Various ointments are offered over the counter for sunburn. Corticosteroid creams are usually not recommended.

DIAGNOSIS AND MANAGEMENT
OF ILLNESS AFTER RETURN

PERSISTENT DIARRHEA

Traveler's diarrhea will persist longer than 2 to 4 weeks in 1 to 2% of patients. Etiologic agents show some differences in persistent diarrhea (Table 30) when compared to acute traveler's diarrhea. The parasitic pathogens should be considered in travelers with persistent (> 14 days) or chronic diarrhea (> 30 days). Prolonged diarrhea may also be caused by a bacterial enteric infection. Other causes include induced lactase deficiency or a transient small bowel bacterial overgrowth syndrome induced by small bowel motility stasis resulting from an earlier enteric infection. Some of these patients have "Brainerd diarrhea," an idiopathic form of chronic diarrhea associated with consumption of untreated water or unpasteurized milk.

Table 30 Etiology of Persistent Diarrhea (> 14 Days)*

Cause of Persistent Diarrhea	Comment
Parasitic agents including *Giardia*, *Cyclospora*, *Cryptosporidium*, *Microsporidium*, *E. histolytica*	Two freshly passed stools should be examined by a competent laboratory for each of the parasitic agents
Bacterial enteropathogens including ETEC, *Shigella*, *Salmonella*, *Aeromonas*, adherent or aggregative *E. coli*, noncholera *Vibrios*	Special studies may be required to identify the enteropathogen
Lactase deficiency and other malabsorption syndromes	Diet alteration may lead to improved symptomatology
Bacterial overgrowth syndrome	Small bowel intubation or breath hydrogen testing is required to make the diagnosis
Idiopathic chronic diarrhea best classified as Brainerd diarrhea	This is an etiology of exclusion after a complete gastroenterologic evaluation fails to show other cause

* In approximate order of importance according to the author's experience.

The patient with persistent diarrhea should be approached sequentially (Figure 54). When seen in a health or travel clinic, these patients have usually not responded to at least one course of antimicrobial therapy. Adult patients, if they have not received antibacterial therapy, may be treated with a fluoroquinolone as in the case of typical traveler's diarrhea. Those who have received one of these drugs before should not receive it again. Etiology of the patient's diarrhea should be assessed if they do not respond to antibacterial therapy. Ideally, two stool

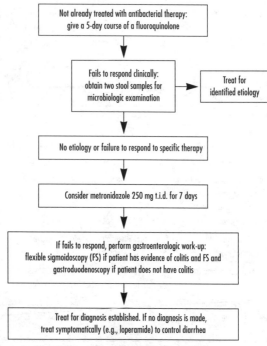

Figure 54 Evaluation of the traveler with persistent diarrhea

samples should be studied for the parasitic and bacterial pathogens listed in Table 30. Etiologic agents identified should be treated. Empiric *Giardia* therapy may be justified if none is identified. Metronidazole may be given empirically for possible giardiasis or bacterial overgrowth. Failure to respond to metronidazole indicates the need for gastroenterologic evaluation. Evidence of colitis, such as fecal urgency and tenesmus, passage of many small volume stools which may contain blood and mucus, or the presence of fecal leukocytes in stool samples, indicates the patient should have a flexible sigmoidoscopy with biopsy of any abnormal tissue. With no evidence of colitis, flexible sigmoidoscopy and an upper gastroduodenoscopy should be performed with biopsy of abnormal tissue, study of duodenal material, and biopsy for *Giardia* and other intestinal parasites. With a negative work-up or only minimal focal colonic mucosal inflammation found (particularly chronic inflammation with lymphocytes), Brainerd diarrhea is suspected. The patient should be reassured that their illness will likely be prolonged but self-limited. In these cases, it is advisable to initiate symptomatic therapy with loperamide-like drugs.

FEVER WITHOUT FOCAL FINDINGS

When fever is reported with focal findings (e.g., respiratory symptoms, jaundice, or eosinophilia), its origin should be identified by carefully considering disorders of the specific organ system. When fever occurs without focal organ system involvement, the diagnosis is more difficult. In the latter case, a systemic approach to evaluation should include the nature of the trip and places visited, with consideration of diseases endemic to regions visited, incubation period of the potential disorder, and patient disorders that may make them more susceptible. Table 31 lists disorders to consider in the patient with fever showing obvious organ system involvement. The laboratory is the key to establishing diagnosis. Blood cultures, blood or cerebrospinal fluid films for parasites, serologic studies, and bone marrow aspiration/ biopsy with histologic and cultural study should be pursued. It is critical to develop an index of suspicion when considering potential diagnoses and ordering appropriate tests.

Table 31 Disorders to Consider in the Febrile Patient without Focal Disease Involvement

Disorders to Consider*	Diagnostic Approach
Bacterial endocarditis, bacterial sepsis, bartonellosis, brucellosis, leptospirosis, listeriosis, melioidosis, meningococcemia, plague, rat bite fever, typhoid fever	Blood cultures
Babesiosis, Borreliae, African and American trypanosomiasis, malaria, microfilariae, visceral leishmaniasis, loiasis	Blood or cerebrospinal films for parasites
Cytomegalovirus infection, Epstein-Barr virus infection, viral hepatitis, leptospirosis, rickettsial infections, viral hemorrhagic fevers, dengue, syphilis, relapsing fever, toxoplasmosis	Serologic procedure
Brucellosis, histoplasmosis, leishmaniasis, tuberculosis, typhoid fever	Bone marrow microscopy and culture

*Treatment of specific conditions may be found elsewhere in the manual or in other texts.

Dermatologic Disorders

Skin involvement may be generalized or localized, macular, papular, or ulcerative. The appearance of the cutaneous process will provide clues as to the cause of the condition. Table 32 provides a partial list of potential causes of cutaneous eruption.

Generalized eruption usually signals systemic disease, often an infection (usually viral). Serologic studies may be helpful in establishing an etiologic diagnosis. With a petechial or ecchymotic skin eruption, dengue and other hemorrhagic fever viruses, meningococcemia, disseminated intravascular coagulation associated with sepsis, and advanced rickettsial infection should be suspected. With a localized skin eruption, especially if the condition is ulcerative, biopsy and histologic examination, and, in selected cases, culture may establish the etiology.

Table 32 Cutaneous Process in a Returning Traveler: Differential Diagnosis

Pattern of Skin Eruption	Differential Diagnosis (Partial List)
Generalized skin rash	Systemic viral infection: measles, rubella, chickenpox, arbovirus, filovirus or Sindbis fever, rickettsial infection, leptospirosis, relapsing fever
Petechial or ecchymotic rash	Viral hemorrhagic fever including dengue, arenaviral infection, meningococcemia and other septicemias, advanced Rocky Mountain spotted fever
Localized maculopapular rash	Onchocerciasis, strongyloidiasis, scabies, lice, cercarial dermatitis in schistosomiasis
Nodular skin lesions	Furuncles, tungiasis, myiasis
Ulcerative or crusted process	Impetigo, primary chancre of African trypanosomiasis, chagoma in Chagas' disease, cutaneous anthrax, fungal, nocardial, or mycobacterial infection, cutaneous leishmaniasis, cutaneous amoebiasis
Serpiginous and migratory processes	Cutaneous larva migrans, loiasis, strongyloidiasis

EOSINOPHILIA

Patients showing >450 eosinophils per microliter of blood have a peripheral eosinophilia. This finding together with a history of international travel suggests a parasitic infection (Table 33). With the exception of *Isospora belli* and *Dientamoeba fragilis*, protozoal parasites do not produce a peripheral eosinophilia. When other protozoal infections are diagnosed (e.g., giardiasis and malaria) in the presence of an eosinophilia, a second parastic infection should be suspected. The nonprotozoal parasites with an extraintestinal migration phase, particularly in association with tissue infection, produce the most intense eosinophilia.

The incubation period of the causes of eosinophilia vary widely. Certain agents may produce illness and eosinophilia years after leaving the endemic area (e.g., onchocerciasis and loiasis) so that a history of remote travel may be important. The traveler who lived under primitive conditions with local populations is at greater risk of parasitic infection. Those exposed to local water sources (local drinking water or an unchlorinated or poorly chlorinated pool) may have schistosomiasis. Diagnosis is suggested by history and place of travel and is confirmed by examination of stool and blood, or tissue biopsy. Treatment depends on the diagnosis.

Table 33 Major Causes of Peripheral Eosinophilia in International Travelers

Clinical Condition	Symptoms and Geographic Region of Occurrence	Diagnosis
Allergic disorder	Rhinitis, respiratory symptoms, hives (worldwide)	History
Bronchopulmonary aspergillosis	Asthma and respiratory symptoms (worldwide)	History plus tissue biopsy
Isospora belli infection	Intestinal symptoms (worldwide)	Stool examination
Dientamoeba fragilis infection	Intestinal symptoms (worldwide)	Stool examination
Ascariasis	Intestinal symptoms, asymptomatic (worldwide)	Stool examination
Hookworm infection	Intestinal symptoms, asymptomatic (worldwide)	Stool examination
Strongyloidiasis	Intestinal symptoms, skin lesion (worldwide)	Stool examination, sputum examination, serology
Trichinosis	Myalgias, intestinal symptoms, periorbital edema (worldwide)	Serology, muscle biopsy
Lymphatic filariasis	Lymphangitis, lymphedema, asymptomatic (tropical regions)	Blood smears, serology, skin biopsy
Onchocerciasis	Nodular skin lesions (Africa and Central and South America)	Skin biospy
Loiasis	Nodular skin lesions, subconjunctival worm (West and Central Africa)	Blood smear, worm identified in eye examination
Mansonellosis	Dermatitis, asymptomatic (Africa and Central and South America)	Blood smear or skin biopsy
Dracunculiasis	Blister/ulcer of skin, fever, generalized urticaria, periorbital edema, and wheezing (Africa, the Middle East, and the Indian Subcontinent)	Clinical diagnosis, visual and microscopic identification of worm or larvae
Tropical pulmonary eosinophilia	Respiratory symptoms (tropical areas, especially Africa)	Serology, clinical history

Table 35 Continued

Clinical Condition	Symptoms and Geographic Region of Occurrence	Diagnosis
Toxocariasis and visceral larva migrans	Intestinal symptoms, fever (worldwide)	Serology, tissue biopsy
Cutaneous larva migrans (creeping eruption)	Serpiginous skin lesion (tropics and subtropics)	Clinical diagnosis
Schistosomiasis	Acute febrile illness or chronic abdominal complaints or hematuria (Africa, Asia, Southeast Asia, South America, Caribbean)	Stool or urine examination, rectal biopsy, serologic study
Fasciolopsiasis	Intestinal symptoms (India, Southeast Asia, Far East)	Stool examination
Echinococcosis	Liver or lung cysts (sheep and cattle raising regions)	Serology
Paragonimiasis	Hemoptysis, respiratory symptoms (West Africa, Far East, India, South and Central America)	Stool or sputum examination
Clonorchiasis	Intestinal symptoms, abnormal liver function tests (Far East, Southeast Asia, Africa, South and Central America)	Stool examination

PART 4

APPENDICES

APPENDIX A:
ABBREVIATIONS

AIDS	acquired Immunodeficiency Syndrome
CDC	Centers for Disease Control and Prevention, Atlanta, GA, U.S.A.
CFR	case fatality rate
CRPF	chloroquine-resistant *P. falciparum*
DEC	diethylcarbamazine
DCS	decompression sickness
G-6-PD	glucose-6-phosphate-dehydrogenase
IAMAT	International Association for Medical Assistance to Travelers
IATA	International Air Transport Association
ID	intradermal (injection)
IHR	International Health Regulations (WHO)
IM	intramuscular (injection)
IV	intravenous (injection)
MMR	measles, mumps, rubella (vaccine)
MMWR	Morbidity Mortality Weekly Report (CDC)
PAX	passenger (airline, ship)
PPM	personal protection measures (against mosquitoes)
SBT/SBET	stand-by (emergency) treatment
SC	subcutaneous (injection)
TB	tuberculosis
TD	travelers' diarrhea
TIM	Travel Information Manual (IATA publication)
UC	unaccompanied children
UK	United Kingdom
U.S.A.	United States of America
WER	Weekly Epidemiological Record (WHO)
WHO	World Health Organization, Geneva, Switzerland
WTO	World Tourism Organization, Madrid

APPENDIX B:
SELECTED INTERNATIONAL AND NATIONAL INFORMATION SOURCES

Published Sources

Textbooks, Manuals

Benenson AS. Control of Communicable Diseases Manual.
Washington: American Public Health Association,
16th edition, 1995

DuPont HL, Steffen R, editors. Textbook of Travel Medicine
and Health. Hamilton: B.C. Decker Inc., 1997 (392 pages,
180 illustrations, over 1000 references)

Wilson ME. A World Guide to Infections. New York: Oxford
University Press, 1991

Publications by International or Selected National Authorities with Regular Updates

CDC. Health Information for International Travel 1996–97.
U.S. Department of Health and Human Services, CDC
Division of Quarantine, Atlanta GA

Department of Health (U.K.). Health Information for Overseas
Travel, 1995 edition. London: HMSO

IATA. Travel Information Manual tim. Amsterdam: International
Airline Publications (monthly, also available as TIMATIC
online in travel agencies)

SMV (France). Médecine des voyages. Guide d'information et
de conseils pratiques, 4ème édition. Saint-Maur: Format
utile, 1998

WHO. International Travel and Health; Vaccination
Requirements and Health Advice. Geneva: World Health
Organization, 1999 (annual)

Electronic media

Only main sources with considerable international impact and generally high quality are included; many more can be found on surfing, using the words "health" and "travel," using net-search programs such as Yahoo, Infoseek, Excite. The sources are subject to frequent changes.

Websites

General Travel Health Information

CDC, in English: Country specific health conditions and
   immunization requirements.
   www.cdc.gov/travel/index.htm

CRM, Centrum für Reisemedizin, in German: country specific
   travel health advice.
   www.crm.de (fee for subscribers)

HEALTH CANADA, in English and French: travel information and advisory report.
   www.dfait-maeci.gc.ca/travelreport/menu_e.htm

MASTA, Medical Advisory Service for Travellers, in English:
   wide range of inquiry options.
   for subscribers only, apply to MASTA, London School of
   Hygiene and Tropical Diseases, Keppel Street, London
   WC1E 7HT, Phone +44-171-631 4408

TRAVAX (Scotland), in English. for subscribers only.

TRAVEL HEALTH ONLINE (SHORELAND), in English:
   CDC-compatible country-specific travel health advice,
   broad in scope.
   www.tripprep.com

TRAVELLERS MEDICAL AND VACCINATION CENTER,
   in English: TMVC, operating travel clinics in Australia,
   travel health advice.
   www.tmvc.com.au

TROPIMED, in English (CDC advice), French (Swiss expert
   group), German (Swiss and German expert groups): country-
   specific travel health advice, broad in scope.
   www.tropimed.com (fee for subscribers)

WHO, in English and French: information limited on annual
publication "International Travel and Health"
www.who.int/ith/index.html

Epidemiology

EUROSURVEILLANCE, in English and French: epidemiological data and reports.
www.ceses.org/eurosurv

OUTBREAK, part of ProMED system (see below) with in-
depth information.
www.outbreak.org/cgi-unreg/dynaserve.exe/index.html

OUTBREAK VERIFICATION LIST, not a Website, in English: Travel health professionals may receive this weekly
WHO list, which is not for public distribution by e-mail;
apply to: *outbreakemc@who.ch*

PROMED (Program for Monitoring of Emerging Diseases,
ProMED), in English: Daily update on epidemiologic
outbreaks, sometimes not validated.
www.healthnet.org./promed

WHO, in English and French: Weekly Epidemiologic Record
and disease outbreak news:
www.who.int/wer/index.htm
www.who.int/emc/outbreak_news/index.html

Vaccines

CDC, in English: fact sheets, safety
www.cdc.gov/nip/vacsafe

Warnings

FRENCH DIPLOMATIC NETWORK
www.France.diplomatie.fr/infopra/avis/index.html

GERMAN FOREIGN MINISTRY WARNINGS, in German:
security risks for specific countries.
www.auswaertiges-amt.de

UK FOREIGN AND COMMONWEALTH OFFICE, in English
www.fco.gov.ujk

US STATE DEPARTMENT, in English: travel warnings, announcements, and information sheets for every country.
www.travel.state.gov/travel_warnings.html

Various

INTERNATIONAL ASSOCIATION FOR MEDICAL ASSISTANCE TO TRAVELERS (IAMAT)
www.sentex.net/~iamat

INTERNATIONAL SOCIETY FOR TRAVEL MEDICINE home page: includes general announcements, professional dialog, research results, and in near future travel clinics worldwide (only ISTM members).
www.istm.org

LONELY PLANET
www.lonelyplanet.com

WHEATHER FORECAST
www.cnn.com

WORLD TOURISM ORGANISATION, tourist statistics and projections, in English.
www.world-tourism.org

Table B–1 Software Sources (status 3/99)

Name	Country of Origin	Price Basic/Annual (US$)	Volume	Update
CATIS	Canada	400/80/year	?	Annual
EDISAN	France	2450/830	100MB	q6 weeks
GIDEON	Israel, USA	797 or 2395 (several users)	6MB	Quarterly
IMMUNIZATION ALERT	USA	500, weekly update 750	?	Weekly
MEDITRAVEL	France, Edisan group	165/80	12MB	q6 months
REISERIX	Germany, SB-Pharma	200	10MB	?
THE MEDICAL LETTER TRAVEL HEALTH	USA, Tropimed group and Medical Letter	Unknown	5MB	Biannual
TRAVAX	USA	595, weekly update	895	?
TRAVEL CARE	USA	399 or 999 (several users)	6MB	Monthly
TRAVELLER	UK, MASTA group	?	?	?
TROPIMED	Germany, Switzerland	150/25 for monthly fax-news	5MB	Biannual
WALKABOUT 2000	Australia	?	?	?

APPENDIX C: COUNTRY-SPECIFIC MALARIA AND VACCINATION RECOMMENDATIONS†

Country N = North S = South W = West E = East	Malaria	Yellow Fever	Hepatitis A	Hepatitis B	Typhoid	Rabies	Meningococcal Meningitis	Japanese Encephalitis	Cholera	Tetanus/Diphtheria	Poliomyelitis	Miscellaneous
AFRICA												
Algeria	—: minimal risk: SE	T1	+		+	R				+	+	
Angola	MP (1–12)	+T1	+	R	R	R				+	+	
Benin	MP (1–12)	requ	+	R	+	R	R:N			+	+	
Botswana	XP (1–12): Boteti, Chiobe, Ngamiland, Okavango, Tutume districts		+	R	R					+	+	
Burkina Faso	MP (1–12)	requ	+	R	R	R	R			+	+	
Burundi	MP (1–12)	+T1	+	R	R	R				+	+	
Cameroon	MP (1–12)	requ	+	R	R	R	R:N			+	+	
Cape Verde Islands	—: minimal risk (9–11) São Tiago Island	T1	+	R	R	R				+	+	

Country N = North S = South W = West E = East	Malaria	Yellow Fever	Hepatitis A	Hepatitis B	Typhoid	Rabies	Meningococcal Meningitis	Japanese Encephalitis	Cholera	Tetanus/Diphtheria	Poliomyelitis	Miscellaneous
Central African Republic	MP (1–12)	requ‡	+	R	R	R				+	+	
Chad	MP (1–12)	requ	+	R	+	R	R			+	+	
Congo-Brazzaville	MP (1–12)	requ	+	R	R	R				+	+	
Congo-Kinshasa (Zaïre)	MP (1–12)	requ	+	R	R	R				+	+	
Comores	MP (1–12)		+	R	R	R				+	+	
Djibouti	MP (1–12)	T1	+	R	R	R				+	+	
Egypt	— : CP or CT* (6–10) El Faiyum area only	T1	+	R	+	R				+	+	
Equatorial Guinea	MP (1–12)	+ T1	+	R	R	R				+	+	
Eritrea	MP (1–12): <2000 m: ø Asmara	T1	+	R	R	R				+	+	

		+T1	+	R	R	R:S		
Ethiopia	MP (1–12): <2000 m: ø Addis Ababa	+T1	+	R	R		+	+
Gabon	MP (1–12)	requ	+	R	R		+	+
Gambia	MP (1–12)	+T1	+	R	+	R	+	+
Ghana	MP (1–12)	requ	+	R	+	R:N	+	+
Guinea	MP (1–12)	requ	+	R	+	R	+	+
Guinea-Bissau	MP (1–12)	+T1	+	R	+	R	+	+
Ivory Coast	MP (1–12)	requ	+	R	+	R:N	+	+
Kenya	MP (1–12): <2500 m: ø Nairobi-City	+T1	+	R	R		+	+
Lesotho	ø	T2	+	R	R		+	+
Liberia	MP (1–12)	requ	+	R	+	R	+	+
Libya	—: minimal risk (2–8): SW	T1	+	R	+	R	+	+
Madagascar	MP (1–12): <1100 m	T1	+	R	R		+	+
Malawi	MP (1–12)	T2	+	R	R		+	+
Mali	MP (1–12)	requ	+	R	+	R	+	+

Country (N = North, S = South, W = West, E = East)	Malaria	Yellow Fever	Hepatitis A	Hepatitis B	Typhoid	Rabies	Meningococcal Meningitis	Japanese Encephalitis	Cholera	Tetanus/Diphtheria	Poliomyelitis	Miscellaneous
Mauritania	MP (1–12): S / MP (7–10): Adrar Inchin	+T2 >2W requ	+	R	+	R	R			+	+	
Mauritius	—: minimal risk (1–12): ø Rodrigues Island	T1	+	R	R	R				+	+	
Mayotte	MP (1–12)		+	R	R	R				+	+	
Morocco	—: minimal risk (5–10)		+	R	+	R				+	+	
Mozambique	MP (1–12)	T1	+	R	R	R			regu	+	+	
Namibia	XP (1–12): Cubango (Kavango) Valley, Kunene Valley, Caprivi Strip: XP (11–6), MT (7–10): other in the N / —: minimal risk S of above areas	T2	+	R	R	R						
Niger	MP (1–12)	requ	+	R	+	R	R			+	+	

Country	Notes	+T2	+	R	+	R	R:N			
Nigeria	MP (1–12)								+	+
Réunion (La)	ø	T1	+	R		R			+	+
Rwanda	MP (1–12)	requ	+	R		R			+	+
São Tomé & Principe	MP (1–12)	requ	+	R	+				+	+
Senegal	MP (1–12)	+T1	+	R	+		R		+	+
Seychelles	ø	T	+	R		R			+	+
Sierra Leone	MP (1–12)	requ	+	R	+				+	+
Somalia	MP (1–12)	+T1	+	R	+				+	+
South Africa	MP (1–12): Kruger and neighboring parks, MP (11–6), MT (7–10): N, NE Kwazulu/Natal (N of Tugela River), E Transvaal	T2	+	R		R			+	
St. Helena	ø	T1	+	R		R			+	+
Sudan	MP (1–12): MT*: Red Sea shores	+T1	+	R	+		R		+	+
Swaziland	MP (11–6), MT (7–10): mainly lowlands	T2	+	R		R			+	+

Country N = North S = South W = West E = East	Malaria	Yellow Fever	Hepatitis A	Hepatitis B	Typhoid	Rabies	Meningococcal Meningitis	Japanese Encephalitis	Cholera	Tetanus/Diphtheria	Poliomyelitis	Miscellaneous
Tanzania	MP (1–12): <1800 m	+T1	+	R	R	R				+	+	
Togo	MP (1–12)	requ	+	R	R	R	R:N			+	+	
Tunisia	ø	T1	+	R	R	R				+	+	
Uganda	MP (1–12)	requ	+	R	R	R	R:N			+	+	
Zambia	MP (1–12): <1000 m	+	+	R	R	R				+	+	
Zimbabwe	MP (1–12): N, Victoria Falls, Zambezi River valley: MP (11–6), MT (7–10): otherwise: <1200 m ø Harare, Bulawayo	T2	+	R	R	R				+	+	
AMERICAS												
Argentina	—: minimal risk (10–5): N: <1200 m		+	R		R				+		
Bahamas	ø	T1	+	R	R	R				+		

Belize	CP or CT* (1–12): ø Belize-District	T1	+	R	R	R			+
Bermudas	ø		+	R	R				+
Bolivia	MP or MT* (1–12): N: <2500 m: CP + MT or MT* (1–12): rest of the country: <2500 m ø cities and provinces of de Oruro and Potosi	+T1	+	R	R				+
Brazil	MP or MT* (1–12): forested areas of Legal Amazonia. <900 m, see map: ø E coast, Iguassu	+T1	+	R	R				+
Caribbean (excl. Haiti and Dominican Republic)	ø	T1	+	R	R				+
Chile	ø		+	R	R				+

Country N = North S = South W = West E = East	Malaria	Yellow Fever	Hepatitis A	Hepatitis B	Typhoid	Rabies	Meningococcal Meningitis	Japanese Encephalitis	Cholera	Tetanus/Diphtheria	Poliomyelitis	Miscellaneous
Colombia	MP or MT* (1–12): rural areas of Urabá-Bajo Cauca, Pacífico, Amazonia: XP or MT* (1–12): other risk areas: ø Bogotá, Caribbean islands (San Andres and Providencia)	+ T1	+	R	R	R				+		
Costa Rica	CP or CT* (1–12): <700 m. ø San Jose		+	R	R	R				+		
Cuba	ø											
Dominican Republic	CP or CT* (1–12): central border with Haiti only: ø coast		+	R	R	R				+		
Ecuador	XP or MT* (1–12): <1500 m: ø Andes highlands, Galapagos	+ T1	+	R	R	R				+		
El Salvador	CP or CT* (1–12): Santa Ana province only: <600 m	T1	+	R	R	R				+		

		requ	+	R	R	R		+
French Guiana	MT (1–12): areas bordering Surinam and Brazil: MP (1–12): rest of the country			R	R	R		+
Guatemala	CP or CT* (1–12): <1500 m: ø Guatemala City	T1	+	R	R	R		+
Guyana	MT or MP* (1–12): ø Georgetown, New Amsterdam	+T1	+	R	R	R		+
Haiti	CP or CT* (1–12): ø Port-au-Prince	T1	+	R	R	R		+
Honduras	CP or CT* (1–12): <1000 m: ø Tegucigalpa	T1	+	R	R	R		+
Mexico	CP or CT* (1–12): <1000 m	T1	+	R	R	R		+
Nicaragua	CP or CT* (1–12): ø Managua	T1	+	R	R	R		+
Panama	CP or CT*(1–12): <800 m: ø Panama, Colon	+	+	R	R	R		+
Paraguay	CP or MT* (10–5): N: ø Iguassu falls	T1	+	R	R	R		+

Country N = North S = South W = West E = East	Malaria	Yellow Fever	Hepatitis A	Hepatitis B	Typhoid	Rabies	Meningococcal Meningitis	Japanese Encephalitis	Cholera	Tetanus/Diphtheria	Poliomyelitis	Miscellaneous
Peru	MP or MT* (1–12): Luciano Castillo, Loreto, Piura: XP or MT* (1–12): rest of the country: <1500 m: ø Lima, Cuzco, Machu Picchu, Ayacucho	+	+	R	R	R				+		
Surinam	MP or MT* (1–12): ø Paramaribo and coast	+ T1	+	R	R	R				+		
Trinidad, Tobago	ø	+ T1	+	R	R	R				+		
Uruguay	ø		+	R	R					+		
Venezuela	MP or MT* (1–12): jungle areas of the Amazonas: XP or MT* (1–12): rest of the country: ø N coast	+	+	R	R	R				+		

ASIA

Afghanistan	XP or MT* (5–11): <2000 m	T1	+	R	R	R			+	+
Armenia	CP or CT*: low risk E borders		+	R	R	R			+	+	B
Azerbaijan	CP or CT*: low risk S borders and N Khachmas region		+	R	R	R			+	+
Bahrein	ø			R	R				+	+
Bangladesh	MP or MT* (1–12): SE: XP or MT* (1–12): rest of the country. ø Dhaka	T1	+	R	+	R			+	+
Bhutan	XP or MT* (1–12): S: <1700 m	T2	+	R	R	R			+	+
Brunei Darussalam	ø	T2	+	R	R	R			+	+
Cambodia	MP or MT* (1–12): ø Phnom Penh DP + MT or MT* (1–12): W border with Thailand (facing Trat province)	T2	+	R	R	R	R		+	+
China (People's Republic)	MP or MT* (1–12): S half of the country: <1500 m: ø Beijing and other major cities	T2	+	R	R	R	R		+	+

Country N = North S = South W = West E = East	Malaria	Yellow Fever	Hepatitis A	Hepatitis B	Typhoid	Rabies	Meningococcal Meningitis	Japanese Encephalitis	Cholera	Tetanus/Diphtheria	Poliomyelitis	Miscellaneous
Hong Kong	— : minimal risk (1–12): N		+	R	R	R				+	+	
India	XP + MT or MT* (1–12): <2000 m. Malaria present also in major cities (Dehli, Bombay, Calcutta, and others): ø Himachal Pradesh, Jammu and Kashmir, Sikkim	T2	+	R	+	R		R		+	+	
Indonesia	XP or MT* (1–12) MP (1–12): ø Jakarta or other major cities and main tourist resorts in Java and Bali	T1	+	R	R	R				+	+	
Irian Jaya, Flores Timor, Sunda Islands	MP (1–12)											
Iran	CP or MT* (3–11): <1500 m: XP or MT* (3–11): SE	T1	+	R	R	R				+	+	

Country	CP or MT* (5–11): <1500 m										
Iraq	ø	T1	+	R	R	R			+	+	C
Israel	ø			R	R	R			+	+	
Japan	ø			R	R				+		
Jordan	ø	T1		R	R	R			+	+	C
Kazakhstan	ø	T1		R	R	R			+	+	C
Kyrgyzstan	ø		+	R	R	R			+	+	
Korea (North)	— : minimal risk: borders to S Korea			R	R	R			+	+	
Korea (South)	— : minimal risk: borders to N Korea			R	R	R			+	+	
Kuwait	ø		+	R	R	R			+	+	
Laos	MP or MT* (1–12): ø Vientiane	T1	+	R	R	R	R		+	+	
Lebanon	ø	T1	+	R	R	R			+	+	
Macao	ø		+	R	R	R			+	+	
Malaysia	XP or MT* (1–12): limited risk in the hinterland: MP or MT* (1–12): Sabah (E Malaysia) ø major cities, coast (W Malaysia)	T1		R	R					+	

Country N = North S = South W = West E = East	Malaria	Yellow Fever	Hepatitis A	Hepatitis B	Typhoid	Rabies	Meningococcal Meningitis	Japanese Encephalitis	Cholera	Tetanus/Diphtheria	Poliomyelitis	Miscellaneous
Maldives	ø	T1		R	R					+	+	
Mongolia	ø		+	R	R	R	R			+	+	
Myanmar (Burma)	MP or MT* (1–12): <1000 m DP + MT or MT* (1–12): NE border with Thailand (facing Tak province) ø Yangoon, Mandalay (City)	T1	+	R	R	R				+	+	
Nepal Terai	XP or MT* (1–12): rural areas of the Terai at SE border with India: <1300 m	T1	+	R	R	R	R	R		+	+	
Oman	XP or MT* (1–12): <2000 m. ø desert	T1	+	R	R	R				+	+	
Pakistan	XP or MT* (1–12): <2000 m	T1	+	R	R	R				+	+	

	Malaria prophylaxis								
Philippines	XP or MT* (1–12): <600 m: ø Manila, Bohol, Catanduanes, Cebu, Leyte	T1	+	R	R	R		+	+
Qatar	ø		+	R	R			+	+
Russian Federation			+	R	R		C	+	+
Saudi Arabia	XP or MT* (1–12): ø Jeddah, Mecca, Medina, Taïf	T1	+	R	R	R	A	+	+
Singapore	ø	T1	+	R				+	+
Sri Lanka	XP or MT* (1–12): ø District of Colombo, Kalutara, Nuwara Eliya	T1	+	R	R			+	+
Syria	CP or CT* (5–10): NE borders only	T1	+	R	R	R	C	+	+
Taiwan	ø		+	R	R		C	+	+
Tajikistan	CP or CT*: Very limited risk: S, borders with Afghanistan and some western and central foci			R	R			+	+

Country N = North S = South W = West E = East	Malaria	Yellow Fever	Hepatitis A	Hepatitis B	Typhoid	Rabies	Meningococcal Meningitis	Japanese Encephalitis	Cholera	Tetanus/Diphtheria	Poliomyelitis	Miscellaneous
Thailand	MP or MT* (1–12): DP + MT or MT* (1–12): borders with Myanmar (Tak province) and with Cambodia (Trat province) ø Bangkok, Phuket, Pattaya, Chiang Mai	T1	+	R	R	R		R:N		+	+	
Turkey	CP or CT* (3–11): SE Anatolia, Amicova and Cucurova plains		+	R	R	R				+	+	
Turkmenistan	ø											
Uzbekistan	ø											
United Arab Emirates	XP or MT* (1–12): limited risk in N Emirates: ø cities, Abu Dhabi Emirate		+	R	R	R				+	+	

										C
Vietnam	MP or MT* (1–12): ∅ cities, Red River delta	T1	+	R	R	R	R		+	+
Yemen	XP or MT* (1–12): ∅ Aden airport perimeter	T1	+	R	R	R			+	+
OCEANIA										
Australia	∅	T1	+	R					+	+
Fiji	∅	T1	+	R	R				+	+
French Polynesia	∅	T1	+	R	R				+	+
Kiribati	∅	T2	+	R	R				+	+
Nauru	∅	T2	+	R	R				+	+
New Caledonia	∅	T1	+	R	R				+	+
New Zealand	∅	T1	+	R					+	
Niue	∅	T1	+	R	R				+	+
Palau	∅	T2	+	R	R			T1	+	+
Papua New Guinea	MP or MT* (1–12): <1800 m	T2	+	R	R				+	+
Pitcairn	∅	T1	+	R	R				+	+
Samoa / U.S. Samoa	∅	T2	+	R	R				+	+

Country N = North S = South W = West E = East	Malaria	Yellow Fever	Hepatitis A	Hepatitis B	Typhoid	Rabies	Meningococcal Meningitis	Japanese Encephalitis	Cholera	Tetanus/Diphtheria	Poliomyelitis	Miscellaneous
Solomon Islands	XP or MT* (1–12):	T2	+	R	R					+	+	
Tonga	ø	T2	+	R	R					+	+	
Vanuatu	XP or MT* (1–12):		+	R	R					+	+	
Wallis and Futuna	ø	T1	+	R	R					+	+	
EUROPE												
Albania	ø	T2	+	R	R					+	+	
Greece	ø	T1	+	R						+	+	
Malta	ø	T2	+	R						+	+	
Moldova	ø	T1	+	R		R			T1	+	+	
Portugal (Azores only, Madeira)	ø	T1		R								

† Adapted from WHO, and from Travel Information Manual for required vaccinations. Status is current as of January 1999. Consult current recommendations in home country.

Malaria

Periods of risk: January–December = (1–12)

Limits of altitude for malaria transmission, in meters=(m)

Chemoprophylaxis, first choice:

Zone A: Chloroquine = CP

Zone B: Chloroquine plus Proguanil = XP. (Note: Proguanil is not marketed in the U.S.; therefore, the CDC recommends MP instead.)

Zone C: Mefloquine = MP, Doxycycline = DP

Stand-by emergency treatment:

Chloroquine = CT, Mefloquine = MT. (Note: In the U.S., CDC does not recommend stand-by emergency treatment as an option, but only CP or MP, respectively. The same applies for various other national expert groups.)

No chemoprophylaxis, no stand-by treatment recommended (risk negligable): —

No malaria = ø. *For low-risk travelers, mainly short travel (<1 week) in risk areas

Yellow Fever

requ = vaccination required (except for airport transits within country)

requ*‡ = vaccination required (including for airport transit within country)

+ = vaccination recommended

T1 = vaccination required if arriving within 6 days after leaving or transiting infected areas (airport transits exempt)

T2 = vaccination required if arriving within 6 days after leaving or transiting infected areas (including airport transits).

Infected areas are countries that have "requ" or "+" in the yellow fever column

Hepatitis A

+ = vaccination recommended for nonimmunes

Hepatitis B

R = vaccination recommended for long-term travelers (>6 months) and for risk groups, such as health care personnel, frequent travelers, young children who will be with other children, travelers likely to engage in casual sex, tattooing, ear piercing, or needle-sharing (often adolescents), and travelers who may need to undergo medical or dental procedures

Typhoid Fever

+ = vaccination recommended

R = vaccination recommended for risk groups, mainly those eating and drinking under poor hygienic conditions and those staying longer than 1 month

Rabies

R = vaccination recommended for risk groups, mainly those with occupational exposure to animals, and those staying longer than 1 month, particularly bicyclists

Meningococcal Meningitis

R = vaccination recommended for risk groups, mainly in the event of epidemics; in Nepal for trekkers; in sub-Saharan Africa during the season of transmission for persons with close contact to the local population (even for short stays, otherwise for stays of over 1 month)

A = vaccination required for pilgrims (Hajj, Umra) and seasonal workers

Japanese Encephalitis

R = vaccination recommended for risk groups: >1 month stay in rural areas. For seasonal information, see Figure 31.

Cholera

requ: vaccination required

R = vaccination recommended for risk groups: e.g., relief workers in refugee camps

T1 = vaccination required if arriving from cholera infected areas

Tetanus and Diphtheria

+ = vaccination recommended for nonimmunes

Poliomyelitis

+ = vaccination recommended for nonimmunes

Miscellaneous

Countries omitted: no special recommendations or requirements

B = no reliable information

C = HIV test may be required for some individuals (information may be obtained at respective embassy)

Bolivia

Malaria Endemic Areas

Endemic area below 2500 m in the departments of Beni, Pando, Santa Cruz and Tarija, and in the provinces of Lacareja, Rurrenabaque, and North and South Yungas in La Paz department

Lower risk exists in Cochabamba and Chuquisaca. Falciparum malaria occurs in Pando and Beni, especially in the localities of Guayaramerin, Riberalta and Puerto Rico

No transmission in big cities, in the highlands of La Paz and in the southwestern provinces.

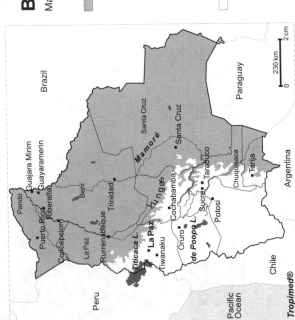

Tropimed®

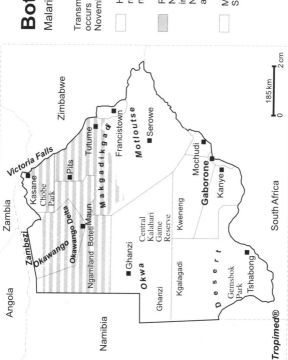

Botswana
Malaria Endemic Areas

Transmission of malaria occurs mainly from November to May/June

High risk areas: Zambezi river valley (1-12) and northern half of country (11-6)

Risk areas:
Northern half of country (7-10) including Boteti, Chobe, Ngamiland, Okawango and Tutume districts/subdistricts

Malaria-free:
Southern half of country

Tropimed®

Brazil

Malaria Endemic Areas

High risk areas:
Rondônia, Roraima
and Acre provinces

Risk of malaria
transmission exists
throughout the states
of the Amazon basin

Malaria-free:
east coast and
cities outside the
Amazon basin

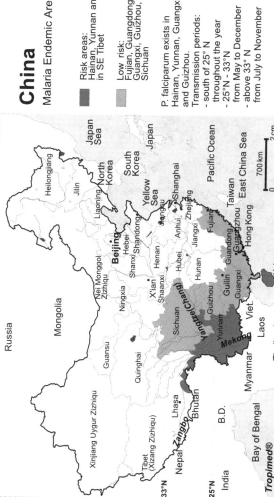

China

Malaria Endemic Areas

Risk areas: Hainan, Yunnan and in SE Tibet

Low risk: Fujian, Guangdong, Guangxi, Guizhou, Sichuan

P. falciparum exists in Hainan, Yunnan, Guangxi and Guizhou.

Transmission periods:
- south of 25° N throughout the year
- 25°N - 33°N from May to December
- above 33° N from July to November

Tropimed®

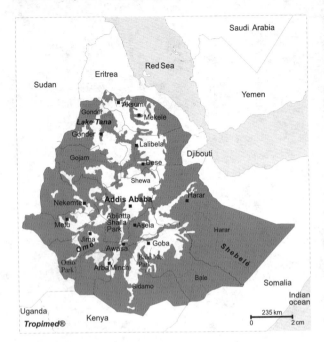

Ethiopia

Malaria Endemic Areas

Malaria exists all year
at altitudes below 2000 m

No transmission above
2000 m

India

Malaria Endemic Areas

High risk in the whole country below 2000 m

Risk in southern coastal areas, along Nepalese border, Calcutta

Malaria-free:
Mountainous areas of: Jammu and Kashmir, Himachal Pradesh, Sikkim
Minimal risk in southern parts of Kerala (Cochin) and Tamil Nadu (Madurai)

Indonesia

Malaria Endemic Areas

High Risk of malaria: Irian Jaya

Malaria risk exists throughout the year in the whole country except in Jakarta Municipality, big cities, and the main tourist resorts of Java and Bali

Pacific Ocean

Thai.
Malaysia
South China Sea

Singapour
Bintan

Medan
Padang
Sumatra

Jakarta
Bandung
Baturraden
Java
Yogyakarta
Wonosobo

Brunei
Malaysia

Kalimantan
Tengah
Banjarmasin

Java Sea

Celebes Sea

Sulawesi
Manadao
Rantepao

Molucca Sea

Ambon

Banda Sea

Jayapura
Wamena
Irian Jaya

Arafura Sea

Flores Sea

Lombok
Kupang

Indian Ocean

0   660 km
2 cm

Tropimed®

Bali

Lovina
Pacung
Candidasa
Denpasar
Kuta
Sanur
Nusa Dua

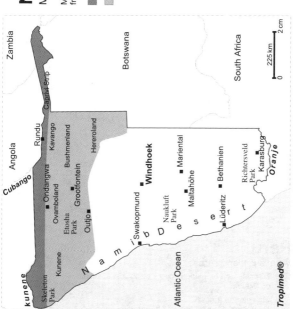

Namibia
Malaria Endemic Areas

Malaria risk exists mainly
from November to June

High risk areas

Risk areas: 11 - 6

Peru
Malaria Endemic Areas

Transmission of malaria occurs below the altitude of 1500 m

Malaria-free areas:
No transmission in Lima and the Andean highlands

Tropimed®

Philippines
Malaria Endemic Areas

Malaria exists all year below 600 m in rural areas of all the islands

Malaria-free:
islands of Leyte, Cebu, Bohol, and Catanduanes
No malaria in urban areas or on the plains > 600 m

South Africa

Malaria Endemic Areas

☐ High risk all year in Krüger National Park
and neighbouring parks, Kwazulu-Natal
and Transvaal (north, east and west)
from November to June

▨ The risk of malaria, mainly P.falciparum,
exists all year in the low altitude
areas of the north, east and west of
Transvaal (1) and in coastal areas
of Kwazulu-Natal (2) north of 28° S,
from July to October

Thailand

Malaria Endemic Areas

■ High risk in: Tak, Mae Hong Son, Prachin Buri, Chanthaburi, Ranong and Trat provinces

■ Risk areas in: Kanchanaburi ("River Kwai"), Prachuap Khiri Khan, Surat Thani and Satun Provinces

▨ Minimal risk

☐ Malaria-free: Cities and major tourist resorts – Bangkok, Chiang Mai, Songkhla, Pattaya, Phuket

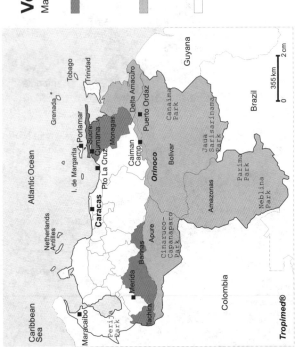

Venezuela
Malaria Endemic Areas

Malaria exists in the rural areas of the territories of:
- Tachira
- Barinas
- Sucre
- Monagas

Minimal risk
- Apure
- Amazonas
- Bolivar
- Delta Amacuro

Malaria-free:
Caracas, central and western coast, Isla Margarita

Tropimed®

APPENDIX D:
MEDICAL EMERGENCY ABROAD:
CALLING AN AIR-AMBULANCE

In the event of serious medical problems abroad, anyone can request assistance by calling an air-ambulance capable of organizing international or intercontinental air-evacuation. Reasons for such a request may be inadequate medical facilities and/or psychological reasons to repatriate a patient with serious injury, acute illness, or deterioration of an existing illness. Many air-ambulance services are also capable of giving medical advice.

One must be ready to answer the following questions:

1. Contact person: full name, phone/fax/telex/e-mail numbers, availability
2. Patient: full name, date of birth, home address
3. Present whereabouts of the patient: address, hospital and ward, phone/fax
4. Doctor attending to the patient: name, language(s), phone/fax
5. Patients condition: presumed diagnosis? conscious? mechanically ventilated?
6. Cause of illness/injury: what happened? when? where?
7. Identification papers: where is the patients passport/ID card, exit visa if applicable?
8. Hospital destination: to which hospital should the patient be transported?
9. Patients' doctor at home: name, address, phone/fax (important in pre-existing illness)
10. Next-of-kin: who needs to be notified? address, phone/fax, e-mail

Based on the information received, the air-ambulance service will decide whether a rescue mission is medically justified and how and when it should be conducted. Whenever possible, the patient will be evacuated aboard a commercial airliner, usually accompanied by trained staff. In case of need, an adequately equipped air-ambulance will repatriate intensive care patients.

Currently, the following major air-ambulance services with international experience and collaboration exist:

Africa

Dakar	Senegalair
Douala	Cameroun Assistance Sanitaire
Harare	Medical Air Rescue
Johannesburg	MRI Medical Rescue International
	National Air-Ambulance
	MedicAir Edenvale
Nairobi	AMREF Flying Doctor Service
	ICAA Intensive Care Air Ambulance

Asia

Bangkok, Beijing, Denpasar, Hanoi, Ho Chi Minh City, Hong Kong, Jakarta, Kuala Lumpur, Seoul, Taipeh	AEA International SOS
Calcutta	ARMS Asia Rescue Medical Services
Delhi	East West Rescue
Mumbai	India Aeromedical Services

North America

Fort Lauderdale, FL	Aero Jet International
St. Petersburg, FL	Care Flight
San Diego, CA	Critical Care Medicine
Alabama	Medjet International

Caribbean

National Air Ambulance

South America

Buenos Aires	Aeromedicos
	Med-Plane
Rio de Janeiro	Lider Air-Ambulance
Sao Paolo	Med Fly Seviços

Australia/New Zealand

Sydney	Royal Flying Doctor Service
Auckland	Pacific Air Ambulance

Europe

Helsinki	Euroflite
Innsbruck	Tyrolean Air-Ambulance
Stuttgart	DRF German Air Rescue
Zurich	REGA Swiss Air-Ambulance

INDEX

The page numbers in italics refer to tables and figures.